CONTEMPORARY
RUSSIAN LITERATURE

CONTEMPORARY LITERATURE
SERIES

CONTEMPORARY
RUSSIAN LITERATURE

1881–1925

BY PRINCE D. S. MIRSKY

LECTURER IN RUSSIAN LITERATURE AT KING'S COLLEGE, LONDON

NEW YORK · ALFRED · A · KNOPF · MCMXXVI

To
MAURICE BARING

PREFACE

The present history of Russian literature since 1881 (the year of Dostoevsky's death) is planned so as to form a continuation of a book which I am preparing on the period preceding that date. The date has been chosen as a convenient landmark, but it is by no means a vital turning-point in the life-story of Russian literature. It marks an end rather than a beginning: the end of the classical age of Russian Realism. For a more thorough dividing line one would have either to go back as far as about 1845, or to advance to about 1895. As it is, the first fifteen years included in this history are a period of senescence: they are the autumn of the great age of Realism: their greatest man is the old Tolstoy, a man of the past generation; their second greatest, the distinctly "autumnal" genius of Chekhov. Only after the rise of the revolutionary realism of Gorky, and still more of the anti-Realist movement of the Symbolists, does a new period begin which is no more an afterglow. All this makes it somewhat difficult to decide which writers are to be included in this volume, and which assigned to the earlier period. With the exception of Tolstoy—a sufficiently big figure to stand an operation of the kind—I have avoided dividing the individual writers between the two volumes. I have left for the other book those writers whose work is a vital part of the movement of the sixties and seventies, and will have to be discussed in any account of that period. Such are, for instance, Saltykov and Gleb Uspensky, though much of their best work appeared after 1881. Other writers, on the contrary, of the same generation, who, like Leskov and Leontiev, were out of tune with the times when they were young, and whose reputation grew in the eighties and has continued growing since their death, have been included here. In a few cases (notably Fet) writers dealt with summarily in this volume will be discussed at greater length in the history of the earlier period.

In presenting modern Russian literature to the English-speaking public, I have tried to keep as near as possible to the facts, and advisedly refrained from generalizations. My book aims at nothing more ambitious than being a *Baedeker* or a *Murray's Guide to Recent Russian Literature*. Bird's-eye views—which are so easily taken by the foreigner who is un-burdened by too much knowledge, and so difficult to the Russian whose wideness of outlook is obscured by a too intimate acquaintance with concrete detail—will be found wanting. I would be happy if the few new facts and points of view offered in these pages will modify the simplified and hasty conclusions which have been arrived at, by Anglo-Saxons and others, on the subject of my country. But I am under no illusion. It has become a tradition for the omniscient geniuses of the West to exercise their intuitive powers on the subject of Russia, where they can move freely, unhampered as they are by any excess of irrelevant and needless information.

Western histories of Russian literature are in the habit of telling their readers, to begin with, that Russian literature is different from every other literature in the world in that it is more closely linked with politics and social history. This is simply not true. Russian literature, especially after 1905, is almost surprisingly non-political, considering the colossal political cataclysms it witnessed. Even when treating "polit-ical" subjects, modern Russian writers are in substance non-political; even when they write propaganda, like Mayakovsky, propaganda in their hands is a means, and not an end. Still I have introduced two interchapters dealing mainly with politics and the interaction of politics and literature. I have done so not because it is more necessary to speak of the two Revolutions when speaking of Andreev and Blok than it is to speak of the Civil War when speaking of Whitman and Whittier, but be-cause (though Russian Revolution is on everyone's lips) very few people born west of Riga know anything at all about the facts that are relevant in this connexion.

If literature in the higher sense has been but little affected by politics, Russian literary *opinion* (which is a very different matter) has always been to a very great extent influenced by political prejudice. This influence has, naturally, grown since 1917. Many pro-Soviet Russians will deny Bunin the title of a great writer because he is on the White side, and in the same way many *émigrés* will deny the title to Gorky because he has supported Lenin. Happily for the future of Russian civilization, there are also people on both sides of the Soviet Pale who have not succumbed to this "Civil War mentality," and their number is steadily growing.

I have not attempted to conceal my own political sympathies, and persons conversant with Russian actualities will easily discover what they are. But I do claim to have kept my *literary* conscience free from political bias, and to have spoken with equal critical integrity of the reactionary Leontiev, of the Liberal Soloviev and of the Bolshevik Gorky; of the "White-guardsman" Bunin and of the Communist Babel. My appreciations and criticisms may be "subjective" and personal, but, if they are, they are the product of literary and "æsthetic" prejudice, not of political party-feeling. Here again I claim an attenuating circumstance: I believe that my taste is to a certain extent representative of my literary generation, and that *on the whole* my appreciations will not seem paradoxical or capricious to the competent Russian reader.

But if the Russian reader will understand me at first sight, I am afraid the Anglo-Saxon intellectual (for, after all, only intellectuals are interested in Russian literature) will find certain of my appreciations startlingly queer. The English and American intellectual, in his appreciations of Russian writers, is about twenty years behind the times, and even twenty years ago some of his preferences would be shared only by the less literate. The prominence I give to Leskov, to Leontiev, to Rozanov, to the Symbolists (and, among them, to Bely rather than to Balmont), and to Remizov reflects what has become a commonplace of Russian literary judgment, and is by no means a bid for originality on my part. In the same way my coolness for Merezhkovsky, for Artsybashev, for Andreev's Symbolism, for Gorky's middle period, and for most of Balmont's poetry is rather a proof of my gregariousness than otherwise. Tastes, of course, are not infallible, and there is no reason to suppose that the later they are, the better. But, after all, we do seem to see better from a distance, and few of us to-day would agree to judge Rogers and Wordsworth as Byron judged them; or Sully-Prudhomme and Mallarmé as the French critics did about 1880.

This book was written in London, and it would not have been written without the help of the British Museum and of the London Library. The British Museum is an invaluable treasure-house for Russian books of the nineteenth century. For the period 1900–1914, it is somewhat less complete, and since the outbreak of war it has almost ceased acquiring Russian books.* But, fortunately for me, the Librarian of the London Library, Dr. Hagberg Wright, is a sympathetic student of things Russian and has made a point of keeping up to date the Russian department of his library, so that its collection of Russian fiction and Russian poetry of the last twenty years is as complete as it can reasonably be expected to be. Suffice it to say that without the London Library certain sub-chapters of my book would have had to remain unwritten.

My principal difficulty was with books published in 1914–1918. Owing to the war conditions then prevalent, they are rare in the libraries of Western Europe. On the other hand, great difficulties have been put up by the Soviet authorities in the way of exportation from Russia of books printed before the Revolution. So it is that I have not been able to use certain important books of reference (including such indispensable works as Brockhaus-Efron's *New Encyclopædia* and Vengerov's *History of Russian Literature in the Nineteenth Century*). The principal effect of this is the paucity of biographical information, especially concerning the writers discussed in Chapter III (Kuprin, Artsybashev, Sergeyev-Tsensky). On the other hand, I flatter myself with giving a tolerably complete and up-to-date account of post-Revolutionary literature.

* Quite recently it seems to have taken measures to renew its supply of Russian books.

I owe my most sincere gratitude to Professor Sir Bernard Pares, without whose energetic promptings this book would never have been written; to Miss Jane E. Harrison, who has had the infinite kindness and patience of reading several chapters of my book and making invaluable corrections in my bad English (which are the chapters that had this good fortune will be easily discovered by the reader); and to my colleague N. B. Jopson for several valuable hints concerning the translation of titles of Russian books.

February, 1925.

marked ones only.

CONTENTS

xiii

CHAPTER I

1. THE END OF A GREAT AGE

THE reign of Alexander II (1855–1881) was an age of great literary achievement, the Golden Age of the Russian novel. It saw the making of almost every one of the great works of Russian fiction, from Turgenev's *Rudin* and Aksakov's *Family Chronicle* to *Anna Karenina* and *The Brothers Karamazov*. The best forces were attracted to the novel, but by its side other forms of imaginative literature continued to flourish, and helped to produce the impression of a Golden Age. But there was a worm in the flower: all this great achievment was due to men of an older generation, and they had no successors. Not one of the younger men who had entered the literary career since 1856 was felt worthy to stand beside them, and as one by one the old men disappeared, there was no one to take their place. The turning-point came soon after 1880: Dostoevsky died in 1881, Turgenev in 1883. Tolstoy announced his withdrawal from literature. The great age was over.

The generation born between 1830 and 1850 was by no means poor in talents, but these talents were directed into other channels than literature. It was a generation of great composers—Musorgsky, Chaikovsky, Rimsky-Korsakov—of great scientists, like Mendeléeff, of eminent painters, journalists, lawyers, and historians. But its poets and novelists were recruited from among the second-rate. It was as if the nation had expended too much of its forces on literature, and was now making up by giving all the genius it had to the other arts and sciences.

But apart from this mysterious process of restoring the balance between various spheres of intellectual activity, there

3

were good reasons why literature should decline. The first is connected with certain essential features of Russian literature itself, and of Russian literary criticism in particular. The great Russian novelists were great masters of their craft, even those of them who, like Tolstoy, most tried to hide it and affected to despise "form." But they did try to hide it and did affect to despise "form." At any rate, before the public they seemed to countenance the view that it was their message that signified, and not their art. The critics went further and crudely identified the value of literary work with the moral or social utility of its message. They "declared war on æsthetics," and proscribed all interest in "pure art." New beginners in literature became easily imbued with the doctrine that form was naught and matter everything. This made the transmission of those traditions of the craft which alone permit the normal development of literary art impossible. The young were prevented from profiting by the example of their elders and betters by a taboo laid on all questions of form. They could only ape them, unconsciously and unintelligently, but not learn from them in any creative sense. The generation of 1860 made an attempt to break away from the established forms of the novel. This attempt promised to develop into a creative quest for new ways of expression, something like a premature Futurist movement. But the atmosphere was unpropitious for such a development and it ended in nothing. The most significant of the young innovators, Pomyalovsky (1835–1863), died very young, and under the general pressure of utilitarianism the movement, instead of leading to a rejuvenation of old forms, resulted in a complete emancipation from all form. This stage is reached in the work of the most gifted democratic novelist of the period—Gleb Uspensky (1840–1902). As for the more traditional and conservative writers, they were able only to repeat the processes and methods of the great realists, vulgarizing and cheapening them. Whether, like Count Salias, they applied the realistic manner to give a fresh appearance to the historical novel, or used it to make propaganda for Radical ideas, like Omulevsky and Scheller, or to combat them, like Avseenko, or to describe the virtues of the Peasant Commune and the vices of capitalistic civilization, like Zlatov-ratsky and Zasodimsky, they are all equally unoriginal, uninteresting and unreadable. They can only be classified, like M.P.'s, according to their political allegiance.

A second reason which accentuated the break of literary tradition was the great social upheaval produced by the Emancipation of the Serfs and the other liberal reforms of the first half of Alexander II's reign. The Emancipation dealt a mortal blow to the economic welfare of the class that had up to that time monopolized all literary culture—the landed gentry. Its middle strata, which were intellectually the most active, suffered most from the blow. A new class arose to replace them—the *Intelligentsia*. The origin of this class was composite. It absorbed many members of the ruined gentry, but the groundwork consisted of men risen from the lower or rather *outer* classes, that had not previously taken part in modern civilization. Sons of the clergy were especially numerous and prominent among the new men of the sixties. One feature is common to all these new intellectuals—complete apostasy from all parental tradition. If he was the son of a priest, he would of necessity be an atheist; if the son of a squire, an agrarian socialist. Revolt against all tradition was the only watchword of the class. To preserve a literary tradition under these circumstances was doubly difficult, and it was not preserved. Only that was retained from the older writers which was considered to be directly useful for the purposes of Revolution and Progress.

The Reforms produced an enormous change in Russian life and opened many new channels to ambitious and vigorous men, who under the preceding régime would most probably have turned to writing verse or fiction. The new law-courts de-manded large numbers of educated and civilized workers. The rapid growth of capitalistic enterprises attracted numer-ous workers, and the number of engineers was many times multiplied. The rise of evolutionary theories made science fashionable and attractive. The whole atmosphere became freer and more propitious for every kind of intellectual activity. Political journalism became possible, and lucrative, and direct revolutionary action absorbed much of the best forces of the younger generation. It would be an error to believe that under freer conditions literature and the arts must necessarily prosper more than under despotism. The contrary is more often the case. When all other activity becomes difficult, they attract all that is ambitious and wants to express itself in intellectual work. Literature, like everything else, requires time and work, and when other work is attractive and is easily found, fewer persons can give their time to the Muses. When new fields of intellectual activity are suddenly thrown open, as was the case in Russia about 1860, the conditions are particularly unfavourable for the progress of literary art. When they are again closed, literature again attracts the intellectual unemployed. Milton was a political pamphleteer and an administrator when his party were in power—and wrote *Paradise Lost* after the triumph of his enemies. The immediate effects on literature of the great liberal Reforms of Alexander II was a shortage of new hands. The sixties and seventies in the History of Russian Literature were a period when work of the first order was done by men of a preceding generation, and the young generation, absorbed by other activities, could give to literature only its second best.

When with the approach of the eighties the atmosphere began to change, the younger generation had still nothing to show to compare with the work of their fathers. The few survivors of the great generation were looked up to as the solitary remnants of a better age, and the greatest of them, Tolstoy, was for many years after his "conversion" without comparison the greatest and most significant figure in Russian literature, a solitary giant incommensurable with the pygmies at his feet.

2. TOLSTOY AFTER 1880

Tolstoy's writings after 1880 are divided by a deep cleft from all his earlier work. But they belong to the same man, and much of that which appeared at first new and startling in the later Tolstoy, existed in a less developed form in the early Tolstoy.* From the very beginning we cannot fail to discern in him an obstinate search for a rational meaning to life; a confidence in the powers of common sense, and of his own reason; contempt for modern civilization with its "artificial" multiplication of needs; a deeply rooted irreverence for all the functions and conventions of State and Society; a sovereign disregard for accepted opinions, and scientific and literary "good form"; and a pronounced tendency to teach. But what was disseminated and disconnected in his early writings was welded after his conversion into a solid consistent doctrine, dogmatically settled in every detail. And the doctrine was such as to surprise and repel most of his old admirers. Before 1880 he had belonged, if anywhere, to the conservative camp. *War and Peace* and *Anna Karenina* first appeared in the magazine of the Reactionary Katkov. Tolstoy's most intimate friends were the poet Fet, a notorious reactionary (and an almost fanatical atheist, or rather heathen), and the critic Strakhov, a strongly anti-Radical Slavophil. Only an exceptionally acute critic like Mikhaylovsky could as early as 1873 discern the essentially revolutionary foundation of Tolstoy's mentality. The general impression was different.

Tolstoy had always been fundamentally a rationalist. But at the time he wrote his great novels his rationalism was suffering an eclipse. The philosophy of *War and Peace* and *Anna Karenina* (which he formulates in *A Confession* as "that one should live so as to have the best for oneself and one's family") was a surrender of his rationalism to the inherent irrationalism of life. The search for the meaning of life was abandoned. The meaning of life was Life itself. The greatest wisdom

* An account of the earlier work of Tolstoy will appear in a book that is being prepared by the present writer on *Russian Literature to the Death of Dostoevsky.* Here it will be sufficient to remind the reader of the principal dates: born in Yasnaya Polyana (province of Tula), in 1828, he served in the army and fought in the Caucasus (1852–1854) and at Sebastopol (1855). His first story, *Childhood,* appeared in 1852. In 1862 he married Sophie Andreevna Behrs and settled down at Yasnaya Polyana. *War and Peace* was published in 1865–1868; *Anna Karenina* in 1874–1876.

consisted in accepting without sophistication one's place in Life and making the best of it. But already in the last part of *Anna Karenina* a growing disquietude becomes very apparent. When he was writing it (1876), the crisis had already begun which is so memorably recorded in *A Confession* and from which he was to emerge the prophet of a new religious and ethical teaching.

The teaching of Tolstoy, as everyone knows, is a rationalized "Christianity," stripped of all tradition and all positive mysticism. He rejected personal immortality, and concentrated exclusively on the moral teaching of the Gospels. Of the moral teaching of Christ the words "Resist not evil" were taken to be the principle out of which all the rest follows. He rejected the authority of the Church, which sanctioned the State, and he condemned the State, which sanctioned violence and compulsion. Both were immoral, like every form of organized compulsion. His condemnation of every form of compulsion authorizes us to classify Tolstoy's teaching, in its political aspect, as Anarchism. This condemnation extended to every State as such, and he had no more respect for the democratic States of the West than for Russian Autocracy. But in practice the edge of his Anarchism was directed against the existing régime in Russia. He allowed that a Constitution might be a lesser evil than Autocracy (he recommended it in *The Young Czar*, written after Nicholas II's accession in 1894), and his attacks were often directed against the same institutions as those of the Radicals and Revolutionaries. His attitude towards the active revolutionaries was ambiguous. He disapproved on principle of violent methods and consequently of political murder. But there was a difference in his attitude towards revolutionary terrorism and governmental suppression. As early as 1881 he remained unmoved by the assassination of Alexander II by the Revolutionaries, but wrote a letter of protest against the execution of the assassins. To all intents and purposes, Tolstoy became one of the greatest forces on the side of Revolution, and the Revolutionaries recognized this and paid homage to the "grand old man," though they did not accept his doctrine of "non-resistance," and

though they treated his followers with contempt. Tolstoy's
agreement with the Socialists was further accentuated by his
own communism, and condemnation of private property, especially in land. The methods he proposed for the abolition of
the evil were different (they included the voluntary abdication
of all money and land), but the negative part of his doctrine
was in this point identical with Socialism.

Tolstoy's conversion was, largely, the reaction of his fundamental Rationalism against the irrationalism into which he
had allowed himself to drift in the sixties and seventies. His
metaphysics may be summed up as the identification of the
principle of life with Reason. Like Socrates, he boldly identifies absolute Good with absolute knowledge. "Reason, i.e.,
Good" is a favourite phrase of his, and occupies as central a
place in his doctrine as *Deus sive Natura* does in Spinoza's.
Knowledge is the necessary foundation of Good, and this
Knowledge is inherent in every man. But it is obscured
and stifled by the evil fogs of civilization and sophistry. It
is only necessary to listen to the inner voice of one's conscience
(which he was inclined to identify with the Practical Reason
of Kant) and not to be misled by the false lights of human
sophistry, which includes the whole of civilization—art, science,
social tradition, law, as well as the historical dogmas of
theological Religion. But for all its rationalism, Tolstoy's
religion is in a sense mystical. It is true that he rejected all
the accepted mysticism of the Churches, declined to recognize
God as a Person, and spoke with satirical scorn (which to
every believer will appear as the wildest blasphemy) of the Sacraments. And yet his final authority (as in fact all the final
authority of every metaphysical Rationalism) is the irrational
human "conscience." He did his utmost to identify it in
theory with Reason. But the mystical *daimonion* constantly
reappeared, and in all his more remarkable later works
"conversion" is described as an essentially mystical experience. It is mystical in that it is personal and unique. It
is the result of an intimate revelation, which may or may
not be prepared by previous intellectual development, but is
essentially, like every mystical experience, incommunicable.

In Tolstoy's own case, as described in *A Confession*, it is led up to by his whole previous intellectual life. But all purely intellectual solutions to the essential question were unsatisfactory, and the final solution is represented as a series of mystical experiences, repeated flashes of inner light. The civilized man lives in a state of unquestioning sin. The questions of meaning and justification arise against his will —as the effect of the Fear of Death—and the answer comes as a ray of inner light—such is the process described more than once by Tolstoy—in *A Confession*, in *The Death of Ivan Ilyich*, in the *Memoirs of a Madman*, in *Master and Man*. The necessary consequence of this fact is that the Truth cannot be preached, but may be only discovered for oneself. This is the doctrine of *A Confession*, which does not attempt to demonstrate, but only to narrate and to "infect." Later on, however, when the original impulse had widened, he attempted to preach it in logical form. He really always disbelieved in the efficacy of preaching. It was his disciples, men of a very different cast, who made Tolstoism a preaching-doctrine and encouraged Tolstoy to preach. In its final form the mystical element of Tolstoy's teaching is practically eliminated, and his Religion becomes an essentially eudæmonistic doctrine—a doctrine founded on the search after happiness. Man must be good because it is the only way for him to be happy. In a typical work of the period when his teaching became crystallized and dogmatic—*Resurrection*—the mystical motive is absent and Nekhlyudov's regeneration is no more than an adaptation of his life to the moral law, in order to free himself from the disagreeable reactions of conscience. In Tolstoy's final conception the moral law, which acts through the medium of conscience, is a law in the strict scientific sense, in the same sense as gravitation, or any other natural law. This is powerfully expressed in the idea—borrowed from Buddhism—of Karma, a conception profoundly different from the Christian in that Karma operates mechanically, without any intervention of Divine Grace, and is a necessary consequence of sin. Morality in the finally crystallized form of Tolstoism is the art of avoiding Karma or of adapting oneself to it.

Tolstoy's morality being a morality of happiness, it is also a morality of purity, not of sympathy. Love of God, i.e., of the moral law inside oneself, is the primary and only virtue, and charity, love for one's fellow creatures, is only a consequence. Charity, the actual feeling of love, is not a necessity for the Tolstoyan saint. He must act *as if* he loves his fellow-men, and that will mean that he loves God and he will be happy. Tolstoism is thus at the opposite pole to the teaching of Dostoevsky. For Dostoevsky, charity, love of men, pity, is the one supreme virtue, and God is revealed only through pity and charity. Tolstoy's religion is entirely egotistic. There is no God except the moral law inside man. The end of good actions is inner peace. This makes us understand the charge of Epicureanism that has been brought against Tolstoy, and also that of Luciferism and measureless pride, for there is nothing *outside* Tolstoy to which he bows.

Tolstoy was ever a great Rationalist, and his Rationalism found satisfaction in the admirably constructed system of his religion. But the irrational Tolstoy remained alive beneath the hardened crust of crystallized dogma. Tolstoy's diaries reveal how difficult it was for him inwardly to live up to his ideal of moral happiness. Except during the first years when he was carried on by the initial mystical impulse of his conversion, he was never happy in the sense he wanted to be. This was partly due to the impossibility he found himself in of practising what he preached, and to the constant and obstinate opposition of his family to his new ideas. But, apart from this, the Old Adam was always alive. The desires of the flesh were active in him till an unusually advanced age, and the desire for expansion, the desire which gave life to *War and Peace*, the desire for the fullness of life with all its pleasure and beauty, never died in him. We catch few glimpses of all this in his writings, for he subjected them to a strict and narrow discipline. But we have a picture of Tolstoy in his old age where the irrational, the complete man stands before us in all the relief of life—this is Maxim Gorky's *Recollections of Tolstoy*, a work of genius worthy of its subject.

When the news of Tolstoy's conversion spread, it became

known that Tolstoy had condemned as sinful all the writings that had made him famous, and decided to abandon all further literary work in the sense of pure and disinterested art. When this news reached Turgenev, who was on his deathbed, he wrote Tolstoy a letter that has been quoted to satiety and which contains a phrase that has become hackneyed to such a nauseous extent that it is impossible to reproduce it. The dying novelist adjured Tolstoy not to abandon literature, and to think of the duty that lay on him as the greatest of Russian writers. Turgenev greatly exaggerated his influence if he hoped that a letter from him might change the decision of a man who had always been noted for obstinacy and who had just emerged from a crisis of immeasurable gravity. But Turgenev saw a danger where there was none: though Tolstoy condemned as sinful (and artistically wrong) *War and Peace* and *Anna Karenina* and subjected all his work henceforth to the exigencies of his moral philosophy, it is ridiculous to think that Tolstoy ever abandoned "art." He soon returned to the narrative form, but even apart from this, even in his polemical writings, he never ceased being supremely artistic. In the most trivial of his tracts against tobacco, he never ceased being, *as a craftsman*, head and shoulders above even the best writers of the "æsthetic" revival of the eighties. *A Confession* itself may without exaggeration be called in some ways his greatest artistic work. It is not a disinterested, self-contained "representation of life" like *War and Peace* or *Anna Karenina;* it is "utilitarian," it is "propaganda work," and in this sense it is less "pure art." But it possesses "æsthetic" qualities that are not present in the great novels. It is *constructed* and constructed with supreme skill and precision. It has an oratorical movement which it would be difficult to expect from the author of *War and Peace.* It is more synthetic and universal, and does not rely for its action on little homely and familiar effects of realism, so abundant in the novels. Its analysis is simple, deep, courageous—and there is nothing in it of that "psychological eavesdropping" (the phrase is Leontiev's) which repels many readers in his earlier works. *War and Peace* and *Anna*

Karenina have been compared, somewhat far-fetchedly, with the poems of Homer. *A Confession* might with more appropriateness be placed by the side of no less supreme "world's books"—*Ecclesiastes* and the *Book of Job*. So it is quite wrong to affirm that in any literary sense the change that overcame Tolstoy about 1880 was a fall. He remained for ever not only the supreme writer but the supreme craftsman of Russian letters. Even the most drily dogmatic of his treaties is a masterpiece of literary ability, and of the best Russian. For all that, the fact remains that henceforward Toltsoy ceased to be a "writer," in the sense of a man who writes for the sake of producing good literary work, and became a preacher. All his writings were now directed towards one end—the elucidation and advancement of his doctrine. And when he turned, as he did very soon, towards imaginative narrative, he wrote stories which, like everything else, were strictly subordinate to his dogmatic teaching and intended to illustrate and to popularize it.

The first of Tolstoy's works in which he preached his new teaching was *A Confession* (begun in 1879 and completed in 1882).* *A Confession* is altogether on a higher level than the rest; it is one of the world's masterpieces, and, as I have already ventured to affirm, is of a class with the *Book of Job*, with *Ecclesiastes*, and with the *Confessions* of St. Augustine. It is a work of art, and Tolstoy's biographer would give proof of too much simple-mindedness if he used it as biographical material in the strict sense of the word. But the work is more important to us than the facts that led up to it. The facts have been, and are no more. Their history in *A Confession* remains as a κτῆμα ἐς ἀεὶ, a perfect work, a living entity. It is one of the greatest and most lasting expressions of the human soul in the presence of the eternal mysteries of Life and Death. It is useless to give any detailed analysis of it here, for all civilized people are presumed to have read it. To give the argument in one's own words would be presumption, to quote passages would be to destroy. For it is

---

* It was not at the time passed by the Russian censorship. It was printed in Geneva, and circulated in manuscript in Russia.

a wonderful whole built with marvellous precision and effectiveness. Every detail, every turn of thought, every oratorical cadence is in its right place to contribute to the one supreme effect. It is the greatest piece of oratory in Russian literature. But it is not conventional eloquence. Its rhythm is a logical, mathematical rhythm, a rhythm of ideas, and Tolstoy scorns all the devices of traditional rhetoric. It is sustained in the simplest of languages, in that wonderful language of Tolstoy, whose secret has not yet been caught, and which is naturally lost in a translation. A good translation (like Mr. Aylmer Maud's) will preserve the oratorical movement of the original, for this is based on the succession of ideas, and large syntactical units, not on the sound and quantity of words. But the effect of Tolstoy's Russian cannot be reproduced in any of the literary languages of the West, for all of them are too far divorced from their spoken forms, and the spoken languages too full of slang. Russian alone has this felicity, that it can use everyday speech to produce effects of biblical majesty. And Tolstoy's favourite device, in *A Confession,* of illustrating his idea by a parable is in complete keeping with the general tone of the work. Tolstoy's language was largely his own creation. He achieved, in *A Confession,* for the language of abstract thought what he had attempted in his pedagogical articles, and achieved for narrative prose, in his novels, the creation of a new literary language free from the bookish traditions of contemporary literature and based entirely on the language actually spoken. The language thus evolved is beyond doubt the best vehicle yet used in Russian for the expression of abstract thought. The extent of Tolstoy's innovation in the literary language is singularly great—it is almost a different language from that of his contemporaries. Many of the principal terms of his teaching are words that had not been used before Tolstoy in literary Russian, and were borrowed by him from the colloquial speech of his class. Such, for instance, is one of his most frequent words—*durno*—bad.

Tolstoy's other moral and religious writings are not on a level with *A Confession,* though they are written in the same

admirable Russian, sometimes with even greater elegance and
precision. In *A Confession* he speaks with the utmost tragical earnestness of a unique and overwhelming experience. In
the latter tracts he lays down the "articles" of a hard and
and narrow creed. They have all the best qualities of Tolstoy
the rationalist, the arguer and the logician, but it would be
quite out of place to compare them, as one can compare *A
Confession*, with the books of the Bible. The first of these
tracts, *What Are We to Do?* (1884), is a kind of continuation
of *A Confession*, but on a less mystical and more social
plane. It is the story of Tolstoy's experience of the slums
and night refuges of Moscow soon after his conversion. His
religious views were systematized in a series of works of which
the first, *What I Believe*, was written in 1884. This was
followed by a *Critique of Dogmatic Theology, The Kingdom
of Heaven Is inside Us, An Exposition of the Gospels*, and
The Christian Doctrine. *What I Believe* is the most comprehensive of his dogmatic writings, it gives the most complete
exposition of his doctrine and is the best-known abroad. What
he gave in *A Confession* in the form of a personal experience,
in its process of becoming, is here crystallized and stabilized
into a settled doctrine. *The Christian Doctrine* (1897) is an
exposition of the same doctrine in a still more logical and
fixed form, after the manner of a catechism. It is a source
of infinite pleasure to those who admire most in Tolstoy his
lucidity and his skill at definition and precise statement.
The Exposition of the Gospels has less of this quality and
more of a very far-fetched and not always *bona fide* interpretation. In *The Critique of Dogmatic Theology* he is a polemist well versed in all the little tricks of argumentative
tactics, a cunning fencer and a consummate ironist. Ridicule
and an appeal to common sense are his favourite polemical
methods. "This is unintelligible nonsense" is his knock-out
argument. His minor tracts are numerous and touch on a
great variety of points of detail, or on topics of current
interest. Such is *Why Do People Intoxicate Themselves?* denouncing drink and tobacco. Such is *I Cannot Be Silent*, a
violent invective against the Russian government and the

numerous executions during the suppression of the First Revolution.

But of all Tolstoy's non-narrative writings, that which is of greatest interest for the literary historian is *What Is Art?* (1897). Tolstoy's taste in literature and in art always drew him towards the classical, the rational, and the primitive. He disliked everything Romantic, everything ornate or exuberant. He had no understanding for "pure poetry." He liked the classic theatre of Racine, the analytical novel of Stendhal, the stories of Genesis, and the songs of the Russian people. He disliked the Elisabethan exuberance of Shakespeare. In his famous attack on Shakespeare, Tolstoy charged him with being not only an immoral writer, but a bad poet. He preferred the pre-Shakespearean *King Leir* to Shakespeare's tragedy because it was more primitive, less exuberant, less baroque. Voltaire would have agreed with much in Tolstoy's criticism of *King Lear*. He had many faults to find in other great writers. Homer was an immoral poet because he idealized wrath and cruelty; Racine and Pushkin were inferior writers because they appealed to a restricted aristocratic audience and were unintelligible to the people. But Shakespeare was a bad writer because he wrote badly, and Tolstoy remained unmoved by his poetry. Now art, according to Tolstoy, is that which "infects" with sympathetic feelings. "If a man is infected by the author's condition of soul, if he feels this emotion and this union with others, then the object which has effected this is art; but if there be no such infection, if there be not this union with the author and with others who are moved by the same work, then it is not art." Shakespeare and Wagner did not infect Tolstoy with their emotion, and as he did not believe in the sincerity of those who pretended to be infected by them—Shakespeare and Wagner were not art. Tolstoy opposes to them the creations of primitive popular art—the story of Joseph, the Hungarian *csardas*, the theatre of a primitive Siberian tribe, the Voguls. He quotes a description of a Vogul drama representing in a very simple and naïve way a reindeer hunt and the anxiety of the doe for her calf as an example of genuine art; "from the mere description, I felt that this was a true work of art," because he was infected by the feelings of the doe. Everything that does not *infect* is not art, and only obscures art. Too much technique, too much magnificence in producing a play, too much realism, obscure and diminish the artistic value of a picture, a play, a book. The simpler, the barer, the better. "The author of the story of Joseph did not need to describe in detail, as would be done nowadays, the blood-stained coat of Joseph, the dwelling and dress of Jacob, the pose and attire of Potiphar's wife, and how, adjusting the bracelet on her arm, she said: 'Come to me,' and so on, because the subject-matter of feelings in this novel is so strong that all details, except the most essential—such as that Joseph went out into the other room to weep—are superfluous, and would only hinder the transmission of feelings. And therefore this story is accessible to all men, touches people of all nations and classes, young and old, and has lasted to our times, and will yet last for thousands of years to come. But strip the best novels of our times of their details, and what will remain?" (*What Is Art?* p. 169). Genuine art may be moral or immoral, according to the moral value of the feelings with which it infects. The *Iliad*, for instance, is *art*, but it is morally bad art because the feelings with which it infects are bad feelings. Much of modern literature, though genuine art, is morally bad because it is class-art, and is intelligible only to the rich and cultivated, and tends to disunite, instead of uniting. Tolstoy excepts very little of modern literature from this general condemnation as immoral. He quotes only a few works—by Schiller (*The Robbers*), Hugo (*Les Misérables*), Dickens (*The Tale of Two Cities, The Christmas Carol,* and *The Chimes*), George Eliot (*Adam Bede*), Dostoevsky (*Memoirs from the House of Death*), and . . . Mrs. Beecher Stowe (*Uncle Tom's Cabin*)—"as examples of the highest art flowing from the love of God and man"—of (as he calls it) "religious art." As examples of an inferior but still good kind of art, of "art transmitting the simplest feelings of common life, but such always as are accessible to all men of the world," he quotes with great reservations *Don Quixote*, Molière, *David Copperfield*, and the *Pickwick Papers*, the tales of Gogol, Pushkin, and Maupassant. But "the exceptional nature of the feelings they transmit, and the superfluity of of special detail of time and locality, and, above all, the poverty of their subject-matter, make them comprehensible only to people of their own circle." His own earlier works Tolstoy condemned on grounds both moral (class exclusiveness and bad feelings) and æsthetic (superfluity of detail, all the paraphernalia of realism). But long before he had completed *What Is Art?* he had already made an effort to produce new works of fiction that would be in harmony with his new ideals. The novelty of Tolstoy's later stories is not only that they are all written with and strongly subordinate to the purpose (many of his early stories, especially those written in 1856–1861 are quite as much "with a purpose"), but that he abandoned in them his early realistic and detailed manner, and endeavoured to approach the chastity and simplicity of outline of his favourite masterpiece—the story of Joseph.

The first stories he wrote after *A Confession* were a series of edifying short stories for the people. They were published in 1885 and the following years by the firm Posrednik, founded for the special purpose of popularizing Tolstoy's teaching. They were written with regard to the existing conditions in Russia, that is, meant to satisfy the censor. Consequently they contain no violent and overt satire of the Church and State. The moral is always plainly present, often in the title, as : *Evil Allures, but Good Endures, God Sees the Truth but Waits*, but is not always peculiarly Tolstoyan. About the time he was writing *Anna Karenina*, Tolstoy had made an attempt at a popular story—this is the only story he excluded from the general condemnation of his earlier work, *The Prisoner in the Caucasus* (1873), which he recognized as belonging to the inferior but still commendable category of "good universal art" (not religious art). The new stories aspired to be religious art. According to Tolstoy's new taste, the narrative in these stories is reduced to the essential subject-matter and stripped of all the superfluous embellish-

read

ments of "realism." But they remain realistic in that they all have for setting the life familiar to the prospective reader —it is Russian peasant life, with sufficient local colour to individualize it as Russian. All these stories are admirably told, and every one of them is a little masterpiece of construction, economy, and adaptation of means to ends. Manner and matter are one organic whole, and the moral tendency does not stand out as something external. One of the best is *Two Old Men*—the story of two peasants who set out on a pilgrimage to Jerusalem, in fulfilment of a vow. One reached his goal and saw the Holy Land, but the other was detained on his way by meeting a starving family, and, in his efforts to save them, spent all his money, lost all his time, and was late for the boat, and returned home without seeing Jerusalem. The other, on his return journey, comes on the family saved from death by his companion, and is brought to understand "that the best way to keep one's vows to God and to do His will is for each man, while he lives, to show love and do good to others."

Later on, as his fame grew and he began to have a public all over the world, he wrote popular stories of a new kind, more universal and generalized. They approach still nearer to his ideal of being comprehensible to all men. Such are his adaptations from the French, *Françoise* (Maupassant's *La Vierge-des-Vents* pruned of all the superfluous realistic excrescences), *The Coffee-House of Surat*, and *Too Dear*, and his still later stories, *King Essarhadon, Work, Death, and Sickness*, and *Three Questions*. In these he approaches the style of the parable, which he had used with such powerful effect in *A Confession*, and of the Oriental apologue.

The stories written with a view to the educated reader are different in manner: they are much longer, much fuller of detail, more "psychological," altogether nearer in style to his earlier work. There are problem stories, written not so much to teach as to communicate his own experience. They may be grouped into two categories, stories of conversion, and stories on the sexual problem. The first group consists of *The Memoirs of a Madman* (unfinished, posthumous, written in 1884); *The Death of Ivan Ilyich* (1886), and *Master and Man* (1895). In all these stories the subject is the conversion of the dark and unregenerated educated or rich man before the face of Death, or Madness. *The Memoirs of a Madman* is very much akin to *A Confession.* It conveys with dreadful force the feeling of elemental metaphysical joylessness and despair before the abysmal meaninglessness of life, the feeling Tolstoy must have himself experienced at the height of his great crisis, and which seems to have returned to him at intervals after his conversion. It is the most genuinely mystical of his writings. He left it unfinished, but yet it cannot be refused a central place in his work, next to, and as a "piece of evidence" even above, *A Confession.* For it is more directly sincere, more of a document, less of a work of art. In *The Death of Ivan Ilyich* the hero is not a thinking and seeking man like Tolstoy of the *Confession* or like the Madman. He is an ordinary, vulgar, average man of the educated classes, a judge (the class Tolstoy detested most of all). The revelation comes to him as the direct consequence of his mortal illness. When he realizes that he is dying, he loses all taste for existence and is plunged into that elemental joylessness which comes from realizing the meaninglessness and emptiness of life. But joy comes back to him in the simple and cheerful charity of his servant Gerasim, the only person who gives him help in his mortal despair. And before he dies he sees the inner light of Faith, Renunciation, and Love. *Master and Man* is again the story of a birth to new life in the face of death. The story is familiar to every reader. It is one of Tolstoy's masterpieces, comparable to *A Confession* in the sustained beauty of its construction and to *The Memoirs of a Madman* in the genuineness of its mystical light. It stands half-way in style between his old realistic and new popular manner, and answers more than anything else of his works not especially intended for the people to his ideal of religious art.

The "sexual" stories are *The Kreutzer Sonata* (1889) and *The Devil* (written the same year, published posthumously). The first, a study of jealousy and a diatribe against the sexual education of young men and women in modern society, is well

known. It is certainly a powerful production but hardly a
perfect work of art. It is not sufficiently concentrated, its
preaching is not always artistically "necessary," its manner
strangely enough reminds one of the untidy and excited manner
of Dostoevsky. *The Devil* is more satisfactory. It is an
extraordinary analysis of that obsession by the desires of the
flesh which was so peculiar to Tolstoy and of which such shrewd
things have been said by Maxim Gorky. It is the story of a
man who loves his young and charming wife, but is impelled
against his will by a purely carnal desire for a peasant woman
with whom he had had relations before his marriage. He is
powerless to combat it and, to save himself from succumbing to
it, in a state of exasperation he kills the woman. Tolstoy was
not completely satisfied by this ending and wrote an alternative
ending, where the hero, instead of killing the object of his
desire, kills himself. In spite of this ambiguous ending, *The
Devil* is one of Tolstoy's greatest masterpieces, both for the
fierce sincerity and the masterly construction: the terrible inevitableness of the hero's fall, his helplessness before his
carnal instinct, grow like a terrible doom and are developed
with supreme mastery.

Of all Tolstoy's late narrative works, the one which attracted
the greatest attention and became most widely known, and is
consequently, more often than not, taken as typical of his last
period, was *Resurrection* (completed and published in 1899).
It is a novel in three parts—by far the longest of all his stories
since 1880, almost comparable in length with *Anna Karenina*
and *War and Peace*. This is the sole reason why it has
usurped a principal position among his later work, and is so
often quoted by the side of the two earlier novels. It has often
been used to prove that Tolstoy's genius declined since he became a preacher. If the imaginative work of his last thirty
years is to stand or fall according to the merit of *Resurrection,*
it will be in somewhat bad case, for it is quite obvious that
Resurrection is very much inferior to *War and Peace* and *Anna
Karenina*. But it is also much inferior to *Master and Man,*
to *Hajji Murad,* and to *The Living Corpse.* In spite of its
size, it is by no means the work into which Tolstoy put the most

work and care. It was written, strange to say, for money, and would probably not have seen the press before his death, were it not for the desire to find funds for the Doukhobors. The Doukhobors, a peasant sect of "Christian communists," were persecuted by the government for their "conscientious objection" to military service. Canada had offered hospitality to them, and the only drawback to their emigration was lack of funds for the transhipment of seven thousand men and women. Tolstoy decided to meet the emergency by finishing in a hurry, and publishing in one of the best-selling Russian papers, a novel he had been working at. So the money was found and the Doukhobors shipped, and settled in Saskatchewan. Thus it is wrong to regard *Resurrection* as the measure of Tolstoy's genius in his later years—it may be considered one of his least satisfactory works. This is what he wrote about it to Chertkov when he decided to finish and publish it: "The novel is in my old manner, which I do not approve of now. If I go on correcting it until I am satisfied, I shall never finish. If I take the obligation of delivering it to the publisher, I shall have to give it to the public as it is." He was working then at *Hajji Murad* and at *Resurrection,* and he chose the latter because he liked it least and had fewer objections to seeing it published in an unsatisfactory form. *Resurrection* is not a perfect work of art: the moral idea, profusely supported by texts from the Gospels, is not organically fused into the fabric. The story of Nekhlyudov's conversion is on an inferior plane to that of Tolstoy's own in *A Confession,* or of Ivan Ilyich's, or of the merchant in *Master and Man.* It is not a revelation of inner light, but a cold decision to adapt himself to the moral law so as to escape the stings of conscience and acquire inner peace. *Resurrection* presents Tolstoy and his teaching from the most unattractive side. For all that, it is a book by Tolstoy. But its best qualities are not characteristic of the later Tolstoy: they are rather, in a minor degree, those of *Anna Karenina* and *War and Peace.* The best thing in the novel are the minor realistic details he condemned so severely in *What Is Art?* The early story of Maslova is the best part of the book. It is full of that elusive poetry which reminds one of the subtle poetic atmosphere that accompanies Natasha in *War and Peace*. The satirical part is also very good. The account of the trial is excellent—sustained, concentrated, unexaggerated satire. It has not been surpassed by Tolstoy, except perhaps in the second part of the same novel, where he satirizes the bureaucratic society of Petersburg. But his satirically blasphemous account of an Orthodox Church service, prohibited by the censorship and absent in pre-Revolutionary editions printed in Russia, can scarcely be qualified otherwise than as a grave lapse from good taste. It is quite gratuitous and unnecessary for the mechanism of the novel.

If in *Resurrection* Tolstoy is at his worst, in its twin-novel he is at his best. *Hajji Murad* was begun in 1896 and completed in 1904. It was published after his death. In it he tried to give a story that would answer to his ideal of "good universal," not religious art. *Hajji Murad* is a masterpiece of the highest order. It is a story of the long-drawn war which the Caucasian mountaineers, under their military and religious leader Shamil, waged against Russia. Hajji Murad, a prominent mountaineer chief, from motives of personal ambition and vengeance deserts Shamil and goes over to the Russians, who receive him with apparent friendliness but with concealed distrust. Hajji Murad's family has remained with Shamil, who keeps them as hostages. The desire of once more seeing his son grows on Hajji Murad, and he decides to escape into the mountains, but is killed in the attempt. Hajji Murad is a savage. His feelings are those of a shrewd, brave, and treacherous warrior with all the virtues and all the vices of a warlike barbarian. The story is told in what Tolstoy called the "peep-show manner"—the scene is constantly shifted and the chapters are like a succession of slides. This method brings forward with great vividness the tragical irony of mutual misunderstanding between men of various classes and nationalities. The story is stirring tragedy conveyed by the simplest means. The final scene—the death of Hajji Murad and his four followers surrounded by hundreds of pursuers—is one of the grandest and most tragical in all literature.

Hajji Murad, as well as *The Memoirs of a Madman* and

The Devil, was published only in 1911, in the collected edition of Tolstoy's posthumous works.* This collection also includes several plays and many other stories and fragments. One of these is *Father Sergius* (1890-1898), the story of an aristocrat who became a monk and a hermit, but, unable to find inner peace in his officially sanctioned sanctity, escapes from his popular cell to become a tramp and, in humiliation and poverty, to find what he could not find in his worldly hermitage. It is a powerful study of spiritual pride, and, once again, of carnal desires. It is also an excellent example of Tolstoy's later rapid and "essential" narrative manner. Still better in this respect is *The False Coupon* (1903–1905), the admirably constructed story of a succession of evils diverging from one initial evil action to converge by a contrasting succession of good actions towards the common salvation of all concerned. It is impossible to list all the numerous minor stories and fragments of these wonderful three volumes. But one at least must be mentioned, one of the shortest—*Alesha Gorshok* (1905). It is a masterpiece of rare perfection. It is the apotheosis of the holy fool, who does not himself realize his goodness. It is the story, told in five or six pages, of a peasant boy who was all his life everyone's drudge, but in his simplicity of soul and meek, unquestioning submission (non-resistance) knew that inner light and purity of conscience, that perfect peace, which was never attained by the conscious, rational, restless soul of Tolstoy. Concentrated into its six pages, *Alesha Gorshok* is one of his most perfect creations, and one of the very few which make one forget the bedrock Luciferianism and pride of the author.

Tolstoy's plays all belong to the period after 1880. He had not the essential qualities that go to the making of a dramatist, and the merits of his plays are not of the strictly dramatic order. In spite of his French education and classical tastes, his plays are constructed in a very un-French and un-classical manner. With the exception of *The Fruits of Enlightenment*, a comedy, or rather a farce, of intrigue, all his plays are built

---

* They were not published during his life, to avoid making the question of their copyright fresh fuel for the war waged by Chertkov and the Countess Tolstoy over the person of their author.

according to the same scheme—which is the "peep-show" scheme
of *Hajji Murad*.   The action is not a continuous development,
but scenes are cut out so as to present the principal moments
of a story, which usually extends over a period of many years.
This construction may in some cases approach the form of a
mediæval morality.   It may also be easily adapted to make a
movie drama.   The first in date of Tolstoy's plays is the
First Distiller, a humorous anti-liquor morality play "for the
people," published originally in 1886 in the same series as the
popular tales.   The First Distiller is of course the devil.   He
has plenty of victims from all the rich and idle classes, but he
cannot succeed in catching a single peasant into his net, for
work is the peasant's safeguard from sin.   He succeeds in
corrupting him only by showing him the way to make spirits.
It is a very amusing little play and, as an English reviewer
has remarked, would raise grave anxiety among the liquor trade
if it were acted in England.   This was followed by *The Powers
of Darkness*, the best-known and most highly esteemed of
Tolstoy's plays (1887).   It is also in essence a morality—but
treated in a very different manner.   It is a tragedy, and a
realistic tragedy.   It represents the life of peasants, but is
intended for the educated public.   There is a profound inner
contradiction in the play.   Planned as a morality, it is
executed as a realistic drama, with all the condemned para-
phernalia of "superfluous details," including phonographically
exact reproduction of peasant dialect, a thing the peasant
spectator resents above all things.   This disharmony of plan
and execution, and this abundant presence of the abominations
of gratuitous realism, made Tolstoy dislike this play and condemn it as belonging to the "bad manner."   Like *Resurrection*,
it is one of Tolstoy's least perfect works, and its great success
only proves how little the Russian and the foreign public were
really in tune with the genius of Tolstoy.   The Russian public
liked it because it was in the familiar realistic "superfluous
detail" style, and because the Russian actors, trained to the
style, acted it well.   Abroad it was received enthusiastically
because its ruthless realism was a new and piquant thing to the
Western palate.   All this is not to say that it has no trace

of genius in it; on the contrary, the scheme of the play is one of Tolstoy's most powerful inventions. It is the best expression he ever gave to his favourite conception of Karma—the mechanical atonement of sin; and of another favourite idea of his—the great evil-begetting power of every evil action, which is expressed in the sub-title, "If a Claw Is Caught, the Bird Is Lost." The tragical atmosphere is thick and dark, and there are few more impressive things in Tolstoy than the third act, where we see Nikita enjoying the first joyless fruit of his initial crime. But the "superfluous detail" is gravely in the way, and the figure of Akim (disfigured by the "realistic" rendering of his speech) is hardly a happy incarnation of the "holy fool." For all its merits, *The Powers of Darkness* cannot take away from a much older play, Pisemsky's *The Hard Lot*, the honour of being the best Russian realistic tragedy. *The Fruits of Enlightenment* (1889) is, after all, but a trifle. As a comedy of intrigue, it is constructed very indifferently. Tolstoy had not in him an ounce of Scribe or Sardou. But the dialogue of the society people is admirable and the satire very pointed. It presents Tolstoy's satirical gift in its lighter mood. The same realistic tendency which mars the dialogue of *The Powers of Darkness* is one of the chief attractions of Tolstoy's society plays. For in the peasant play he tried to ape a dialect that was not his, in *The Fruits of Enlightenment* and in the posthumous plays he made his characters talk his own everyday language. These two plays, *The Light Shines in the Darkness* and *The Live Corpse*, are remarkable for their dialogue, which reproduces the actual spoken language of the Russian upper classes with all the illogicalness and formlessness of actual life, and seems to have on the printed page all the rhythms and intonations of the individualities. *The Light Shines in the Darkness* (begun in the early eighties and continued in 1900–1902) remained unfinished. It has the appearance of autobiography—for it is the story of a Tolstoyan moralist who is surrounded by an unsympathizing family, and whose followers are sent to prison for practising what he preaches. But it must be said in all fairness that Tolstoy does much less than justice to himself in the character of Saryntsov.

Saryntsov is not the giant of Yasnaya Polyana, but a narrow, cold, hard, pedantic fanatic—perhaps more like some inferior Tolstoyan—Chertkov, for instance. A very different thing is *The Live Corpse*, one of Tolstoy's most attractive and lovable works. There is in it what we meet with in a very few of his works, a distinct note of human sympathy, free from all moralizing dogmatism. There is in it also what one could hardly suspect in Tolstoy, a vast mellow pity for the misformed and erring human race, a respect for the sufferings of man, even of the abandoned drunkard, even of the proud society mother. It is at the opposite pole to *Resurrection*. It is, even more than *Hajji Murad*, the most *disinterested* of all Tolstoy's later works. It is rather loosely constructed, after the familiar "peep-show" plan, and it can hardly be called a drama in any strict sense of the word. But it has been produced, and in the hands of a cast like Stanislavsky's Moscow Art Theatre it acts very well. *The Live Corpse* may be taken as the last expression of Tolstoy's genius. It is distinctly a very old man's work, with that broadness and mellowness of outlook which, if it comes, is the best ornament of old age.

The life of Tolstoy since his conversion can be given here only in the briefest ontline. Soon after *A Confession* became known, he began, at first against his will, to recruit disciples. The first of these was the notorious and sinister V. G. Chertkov,* an ex-officer of the Horse Guards, a narrow fanatic, and a hard despotic man, who exercised an enormous practical influence on Tolstoy, and became a sort of Grand Vizier of the new community. Other disciples came, among whom P. I. Biryukov may be mentioned, the author of a *Life of Tolstoy*, the official life, written throughout in a tone of panegyrical admiration like the life of a saint, but valuable for its wealth of information. Tolstoy also established contact with certain sects of Christian communists and anarchists, like the Doukhobors. The external action of Tolstoy's new doctrine found its principal expression in cases of conscientious ob-

---

* Chertkov was the grandson of the landlord whose serf was Ephim Chekhov, the father of the writer.

jection to military service, which sent many men to prison and Siberia. But Tolstoy himself was unmolested by the government. Only in 1901 the Synod excommunicated him. This act, widely but very unjudiciously resented both at home and abroad, merely registered a matter of common knowledge, that Tolstoy had ceased to be an Orthodox Churchman.

The dogmatic followers of Tolstoy were never numerous, but his reputation among people of all classes grew immensely. It spread all over the world, and by the last two decades of his life Tolstoy enjoyed a place in the world's esteem which had not been held by any man of letters since the death of Voltaire. Yasnaya Polyana became a new Ferney, or even more than that, almost a new Jerusalem. Pilgrims from all parts flocked there to see the great old man. But Tolstoy's own family remained hostile to his teaching, with the exception of his youngest daughter, Alexandra. Countess Sophie Andreevna especially took up a position of decided opposition to his new ideas. She refused to give up her possessions and asserted her duty to provide for her large family. Tolstoy renounced the copyright of his new works, but had to surrender his landed property and the copyright of his earlier works to his wife. This produced an external contradiction between Tolstoy's preaching of communism and contempt of material riches, and the easy and even luxurious life he led under the régime of his wife—for Sophie Andreevna was the embodiment of Tolstoy's earlier philosophy of *War and Peace*, "that one should live so as to have the best for oneself and one's family." This contradiction weighed heavily on him, and the consciousness of it was carefully fostered by Chertkov. This man and Countess Tolstoy became the heads of two hostile parties who disputed the possession of Tolstoy. Tolstoy was remarkably healthy for his age, but he fell seriously ill in 1901 and had to live for a long time in the Crimea. Still he continued working to the last and never showed the slightest sign of any weakening of brain-power. The story of his "escape" and death is familiar to all. Ever more oppressed by the contradiction of his private life, urged on by Chertkov, full of a growing irritation against his wife, he left Yasnaya in the company of his daughter Alexandra and his doctor, for an unknown destination. After some restless and aimless wandering, he had to stop at Astapovo Junction (province of Ryazan). There he was laid up in the station-master's house, and died on November 7 (O.S.), 1910.

3. LESKOV (1831–1895)

Leskov was only three years younger than Tolstoy, but he was past thirty when he first appeared before the public, and the time was no longer the same as had given such a whole-hearted and generous reception to the great generation of novelists. It was a time of intense party strife when no writer could hope to be well received by all the critics, and only those who identified themselves with a definite party could hope for even a partial recognition. Leskov never identified himself with any party and had to take the consequences. His success with the reading public was considerable, but the critics continued to neglect him. Even now, when his place as a classic has been established beyond dispute, and he is better known and much more widely read than, say, Goncharov or Pisemsky, he has not yet received "official" recognition, with a permanent place in the text-books. Leskov's case is a striking instance of the failure of Russian criticism to do its duty. His reputation was made by the readers in spite of the critics.

Nikolay Semenovich Leskòv (Lyeskov) was born in the province of Orel in 1831. His father was a civil servant, and the son of a priest. His mother was of a family of gentry, and his early life was that of an average squire's son. One of the lasting influences of his early life was his Aunt Polly, who had married an Englishman, and followed the Quaker rule. When he was sixteen, his parents died and he found himself alone in the world and under the necessity of earning his own bread. He had to leave school and enter the civil service. He served as a copying clerk in various provincial government offices. In this service he acquired an extensive first-hand acquaintance with various aspects of Russian reality. This knowledge of life was still more widened when he left the civil service and was employed by an Englishman, a Mr. Scott, a Nonconformist like Aunt Polly, and chief steward of the estates of a rich nobleman. In this employment Leskov acquired a far wider outlook on Russian life, and one very different from that of the typical educated gentleman of the day. Owing to this training, Leskov is one of those Russian writers whose knowledge of life was not founded on the possession of serfs, to be later modified by university theories of French or German origin, like Turgenev and Tolstoy, but on a practical and independent knowledge of life. This is why his view of Russian life is so unconventional and so free from that attitude of condescending and sentimental pity for the peasant, which is typical of the liberal and educated serf-owner. His first literary work consisted of business reports to Mr. Scott, who was quick to appreciate the wealth of common sense, the power of observation, and the knowledge of people displayed in them. Leskov was twenty-nine when, in 1860, he first engaged in journalism. At first he only wrote between times communications to the daily press, and articles on affairs of practical and everyday interest. But he soon abandoned his other work, came to Petersburg, and became a professional journalist. This happened in 1862. It was a time of intense public excitement. Leskov was absorbed by public interests as much as anyone, but his eminently practical mind and training made it impossible for him to join unreservedly any of the very unpractical and hot-headed parties of the day. Hence his isolation when the incident occurred which left such a lasting trace in his career. He wrote an article on the great fires which had in that year destroyed a large part of Petersburg and which popular rumour was inclined to impute to the "nihilists" and radical-minded university students. Leskov did not support this rumour, but he mentioned it in an article and demanded that a thorough investigation should be carried out by the police in order that it might be either confirmed or confuted.

This demand produced in the Radical press the effect of a bombshell. Leskov was accused of inciting the populace against the students and of "informing" to the police. Leskov was put under boycott, and expelled from the progressive papers. Meanwhile he passed from journalism to fiction. His first short story (*The Oxibos*) appeared in 1863. It was followed by a long novel, *No Way Out* (1864). This novel led to further misunderstandings with the Radicals, who affected to recognize in some of its characters slanderous caricatures of their friends, and this sufficed to stamp Leskov as a vile and libellous reactionary, though the principal Socialist characters in the book were represented as little short of saints. In his next "political" novel, *At Daggers Drawn* (1870–1871), Leskov went much further in the representation of the "nihilists" as a set of blackguards and scoundrels. These "political" novels are not among Leskov's masterpieces, and they had no part in the great reputation he enjoys to-day, which is based on his short stories. But they were sufficient to make Leskov the nightmare of all the Radical literature and to make it impossible for the most influential critics to treat him with any amount of fairness. The great Slavophil critic Apollon Grigoriev, a man of extraordinary but erratic genius, was the only critic to welcome Leskov, to appreciate and to encourage him. But Grigoriev died in 1864 and all Leskov's subsequent popularity was entirely due to the unguided good taste of the public.

This popularity began especially after the publication of his "chronicle" *Soboryane* in 1872 and the series of stories, largely of ecclesiastical life, which followed it in remarkable succession till the end of the seventies. In these stories Leskov appeared as a champion of Orthodoxy and Conservative ideals and they attracted towards him the goodwill of many high-placed persons, in particular of the Empress Marie Alexandrovna, the wife of Alexander II. It was through her interest that Leskov got an official appointment in an advising board of education, practically a sinecure. In the later seventies he joined in a campaign in favour of Orthodoxy against the pietist propaganda of Lord Radstock. But

Leskov never became a thorough conservative, and even in his support of Orthodoxy against Protestantism his principal arguments were the democratic humility of the first and the aristocratic individualism of the "Society schism," as he called Radstock's sect. His attitude towards the official government of the Church was never quite docile, and gradually his Christianity became less traditional and more critical. His stories of clerical life, written in the early eighties, were largely satirical, and for one of these he was asked to leave his government post. He came under the growing influence of Tolstoy and towards the end of his life became a devoted Tolstoyan. This change of attitude towards the conservative principles pushed him back towards the left wing of journalism and in his later years he contributed mainly to moderate Radical magazines. But the dictators of literary opinion still reserved their judgment and were more than cold to him. When he died in 1895, he had many readers all over Russia, but few friends in the literary press. Not long before his death he is reported to have said: "Now I am read for the beauty of my imaginative work, but in fifty years hence this beauty will have faded, and my books will be read only for the ideas contained in them." This was a singularly bad prophecy. More than ever Leskov is read to-day for his qualities of form, style, and narrative, and less than ever for his ideas. In fact very few of his admirers realize what his ideas were. Not that his ideas are at all obscure or concealed, but simply that the attention is concentrated on something different.

Leskov's most striking originality lies in his Russian. His contemporaries wrote and tried to write in a level and even style, avoiding anything too striking or questionable. Leskov avidly absorbed every unexpected and picturesque idiom. All the various forms of professional and class language, every variety of slang, were welcome to his pages. But his especial favourites were the comic effects of colloquial Church Slavonic, and the puns of "popular etymology." These effects are of course untranslatable. Like O. Henry, he allowed himself great liberties in this direction, and was the inventor of many successful and unexpected deformations of familiar sense or familiar sound. Another striking peculiarity which Leskov alone of all his contemporaries possesses is a superlative narrative gift. As a story-teller he is easily first among modern Russian writers. His stories are mere anecdotes, told with enormous zest and ability, and even in his longer works his favourite way of characterizing his characters is by a series of anecdotes. This was quite contrary to the traditions of "serious" Russian fiction and induced the critics to regard Leskov as a mere jester. His most original stories are packed with incident and adventure to an extent that appeared ludicrous to the critics, who regarded ideas and messages as the principal thing. It is too evident that Leskov revels in this wealth of incident, as also in the sounds and the grotesque appearances of words. However sincerely he tried to be a moralist and a preacher, he could not refrain from making the most of every opportunity of making puns and multiplying anecdotes. Tolstoy liked Leskov's stories and enjoyed his verbal gambols, but he censured him for his exuberance. His chief fault, Tolstoy thought, was that he could not keep his talent in bounds and that there were too many good things in his stories. This taste for verbal picturesqueness and rapid and complicated narrative are in striking contrast to the habits of almost every other Russian novelist, especially of Turgenev, Goncharov, or Chekhov. There is no haze, no atmosphere, no mellowness in Leskov's vision of the world: he chooses the most crying colours, the boldest relief and the sharpest outline. His figures stand out in a crude daylight. If Turgenev's or Chekhov's world may be compared to a landscape by Corot, Leskov's is a picture by Breughel the Elder, full of gay and bright colours and grotesque forms. There is no drabness in Leskov, and the characters he finds in Russian life are picturesque, striking, and vigorously drawn. Great virtue, extraordinary originality, strong vices, powerful passions, and grotesque humours are his favourite matter. He is at once a hero-worshipper and a humorist. It can almost be said that the more heroical his heroes, the more humorously he treats them. This humorous hero-worship is Leskov's most original feature.

Leskov's political novels, which brought on him the hostility of the Radicals, may be safely left out of account. Their level is no higher than that of the average "reactionary" novels of the sixties and seventies. They are deservedly forgotten and have no part in his present fame. But the short stories he wrote at the same time are very good. They are not so rich in verbal felicity as the stories of his mature period, but they present in an eminent degree his qualities as a story-teller. Unlike his later work, they are pictures of almost unrelieved wickedness and passion. A typical instance is *A Lady Macbeth of the Mtzensk District* (1866), which has been translated into the English. It is a powerful study of the criminal passion of a woman, and of the gay and cynical callousness of her lover. It is bathed in a cold and crude light and written with sustained, "naturalistic" objectivity. Another remarkable story of this period is *The Amazon* (*Voïtelnitsa*), the racy study of a Petersburg procuress, who regards her profession with a deliciously naïve cynicism, and is sincerely and deeply hurt by the black "thanklessness" of one of the victims, whom she had first pushed into the ways of shame.

These early stories were followed by a series of "Chronicles" of the imaginary town of Stargorod, which may be called a Russian Barchester, as an English reviewer has honoured Leskov on account of one of these with the title of a Russian Trollope. They form a trilogy—*Old Years in Plodomasovo* (1869), *Soboryane* (Cathedral, or rather Minster, folk—1872), and *A Decayed Family* (1875). The second of these chronicles is the most widely popular of all Leskov's works. It deals with the Stargorod clergy. Its head, the Archpriest Tuberozov, is one of Leskov's most successful and noble portraits of a "just man." The deacon Akhila is his greatest character creation. It is one of the most wonderful of the whole portrait-gallery of Russian literature. The comic escapades and unconscious mischief-making of this enormous, exuberant, very unspiritual, and quite childlike deacon and the constant reprimands his behaviour draws from Father Tuberozov are familiar to every Russian reader, and Akhila himself is a universal favourite. But *Soboryane* is not at all points representative of their author—it is too leisurely, too uneventful, too placid to be really quite Leskovian. The very idea of a comparison with Trollope would be ridiculous in reference to one of his more typical tales.

Such a typical tale is *The Enchanted Wanderer* (1874). Here his narrative power reaches the high-water mark. In a little over a hundred pages are told the eventful life and extraordinary adventures of an unwilling adventurer, who comes under a spell and all his life, willy-nilly, is tossed from adventure to adventure. The adventures follow in breathless succession and each of them is told in extraordinary rapid tempo, and saturated with expressive and picturesque detail. The story is told in the first person—and this is Leskov's favourite way of giving free play to all his power of verbal invention. *The Enchanted Wanderer* was followed in the same year by *The Sealed Angel*, another breathless story of adventure told in the racy language of an Old Believer—the thrilling story of the recovery of a holy image confiscated by the authorities. In these stories, as in so many others, Leskov has for his subject the religious life of the Russian people. His ideal, at first very close to that of Orthodox Churchmen, in his later stories becomes more purely ethical and less Orthodox. Such already is *On the Edge of the World* (1876), the story of how a Russian missionary bishop was saved from death in the Siberian wilderness by a heathen native, and how he came to the conclusion that mission work as it was conducted worked only ill to the natives. Next came *The Just Men*, a series of extraordinary puritan and Christian virtue among most various classes of Russian Society. In them, as well as in the humorous and satirical *Details of Episcopal Life*, Leskov tends to approach pure journalism. There is no invention in these stories. The limits of the narrative form become less distinct and the narrative is often interrupted by discussions. Soon after this, Leskov came under the influence of Tolstoy, but he never abandoned his own idiosyncrasies and it was in the eighties that his most exuberantly original stories were written. In such stories as *The Left-handed Smith and the Steel Flea* (1882), *A Robbery* (1887), or in most stories from the collection of *Christmas Stories* (1886) and *Appropriate Stories* (1887), there is nothing except a sheer delight in story-telling. *The Left-Handed Smith* is the most extraordinary of these productions. It tells of how a Steel Flea of life size was made by an English smith and presented to the Emperor Alexander I. The Emperor challenges the smiths of Tula to go one better—this they do by shoeing every one of the English Flea's feet in gold. The Left-handed Smith is taken to England but, on returning to Russia, gets into the lock-up for drunkenness. The story is told in the most wonderful language, where almost every other word is an extraordinary funny invention of Leskov's. It stands next to *Soboryane* in the favour of the general reader.

Still most of his later works are profoundly impregnated with his "new Christianity," which he himself identified with Tolstoy's teaching. This identification cannot be quite endorsed. Leskov's Christianity, like Tolstoy's, is anticlerical, undenominational, and purely ethical. But here the identity ends: the dominant ethical note is different. It is the cult not of moral purity and of reason, but of humility and charity. "Spiritual pride," self-conscious righteousness, is for Leskov the greatest of crimes, and it is doubtful whether he would have liked the hero of *The Light Shines in the Darkness*. Active charity is to him the principal virtue and he attaches very little value to moral purity, still less to physical purity. The charity of his harlots is often pointedly contrasted with the proud and cold virtue of matrons. His women do not shrink from prostitution to save those whom they love. And one of his most holy characters is the Mime Pamphalon (in the story of the same name), who spends all his life in procuring frivolous and by no means virtuous amusement for the rich, but, when the occasion comes, does not for a moment waver before sacrificing all his hard-won savings to save a human soul in distress. This feeling of sin as the necessary soil for sanctity, and the condemnation of self-righteous pride as the sin against the Holy Ghost, is intimately akin to the moral sense of the Russian people and of the Eastern Church, and very different from Tolstoy's proud protestant and Luciferian ideal of perfection. Many of Leskov's stories of his last years written in his early manner are among his best, and one of these is his last, bearing the title so characteristic of his cult of humility—*The Lady and the Slut*.

But the most characteristic work of his last few years, his stories of early Christian life * (*The Mountain, The Brigand of Ascalon, The Beautiful Aza*), are written in a new manner. The subject-matter and setting prevented Leskov from giving rein in these stories to his usual verbal liberties and eccentricities. But his exuberance did not forsake him, and for all his admiration of Tolstoy, Leskov did not seek to imitate the "classical" manner of his popular tales. His narratives are as picturesque, as varied, and as complicated as ever. He develops a new and unexpected quality, a wonderful power of imagination. He conjures up a vivid and splendidly coloured pageant of life under the late pagan or early Byzantine Emperors. He has very little exact knowledge of the period, he commits glaring anachronisms, and is rather at sea in ancient geography. The world he evokes owes much to the Lives of the Saints, something to Flaubert, and much to his own imagination. There is a charming, ever-present undercurrent of humour and finesse. The result is altogether queer and baroque. What was particularly new in them to the Russian reader was a boldly outspoken treatment of sensual episodes. The prudish Russian critics of the time cried out against this licence, which seemed strange in a Tolstoyan. They charged Leskov with insincerity, with treating his moral subjects as nothing but pretexts for the display of voluptuous and sensuous scenes. Leskov, however, was quite sincere, and the morals of his stories were the most

---

* These are for the most part borrowed from the *Prologue,* a Slavonic collection of edifying readings for every day (mainly from the Greek), which was very popular in old Russia, and is still held in high esteem by the Old Believers.

important thing in them to his conscious self. But there was more complexity in the marvellous story-teller than in his simple-minded critics, and his subconscious artistic self took quite as much pleasure in the descriptions of the doings of the Alexandrian flower-girls as in the sublime humility of his chief characters. He had seen Russian life as a violent, crude, parti-coloured pageant of crime, horseplay, and heroism. And now he had created for himself an equally magnificent and indecent Roman Orient. For if there was one thing he hated in the world, it was self-centred and self-satisfied respectability.

To his last years belongs also *The Hare Park* (*Zayachi Remiz*), which was published only posthumously in 1917 (in book form in 1923). It is one of his most remarkable works, and his greatest achievment in concentrated satire. It is the story, told for the greater part in his own words, of Onopri Opanasovich Peregud, an inmate of a lunatic asylum. In his former life he was the son of a petty Little-Russian squire, and was made police-inspector through the influence of the bishop, who happened to be a schoolfellow of his father's. Onopri Opanasovich, who is a quite unusually weak-minded and imbecile creature, got on all right with his responsible post until the beginning of the Revolutionary movement of the sixties, when he succumbed to the ambitious desire of catching a Nihilist. He gets hold of several Nihilists, who turn out to be law-abiding citizens (and one of them even a detective who is himself hunting for Nihilists), and is ultimately hoodwinked by his own coachman, who turns out to be a genuine Nihilist. The unexpected result unhinges him and so he comes to the lunatic asylum. The story contains all the best features of Leskov's manner: wonderful racy diction, boisterous farce, extraordinary anecdotes; but it is subordinated to a unifying idea, and the figure of the hapless police-inspector grows into a symbol of vast historical and moral significance.

Leskov, in spite of the admiration for him of some English critics, like Mr. Baring, has not yet come into his own with the English-speaking reader. Two volumes of translations of his work have appeared within these last three years (*The*

Sentry, and Other Stories, tr. A. E. Chamot, and *The Cathedral Folk,* tr. Isabel F. Hapgood), but they have attracted little attention. This is largely due to the inadequacy of the translations. The choice of short stories is also not of the happiest—it represents Leskov exclusively from his more gloomy and serious side, and leaves his humorous gift unrecognized. But there is also a deeper cause for this—the Anglo-Saxon public have made up their mind as to what they want from a Russian writer, and Leskov does not answer to this idea. But those who really want to know more about Russia must sooner or later recognize that Russia is not all contained in Dostoevsky and Chekhov, and that if you want to know a thing you must first be free of prejudice and on your guard against hasty generalizations. Then they will perhaps come nearer to Leskov, who is generally recognized by Russians as the most Russian of Russian writers and the one who had the deepest and widest knowledge of the Russian people as it actually is.

4. POETRY: SLUCHEVSKY

Poetry, in the reign of Alexander II, suffered from the same causes as prose, but in a much greater degree. Russian "Victorian" poetry was not in itself a very vigorous growth. It was eclectic; it had degenerated from the high standard of the age of Pushkin, it did not believe in its own right to be, and tried to discover a compromise between pure art and public utility. The typical Russian "Victorians" —Polonsky, Maykov, Alexis Tolstoy—wrote some very good verse, but they were distinctly minor men in comparison with their great prose-writing contemporaries, and not only minor in genius but minor in craftsmanship. Poetry as it existed in their hands was incapable of further development. But there were beside them other poets, who, breaking away in exactly opposite directions from the "Victorian compromise," produced poetry of a more vigorous, less decadent, and more fruitful kind. These were Nekrasov and Fet.

Nekrasov (1821–1877) rejected all the stock-in-trade of

conventional poetry and attempted to introduce a new style full of Realism and daring modernity. His vigorous and unrefined genius produced work of extraordinary power, but his would-be disciples were incapable of learning from him, as much as he was incapable of teaching them. They could adopt only his subject-matter—"the sufferings of the people" —but not his violent and impulsive originality. Nekrasov was despised by the "æsthetes," and though he was admired by the Radicals, they admired him chiefly for his noble civic feelings. His verse, they admitted, was uncouth, but all its shortcomings might be pardoned for the noble feelings it expressed. Only our time has discovered that Nekrasov was not only a good Democrat (as a matter of fact, he was a very bad one), but a great and startlingly original poet as well. At the time, no one was capable of even imitating him, and "civic" poetry sank in the hands of his successors to absolute insignificance. Fet (1820–1892), on the other hand, rejected the compromise in favour of pure poetry. He divorced poetry from life, or at least from everyday life. Poetry was to him a pure essence, like the rarefied air of the mountain tops—it could not be one's home, but only a sanctuary. His early poetry (1840–1860) is purely musical and in many respects anticipates the most original features of Verlaine. In the sixties he was hissed out of literature by the anti-æsthetic critics, and ceased publishing. He lived the life of a country squire, keeping up relations with Tolstoy and putting into practice his conviction that life and poetry were to be kept apart. He applied himself to increasing his income, and only at rare intervals climbed the mountain tops of poetry. For twenty years he published nothing. When he appeared before the public again with the distilled produce of those twenty years, he had become another poet. His late poetry contained in the four issues of *Evening Lights* (1883–1891) is less musical, more tense, more packed, and more intellectual than his early songs. It achieves the ideal of pure poetry in a way somewhat similar to that of Mallarmé and Paul Valéry. It is like pure gold, with no dross in it. These short poems, seldom more than twelve lines long, are tight with poetical significance, and though he uses as his subject-matter themes of emotion and passion, the real content of his poems is the creative process, which distils from the raw matter of emotion the pure essence of poetry. Fet was highly esteemed by all those who did not measure poetry by the scale of civic progressiveness. But the principles of his late work were creatively adopted only by the Symbolists, who from the very beginning recognized him as one of their greatest masters.

But, apart from Fet, "art for art" poetry fell as low as civic poetry. Even if compared with the novelists of the time, the poets born between 1830 and 1850 are utterly contemptible. The chief reason was again the consistent neglect of craftsmanship. This is best seen in the work of Constantine Sluchévsky (1837–1904), who had in him the germs of genius, but was incapable of expressing himself otherwise than in a stammer. He began publishing verse very early, but, like Fet, he was hissed into silence by the Nihilist critics and, like Fet, ceased publishing. When the atmosphere became more propitious for poetry, he reappeared before the public and in 1880 published a collected edition of his poems. The Radicals did not give him a better reception than that of twenty years earlier, but there was now a larger public who could appreciate him apart from the utilitarian considerations. He even became a sort of head of a school and was sometimes honoured with the title of King of Poets, but, being what he was, a stammerer innocent of the principles of his craft, he was incapable of becoming a fruitful influence.

In spite of the low level of his poetical workmanship, Sluchevsky is a true poet and a poet of outstanding interest. Like Nekrasov, though in another way, he tried to spring the fetters of romantic convention and annex to poetry provinces that had hitherto been considered foreign. He had a philosophical mind and was deeply read in modern science. He had a wonderful vision of the world and delighted in the boundless multiplicity of beings and things. His "geographical" poems, especially those inspired by the North of Russia and the Murman Coast, are among his best. But he was still more powerfully attracted by the eternal problems of Good and Evil, and of Life and Death.   He brooded over the problem of personal immortality, and some of his poems on the subject are most striking.   He had a wonderful way of expressing his faith in lines of memorable pointedness.   In one of his *Easter Poems* the Marys discover that Christ is not in his grave:

> "They hasten, silent.   They dare not realize
> That Death is no more.   That the hour is nigh
> Their graves will also become empty
> To the light of the heavens on fire."

And as a contrast to this, in another poem he has a terrible vision of Judgment: "In the green light that proceeded not from the extinguished suns, but from the wrath of God," the Lord, as in the Judgment of Michael Angelo, rises to pronounce the damnation of the whole of mankind, "for Grace is useless, since it could be accorded only to the babe unborn." Another terrible vision is *After an Execution in Geneva*, where the poet dreams that he has become a "sounding sensitive chord" strung on a guitar as on a rack, and some "fearful hag" playing a psalm on it.   And by the side of this poem, so symbolically pregnant (and so highly esteemed by the Symbolists), *Parson Elisey*, a tale in verse in the style of Nekrasov, on a subject strikingly reminiscent of Tolstoy's *The Devil*. Flashes of genius are frequent in his work, but on the whole it is ineffective and irritating, for one feels all the time that all this might have been expressed much better if Sluchevsky had not lived in such a degenerate age.

5. THE LEADERS OF THE INTELLIGENTSIA: MIKHAYLOVSKY

The word *Intelligentsia* has two meanings.   In the broader sense it includes all the educated and professional classes, irrespective of their political feelings and degree of political activity.   In a narrower sense it is used to denote a special section of these classes—that which is intensely and actively interested in political and social issues.   By a still narrower application it came to be applied in pre-

Revolutionary Russia to those groups only which were more or less radically inclined. Slavophils and Conservatives were not "intelligentsia." The Intelligentsia in this sense is an inner circle, a sect, almost an order of knighthood. The Russian intelligentsia assumed this form in the sixties and it subsisted till the Bolshevik Revolution. It never included the whole, and probably even never the majority, of the intelligentsia in the wider sense. But it was a centre, a sort of magnetic pole towards which the majority were attracted. Its influence was large. University students formed the main army of Radicalism, but it was led by the literary press. There was inside this "Church" a great variety of opinion in detail, but all were united in several essential tenets. These were: hostility to the existing régime; faith in Progress and Democracy; a feeling of duty towards what was called in the sixties "the younger brother"—the uneducated working-classes. Most of the Radicals were Socialists, but they regarded the more advanced liberals as "theirs" if they were sufficiently anti-government. The history of the ideas that dominated the Intelligentsia has been many times written, and intelligentsia historians have often tried to identify the history of these ideas with the history of Russian literature. This is a gross falsification. But no literary history can overlook the main lines of the development.

In the sixties and seventies there were two main shades of Radical opinion—the Nihilists (or "Thinking Realists," as they called themselves) and the Populists (Narodniks). The Nihilists laid stress on materialism and agnosticism. Science, especially Natural Science (Darwin), was their chief weapon. They carried furthest the anti-æsthetic movement. They were Socialists, but their Socialism stood in the background. Their first duty was to enlighten the people with practical knowledge and evolutionary science. Their influence was paramount in the sixties, when they had a gifted leader in the brilliant pamphleteer Pisarev (1840–1868), but it declined after his death and had almost disappeared towards the beginning of our period. The Populists were more pronounced Socialists. Their name came from their cult of the People—

identified with the working-classes, and more especially with the peasants. Many of them were "conscience-stricken noblemen," that is, members of the gentry who were obsessed by the idea of sacrificing all their lives to the People in expiation of the wrongs of serfdom. At first they were largely non-political and hoped to achieve social revolution by some internal process in the existing peasant land-commune. But towards the end of the seventies they gave birth to the "People's Will" party, which adopted more active revolutionary methods and organized the assassination of Alexander II. The reaction of the eighties put an end for a time to all active revolutionism, but the Narodniks remained the most influential and numerous group of the intelligentsia. They retained their hegemony over the Radical intelligentsia till the advent of Marxism in the nineties. Some of them, after the defeat of the Terrorists, shifted towards a more non-political attitude, and many Populists of the eighties approached Tolstoy in his passive Anarchism, or even the more conservative and Slavophil anarchism of Dostoevsky. But all of them retained the cult of the virtues of the Russian People, and the motto "Everything for the People." Populism was, after all, the form taken in Russia by the teaching of Jean Jacques Rousseau.

The leaders of Populism in the sixties and seventies were the poet Nekrasov and the novelist Saltykov. They gave the tone to the great majority of the young generation, but as they were imaginative writers and not theoreticians, they could play but a small part in settling the detail of the Populist dogma. The great "Doctor" of the Populist "Church" was a younger man—Nikolay Konstantinovich Mikhaylòvsky (1842–1904), the all-authoritative expounder of its doctrine, and in his last years, especially after the death of Saltykov in 1889, the grand old man of Russian Radicalism. He was a sociologist, and his book on *What is Progress* is still considered by the successors of the Populists as the *Summa Theologiæ* of their doctrine. Mikhaylovsky called his method in sociology the "subjective" method, which meant that social science was to be studied not disinterestedly like natural science, but in terms of human progress. Progress for him meant the greatest happiness not of the greatest number, but of all men, for human individuality was the supreme and only value and could not be sacrificed to society. Socialism was precisely the only order which allowed for the happiness of all and for the full expansion of every individuality. The means of achieving progress was the conscious action of individual persons inspired with Faith and with a sense of duty towards the People. Populism as expounded by Mikhaylovsky differs from Marxian Socialism principally in two things—in its ethical foundation and in its faith in human individuality. It knows nothing either of the class-morality or of the superstitious faith in the laws of evolution of Marxism.

Besides his sociological writings, Mikhaylovsky was a great journalist; his polemical writings (though, as is the case with most polemical writings, they are often not fair play) are always brilliant and full of point. He was also a critic, and though, like all the critics of his time, he considered in the writers he criticized only their "message" and their degree of public utility, he had a wonderfully acute critical insight. He was able as early as 1873, from certain pedagogical articles by Tolstoy, to discern the essentially destructive and anarchical nature of Tolstoy's doctrine and largely to predict the development taken by him after 1880 (*The Left and Right Hand of Count Leo Tolstoy*). Mikhaylovsky's critical masterpiece is his essay on Dostoevsky (*A Cruel Talent*, 1882). It is full of suppressed but unmistakable hostility to the ideas and person of Dostoevsky, but with wonderful precision he lays his finger on the writer's love of suffering and connects it with his morbid "sadism." He was the first to bring out the importance of *The Memoirs from Underground* and recognize the central position they occupied in Dostoevsky's work.

6. THE CONSERVATIVES

In political life the Radicals were the opposition. But in literature they were the majority, and the supporters of the existing order were, in their turn, the opposition. Conservative writers had a considerable influence on the Government, but they had fewer readers than the Radicals. The Polish revolt of 1863, and still more the assassination of Alexander II in 1881, had turned the bulk of the upper and middle classes away from Radicalism in practical politics, and the reactionary policy of Alexander III's Government found substantial support in the country. But this conservatism (as conservatism so often is) was merely the outcome of fear and inertness. It was not interested in conservative *ideas*. The intellectually active part of the Nation remained largely Radical and atheistic. Only a small minority of thinking people, but among them perhaps the most independent, original, and sincere minds of the day, showed a critical attitude towards the dogma of Agnosticism and Democracy, and strove towards a creative revival of Christian and national ideas. But the public had little use for independent thought—they preferred either Radicalism or Radicalism-and-water, and independent Conservative writers—like Grigoriev, Dostoevsky, Leontiev, Rozanov—had to struggle against general indifference and its consequences, unemployment and poverty. Dostoevsky was alone successful in this struggle. Only the big men of the political press, the spokesman of one of the two large sections of conservative opinion, could command a hearing.

These two sections were Slavophils, represented by Aksakov, and practical Government nationalists, headed by Katkov. Ivan Aksakov (1823–1886), the son of the great memoirist, was the last remnant of the old idealistic Slavophilism of the forties. He was a brilliant and outspoken publicist and orator, and his political influence, especially during the Turkish crisis of 1876–1878, was enormous. But he was not a creator of ideas. Katkov (1818–1888) was still less creative. He was an eloquent and determined journalist, and his force of will and fixity of purpose often compelled the Government to be firmer in its policy than it would have been without his support. But he was only the watchdog, not the philosopher of Reaction. This title might rather be assigned to the famous Pobedonostsev (1828–1910), "Ober-procuror" of the Synod for thirty years, and an enormous political influence under Alexander III and especially in the first years of

Nicholas II. But his conservatism was merely negative; it arose out of a profound disbelief in every reform; it was the outcome of a scepticism that did not believe in the possibility of any rational betterment. He was at bottom a nihilist, who thought that the existing order was as good as any other, and that it was better to support it by all possible means than to launch out on any uncertain experiment.

But among those less closely connected with the Government and with politics, there were men who had better and more positive reasons for defending the traditional groundwork of Russian State and Church. Of the old Slavophils, romantic idealists, who believed in the inherent, God-ordained superiority of the Russian nation, and in the great responsibility of Russia for this dangerous gift of Providence, Aksakov was the last. A later phase of Slavophilism, more democratic and less exclusive, had lost its greatest leaders in Grigoriev (1822–1864) and Dostoevsky. It was still represented by Stràkhov (1828–1895), a philosopher and critic, who had been the journalistic ally of Dostoevsky, but had retained little enthusiasm for his great associate: of all those who knew Dostoevsky, Strakhov had had the most illuminating and terrible glimpses of the dark, "infernal, underground" soul of the creator of Stavrogin. Strakhov's philosophical work does not belong here, and as a critic he was not strikingly great. But he was the centre of anti-Radical idealism in the eighties, the principal link between the Slavophils and the mystical revival of the nineties. His place is greater in literary biography than in literary history. Besides his association with Dostoevsky, he was an intimate friend of Tolstoy, and he became the literary godfather of the greatest writer of the mystical revival—Rozanov.

Another interesting figure was Nicholas Danilévsky (1822–1885), the creator of scientific Slavophilism. He was a naturalist by training, passed most of his life in combating the phylloxera in his Crimean property, and gave his nationalism a biological foundation. His book on *Russia and Europe* (1869) develops the theory of individual, mutually watertight civilizations. In Russia and Slavdom he saw the germs of a new civilization that was to displace that of the West. He did not consider Russia in any way superior to, but merely different from, the West, and Russia's duty was to be herself not because by being herself she would be better and holier than the West, but because as she was not of the West she could never by imitating the West become anything but an imperfect ape, not a real member of Western civilization.* Danilevsky's ideas had a great influence on Leontiev, the only conservative philosopher of the period, who had real genius.

7. CONSTANTINE LEONTIEV

Constantine Nikolaevich Leòntiev was born in 1831, on his paternal estate of Kudinovo (province of Kaluga). He has left us in his memoirs a vivid picture of his mother, who was the principal influence in his childhood, and for whom he ever retained a deep affection. In due course he went to school, and afterwards to the University of Moscow, where he studied medicine. He came under the influence of the "philanthropic" literature of the time and became an ardent admirer of Turgenev. In 1851, under this influence, he wrote a play full of morbid self-analysis. He took it to Turgenev, who received him, liked it, and used his influence to place it in a magazine. But it was not passed by the censor. Turgenev continued patronizing Leontiev and at one time considered him, next to Tolstoy (whose *Childhood* appeared in 1852), the most promising young writer of the time. In 1854, when Leontiev was in his last year, the Crimean War broke out, and medical students in their last year were allowed, if they went to the front, to take their degree without completing their studies. Leontiev volunteered and joined the Crimean army as a military surgeon. He worked for the most part in hospitals, and worked hard, for he was passionately interested in his work. About this time he developed a paradoxical theory of æsthetic immoralism, which took strange forms at

---

* There can be no doubt that Danilevsky's book (which has been translated into German) is the principal source of the ideas of Oswald Spengler, whose *Untergang des Abendlandes* produced such a sensation in Germany.

times—thus on two occasions, as he tells us in his wonderful memoirs, he encouraged marauding in the Cossacks of a regiment he was attached to. But he remained himself scrupulously honest. He was one of the few non-combatants connected with the Crimean army who had the opportunity of enriching themselves and did not.

So when the war was over he returned to Moscow penniless. He continued practising as a doctor, and published in 1861–1862 a series of novels which had no success. They are not great novels, but remarkable for the fierce intensity with which he expressed in them, always in the most striking and provoking manner, his æsthetic immoralism. "All is good which is beautiful and strong, whether sanctity or debauch, whether reactionary or revolutionary—no matter" "That nation is great which is great both in good and evil." This strange immoralistic pathos is best of all seen in the very remarkable story *A Husband's Confession,* where a middle-aged husband encourages the misconduct of his young wife, not from any idea of the "rights of woman" in the style of George Sand, but because he wants her to live a full and beautiful life of passion, ecstasy, and suffering. All these novels passed at the time unnoticed. At this period of his life he began to be attracted by the Slavophils for their respect and love of the originality of Russian life, but their moral idealism remained quite alien to him.

In 1861 he married an uneducated Greek girl from the Crimea. He could not live on literature, so he began to look out for some better employment. In 1863 he was admitted to the consular service and was appointed secretary and dragoman to the Russian consulate at Candia. He did not stay long at Candia, for he soon had to be transferred for horsewhipping the French vice-consul. This, however, did not impede his career. He moved up the ladder of consular service with great rapidity and was in 1869 appointed to the important and independent post of consul at Yanina, in Epirus. All this time his behaviour was far from exemplary. His hero was Alcibiades and he tried to live up to his standard of "full" and beautiful life. He lived passionately and expensively. He was always in some love affair—and confided them to his wife. She did not like it, and it would seem that these confidences were the cause of her mental illness. For since 1869 she became, with intervals, a permanent mental invalid. This was the first shadow on the wall. In 1871 came the next, the death of his mother.

In the same year he was transferred to Salonika and almost immediately had a very severe attack of local malaria. He was in imminent danger, and on his bed of sickness made a vow to go to Mount Athos to expiate his sins. As soon as he was well enough, he fulfilled his vow and spent about a year at Athos submitting to the severe rule of the monastery and to the strict spiritual guidance of an "elder." From this time he recognized as sinful his Alcibiades-like life of the previous years and all his immoralistic writings, and became converted to the strictest and most ascetic form of Byzantine and monastic orthodoxy. But his æsthetic immoralism remained in substance unchanged, it only bowed down before the rule of dogmatic Christianity. In 1873, finding himself in disagreement with the ambassador Ignatiev about the Græco-Bulgarian church schism, he left the consular service. Ignatiev, like the Slavophil he was, and like all official Russia, took the side of the Bulgarians because they were Slavs. To Leontiev the Bulgarians, Slavs or no Slavs, were democrats and rebels to their lawful spiritual lord, the Œcumenical Patriarch. This was characteristic of Leontiev—he had no interest in mere Slavdom. What he wanted was a firm conservatism in the matter of national originality and tradition, and of this he found more in the Greeks than in the Bulgarians, whom with complete justice he suspected of being easily Europeanized and reduced to the common level of Western democratic civilization. But the Greeks—the conservative Greek peasants, rural tradesmen, and monks—he loved passionately. They were to him the bulwark of what was to him the greatest of values—Byzantine civilization.

About the same time he became acquainted with Danilevsky's *Russia and Europe*, which produced on him a strong impression by its scientific-biological treatment of the history of civilizations. The idea of the individual civilization as a complete and self-contained organism became his own and he gave it a brilliant development in his remarkable essay on *Byzantinism and Slavdom*. In it he confuted Danilevsky's idea of the Slavs' being an independent cultural entity and saw the originality of Russia in her being the pupil and heir of Byzantium. Unlike the Slavophils, Leontiev did not condemn Western civilization as a whole, but only in its last stage. Mediæval and seventeenth-century Europe was as good as Byzantium, but civilizations were like living beings and passed with the necessity of a natural law three inevitable phases of development. The first phase was initial or primitive simplicity; the second, exuberant growth and complexity of creative and beautiful inequality. This was the only valuable stage. It had lasted in Europe from the eleventh to the eighteenth century. The third phase was the "secondary simplification" of dissolution and putrefaction. These phases in the life of a nation were equivalent in the life of an individual to those of embryonic life, of life, and of dissolution after death, when the complexity of a living organism is again reduced to its constituent elements.* Europe was since the eighteenth century in the third stage, and there was reason to believe that Russia was already infected by this putrefaction.

The essay passed unnoticed, and altogether, after leaving the consular service, Leontiev fell on evil times. His income was insignificant and in 1881 he had to sell his estate. He passed much of his time in monasteries. At one time he was sub-editor of a provincial official paper. Then he was appointed censor. But up to his death he was in constant difficulties. During his life in Greece he had worked at a series of stories of modern Greek life. In 1876 he published them in book form (*From the Life of Christians in Turkey*, 3 volumes). He placed great hopes on the success of this work but it fell flat, and the few people who noticed it admired it only as good descriptive journalism. In the eighties, with

---

* This theory is again strikingly reflected in those of Oswald Spengler. Leontiev's three phases are Spengler's *Vorkultur, Kultur,* and *Zivilisation.*

the growth of reaction, Leontiev felt himself a little less out
of tune and less alone. But though the reactionaries re-
spected him and opened to him their columns, they did not
gauge the originality of his genius and regarded him as rather
a doubtful and dangerous ally. Still, in the last years of his
life he found more sympathy than before. And before he
died he was surrounded by a small number of devoted followers
and admirers. This brought some consolation to his last
years. He spent more and more time in Optina, the most
famous of Russian ascetic monasteries, and in 1891, with the
permission of his spiritual father, the "elder" Father Ambrose,
he took monastic vows with the name of Clement. He settled
in Troitsa (the ancient Trinity Monastery near Moscow),
but had not long to live. He died on November 12, 1891.

Leontiev's writings, apart from his early novels and his
stories of Greek life, are of three kinds: those in which he
expounds his political and religious ideas; works of literary
criticism, and memoirs. His political writings (including
Byzantinism and Slavdom) were published in two volumes
under the title of *Russia, the East, and the Slavs* (1885–1886).
They are written in a vehement, nervous, hurried, disrupted,
but vigorous and pointed style. The nervous uneasiness
reflected in it reminds one of Dostoevsky. But, unlike Dostoevsky, Leontiev is a logician, and the outline of his argument
through the agitated nervousness of his style is almost as clear
as Tolstoy's. Three elements form the philosophy (if it may
be called a philosophy) of Leontiev. First came a biological
foundation due to his medical training, which made him look for
and believe in natural laws in the social and moral world. It
was strengthened by the influence of Danilevsky. It found
expression in his law of the "triune process"—gestation—
life—dissolution of societies. Next came his temperamental
æsthetic immoralism, which made him passionately enjoy the
multiplicity and varied beauty of life. And at last his unconditional submission to the guidance of monastic orthodoxy which
dominated his later years; it was rather a passionate desire than
the actual presence of faith, but this only made it more
vehement and uncompromising. These three influences resulted

in his final political doctrine of extreme Reaction, and nationalism. He hated the modern West both for its atheism and for its democratic, levelling tendencies which destroyed the complex and varied beauty of social life. The chief thing for Russia was to stop the process of dissolution and putrefaction coming from the West. This is expressed in the words (attributed to Leontiev, though they do not occur in his works), "We must freeze Russia, to prevent her from rotting." But in his biological heart of hearts he did not believe in the possibility of stopping the natural process. He was a profound anti-optimist. He not only hated democratic progress, but he disbelieved in the realization of his own ideals. He did not want the world to be better. He thought pessimism *here* an essential part of religion. His political "platform" is stated in his characteristic agitated and broken style in the following formulas.

"(1) The State must be many-coloured, complex, strong, based on class privileges, and change with circumspection; on the whole, harsh, even to fierceness. (2) The Church must be more *independent* than at present. The Episcopate must be bolder, more authoritative, more concentrated. The Church must act as a moderating influence in the State, not the contrary. (3) Life must be poetical, multiform in its national —as opposed to the West—unity (for instance, either not dance at all, but pray to God, or else dance, but in our own way; invent or develop our national dances to a beautiful refinement). (4) The Law, the principles of government, must be severer; individuals must try to be personally kinder; one will counterbalance the other. (5) Science must develop in a spirit of profound contempt for its own utility."

In all Leontiev did and wrote, there was such a profound contempt for mere morality, such a passionate hatred of the democratic herd, and such a violent assertion of the aristocratic ideal, that he has been more than once called the Russian Nietzsche. But Nietzsche's impulse was religious and Leontiev's was not. He was a rare instance in modern times (the thing was a rule in the Middle Ages) of an essentially unreligious man submitting consciously and obediently to the hard rule of dogmatic and exclusive religion. But he was not a seeker after God, or after the Absolute. Leontiev's world is a finite world, a world whose very essence and beauty lie in its finiteness and in its imperfection. *Die Liebe zum Fernen* was quite unknown to him. He accepted and loved Orthodox Christianity not for the perfection it promised in heaven and announced in the Person of God, but for the stress it laid on the imperfection of earthly life. And this imperfection was what he loved above all things, with all the variety of forms implied in it—for he was a Pluralist, if ever there was one. Those who believed in progress and wanted to introduce their paltry and inferior perfection into this splendidly imperfect world were his worst enemies. He treats them with splendid scorn, quite worthy of Nietzsche, in his brilliant satire *The Average European as the Means and End of Universal Progress.*

Though Leontiev preferred life to art and liked literature in the measure it reflected beautiful, that is, organic and varied, life, he was perhaps the only genuine literary critic of his time. For alone of all his contemporaries he was capable of going to the essential facts of literary art, apart from the *message* of the author. His book on the novels of Tolstoy (*Analysis, Style, and Atmosphere in the Novels of Count L. N. Tolstoy,* 1890) is for its penetrating analysis of the novelist's means of expression the masterpiece of Russian criticism. In it he condemns (as Tolstoy did himself a few years later in *What Is Art?*) the superfluous-detail manner of the Realists and praises Tolstoy for abandoning it in his then recently published stories for the people. This is characteristic of Leontiev's critical fairness: he censures the style of *War and Peace,* though he likes its philosophy, and praises the style of the popular stories, though he hates their "new Christianity."

During the last years of his life Leontiev published some fragments of his personal recollections, which for the general reader are his most interesting work. They are written in the same agitated and nervous manner as are his political essays. This nervous style, the great vividness of the story, and their unlimited sincerity give them a unique place among

Russian memoirs. The best fragments are those which were to contain a complete history of his religious life and conversion (but stop short with the first two chapters describing his childhood and his mother; the story of his literary relations with Turgenev); and the wonderfully vivid account of his part in the Crimean War and of the descent of the Allies on Kerch in 1855. It is truly "infectious." The reader himself becomes part of the agitated, passionate, impulsive soul of Leontiev.

In his lifetime Leontiev was judged exclusively on party lines, and as he was nothing if not paradoxical, he earned little else than ridicule from his opponents, and qualified praise from his friends. The first man who recognized his genius without sympathizing with his ideas was Vladimir Soloviev, who was struck by the powerful originality of his personality, and after his death did much to keep his memory green by writing a sympathetic and detailed notice of him for the standard Russian *Encyclopædia*. Since then he has been revived. In 1912 and following years there appeared a collected edition of his works (in nine volumes), in 1911 a collection of memoirs dedicated to him, preceded by an excellent *Life of Leontiev* by his disciple Konoplyantsev. He has become generally (though sometimes tacitly) recognized as a classic. The originality of his thought, the individuality of his style, the acuity of his critical judgment have become points of commonplace. The literary historians of the young school consider him the best, the only genuine critic of the second half of the nineteenth century; his high literary merits are recognized even by Bolshevik critics; and the "Eurasians," the only original and vigorous school of thought produced since the Revolution by the anti-Bolsheviks, regard him as one of their greatest teachers.

CHAPTER II

1. THE EIGHTIES AND EARLY NINETIES

THE reign of Alexander III (1881–1894) was a period of reaction in political life. The assassination of Alexander II marked the crest of the great revolutionary wave and was followed by a collapse of the whole movement. The Government opened an energetic campaign of suppression and found substantial support in the opinion of the upper and middle classes. In two or three years it succeeded in making a clean sweep of all revolutionary organizations. By 1884 all active revolutionaries were either in Schlüsselburg and Siberia or abroad. For almost ten years there was no revolutionary activity to speak of. The more law-abiding Radicals also suffered from the reaction. Their leading magazines were suppressed, and they lost most of their hold on the masses of the intelligentsia. Peaceful and passive, non-political aspirations were the order of the day. Tolstoism became popular, not so much for its sweeping condemnation of State and Church, as for its doctrine of non-resistance—precisely the point in which it differed from Revolutionary Socialism. The great majority of the middle class subsided into a life of humdrum boredom and impotent aspirations—a life familiarized to the English reader by the stories of Chekhov. But the end of the reign also saw the beginning of a new upheaval of capitalistic enterprise.

In literature the eighties were a period of "æsthetic" reaction against the utilitarian practice of the sixties and seventies. This reaction began before 1881, so it cannot have been the result of political disillusionment. It was merely the natural and essentially healthy protest of the literary spirit against the all-pervading utilitarianism of the preceding age. The movement, as a whole, did not proclaim the doctrine of "art

56

for art's sake," but writers began to show a greater interest in things other than immediate public utility—a greater interest in form, and for the "eternal" problems of Life and Death, of Good and Evil, apart from their social implications. Even those writers of the eighties who were most "with a purpose" were at pains not to let it be seen too crudely. Poetry was revived. In prose the new writers tried to avoid the formlessness and untidiness of the "tendentious" novelists and the journalistic tendencies of Saltykov and Uspensky. They reverted to the examples of Turgenev and Tolstoy, and tried to be what is called in Russian *khudozhestvenny*. This word really means "artistic," but owing to the use it was put to by the idealist critics of the forties (Belinsky), it has a very different emotional "overtone" from its English equivalent. Among other things, it conveyed to the late nineteenth-century Russian "intelligent" a certain mellowness and lack of crudeness, an absence of too apparent "purpose," and also an absence of intellectual elements—of logic and "reflection." It was also coloured by Belinsky's doctrine that the essence of "art" was "thinking in images," not in concepts. This idea is partly responsible for the great honour in which descriptions of visible things were held—especially emotionally coloured descriptions of Nature in the style of Turgenev.

For all this reversal to "form" and to "eternal ideas" this movement was very little of a renascence. It lacked force and originality. It was conservative and placid, eclectic and timid. It strove rather after the absence of great ugliness than after the presence of great beauty. The revival both of a really active feeling for form, and of really daring metaphysical speculation, came only later, in the nineties and in the early years of this century.

2. GARSHIN (1855–1888)

The first in date, and in many ways the most representative, of the novelists of the eighties was Vsevolod Mikhaylovich Gàrshin. He came of a family of country gentry and was born in 1855 in the Donets district. He went to school in Kharkov, and from there in 1873 to the High School of Mines in Petersburg, but did not complete his studies there. He was a man of extraordinary acute moral sensitiveness, and, brought up as he was in the period immediately following the emancipation of the serfs, he naturally enough acquired the mentality of a "conscience-stricken nobleman." It did not take the direction of political work for the people, but when war broke out with Turkey (1877) he enlisted as a private soldier. He did not do this from motives of patriotism, or for the love of adventure, but under the intense conviction that if the people were suffering at the front, it was his duty to suffer with them. Garshin did well as a soldier. He was mentioned in dispatches and promoted to the grade of sergeant. In August, 1877, he was wounded in the leg and invalided to Kharkov. There he wrote *Four Days*, a short story about a wounded soldier who remained four days on the battlefield, unable to move, and next to the putrefying corpse of a dead Turk. The story appeared in October, 1877, and created a sensation. It established Garshin's reputation once for all. He became a professional writer. Gradually his delicate moral constitution took a morbid turn, and developed into a permanent and agonizing dissatisfaction with the whole of the world order. He was constantly on the brink of a mental breakdown. His conduct became eccentric. One of his first eccentricities was his visit to the Prime Minister Loris-Melikov, whom he endeavoured to convince of the necessity of "making peace" with the revolutionaries. His personal acquaintance with morbid states of mind helped him to write *The Red Flower* (1883), the most remarkable of all his stories. As time went on, his nervous state grew worse. He began to feel the imminent approach of madness. This aggravated his melancholy and brought him to suicide. After a particularly bad access of despair, he threw himself down a staircase and broke his leg. He did not recover, and, after an agony of five days, died on March 24, 1888. All those who knew him testify to the extraordinary purity and charm of his person. His eyes especially are said to have been unique and unforgettable.

The essence of Garshin's personality is a "genius" for pity

and compassion, as intense as Dostoevsky's but free from all the "Nietzschean," "underground," and "Karamazov" ingredients of the greater writer. This spirit of compassion and pity pervades all his work. This is not voluminous: it consists of some twenty stories, all of them contained in a single volume. In most of them he is an intelligent pupil of Turgenev and the early Tolstoy. In a few (*The Signal, The Legend of Proud Aggey*) he follows the lead given by Tolstoy's "popular" stories. *That Which Was Not* and *Attalea Princeps* are fables with animals and plants in human situations. The second of these two stories is one of his best—it is saturated with a spirit of tragical irony. In *Officer and Servant* he is a forerunner of Chekhov—it is an excellently constructed story of "atmosphere," an atmosphere of drab gloom and meaningless boredom. In *A Very Short Novel* he treats, with greater felicity, the subject of Artsybashev's *War*, the infidelity of the woman to the crippled hero. It is a little masterpiece of concentration and lyrical irony. His best-known and most characteristic story is *The Red Flower*, the first in a long row of lunatic-asylum stories (the next in time was Chekhov's *Ward No. 6*). In it Garshin's morbid and high-strung moral sensitiveness reaches its highest pitch. It is the history of a madman who is obsessed by the desire to challenge and defeat the evil of the world. He discovers that all evil is contained in three poppies growing in the middle of the hospital garden, and with infinite astuteness and cunning succeeds in defeating the vigilance of his warders and picking the flowers. He dies from nervous exhaustion, but dies happy and certain of having attained his end. The story is gloomy and powerful. The oppressive atmosphere of the asylum is conveyed with effective skill. The end comes as a relief, like death to a martyr, but there is in it also a pang of bitter irony.

Garshin is hardly a great writer. His manner is too much that of a degenerate age. His technique is insufficient, and even in *The Red Flower* there are irritating lapses into the inadequate. But his style is sober and sincere, and even his occasional clumsiness seems preferable to the fluent rhetoric and cardboard dramatism of the school of Andreev.

3. MINOR NOVELISTS

In the eighties and nineties there was a considerable output of Russian fiction. It was not of a very high quality, and even at the time no one thought that a great literary revival was going on. But some of it is not altogether insignificant. There is no need to give much attention to the novelists of the eighties, and a brief survey will suffice. The oldest of them (for many years the Dean of Russian Letters), P. D. Boborỳkin (1836–1921), was a journalist rather than a novelist; his novels are snapshots of the various states of mind through which the typical "intelligent" passed, and of various new social phenomena, such as the "cultured merchant." They are written in an "objective" style imitated from the French naturalists. A journalist of another sort was Vasili Nemiròvich-Dànchenko (b. 1848, to be distinguished from his brother Vladimir, founder of the Moscow Art Theatre), who led the Russian reader on tours all round the world, with just a touch of primitively mild sensationalism. He was read by the unsophisticated, who also enjoyed the historical novels of Vsevolod Soloviév (1849–1903), the brother of the famous philosopher. But to indulge in this sort of literature was "bad form" for the self-respecting intellectual.

The influence of Dostoevsky is discernible in the work of M. N. Àlbov (1851–1911), who described at great length the morbid states of mind experienced by priests and clerics; and in that of Prince D. P. Golìtzyn Muràvlin (b. 1860), who, starting from the character of Prince Myshkin, attempted to portray pathological types of the aristocracy. Another side of Dostoevsky is reflected in the work of K. S. Barantsévich (b. 1851), who wrote stories in the respectable tradition of *Poor Folk*, describing the sufferings of the poor and the oppressed. A sterner note sounded in the stories of D. N. Màmin-Sibiryàk (1852–1912), who drew unsweetened pictures of the hard and joyless life of the miners in the Ural. Ieronim Yasìnsky (b. 1850) was a naturalist of the French type who early proclaimed the rights of Art for Art's sake. He was the first Russian writer to approach sexual subjects, and in 1917 the first non-party intellectual to join the Bolsheviks. The humorous South Russian nature found expression in the unpretending stories of I. N. Potàpenko (1856–1915). Another popular humorist of the time was Chekhov's friend Shcheglòv (pseud. of I. L. Leòntiev, 1850–1910). His *Suburban Husband,* an amusing picture of Russian Suburbia, became a favourite catchword, almost a new word. Another famous humorous type was created by Mme. Mikùlich (pseud. of Lydia I. Veselìtsky, b. 1857). Her *Mimochka* is a witty picture of the average *jeune fille* of Petersburg bureaucratic society—the incarnation of placid futility.

More important than any of these writers was Alexander Ivanovich Értel (1855–1908). He was a Populist, but in his later years he abandoned the usual agnosticism of the Russian "intelligent" and tried to evolve a more spiritualist philosophy. This caused a considerable revival of interest in him about 1910 when the revival of religion was the watchword—his collected works and his letters were published then and had a considerable success. His first stories appeared in 1880 but his best and best-known novel is *The Gardenins, Their Retainers, Their Friends, and Their Enemies,* in two volumes (1898). It had the honour, when reprinted in 1908, of a preface by Tolstoy. Tolstoy gave especial praise to Értel's art of dialogue. Referring to it, Tolstoy said: "Such good Russian is not to be found in any writer, old or new. He uses the people's speech not only with accuracy, force, and beauty, but with infinite variety. . . . Who wants to know the language of the Russian people . . . must not only read but study Értel's Russian." Apart from this, *The Gardenins* is one of the best Russian novels written since the great age. It is a vast panorama of life on a big estate in South Central Russia. The hero is the son of an estate-agent (like Értel himself). The characters of the peasants are infinitely varied, and splendidly individualized. So are those of the rural middle class and of the rural police, which of course is presented in a satirical light. But the Gardenins themselves, one of whom is a "conscience-stricken" aristocrat, are much less happily portrayed. The novel is transfused with a very keen poetical sense of nature. One of the most memorable episodes is the account of a trotting-match at Khrenovaya, which holds its own even by the side of the race-scene in *Anna Karenina*.

Another writer whose work has not lost its charm was Nikolay Georgievich Mikhaylòvsky, who wrote under the pseudonym of N. Gàrin (1852–1906). He was a railway engineer by profession, and took to literature rather late in life. His principal work is a trilogy describing the early life of Tema Kartashov—*Tema's Childhood* (1892), *Schoolboys* (*Gimnazisty*, (1893), and *Students* (1895). The series has great charm, is written in a simple and sincere style, and was immensely popular in its day. The characters which go through the three books are drawn with great warmth, and the reader soon feels towards them as if they were boys he knew in real life. Apart from the literary qualities of the trilogy, it is an important historical document, for it is the "natural history" of a typical *intelligentsia* education, a school of morally inefficient and nervously unstable men.

This enumeration of minor writers may be completed by the name of Peter Filipovich Yakubòvich (1860–1911), the only active revolutionary among them. He joined the People's Will party (after March 1st), was arrested in 1884, spent three years in St. Peter's and St. Paul's Fortress, and eight years (1887–1895) as a convict in Siberia. This record did not allow him to appear in literature under his own name, which has remained comparatively unknown, though his two pseudonyms P. Ya. and L. Melshin became very popular. He used the first to sign his poetry, which is "civic" and very poor. Under the second he published in 1896 a remarkable book of stories of convict life, *A World of Outcasts*, the first book of its kind since Dostoevsky's *House of Death*. Though, of course, on a much inferior level to Dostoevsky's, Melshin's book has considerable merit. Its attitude is characteristic of the Russian revolutionary idealist. He paints the most repulsive criminals, with uncompromising objectivity, as they are, with all their crimes and cynical heartlessness, but he descries in them flashes of humanity, and the message of the book is a firm belief in human nature and a firm respect for human individuality even in the deepest degradation.

4. THE ÉMIGRÉS

Those revolutionaries who did not go to Siberia or to Schlüsselburg found refuge abroad. Their place in literary history is not great. Their political press between 1881 and 1900 was not very active, and even afterwards it produced nothing to compare with Herzen's *Bell*. But this period of calm produced an interesting series of memoirs. Now at rest, the active fighters of yesterday sat down to record their experiences of the great struggle. Their memoirs were largely intended for a foreign audience (before 1905 they could not be imported into Russia), and much of it was even written in some foreign language. The idea Western people made themselves of the revolutionary movement (in so far as it was not quite fantastic) was derived from the works of Sergey M. Kravchìnsky, who wrote under the pseudonym of S. Stepniàk (1852–1895). He was a terrorist: he had taken part in 1878 in the assassination of General Mezentsov, chief of the political police. In 1882 he published in Italian *La Russia Sotteranea* (*Underground Russia*), which he himself translated into Russian. Later on he settled down in England and wrote *The Career of a Nihilist* (1889) in English. His stories were well suited to the taste of the Western reader—they were vivid, and thrilling. But they have very little value as documentary evidence. From this last point of view the memoirs of Vladimir Debogòri-Mokriévich (b. 1847) are much more valuable. Nor are they without purely literary merits: their narrative is easy, straightforward, and full of humour, the almost inevitable virtue of all Southern Russians.

The most eminent of the Russian *émigrés* of this period was Prince Peter Kropòtkin (1842–1921). He was the descendant of a very ancient family, and received his education at the Corps des Pages. He served in a Cossack regiment in Siberia, and made himself a name as a geographer. In the seventies he joined the revolutionary movement, was arrested, and finally escaped over the frontier. At first he lived in Switzerland and in France, but was expelled from the former and sentenced to imprisonment in the latter, in both cases for Anarchist propaganda. For he had become the leader and theoretician of Anarchism. In 1886 he came to London, where he lived till 1917. He was a man of aristocratic manners and great personal charm and found many friends in various classes of English society. During the great war his attitude was patriotic. In 1917 he returned to Russia. He remained hostile to the Bolsheviks, and rejected all Lenin's approaches. He died in 1921, near Moscow. His work is voluminous: it includes, besides geographical works, propaganda tracts and more elaborate expositions of his Anarchism; an optimistic philosophy based on evolutionary theories; a history of the French Revolution and a history of Russian literature.* Practically all of it is in French or English. The most interesting of his books (also originally in English) is *The Memoirs of a Revolutionary* (1899), a first-class autobiography, the most remarkable work of its kind since Herzen's *My Past and Thoughts*.

Here perhaps would also be the place to mention (only mention) the name of Marie Bashkírtseva (Baschkirtseff, 1860–1884). Though she was not a political *émigrée*, she lived and wrote in France and in French. Her *Journal* published posthumously in 1887 produced a sensation in Europe and has been translated into many languages (into Russian later than into English and German). It is certainly a remarkable human document, and gives proof of more than ordinary power of self-observation. But its importance has probably been overrated, and in any case it stands entirely outside the line of development of Russian literature.

5. KOROLÉNKO (1853–1921)

Vladimir Galaktionovich Korolénko is undoubtedly the most attractive representative of idealist Radicalism in Rus-

* Most of the articles on Russia in the *Encyclopædia Britannica* are from his pen.

sian literature. If Chekhov had never lived he would also
have been *facile princeps* among the novelists and poets
of his time. He was born in 1853 in Zhitomir, the capital of Volynia, then a semi-Polish city. His father was
a judge (in those days a civil servant with approximately the
competence of a Justice of the Peace), his mother a Polish
gentlewoman. In his childhood Korolenko did not very well
know to which nationality he belonged, and learned to read
Polish before he did Russian. Only after the Revolt of 1863
did the family have definitely to "choose" its nationality, and
became Russians. In 1870 Korolenko went to Petersburg and
became a student of the Institute of Technology, and afterwards of the Moscow School of Agriculture, but he did not
complete his studies at either: he was expelled for belonging
to a secret political organization. In 1879 he was arrested and
deported to north-eastern Siberia, and spent several years in
a far-off part of the Yakut province. In 1885 he was allowed
to come to Russia and settled in Nizhni-Novgorod. The same
year he reappeared in literature,* with *Makar's Dream*, the
story of a Yakut. The next ten years he spent in Nizhni,
where he wrote almost all his best stories. During the famine
of 1891–1892 he took part in the relief work and published
a volume of impressions. In 1895 he was allowed to come to
Petersburg. In 1900 he was elected a Member of the Academy,
but resigned the title, after the incident with Gorky's election
(*vide infra*). In 1900 he settled in Poltava, where he lived
until his death. After the death of Mikhaylovsky he became
the most prominent figure in the Populist camp. Ever since
1895 he almost abandoned literature, and devoted himself to
the disclosure and exposition of injustices committed by the
law courts and the police. After 1906 he headed the campaign
against military law and capital punishment. The only work
of his last period (and perhaps his best) was a sort of autobiography, *The History of My Contemporary*, the first part
of which appeared in 1910, and the other parts posthumously
in 1922. In 1917 and after, he remained hostile to the Bol-

* He had begun publishing before his exile, but he never allowed this
early work of his to be reprinted.

sheviks, and his last published work was a series of letters to Lunacharsky denouncing the Bolsheviks as the enemies of civilization. He died in December, 1921, in Poltava, which during the last few years of his life had more than once been taken and retaken by the various parties in the Civil War.

Korolenko's work is very typical of what the eighties and nineties called "artistic" in the peculiar sense explained above. It is full of emotional poetry and of Nature introduced in the way Turgenev used to. This lyrical element seems to-day a little stale and uninteresting, and most of us will prefer to all his earlier work his last book, where he has almost freed himself of this facile poetry. But it was this poetry which appealed so strongly to the tastes of the Russian reading public thirty and forty years ago. The age that made the reputation of Korolenko also revived the cult of Turgenev. Though everyone knew that Korolenko was a Radical and a revolutionary, he was received with equal enthusiasm by all parties. This non-party reception given to writers in the eighties was a sign of the times. Garshin and Korolenko became recognized as (minor) classics before Leskov, a much greater man, but born in worse times, was given anything like justice. Korolenko's poetry may on the whole have faded, but his best early work still retains much of its charm. For even his poetry rises above the level of mere prettiness when he has to do with the more majestic aspects of Nature. The north-east of Siberia with its vast and empty spaces, its short sub-polar days, and its dazzling wilderness of snow, lives in his early stories with impressive grandeur. He is a master of atmosphere. All who have read it remember the romantic island with the ruined castle and the tall poplars rustling in the wind in *In Bad Society*. But what gives Korolenko his unique flavour is the wonderful blend of his poetry with a delicate humour and with his undying faith in the human soul. Sympathy and faith in human goodness are characteristic of the Russian Populist—Korolenko's world is a fundamentally optimistic world, for man is good by nature, and only the evil conditions created by despotism and the brutal selfishness of capitalism make him what he is—a poor, helpless,

absurd, pitiful, and irritating creature. There is a mighty
poetry in Korolenko's first story, *Makar's Dream*, which is
due not only to the suggestive painting of the Yakut landscape,
but still more to the author's profound, indestructible sympathy
with the dark and unenlightened savage, whose mind is so
naïvely selfish and who yet has in him a ray of the divine
light. Korolenko's humour is especially delightful. It is free
from all satirical intent and sophistication. It is wonderfully easy and natural—it has a lightness of touch which is
rare in Russian authors, and in which he is surpassed only
by that wonderful and still unappreciated writer, Kushchevsky,
who wrote only one book and died of drink at the age of
twenty-nine (1847–1876). In Korolenko this humour is often
subtly interwoven with poetry—as in the delightful story *At
Night*, where a family of children discuss in their bedroom the
absorbing question of how babies are made. *The Day of
Atonement* with its funny old Jewish devil has that blend of
humour and phantasy which is so delightful in Gogol's early
stories, but Korolenko's colours are mellower and quieter, and
though he has not an ounce of the creative exuberance of his
great countryman, he has much more human sympathy and
warmth. The most purely humorous of his stories is *Tongue-
less* (1895), the story of three Ukrainian peasants who emigrated to America without knowing a word of any language
but their own. Russian critics have called it Dickensian, and
this is true in the sense that in Korolenko as in Dickens the
absurdity of his characters does not make them less lovable.

Korolenko's last work is an autobiography, which seems to be
even a singularly exact and truthful account of his life but
which for some supersensitive scruple he called the history not
of himself, but of his contemporary. It is less poetical and
barer than his early work, but his two principal qualities—humour and sympathy—are very much present. He gives a delightful picture of life in yet semi-Polish Volynia—of his
scrupulously honest but wilful father. He records his early
impressions of country life, of school, of the great events he
had to witness—the Emancipation and the Polish Revolt. It is
full of wonderfully vivid, grotesque figures of cranks and origi-

nals, perhaps the best in his whole portrait gallery. It is certainly not thrilling, but it is a deliciously quiet story, told by an old man (he was only fifty-five when he began it, but there always was something of the grandfather in Korolenko) who has ample leisure and goodwill, and finds pleasure in reviving the vivid memories of fifty years ago.

6. THE LITERARY LAWYERS

One of the most important changes introduced into Russian life in the reign of Alexander II was the Reform of the Law Courts. It substituted for the old secret process a public procedure after European models. It made the judges independent of the executive and introduced a corporation of the bar. The independence of the judges was practically done away with under Alexander III, but the bar flourished from the very beginning and turned out an important nursery of general culture. The most brilliant men of the generation adopted this profession, and many advocates soon won an all-Russian reputation by their eloquence. Contrary to what was going on elsewhere, they did not neglect to work at the form of their utterances, and more workmanship was displayed in this field than in any department of imaginative literature. The names of the advocates W. D. Spasòvich, Prince A. I. Urùsov, and the crown prosecutor (later on, Minister of Justice) N. V. Muraviev may be mentioned as those of the most brilliant speakers of the time. Nor did the lawyers neglect more strictly literary work. Spasòvich wrote notable essays on Pushkin and Byron; Anatoli F. Koni (b. 1844), who is to-day the oldest living Russian writer, made a name by his life of Dr. Haas, the philanthropist, and still more by several volumes of recollections. They are written in an easy and limpid style, agreeably reminiscent of the fragmentary memoirs of Turgenev. The æsthetic revival of the eighties and nineties owes much to Prince Urùsov (1843–1900). He introduced into Russia the cult of Flaubert and of Baudelaire, and was one of the best critics of literature of his time, though all his criticism was contained in conversation and private letters.

But the most remarkable of all these literary lawyers was Sergey Arkadievich Andreévsky (1847–1920). He was one of the most successful advocates of his day, but his name will be remembered rather for his literary work. His verse, like practically all the verse of his time, is insignificant. But his critical essays were an important event in their day—he was the first critic to give Dostoevsky his due place (essay on *The Brothers Karamazov*, 1888) and to begin the revival of the older poetical tradition—he "discovered" Baratynsky. But his most important work is *The Book of Death*, which was published only posthumously (Reval, 1922). It reveals him as a delicate and refined prose-writer, a diligent and intelligent pupil of Lermontov, Turgenev, and Flaubert. The first part, written about 1891, is the most remarkable. It is the history of his first experiences of death. It contains passages of singular force and sustained beauty. Such is the wonderful chapter about his elder sister Masha, his morbid affection for her, her strange mental malady and early death. This chapter deserves a high place in Russian literature. It is wonderful for the sincere analysis of his own feelings, for the vividness of the narrative, and for the sustained rhythm, for which there is no precedent in Lermontov or Turgenev. The whole chapter (some fifty pages) is one rhythmical whole. The rhythm is all the more perfect for being quite unobtrusive —the turn of phrase is so colloquial that an untrained ear might not suspect, or a deliberately unrhythmical delivery might not convey to the listener, that there was anything peculiar about it. It is one of the finest achievements of Russian prose.

7. POETS

Andreévsky was typical of his time when in one of his essays he said that the only legitimate subject-matter for poetry was "beauty and melancholy." These two words effectively sum up the poetical work of the eighties and early nineties. The revival of poetry began a few years before 1881 and affected both the civic and the "art-for-art's sake" school. But there is very little difference between these two "schools." Their style is indistinguishable. The "civic" poets concentrated on melancholy caused by the evils of despotism and social injustice, but they had nothing of the vigorous, daring realism of Nekrasov, whom they affected to recognize as a master. The "art-for-art's sake" poets preferred to dwell on beauty and on melancholy arising from sentimental causes, but they had neither the high craftsmanship of Fet nor the range of interest of Sluchevsky.

Among the "civic" poets, the most famous was Semen Yakovlevich Nàdson (1862–1887), a young man of semi-Jewish descent who died of consumption at a very early age. His poetry is inspired by the impotent desire to make the world better and the burning consciousness of his own impotence. This makes him akin to Garshin, but he had neither Garshin's imaginative power nor his great spiritual intensity. Nàdson's verse is smooth and skeletonless, it avoids ugliness, but it is quite devoid of all life and strength. It marks the low-water mark of Russian poetical technique, and his great popularity the low-water mark of Russian poetical taste. His jelly-fish poetry was preferred to everything else, every school-girl and student knew by heart hundreds of lines from him, and his collected poems ran into several tens of thousands before the end of the century. His only rival was Mìnsky (pseud. of N. M. Vilénkin, b. 1855), the first full-blooded Jew to win a reputation in Russian letters. He began before Nàdson, but could not compete with him—his poetry seemed cold and intellectual. We shall meet him once again in a later chapter. In the late eighties he abandoned "civic" poetry and became the first swallow of the Modernist movement, together with Merezhkovsky, who also began under the auspices of Nàdson as a civic poet. But Merezhkovsky from the very first gave proof of a poetical culture superior to that of his contemporaries.

The most popular of the non-civic poets was Alexey Nikolaevich Apùkhtin (1841–1893). He was the friend and schoolfellow of Chaikovsky, and a popular figure in Petersburg society, where he was noted for his abnormal stoutness. He was a sort of aristocratic counterpart of Nàdson—what Nàdson's poetry was to the Radical intelligentsia, Apukhtin's was to the gentry and official classes. It is also a poetry of impotent regret, but his regret is for the days of his youth when he could better enjoy the love of women and the taste of wine. It is the poetry of a man who has ruined his health by too much indulgence. It is less colourless and jelly-like than Nàdson's, for he does not so studiously shun all realism and all concrete detail. Some of his lyrics have become very popular as songs, as the well-known *Sleepless Nights*, one of the most popular things in the "gipsy" repertoire. A more dignified poet was Count A. A. Golenìshchev-Kutùzov (1848–1912). He has been called the poet of Nirvana. He tried to revive a severe and "classical" style, but it is merely still and lifeless in his hands. He is at his best when he speaks of death and destruction. The description of a snow-storm in one of his poems is not without merit. But his principal title to glory is that some of his poems were put to music by Musorgsky, who had a peculiar weakness for his poetry. Another aristocrat who wrote poetry was Count P. D. Buturlìn (1859–1895). He was more than half a foreigner, with Italian and Portuguese blood in him, and an English education. His first work was a book of English verse printed in Florence. He contributed to the *Academy* and other English papers. He never learnt properly to speak the language of his country. This makes his poetry inadequate, but it is interesting as an isolated instance of English influence—Buturlìn was a devoted follower of Keats and of the pre-Raphaelites.

In the later eighties the anti-Radical critics tried to create a boom round the poetry of Konstantine Mikhailovich Fòfanov (1862–1911). Quite uncultured and uneducated (he was the son of a small shopkeeper in a Petersburg suburb), he possessed what none of his contemporaries possessed—a genuine gift of song, very much akin to Mr. Davies's. His poetry is all about stars, and flowers, and birds—it is sometimes quite genuine, but on the whole rather uninteresting, and as he was a very poor craftsman it is singularly unequal. The next poetical boom was around Myrrha Lókhvitsky (1869–1905), who appeared in 1895 with a volume of passionate and exotic feminine poetry. Her poetry and Fòfanov's seemed the last word of beauty in the nineties, when the real revival of poetry began with the rise of the Symbolist movement.

8. VLADIMIR SOLOVIEV (1853–1900)

The eighties were a period of (mild) reaction against the Utilitarian Positivism of the preceding age. This reaction found expression in the anæmic revival of poetry, and in a somewhat more vigorous revival of religious idealism. The Radicals were, by temperament, Idealists, but their idealism was based (to quote a joke of Soloviev's) on the rather unjustifiable syllogism, "Man is descended from monkeys: consequently we must love each other." The eighties attempted to give this piece of reasoning a more plausible foundation. Their religious idealism found its most popular expression in the teaching of Tolstoy, which influenced contemporaries precisely in so far as it was religious and a reaction against Radical materialism. Another and more orthodox expression of the same tendency is the work of Vladimir Soloviev. The influence of Soloviev's religious philosophy, at first insignificant, in the long run proved more important than that of Tolstoism. Soloviev's place in the history of Russian thought is defined by the fact that he was the first Russian thinker to divorce mystical and orthodox Christianity from the doctrines of Slavophilism. He was to a certain extent the continuer of the less exclusive and more "occidentalist" wing of Slavophilism, which found its most complete expression in the ideas of the publicist Dostoevsky. But there is between the two a substantial difference: to Dostoevsky the supreme sanction of orthodox Christianity was that it expressed the religious intuition of the *Russian people*. He was a nationalist in religion, a mystical Populist: orthodoxy was true *because* it was the faith of the Russian people. Soloviev was quite free from this mystical nationalism, and whether he based his religion on the deductions of Idealist philosophy, or on the authority of the Œcumenical Church, the religious opinion of the Russian people is to him a matter completely irrelevant. His orthodoxy had a strong leaning towards Rome, as the symbol of Christian Unity, and in politics he was a westernizing Liberal. This was the chief element in his early success, for the Liberals found him a valuable ally in their campaign against the Government and the Slavophils, all the more valuable because in his indictment of the existing political order he appealed not to Darwin or Marx, but to the Bible and to the Fathers. His help came from an unexpected quarter and for that reason was especially welcome.

Vladimir Sergeevich Soloviév was born in Moscow in 1853. He was one of a numerous family. His father was the eminent historian S. M. Soloviev, and he grew up in the atmosphere of the Moscow University. He belonged to that class of Moscow society which included the élite of the cultured nobility and the pick of the higher *intelligentsia*. He early joined a highly gifted set of humorists, who called themselves the Shakespeare society and indulged in writing nonsense verse and staging parody plays. The most brilliant of this set was Count Theodore Sologub, the best Russian nonsense poet since "Kusma Prutkov." Soloviev himself was all his life an adept in this art. At the same time his scholarship was brilliant and precocious. As early as 1875 he published his Ph.D. thesis on *The Crisis of Western Philosophy*, directed against Positivism. In the same year he went to London, where he spent all his time in the British Museum studying the mystical doctrine of Sophia the Divine Wisdom. There, in the reading-room, he had a vision, and received the mystical command to go immediately to Egypt. In the desert near Cairo he had his most important and completest vision, which revealed to him the Person of Sophia. This voyage into the desert was accompanied by amusing incidents with the Arabs. It is highly characteristic of Soloviev that twenty years later he described these visions (including an earlier one of 1862) in a humorous poem, *Three Meetings*, in which the highly lyrical and esoteric description of the visions is surrounded by verse in the style of *Beppo* and *Don Juan*. On his return to Russia, Soloviev was appointed reader of philosophy at Moscow, and soon afterwards at Petersburg. His university career was a short one: in March, 1881, he made a speech against capital punishment, in which he tried to persuade the new emperor not to execute the assassins of his father. His motive was that by going "counter to the natural inclination of his heart and to every consideration of earthly wisdom, the Czar would rise to a superhuman level, and in the very fact demonstrate the divine source of his royal power." In spite of this motive, he found himself compelled to leave the university. During the eighties he worked at the idea of a Universal Theocracy, which brought him nearer and nearer to Rome. He went to Zagreb and became intimate with Bishop Strosmayer, the opponent in 1870 of papal infallibility, but by now a docile servant of the Vatican. The work of this period is summed up in his French book *La Russie et l'Eglise Universelle* (1889), where he took up an extremely pro-Roman position, defending both the infallibility and the Immaculate Conception, describing the Popes as the only rock of Orthodoxy throughout the ages, and denouncing the Russian Church as State-governed. The book could not appear in Russia, but produced a certain sensation abroad. However, Soloviev never actually became a Roman Catholic, and the appellation of a "Russian Newman" given him by the French Jesuit d'Herbigny (in his book *Un Newman Russe*) is grossly misleading. *La Russie et l'Eglise Universelle* marks the high-water mark of his Romish tendencies. They soon began to decline, and in his last work he represented the final Union of Christian Churches as a union between three *equal* Churches—Orthodox, Catholic, and Protestant, with the Pope as only *primus inter pares*. In the late eighties and nineties he conducted an energetic campaign against the nationalist policy of Alexander III's Government. These articles brought him a high reputation in Liberal spheres. His mystical life, however, continued, though his visions of Sophia ceased with the Egyptian one. In the nineties his mysticism became less Orthodox and took the form of a strange "mystical love affair" with the

Finnish Lake Saima, which found abundant expression in his poetry. He had also diabolical visitations: there is a story of how he was attacked by a devil in the form of a shaggy animal. Soloviev tried to exorcize him by telling him that Christ had risen. The devil retorted: "Christ may have risen for all I know, but you will be my prey." In the morning Soloviev was found lying on the floor unconscious. In the last year of his life he entered on a correspondence with Anna Schmidt, a provincial newspaper hack who believed herself to be the incarnation of Sophia, and Soloviev of the Person of Christ. (There is a striking chapter on Anna Schmidt in Gorky's *Fragments from a Diary*.) Soloviev's answers to her were humorous in form, but sympathetic in substance, and he lent himself to her singular adoration. But his mystical life remained little known to his contemporaries. They knew him as an Idealist philosopher and an outspoken Liberal polemist. This last capacity placed him high in the eyes of the *intelligentsia*, and he was invited by the Radical editors of the standard encyclopædia to be editor of the philosophical department, which was consequently conducted in a spirit strongly opposed to agnosticism and materialism. He also found more devoted followers who took up and developed his philosophical doctrines. First among them were the brothers Prince Serge and Prince Eugene Troubetzkoy. In 1900 he published his last and from the literary point of view most important work, *Three Conversations on War, Progress, and the End of Human History, to which is added a Short History of Antichrist*. The conversations were at once recognized as masterpieces, but the *Story of Antichrist* produced a certain consternation by its strangely concrete faith in that personage. Soloviev was by this time worn out by a too intense intellectual, spiritual, and mystical life. He went to seek repose in Uzkoe, the Troubetzkoys' estate near Moscow. There he died on July 31, 1900, of general exhaustion.

Soloviev's personality was extraordinarily complex, and its variations and contrasts are greater than we usually allow of in a single man. It is difficult to include in one formula this strange and inseparable blend of high-strung religious and

moral earnestness, with an invincible turn for the most nonsensical humour; his extraordinarily acute sense of Orthodoxy
with curious proclivities towards gnosticism and undisciplined
mysticism; his equally acute sense of social justice with the lack
of fair play in his polemical writings; his profound faith in
personal immortality with utterances of gaily cynical nihilism;
his earthly asceticism with a morbidly developed erotical mysticism.   This complexity and multiplicity of his person seems
to have found its expression in his laugh, which was that
in him which all who knew him considered most striking and
unforgettable.   It has been variously described, and many
witnesses testify to the weird, uncanny impression it produced.

  Soloviev was a most brilliant writer, brilliant in everything
he undertook; he was always successful, and met with applause
and admiration wherever he appeared.   In prose he commanded
a trenchant and coldly splendid style, especially suited for
polemics.   His more serious prose works are perhaps his least
characteristic, for in them he had to suppress both his merriment
and his mysticism.   But they are important for their ideas
and of course it was on them that his reputation grew and is
still largely based.   His early works are devoted to the enun-
ciation of the first principles of his philosophy; those written in
the eighties deal chiefly with questions of Church policy *sub
specie æternitatis. The Justification of Good* (1898) is a
treatise on moral theology, mainly directed against the "non-
resistance" teaching of Tolstoy.   Soloviev is considered Russia's most important philosopher in the "professional" sense
of the word.   He was a great scholar in philosophy, and his
knowledge of ancient and modern philosophy was enormous, but
he cannot in any sense be put on a level with the world's greatest
philosophers, and in a universal history of philosophy he may
be overlooked.   His philosophy was Neo-Platonic, and the
Gnostics had always a great attraction for him.   But I am in
no way competent, and it is in the present connexion irrelevant,
to give any epitome of his metaphysics.   As for his theology,
his relations with Roman Catholicism have already been mentioned.   He is studied in Roman Catholic schools, though of
course he is not recognized as a Doctor.   In the Orthodox

Church his position is ambiguous—it is recognized that he gave the best existing definitions of Orthodoxy as opposed to every individual heresy, but his leanings towards Rome and visible Unity, as well as the undisciplined and dubious character of his mystical life, make him suspect.

The cold brilliancy of his manner is nowhere more apparent than in his polemical writings. They are splendid examples of the higher journalism, but, as has already been pointed out, when disputing with opponents who had no support in public opinion (e.g., Strakhov, Rozanov, the Decadents), he preferred to use arguments that were most likely to give him easy victory in the eyes of the reader, than to go out of his way to be intellectually fair. Far more remarkable from the literary point of view than his other prose writings are the *Three Conversations*, a true masterpiece in a difficult kind. In them he gave free rein to his exuberant humour and to his sparkling wit, and succeeded in creating a work which is at once as amusing as Mark Twain and as earnest as William James. And this he achieves without the aid of paradox, that favourite weapon of all "laughing philosophers." He revels in puns and anecdotes and quotations from nonsense verse, and each of the personages in the dialogue is delightfully individualized. But each (except the purely ridiculous Lady "to whom nothing human is alien") supports his thesis with admirable logic and consistency, and uses his best arguments. The *dialogi personæ* are (besides the Lady) the General, who maintains the rights of force as the just chastiser of brute evil; the Politician, who supports modern civilization as an advance against savagery; the Prince, who is a Tolstoyan, and preaches non-resistance and who is the villain of the play, and Mr. Z., who is Soloviev's mouthpiece, and recognizes the General and the Politician as the exponents respectively of a *partial* truth which must be merged in the higher synthesis of active Christianity. The *Conversations* are followed by the *Story of Antichrist*. This is a curiously vivid and detailed story of the end of the world and of the events immediately preceding the Day of Judgment. Soloviev saw in the rise of China and Japan (he wrote in 1900) a great danger for Christendom, and considered it one

of the precursors of Antichrist. But Antichrist himself is a
European, a philologist and a Roman bishop *in partibus* who is
also a magician and a Superman according to Nietzsche.

Those admirers of Soloviev who think his mysticism the
principal thing in him lay a particular value on his poetry.
In this art he was a follower of Fet, with whom he was on
intimate terms, and whose militant atheism he deplored as pre-
cluding any chance of their meeting in the next world. But,
like all his contemporaries, he was incapable of acquiring
(perhaps even of distinguishing) Fet's superior technique, and,
like all of them, he suffered from a slackness and thinness of
form. Still he was a true poet, certainly the best poet of his
generation. He used the usual romantic vocabulary, but in his
hands it received a new significance, for its hackneyed stock
words were used to denote concrete mystical facts. His poetry
is mystical throughout and for a complete understanding of it
the fundamental conceptions of his mystic experience must be
constantly kept in mind. His most productive period was in the
early nineties, when he wrote the beautiful series of lyrics addressed to Lake Saima, of which he speaks as of a living being.
Those who want to understand anything in Soloviev must realize that it is no poetical metaphor, but the actual feeling of a
mystical person, when he addresses the lake as "gentle lady"
and speaks of its eyes, of its moods, and of its dreams. His
longest poem, *Three Meetings*, though not the best, is in many
ways the most characteristic, for in it his mysticism is closely
elbowed by his humorous irreverence. He describes his vision
in the desert in terms of sublime mystical poetry:

> "I saw All, and All was but One,
>   One vision of feminine beauty. . . .
>   The infinite was contained in its limits—
>   Before me, in me—was only Thou";

and, in almost the next stanza, on his return to Cairo he hears
from his hotel neighbour:

> "Though great brains give one the right to be stupid,
>   My advice is not to abuse of this right.

.   Human dullness is not quick at discerning
With exactness all the varieties of folly."

But quite apart from this humorous frame of his mystical poem, Soloviev was prolific in the purest nonsense verse. It is infinitely varied and, though it has not been collected, might make a .handsome volume. It includes witty parodies, biting satire, "cautionary tales," and the Russian equivalent of limericks, but the element of pure nonsense and reckless absurdity is always very apparent. By a procedure opposite to that of *Three Meetings*, he introduced into one of his most nonsensical plays (*The White Lily*) passages of intense mystical significance and gave the whole play a mystical "second meaning." His love of nonsense is also apparent in his letters, which seethe with puns (he was an incorrigible punster) and delightfully irrelevant quotations. Most people's letters written with the view of amusing the addressee, when they are published fail to amuse the reader, who has the disagreeable feeling that he is required to laugh and does not feel inclined to. Soloviev's fun is always as amusing to the general reader, unless he feels an aversion to all forms of nonsense, as it was to the person who first read it. Only in writing to such particularly important and respectable people as Bishop Strosmayer does Soloviev refrain from his jokes. But even apart from their nonsense his letters are full of wit and humour, and are delightful reading. Next to Pushkin (who has no rivals), Soloviev is no doubt the best of Russian letter-writers, with Chekhov as a good third.

9. CHEKHOV (1860–1904)

Anton Pavlovich Chékhov was born on January 17, 1860, at Taganrog, on the sea of Azov. His grandfather had been a serf on one of the enormous estates of the province of Voronezh, but had acquired considerable wealth by trade and was able to purchase his freedom and that of all his family. His son Paul, the writer's father, was a boy of nine when he ceased to be a serf. Afterwards he settled down as a merchant at Taganrog and carried on a prosperous trade. Both he and his wife were simple, half-educated, very religious people, with a strong family feeling. The favourite occupation of Paul Chekhov was to sing church hymns in chorus with his family. In the late nineties, when Anton Chekhov was already the author of most of his masterpieces, we still find the Chekhovs singing the Church service in chorus under the direction of their father. The family consisted of several sons and a daughter. They were all given a liberal education. Anton, who was the youngest but one, was sent to the gymnasium (secondary school) of Taganrog. But while he was there, the prosperity of the Chekhovs came to an end. The building of a railway through the neighbouring Rostov was a severe blow to the commerce of Taganrog, and Paul Chekhov soon saw himself forced to close his business. In 1876 he left Taganrog and went to seek employment in Moscow, where his elder sons were studying. Anton remained alone in Taganrog. In 1879 he finished his time at the gymnasium and went to Moscow to join his family. He was matriculated as a student of the Faculty of Medicine. After the normal course of five years, he took his degree in 1884. From his arrival in Moscow to his death, he never parted from his parents and sister, and as his literary income soon became important, he early became the mainstay of his family. The Chekhovs were an exceptionally united family—a case exceedingly rare among the *intelligentsia*, and due of course to the peasant and merchant origins of the family.

Chekhov began working in the comic papers the year he came to Moscow, and before he left the university he had become one of their most welcome contributors. So on taking his degree he did not settle down to practise as a doctor, but fell back on his literary work for subsistence. In 1886 some of his comic stories were collected in book form. The book had an immediate success with the public and was soon followed by another volume of comic stories. The critics, especially the Radical critics, took little notice of the book, but it attracted the attention of two influential men of letters—of the veteran novelist Grigorovich and of Suvorin, editor of the pro-

Government *Novoe Vremya*, the largest daily paper of the day. This shrewd and clever man at once saw the great possibilities of Chekhov and invited him to contribute to his paper, where he even started a special weekly literary supplement for Chekhov. They became close friends and in Chekhov's correspondence his letters to Suvorin form undoubtedly the most interesting part. Chekhov had now gained a firm footing in "big literature" and was free from the tyranny of the comic papers. This change in his social position was followed by a change in his work—he abandoned comic writing and developed that style which is most characteristically his. This change is apparent in the stories written by him in 1886–1887. At the same time Chekhov wrote his first play, *Ivanov*, which was produced in Moscow in December, 1887, and in Petersburg a year later. It is characteristic of this period of transition that Chekhov continued working at these works after their first publication: *The Steppe* and *Ivanov* that are now reproduced in his *Works*, are very different from what first appeared in 1887. Henceforward Chekhov was a writer with an established reputation, and he and his people were able to live a comparatively easy life. This life is rather uneventful, and what events there are, are closely connected with his writings. An isolated episode was his journey to Saghalien, the Russian Botany Bay. He went there in 1890, travelling through Siberia (before the days of the Trans-Siberian) and returning by sea *via* Ceylon. He made a very thorough investigation of convict life and published the result of it in a separate book (*Saghalien Island*, 1891). It is remarkable for its thoroughness, objectivity, and impartiality, and is an important historical document. It is supposed to have influenced certain reforms in prison life introduced in 1892. This journey was Chekhov's greatest practical contribution to the humanitarianism that was so near to his heart. In private life he was also very kind-hearted and generous. He gave away much of his money. His native town of Tanganrog owes him a library and a museum.

In 1891 Chekhov was rich enough to buy a piece of land at Melikhovo, some fifty miles south of Moscow. There he settled down with his parents and sister and younger brother, and lived for six years. He took part in local life, and spent much money on local improvements. In 1892–1893, during the cholera epidemic, he worked as the head of a sanitary district. Here it was he wrote many of his best and most mature stories. He remained at Melikhovo till 1897, when the state of his health forced him to move. Consumption had set in, and he had to spend the rest of his life mainly between the south coast of the Crimea and foreign—French and German—health resorts. This was not the only change in his life. All his surroundings changed, owing to his new connexion with the Moscow Art Theatre and his more decided political orientation towards the left. This latter led to his breach with Suvorin, to whom he wrote a very angry letter in connexion with the Dreyfus affair (even in Russia the *Affaire* was a hotbed of quarrel!) and to his friendship with the younger generation of writers, headed by Gorky and distinctly revolutionary. During these last years (especially after 1900, when he settled down in Yalta) he saw much of Tolstoy. In the popular opinion of that time, Chekhov, Gorky, and Tolstoy formed a sort of sacred Trinity symbolizing all that was best in independent Russia, as opposed to the dark forces of Czarism. Chekhov lived up to his Liberal reputation, and when the Academy, following a hint of the Government, excluded Gorky from its membership almost immediately after electing him, Chekhov, like the veteran Socialist Korolenko, resigned his membership. But from the literary point of view this phase is hardly of much importance—it introduced no new elements into his work. Far more important is his connexion with the Art Theatre. After *Ivanov,* Chekhov had written several light one-act comedies that had a considerable success with the public, but added little to his intrinsic achievement. In 1895 he turned once more to serious drama and wrote *The Seagull* (as it is called in the English translation, rather absurdly: the Russian *Chaika* means just *Gull*). It was produced at the State Theatre of Petersburg in 1896. It was badly understood by the actors and badly

acted.   The first night was a smashing failure.   The play was
hissed down, and the author, confounded by his defeat, left
the theatre after the second act and escaped to Melikhovo,
vowing never again to write a play.   Meanwhile K. S.
Stanislavsky (Alekseev), a wealthy merchant of Moscow, and
the dramatist Vladimir Nemirovich-Danchenko founded the
Art Theatre which was to be such an important landmark
in the history of the Russian stage.   They succeeded in getting
The Seagull for one of their first productions.   The cast
was exceptionally good and quite in tune with the play they
were to produce.   They worked at it with energy and understanding, and when the play was acted by them in 1898 it
proved a triumphant success.   Stimulated by this success,
Chekhov turned with new energy towards dramatic writing,
and wrote his most famous plays with a direct view to
Stanislavsky's cast.   *Uncle Vanya* (which had been planned as
early as 1888) was produced in 1900, *The Three Sisters* in
1901, and *The Cherry Orchard* in January, 1904.   Each play
was a greater triumph than the preceding one.   There was
complete harmony among playwright, actors, and public.
Chekhov's fame was at its height.   Together with Tolstoy and
Gorky he was universally accepted as the great man of Russian
letters.   However, he did not become so rich as to compare
with Mr. Rudyard Kipling or Gabriel d'Annunzio, nor even
with Gorky.   For like his favourite heroes he was eminently
unpractical: in 1899 he sold all the works he had hitherto
written to the publisher Marx for 75,000 r. ($37,500).   It
turned out after the transaction that Marx was not aware of
the extent of his writings—he had reckoned on four volumes
of short stories, and he had unconsciously bought nine!   In
1901 Chekhov married an actress of the Art Theatre, Olga
L. Knipper, so that his life became further changed.   These
last years he lived mostly at Yalta, where he had built a villa.
He was constantly besieged by importunate admirers, with
whom he was also very patient and kind.   His health went
from bad to worse.   In June, 1904, his illness had so advanced
that he was sent by the doctors to Badenweiler, a small health

resort in the Black Forest. There it was he died on July 2, 1904. His body was brought to Moscow and buried by the side of his father, who had preceded him in 1899.

Chekhov's literary career falls into two distinct periods: before and after 1886.* The English reader, and the more "literary" Russian public, know him by his later work, but it may be safely asserted that a much greater number of Russians know him as the author of his early comic stories than as the author of *My Life* and *Three Sisters*. It is a characteristic fact that the most popular and typical of his comic stories, precisely those which are sure to be known to every middle-class or semi-educated Russian (i.e., *A Horse Name*, *Vint*, *The Complaint Ledger*, *Surgery*, etc.), have not been translated into English. It is true that some of these stories are very difficult to translate, so topical and national are the jokes. But it is also evident that the English-speaking admirer of Chekhov has no taste for this buffoonery, and looks to Chekhov for commodities of a very different description. The level of the comic papers in which Chekhov wrote was by no means a high one. They were the sanctuary of every kind of vulgarity and bad taste. Their buffoonery was vulgar and meaningless. They lacked the noble gift of nonsense which of all things elevates man nearest the gods; they lacked wit, restraint, and grace. It was mere trivial buffoonery, and Chekhov's stories stand in no striking contrast to their general background. Except for a higher degree of craftsmanship, they are of a piece with the rest. Their dominant note is an uninspired sneer at the weaknesses and follies of mankind, and it would need a more than lynx-eyed critic to discern in them the note of human sympathy and of the higher humour which is so familiar to the reader of Chekhov's mature work. The great majority

---

* A great inconvenience of the English edition of Chekhov is that it entirely disregards dates. The tales are arranged in an arbitrary order, and Mr. Edward Garnett, in his preface to vol. xiii of *The Tales of Tchehov*, even affirms that "it is impossible to obtain the necessary information for a chronological list" of his works. Meanwhile, in the Russian editions they are all arranged in a strictly chronological order, and a few hours in the British Museum would suffice to draw up a complete list of their dates.

of these stories were never reprinted by Chekhov, but still the first and second volumes of his collected edition contain several dozen of the kind. Only a few, and all of them of a less crude variety, have had the honour of an English translation. But even in the crudest, Chekhov stands out as a superior craftsman and in the economy of his means there is a promise of *Sleepy* and *At Christmas-time*. Before long, Chekhov began to deviate from the straight line imposed on him by the comic papers, and as early as 1884 he could write such a story as *The Chorus Girl*, which may yet be still a little primitive and clumsy in its lyrical construction, but on the whole stands almost on a level with the best of his mature work. *Parti-coloured Stories*, which appeared in 1886 and laid the foundation of Chekhov's reputation in the literary circles, contained, besides many exercises in crude buffoonery, stories of a different kind which presented a gay appearance but were sad in substance—and which answered admirably to the hackneyed phrase of Russian critics, "tears through laughter." Such, for instance, is *Misery:* on a wet winter night a cabman who has just lost his son tries to tell his story to one after another of his fares, and does not succeed in kindling their sympathy.

In 1886, as has been said, Chekhov was able to free himself from the comic papers and could now develop a new style which had begun to assert itself somewhat earlier. This style was (and remained) essentially poetical, but it was some time before he finally settled the main lines of what was to be the characteristic Chekhovian story. In his stories of 1886–1888 there are many elements that have been yet imperfectly blended —a strain of descriptive journalism (in its most unadulterated form in *Uprooted*); pure anecdote, sometimes just ironical (*The First-Class Passenger*), sometimes poignantly tragi-comical (*Vanka*); the lyrical expression of atmosphere (*The Steppe, Happiness*); psychological studies of morbid experience (*Typhus*); parables and moralities laid out in a conventional, un-Russian surrounding (*The Bet, A Story without a Title*). But already one of the favourite and most characteristic themes asserts its domination—the mutual lack of understanding between human beings, the impossibility for one person to feel in tune with another. *The Privy Councillor, The Post, The Party, The Princess* are all based on this idea —which becomes something like the *Leitmotiv* of all Chekhov's later work. The most typical stories of this period are all located in the same country, the country of his early life, the steppe between the Sea of Azov and the Donets. These are *The Steppe, Happiness, The Horse-Stealers.* They are planned as lyrical symphonies (though the last one is also an anecdote). Their dominant note is superstition, the vague terror (Chekhov makes it poetical) before the presences that haunt the dark and empty steppe, the profound uninterestingness and poverty of the steppe peasant's life, a vague hope of a happiness that may be discovered with the help of dark powers, in some ancient treasure-mound. *The Steppe*, at which Chekhov worked much and to which he returned again after its publication, is the central thing in this period. It lacks the wonderful architecture of his short stories—it is a lyrical poem, but a poem made out of the substance of trivial, dull, and dusky life. The long, monotonous, uneventful journey of a little boy over the endless steppe from his native village to a distant town is drawn out in a hundred pages to form a languid, melodious, and tedious lullaby. A brighter aspect of Chekhov's lyrical art is in *Easter Eve*. The monk on night duty on the ferry-boat tells a passenger about his dead fellow-monk, who had the rare gift of writing lauds to the saints. He describes with loving detail the technique of this art, and one discerns Chekhov's sincere sympathy for this unnoticed, unwanted, quiet, and unambitious fellow-craftsman. To the same period belongs *Kashtanka*, the delightful history of a dog that was kidnapped by a circus clown, to form part of a troupe of performing animals, and escaped from him in the middle of a performance to her old master. The story is a wonderful blend of humour and poetry, and though it certainly sentimentalizes and humanizes its animals, one cannot help recognizing it as a masterpiece. Another little gem is *Sleepy*, a real masterpiece of concentration, economy, and powerful effectiveness. The story is so short that it cannot be summarized, and so good that it cannot be left unread.*

In some stories of this period we find already the manner which is especially characteristic of him and which is pre-eminently Chekhovian. The earliest story where it is quite distinctly discernible is *The Party* (1887), on which Chekhov himself laid a great value, but which is not yet perfect; he confesses in a letter to Suvorin that he "would gladly have spent six months over *The Party.* . . . But what am I to do? I begin a story on September 10th with the thought that I must finish it by October 5th at the latest; if I don't, I shall fail the editor and be left without money. I let myself go at the beginning and write with an easy mind; but by the time I get to the middle, I begin to grow timid and fear that my story will be too long. . . . This is why the beginning of my stories is always very promising . . . the middle is huddled and timid, and the end is, as in a short sketch, like fireworks." † But the essential of Chekhov's mature style is unmistakably present. It is the "biography" of a mood developing under the trivial pinpricks of life, but due in substance to a deep-lying, physiological or psychological cause (in this case the woman's pregnancy). *A Dreary Story*, published in 1889, may be considered the starting-point of the mature period. The *Leitmotiv* of mutual isolation is brought out with great power. We may date the meaning which has come to be associated in Russia with the words "Chekhovian state of mind" (*Chekhovskoe nastroenie*) from *A Dreary Story*. The atmosphere of the story is produced by the professor's deep and growing disillusionment as to himself and the life around him, the gradual loss of faith in his vocation, the gradual drifting apart of people linked together by life; a gradual dawning on him of the utter vulgarity and insignificance of the people nearest him. The professor realizes the meaninglessness of his life—

---

* Tolstoy is said to have held this story in high esteem, and one cannot help noticing a certain similarity it bears to his own masterpiece, *Alesha Gorshok*, written eighteen years later.

† Letters of Anton Tchehov, tr. by Constance Garnett, p. 101. (Chatto & Windus.)

and the "giftlessness" (*bezdarnost*—a characteristically Chekhovian word) and dullness of all that surrounds him.   His
only remaining friend, his former ward, Katya, an unsuccessful
disillusioned actress, breaks down under an intenser experience
of the same feelings.   And though his affection for her is
sincere and genuine, and though he is suffering from the same
causes as she is, he fails to find the necessary language to
approach her.   An unconquerable inhibition keeps him closed
to her, and all he can say to her is:

"Let us have lunch, Katya."

"No, thank you," she answers coldly.

Another minute passes in silence.

"I don't like Kharkov," I say; "it is so grey here—such a grey
town."

"Yes, perhaps. . . . It's ugly. . . . I am here not for long,
passing through.   I am going on to-day."

"Where?"

"To the Crimea . . . that is, to the Caucasus."

"Oh! For long?"

"I don't know."

"Katya gets up and, with a cold smile, holds out her hand, looking at me.   I want to ask her: "Then you won't be at my funeral?" but she does not look at me; her hand is cold and, as it
were, strange.   I escort her to the door in silence.   She goes out,
walks down the long corridor, without looking back.   She knows
that I am looking after her, and she will look back at the turn.
No, she did not look round.   I've seen her black dress for the last
time; her steps have died away! . . . Farewell, my treasure!" *

This ending on a minor note is repeated in all Chekhov's
subsequent stories, and gives the keynote to his work.

A Dreary Story opens the succession of Chekhov's mature
masterpieces.   Besides the natural growth of his genius, he
was now free to work longer over them than he could when
he was writing *The Party*.   So his stories written in the
nineties are almost without exception perfect works of art.
It is mainly on the work of this period that Chekhov's reputa-

* *The Wife and Other Stories,* tr. by Constance Garnett, pp. 218–219.
(Chatto & Windus.)

tion now rests. The principal stories written after 1889 are, in chronological order, *The Duel, Ward No. 6* (1892), *An Anonymous Story* (1893), *The Black Monk, The Teacher of Literature* (1894), *Three Years, Ariadne, Anna on the Neck, An Artist's Story* (in Russian: *The House with the Maisonette), My Life* (1895), *Peasants* (1897), *The Darling, Ionich, The Lady with the Dog* (1898), *The New Villa* (1899), *At Christmas-time, In the Ravine* (1900). After this date (it was the period of *Three Sisters* and *The Cherry Orchard*) he wrote only two stories, *The Bishop* (1902) and *Betrothed* (1903).

Chekhov's art has been called psychological, but it is psychological in a very different sense from Tolstoy's, Dostoevsky's, or Marcel Proust's. No writer excels him in conveying the mutual unsurpassable isolation of human beings and the impossibility of understanding each other. This idea forms the core of almost every one of his stories, but, in spite of this, Chekhov's characters are singularly lacking in individual personality. Personality is absent from his stories. His characters all speak (within class limits and apart from the little tricks of catchwords he lends them from time to time) the same language, which is Chekhov's own. They cannot be recognized, as Tolstoy's and Dostoevsky's can, by the mere *sound of their voices*. They are all alike, all made of the same material— "the common stuff of humanity"—and in this sense Chekhov is the most "democratic," the most "unanimist," of all writers. For of course the similarity of all his men and women is not a sign of weakness—it is the expression of his fundamental intuition of life as a homogeneous matter, but cut out into watertight compartments by the phenomenon of individuality. Like Stendhal and the French classicists, and unlike Tolstoy, Dostoevsky, and Proust, Chekhov is a student of "man in general," of the genus *Homo*. But unlike the classicists and like Proust, he fixes his attention on the infinitesimals, the "pinpricks" and "straws" of the soul. Stendhal deals in psychological "whole numbers." He traces the major, conscious, creative lines of psychical life. Chekhov concentrates on the "differentials" of mind, its minor, unconscious, involuntary, destructive, and dissolvent forces. As art Chekhov's method is active, more active than, for instance, Proust's, for it is based on a stricter and more conscious *choice* of material and a more complicated and elaborate disposition of it. But as "outlook," as "philosophy," it is profoundly passive and "non-resistant," for it is a surrender to the "micro-organisms," of the soul, to its destructive microbes. Hence the general impression produced by the whole of Chekhov's work that he had a cult for inefficiency and weakness. For Chekhov has no other way of displaying his sympathy with his characters than to show in detail the process of their submission to their microbes. The strong man who does not succumb in this struggle, or who does not experience it, is always treated by Chekhov with less sympathy and comes out as the "villain of the play"—in so far as the word "villain" is at all applicable to the world Chekhov moves in. The strong man in this world of his is merely the insensate brute, with a skin thick enough not to feel the "pinpricks" which are the only important thing in life.

Chekhov's art is constructive. But the construction he uses is not a narrative construction—it might rather be called musical, not, however, in the sense that his prose is melodious, for it is not. But his method of constructing a story is akin to the method used in music. His stories are at once fluid and precise. The lines along which he builds them are very complicated curves, but they have been calculated with the utmost precision. A story by him is a series of points marking out with precision the lines discerned by him in the tangled web of consciousness. Chekhov excels in the art of tracing the first stages of an emotional process; in indicating those first symptoms of a deviation when to the general eye, and to the conscious eye of the subject in question, the nascent curve still seems to coincide with a straight line. An infinitesimal touch which at first hardly arrests the reader's attention gives a hint at the direction the story is going to take. It is then repeated as a *Leitmotiv* and at each repetition the true equation of the curve becomes more apparent, and it ends by shooting away in a direction very different from that of the original straight line. Such stories

as *The Teacher of Literature, Ionich, The Lady with the Dog,*
are perfect examples of such emotional curves. The straight
line, for instance, in *Ionich* is the doctor's love for Mlle.
Turkin; the curve, his subsidence into the egoistical com-
placency of a successful provincial career. In *The Teacher
of Literature* the straight line is again the hero's love; the
curve, his dormant dissatisfaction with selfish happiness and
his intellectual ambition. In *The Lady with the Dog* the
straight line is the hero's attitude towards his affair with the
Lady as a trivial and passing intrigue; the curve, his overwhelming and all-pervading love for her. In most of Chekhov's stories these constructive lines are complicated by a
rich and mellow atmosphere, which he produced by the
abundance of emotionally significant detail. The effect is
poetical, even lyrical: as in a lyric it is not interest in the
development that the reader feels, but "infection" by the
poet's mood. Chekhov's stories are lyrical monoliths, they
cannot be dissected into episodes, for every episode is strictly
conditioned by the whole and is without significance apart from
it. In architectural unity Chekhov surpasses all Russian
writers of the Realistic age. Only in Pushkin and Lermontov
do we find an equal or superior gift of design. Chekhov
thought Lermontov's *Taman* was the best short story ever
written, and this partiality was well founded. *Taman* fore-
stalled Chekhov's method of lyrical construction. Only its
air is colder and clearer than the mild and mellow "autumnal"
atmosphere of Chekhov's world.

Two of his best stories, *My Life* and *In the Ravine,* stand
somewhat apart from the rest of his mature work. *My Life*
is the story of a Tolstoyan, and one cannot help thinking
that in it Chekhov tried to approach the clearer and more
intellectual style of Tolstoy. There are a directness of narrative and a thinness of atmosphere which are otherwise rare
in Chekhov. In spite of this relative absence of atmosphere,
it is perhaps his most poetically pregnant story. It is convincingly symbolical. The hero, his father, his sister, the
Azhogins, Anyuta Blagovo stand out with the distinctness of
morality characters. The very vagueness and generality of

its title helps to make it something like an *Everyman*. For poetical grasp and significance, *My Life* may be recognized as the masterpiece of Chekhov—unless it is surpassed by *In the Ravine*. This, one of his last stories, is an amazing piece of work. The scene is the Moscow industrial area—it is the history of a shopkeeper's family. It is remarkably free from all excess of detail, and the atmosphere is produced with the help of only a few descriptive touches, by the movement of the story. It is infinitely rich in emotional and symbolical significance. What is rare in Chekhov, in both these stories there is an earnestness and keenness of moral judgment which raises them above the average of his work. All Chekhov's work is symbolical, but in most of his stories the symbolism is less concrete and more vaguely suggestive. It is akin to Maeterlinck's, in spite of the vast difference of style between the Russian realist and the Belgian mystic. *Ward No. 6*, the darkest and most terrible of all Chekhov's stories, is an especially notable example of this suggestive symbolism. It is all the more suggestive for being strictly realistic. (The only time he attempted to step out of the limits of strict realism, Chekhov wrote the only story that is quite certainly a failure—*The Black Monk*.) But this symbolism reached its full development in his plays, beginning with *The Seagull*.

Chekhov's first attempt to use the dramatic form was *On the High Road* (1885). This is an adaptation of an earlier story of his. It did not see the stage: it was suppressed by the dramatic censorship as too "gloomy and filthy." It was published only after his death. In 1886 Chekhov wrote his first full-size play, *Ivanov*. Like *The Party* and other stories of the period, *Ivanov* is a transitional work, and betrays a somewhat wavering hand which has not yet acquired a complete command of its material. *Ivanov* was successful on the stage, and, stimulated by success, Chekhov almost immediately began writing a new play, *The Forest Spirit*. But the cold reception given it by the few friends he showed it to, made him put it aside and abandon serious dramatic work. Instead he wrote a series of one-act comedies (*The Bear, The Wedding,* etc.) in a style closely connected with his early comic stories. These comedies were well received by the admirers of Chekhov's comic writings and became widely popular. They are still a favourite item in every provincial repertoire, and especially often staged in private theatricals. In 1896 Chekhov returned to serious drama—and produced *The Seagull*. I have already told the story of its original failure and subsequent success. After that, Chekhov returned to *The Forest Spirit*, which became *Uncle Vanya*, and was followed by *Three Sisters* and *The Cherry Orchard*. These four famous plays form Chekhov's Theatre. They have received, especially the two last ones, even extravagant praise from English critics, who seem to lose the famous English virtue of "understatement" the moment they have to do with Chekhov. *The Cherry Orchard* has been described as the best play since Shakespeare, and *Three Sisters* as the best play in the world. Tolstoy thought differently, and though he had an intense dislike for Shakespeare, he preferred his plays to Chekhov's. Tolstoy, who considered subject-matter the chief thing in plays and novels, could not have thought otherwise: there is no subject-matter in Chekhov's plays, no plot, no action. They consist of nothing but "superficial detail." They are, in fact, the most undramatic plays in the world (if, however, they are not surpassed in this respect by the plays of Chekhov's bad—they were all bad—imitators). This undramatic character is a natural outcome of the Russian realistic drama. The plays of Ostrovsky, and especially of Turgenev, contain the germs of much that reached its full development in Chekhov. The Russian realistic drama is essentially static. But Chekhov carried to the extreme limit this static tendency, and gave his name to a new type in drama—the undramatic drama. On the whole, his plays are constructed in the same way as his stories. The differences are due to the differences of material and are imposed by the use of dialogue. As a general rule, it may be said that the principal difference is that the plays have less backbone, less skeleton, than the stories, and are more purely atmospheric creations. In his stories there is always one central figure which is the main element of unity—the story is conducted from the standpoint of this central figure. But the use of dialogue excludes this monocentric construction, and makes all the characters equal. Chekhov amply avails himself of this fact, and distributes the spectator's attention among all his people with wonderful fairness. His *dramatis personæ* live in a state of ideal democracy—where equality is no sham. This method was admirably adapted to the principles of the Moscow Art Theatre, which aimed at creating a cast where there would be no stars but all the actors would be equally excellent. The dialogue form is also admirably suited to the expression of one of Chekhov's favourite ideas: the mutual unintelligibility and strangeness of human beings, who cannot and do not want to understand each other. He constantly makes his characters exchange entirely unrelated remarks. Each character speaks only of what interests him or her, and pays no attention to what the other people in the room are saying. Thus the dialogue becomes a patchwork of disconnected remarks, dominated by a poetic "atmosphere," but by no logical unity. The effect is familiar and plays a principal part in producing the general "Chekhov" effect. Of course this system is entirely an artistic convention. No one in real life ever spoke as Chekhov's people do. Again it reminds one of Maeterlinck, whose plays (as Mr. Chesterton has remarked) have a meaning only if one is quite in tune with the poet's very exclusive mood; otherwise it is mere nonsense. It is the same with Chekhov. His plays are "infectious," as Tolstoy wanted all art to be, in fact nothing if not infectious. But, though the moods are perhaps less exclusive and more universal than Maeterlinck's, unless one has a sympathy with his moods the dialogue is meaningless. Like his stories, Chekhov's plays are always saturated with emotional symbolism, and in his research for suggestive poetry he sometimes oversteps the limits of good taste—such lapses are, for instance, the bursting of a string in *The Cherry Orchard*, and the last scene in the same play—when Firs, the old servant, is left alone in the deserted house where he had been locked in and forgotten. Even more consistently than in his stories, the dominant note of Chekhov's plays is one of gloom, depression, and hopelessness. The end of every one of them is managed in the same way as the end of *A Dreary Story*. They are all in the minor key, and leave the spectator in a state of impotent—perhaps deliciously impotent—depression. Judged by their own standards (which can hardly be accepted as the normal standards of dramatic art), Chekhov's plays are perfect works of art, but are they really as perfect as his best stories? At any rate, his method is dangerous, and has been imitated only at the imitator's imminent peril. No play written by an imitator of Chekhov is above contempt.

Chekhov's English admirers think that everything is perfect in Chekhov. To find spots in him will seem blasphemy to them. Still it is only fair to point out these spots. I have already referred to the complete lack of individuality in his characters and in their way of speaking. This is not in itself a fault, for it belongs to his fundamental intuition of life which recognizes no personality. But it is not a virtue. It is especially noticeable when he makes his characters speak at length on abstract subjects. How different from Dostoevsky, who "felt ideas" and who made them so splendidly individual! Chekhov did not "feel ideas," and when his characters give expression to theirs they speak a colourless and monotonous journalese. *The Duel* is especially disfigured by such harangues. This is perhaps Chekhov's tribute to a deep-rooted tradition of Russian *intelligentsia* literature. Their speeches may have had some emotional significance in their time, but certainly have none to-day. Another serious shortcoming is Chekhov's Russian. It is colourless and lacks individuality. He had no feeling for words. No Russian writer of anything like his significance used a language so devoid of all raciness and nerve. This makes Chekhov (except for topical allusions, technical terms, and occasional catchwords) so easy to translate. Of all Russian writers, he has the least to fear from the treachery of translators.

Chekhov's direct influence on Russian literature was not important. The success of his short stories contributed to the great popularity of that form, which became the predominant form in Russian fiction. Gorky, Kuprin, Bunin, to name but the foremost, look to him as to a master, but can hardly be recognized as his pupils. Certainly no one learned from him the art of constructing his stories. His dramas, which looked so easy to imitate, were imitated, but the style proved a pitfall. To-day Russian fiction is quite free from any trace of Chekhov's influence. Some of the younger writers began before the Revolution as his more or less unintelligent imitators, but none of them has remained true to him. In Russia, Chekhov has become a thing of the past, of a past remoter than even Turgenev, not to speak of Gogol or Leskov. Abroad, things stand differently. If Chekhov has had a genuine heir to the secrets of his art, it is in England—where Katherine Mansfield did what no Russian has done, learned from Chekhov without imitating him. England is to-day the country where Chekhov has the most devoted and enthusiastic admirers. There, and to a lesser degree in France, the cult of Chekhov has become the hall-mark of the highbrow intellectual. Curiously enough, in Russia Chekhov was always regarded as a distinctly "lowbrow" writer; the self-conscious intellectual élite was always conspicuously cool to him. The highbrows of twenty years ago even affected to (or sincerely did) despise him. His real stronghold was in the heart of the honest Philistine in the street. Nowadays Chekhov has of course become the common property of the nation. His place as a classic, a major classic, one of the "ten best," is not challenged. But he is a classic who has been temporarily shelved.

INTERCHAPTER I

THE FIRST REVOLUTION

THE history of Russia since the beginning of the nineteenth century may be represented as a succession of revolutionary waves and interrevolutionary troughs. Each of these waves rose higher than the one that preceded it. The first wave broke in 1825, in the entirely unsupported and unsuccessful mutiny of the Decembrists. It was followed by the long reaction of the reign of Nicholas I, during which rose the second wave. Gradually and slowly developing, it was at once held back and powerfully seconded by the liberal reforms of the sixties, reached its climax in the activity of the People's Will party, and broke in 1881 in the assassination of Alexander II. The succeeding calm was neither so long nor so complete as that which preceded it. The Revolution regained strength by the nineties (largely owing to the effect of the hunger year 1891–1892), rose to an unprecedented height, and broke with a terrible crash in 1905. The movement was again suppressed, only to reappear during the War and finally to triumph in 1917. The third of these waves was the first to be supported by a wide-spread *popular* movement, and its crest is known by the name of the First Revolution.

This Revolution of 1905, in so far as it was a conscious effort to attain definite ends, was entirely the result of the development of the revolutionary ideas of the *intelligentsia*, supported at a critical moment by a refusal of the propertied classes to defend autocracy. But it would have remained ineffective had it not found an army in the recently developed class of industrial workmen. This class, in its turn, was the direct outcome of the rise of capitalism in the second half of the nineteenth century. Russian capitalism was born in the age of reform under Alexander II, but it grew by leaps and bounds in the eighties and nineties, largely owing to the protectionist policy of the Government, embodied in the person of Count Witte. The rise and growth of Russian capitalism out of the conservative forms of pre-reform trade and commerce is a matter of absorbing, but here irrelevant, interest. It is not lacking in traits of considerable picturesque and literary value, and has more than once been treated in literature—perhaps by no one with more effect than by Gorky (who, for all his Marxian allegiance, has a distinct sympathy with the creative impulse of capitalism) in *Foma Gordeev*, and in a chapter of *Fragments from a Diary* dealing with the millionaire Old-Believer Bugrov, of Nizhni Novgorod. The merchant princes of Moscow played an important part in the nineties and after as patrons of art and literature: the æsthetic revival was largely financed by them.

One of the earliest effects of capitalism in literature was the rise of the big daily press. The first journalist of this period was Aleksey Sergeevich Suvòrin (1833–1911), the founder of the *Novoe Vremya*—for many years the best-equipped of Russian papers and the only one that had a certain influence on the Government. Suvorin's *Diary* (published recently by the Soviet Government) is a document of first-class importance, but on the whole he is interesting chiefly as a figure in life, and his place as a writer is insignificant. Only his connexion with Chekhov and with Rozanov gives him an honourable place in Russian literature. The greatest literary exponent of Russian capitalism and industrialism was no lesser man than the great chemist Dmitri Ivanovich Mendeléeff. It may be said that he was passionately in love with the productive forces of his country, and was their champion and troubadour. Though there can be no question of comparing his literary to his scientific importance, he was a writer of powerful temperament and genuine originality. His daughter was married to Alexander Blok, and though the poet was inspired by very different ideas, once at least he struck a note which would have pleased his father-in-law in his grave—in his poem *The New America*, where he sings the praise of the Donets coal, "the black coal, our subterranean Messiah." Count Witte, the good genius of Russian industrialism, wrote three very remarkable volumes of memoirs. Though clumsily composed and almost illiterate, they also reveal a very personal temperament, which make them an interesting book quite apart from their documentary value. Unfortunately, in the English translation they have been outrageously "amended" and "adapted"—all the most racy and unconventional passages having been mercilessly cut out by their American editor, Mr. Yarmolinsky.

The reverse of the capitalistic medal was the rise of Russian Marxism, which became a strong movement towards 1894. It is not necessary to impress the reader with the importance of this movement in Russian history—it is sufficient to say that Lenin was one of the original Marxists of the nineties. But apart from its rôle in 1905 and 1917 and since that date, it was an important stage in the intellectual history of the *intelligentsia*. In the nineties Marxism was a progressive and a liberating force because it brought with it an emancipation from the routine of Populism. It appealed to the Russian intellectual, *rerum novarum cupidum*, as a fundamentally scientific doctrine. What impressed him most in it was its "dialectical method" and the conception of history as a process which obeyed fixed and immutable laws. It divorced politics from ethics, and if this had its bad side in the development of an exclusive class morality (the results of which are apparent in the U.S.S.R.), it had, at first, also a good effect, for it freed the student of political science from the blinkers of a too narrow idealism. The chief exponent of Russian Marxism, its prophet and doctor, was a man of an older generation, Georgi Valentinovich Plekhànov (1852–1918), during the Great War the leader of the patriotic Socialists. In spite of this, the Communists consider him a teacher of Marxism second only to Marx and Engels themselves. He is universally accepted as one of the biggest brains of the Russian *intelligentsia*. Lenin himself began his journalistic career in the mid nineties. But from the literary point of view the most interesting Marxist writers were a group of young men known by the name of "legal Marxists" (for they worked in the "legal," that is, the home press). Their brilliant spokesman was Peter Struve (b. 1870), whose influence as a Marxist was second in the nineties only to that of Plekhanov. But early in the twentieth century he abandoned Socialism, and his writings after 1905 will have to be mentioned in a very different connexion, for he became the leader of the National Liberalism which opposed the old agnostic idealism of the Radical *intelligentsia*. This shows how important Marxism was as an emancipation from the conventions of Populist idealism, and what a powerful leaven of independent thought it could be.

By the end of the nineties the Marxists succeeded in laying the foundations of a successful propaganda among the working-classes, and organized themselves into the Social Democratic Party of Russia. The Populists imitated them, and became the Party of Socialist Revolutionaries. These two parties became known respectively as the S.D.'s, and the S.R.'s, and played a principal part in the events of 1905–1906. The S.D.'s, as Marxists, did not believe in the efficacy of individual action, and consequently condemned terrorism. They laid their hopes on mass action, especially on strikes. In 1903 they became divided (on points the details of which would be irrelevant) into two factions, the Mensheviks (minority men) and the Bolsheviks (majority men, *not* maximalists, the names referring merely to the number of votes given respectively to the two shades of opinion at a particular party congress). But the Bolsheviks did not become widely influential or strongly individualized till much later, during the Great War, and the S.D.'s remained in substance one party. The S.R.'s who, following the older Populists, believed in the importance of the "critically thinking individual" organized from 1900 to 1906 a series of political assassinations. They were the romantic party which attracted all the hot-headed and adventurous youth.

A few years before 1905 Russian Liberalism, which had always had a rather valetudinarian existence, rallied its forces, and for a few years rivalled Socialism in active opposition to the Government. A revolutionary organization of Liberals was formed—the Union for Liberation (*Soyuz Osvobozhdenia*)—and Peter Struve, a valuable and recent recruit to Liberalism from Marxism, left Russia and founded in Stuttgart an uncensored Liberal paper, *Liberation,* which for a moment almost rivalled the popularity of Herzen's *Bell* of forty-five years earlier. The unsuccessful war with Japan (1904–1905) seconded very powerfully the growth of opposition, and a pact for co-operating against the Government was formed between the three parties—S.D., S.R., and Union for Liberation. During the first period of Revolution the three parties went hand in hand, and the great strike of October, 1905, which was the immediate cause of the granting of the Charter of October 17th, was materially helped by the Union of Unions, an organization of the professional classes, headed by the Liberal leader, Paul Milyukov. But after the 17th of October the ways of Liberalism and Socialism began to diverge. The Liberals took no part in the armed Rising of December, 1905, and the Socialists boycotted the Duma elections in the spring of 1906. The Liberals formed a party which took the name of Constitutional Democrats, and became known by its Russian initials, K.D., or Cadets. The most influential figure of Russian Liberalism from the nineties to 1917 was Professor Paul Milyukov (b. 1856), a Positivist and a confirmed Westernizer. He began by making a name as an historian (*Sketches from the History of Russian Civilization* has become a standard work), and after 1905 directed all the activities, parliamentary and journalistic, of the Cadet party. He had a decided genius for organization, but also a certain unconquerable stolidity which has won him the name of "a genius of tactlessness." Milyukov is typical of the traditional positivism and agnosticism of the older Russian Liberals, but already before 1905 a new movement began, which proceeded from Soloviev and tended to identify Liberalism with Christian Idealism and, by a strange, if natural, association, with Patriotism and Imperialism. This movement found its most gifted expression in the work of Peter Struve, the ex-Marxist, and of his associates, the authors of

Landmarks, of whom I shall have more to say in my fourth chapter.

The First Revolution was a deep-reaching and infectious movement. For a moment it dominated the whole of Russian intellectual life, and even the Symbolists, who had made a point of being non-political, became revolutionaries and "mystical anarchists." But this momentary excitement was followed by a depression of political, especially of Radical, feeling. The years following the suppression of the Revolution were a period of anti-political individualism, which found its expression in the growth of æstheticism and sexual freedom on the one hand, and of the productive forces of capitalism on the other. There was a profound disillusionment in Radicalism and in all the traditional ideas of the *intelligentsia.* This feeling was strongly supported by the revelations of Burtsev, who denounced Azef (a prominent and influential member of the S.R. party who had organized several political assassinations) as an agent of the Secret Police—a revelation that was followed by a deep-going disintegration of the revolutionary parties. By 1914 they had lost most of their prestige and influence, and the *intelligentsia* was well on its way towards patriotism and imperialism.

An important result of the Revolution was the relative (in 1905–1906, much more than relative) freedom of the press. The censorship disappeared, and though the Government always found means of coercing the opposition papers, it became possible to treat practically all political issues in the press. This naturally raised the importance of the daily papers and relatively diminished that of the monthly papers, the bulwark of *intelligentsia* idealism. Politics and literature became more easily divorced. Politics became more practical, and literature was largely emancipated from the obligation of serving party ends.

The most important result of the Revolution was the establishment of a Parliament, with limited functions—the Duma. But the Duma has little to do with literature. Unlike the opening of the new law courts forty years earlier, it did not become the starting-point for a revival of public eloquence.

There is little to be said of the Duma orators from the literary point of view. The Cadets were the best. But their most famous orator, V. A. Maklakov, was a lawyer with a settled reputation before he was returned to the Duma. And many of those who attended the Duma sittings hold that the best orator they ever heard was not a member of the Duma, but the Prime Minister P. A. Stolypin.

CHAPTER III

1. PROSE FICTION AFTER CHEKHOV

BEFORE Chekhov died it seemed as if his example had brought into life a new golden age of Realism, of which he was to be but the precursor. Between 1895 and 1905 there appeared one after the other a succession of young writers (born between 1868 and 1878) who attracted all the literary limelight, won world-wide reputations, and sold better than Turgenev or Dostoevsky had ever sold. The most prominent were Gorky and Andreev—and the whole movement may be called the Gorky-Andreev school. It may be called a school, without unduly straining the facts, for all the writers who constituted it have sufficient features in common to mark them off from the older pre-Chekhov school of fiction whose last considerable representative was Korolenko, as well as from the Symbolists and the modern movement in prose which has been more or less affected by Symbolist influences.

Gorky is the earliest in date and the most significant writer of the school we are speaking of, and to a certain extent his influence is traceable in most of its other members. This influence is largely due to the fact that he was the first to free Russian Realism from its former "genteel" and "puritan" characteristics. Russian Realism had always been morally delicate, and avoided the crudity and outspokenness of French novelists. Less reticent in appearance, it was as delicate in substance as the English Victorian novel. Ugliness and filth, and the physical side of sexual relations, were, on the whole, taboo to the old Russian novelist. The convention was broken by Tolstoy, who was the first to speak of the physical horrors of disease and death in *The Death of Ivan Ilyich* and of the physical foundation of love in *The Kreutzer Sonata*. He thus contributed very substantially to the destruction of nineteenth-century taboos and conventions, and his influence on Russian fiction was not entirely different from the parallel influence of Zola, whom he hated. This is one of the "little ironies" of history: the "classical" and "religious" art of Tolstoy's last years was a step in the direction of *Sanin*. The taboo-lifting work begun by Tolstoy was continued by Gorky, Andreev, and Artsybashev. Beside this, Tolstoy's influence was also considerable as the founder of a new genre—the metaphysical and moral problem story which flourished especially in the hands of Andreev and Artsybashev. The great extent of his influence on these two writers will appear later on. The influence of Chekhov was of a different kind—more technical and formal. It was partly owing to him that the short story became a favourite form with the young writers. They also tried to imitate his artistic economy—his avoidance of empty places in a story, and his care to charge every portion of it with equal significance and expressiveness. In this respect he remained an unattainable ideal, and though his turns of phrase and idiosyncrasies of expression abound in the work of the young novelists, the secret of Chekhov's narrative art was never discovered by them.

Between 1900 and 1910 Russian literature was divided into two distinct and mutually watertight parts—the Gorky-Andreev school on the one side, and the Symbolists with their following on the other. The separation was almost absolute. At first the Gorky-Andreev group obscured the Symbolists almost completely; but with time the situation was reversed and to-day the first decade of this century appears to us as the Age of Symbolism. To-day it is almost an axiom that of the two movements Symbolism was far the more significant. It is possible that some future age will again reverse the judgment, and find more attractions in Kuprin and Sergeev-Tsensky than in Balmont and Bryusov. But the main issue between the two schools has nothing to do with the talents of the two parties—it is a matter of cultural level: the Gorky-Andreev school are the successors of the old *intelligentsia* who had lost much of the ethical education of the old Radicals and acquired nothing in return beyond a "craving void" of pessimism and unbelief. The Symbolists were the pioneers of a new culture which, though one-sided and imperfect, infinitely widened and enriched the Russian mind and made the *intelligentsia* at once more European and more national.

By 1910 the work of the Gorky-Andreev school was done. Since then it has ceased to be a living movement and a literary influence. This, however, does not mean that individual members have not produced works of permanent and lasting value: within the last decade or so books have been written by them that will in all probability eclipse the earlier efforts of their authors. But they are works of isolated and disinterested maturity. Such are Bunin's stories, including *The Gentleman from San Francisco;* Gorky's autobiographical books and memoirs, which give him a safe place among the classics, and outweigh in intrinsic significance his early fiction; and the latest works of Sergeev-Tsensky, who after almost ten years' silence has unexpectedly revealed himself as one of the most vigorous and *promising* writers of to-day.

2. MAXIM GORKY

The greatest name in the realistic revival is Maxim Gorky's. Next to Tolstoy he is to-day the only Russian author of the modern period who has a really world-wide reputation and one which is not, like Chekhov's, confined to the *intelligentsias* of the various countries of the world. Gorky's career has been truly wonderful; risen from the lowest depths of the provincial proletariate, he was not thirty when he became the most popular writer and the most discussed man in Russia. After a period of dazzling celebrity during which he was currently placed by the side of Tolstoy, and unquestionably above Chekhov, his fame suffered an eclipse, and he was almost forgotten by the Russian educated classes. But his fame survived abroad and among the lower classes at home, and after 1917 his universal reputation and his connexion with the new rulers of Russia made him the obvious champion of Russian literature. However, this new position was due to his personal rather than to his literary merits, and though in the general opinion of competent people Gorky's last books (beginning with *Childhood*, 1913) are superior to his early stories, his literary popularity is to-day quite out of proportion to what it was a quarter of a century ago. And those works by which he is most likely to survive as a classic will never have known the joy and wonder of immediate success.

Maxim Gorky's real name is Aleksey Maksimovich Péshkov. His father, Maxim Peshkov, was an upholsterer, who by dint of hard work rose to be a shipping agent at Astrakhan. He was married to the daughter of Vasili Kashirin, a dyer of Nizhni-Novgorod. The writer was born in that city on March 14, 1869. He was taken to Astrakhan, but there when he was five his father died, and his mother brought him back to Nizhni to the house of his grandparents. Gorky has told us the story of his *Childhood* and drawn unforgettable portraits of his close and harsh grandfather and of his charming, beauty-loving, and kind grandmother. The Kashirins were on the decline when the Peshkovs came to live with them, and as the boy grew up, the atmosphere of increasing poverty and squalid selfishness grew denser round him. His mother married again—a "semi-intelligent" for whom Gorky has little good to say. She died before long. His grandfather sent him out into the world to earn his bread, and for more than ten years he made the acquaintance of every conceivable kind of drudgery. He began as a boy at a bootmaker's shop. Then he was one time pantry boy on a Volga steamer where the cook, a drunken old ex-corporal of the Guards, taught him to read and write and laid the foundations of his literary education. One of the first books he read was *The Mysteries of Udolpho*, and for a long time his reading was very largely of the blood-and-thunder popular romance type—a fact that did not remain without its influence on his early work. At fifteen Gorky tried to get into a school at Kazan, "but as," he says, "it was not the fashion to give education for nothing," he did not succeed in the attempt, and instead, to save himself from starving, he had to work in an underground bakery so memorably described in *Twenty-six Men and a Girl*. In Kazan he came into contact with students who sowed in him the seeds of his future revolutionism, and also became familiar with the life of those "ex-people" who were to become his stepping-stone to celebrity. Leaving Kazan, he moved from place to place over the whole of South-east and South of Russia, taking up odd jobs, working hard, and often remaining without work. In 1890 he came to Nizhni to present himself for conscription but was released on grounds of illness. Instead he became clerk to the Nizhni advocate, M. A. Lanin, who did much for his education, and whom he later on always remembered as his greatest benefactor.* But he soon left his work and again went wandering over Russia. During these wanderings he began to write. In October, 1892, when he was working at the railway depot in Tiflis, his first story, the intensely romantic *Makar Chudra*, was accepted and printed by the local daily paper, *Kavkaz*, over the signature that has since become so famous.† In the following years he continued writing for the provincial press and was soon able to rely on his literary work for a livelihood. But it was not till 1895, after he had once more returned to Nizhni, that he definitely entered into the "big literature." Korolenko, who was then living in that city, had one of his stories (*Chelkash*) printed in the influential monthly *Russkoe Bogatstvo*. Though he continued working for the provincial press, he was now a welcome guest in the Petersburg magazines. In 1898 his stories came out in book form (2 volumes).

Their success was tremendous and, for a Russian author, unprecedented in the strict sense of the word. From a promising provincial journalist Gorky became the most famous writer of his country. From this date to the First Revolution, Gorky was, next to Tolstoy, the figure in Russia which aroused the greatest public interest. Interviews and portraits of him flooded the press, and everyone thought it his duty to have a look at his person. International fame was not slow to follow. Germany especially went mad over him

* The first volume of his *Stories* is dedicated to Lanin.
† Gorky (or, in strict transliteration, Gor'kiy) means (1) bitter, (2) miserable.

—in 1903–1904 his famous play *Na Dne* (*The Lower Depths*) had an uninterrupted run of over 500 nights in Berlin.

In Petersburg Gorky came in contact with the Marxists and became himself a Marxist and a Social Democrat. His works became the *pièce de résistance* of the Marxist review *Zhizn,* to which he gave *Foma Gordeev* and *Three of Them* (1899–1901). It was also for a poem by Gorky that the review was suppressed. This poem was the *Song of the Petrel:* the Russian name for "petrel" means storm messenger, and the *Song* was a very transparent allegory of the coming revolutionary storm. Gorky was now one of the foremost figures in the Russian Radical world. He was also one of the financial powers behind the movement: his very considerable literary income was systematically drawn on by his political friends for the promotion of Revolution. This state of things continued till 1917, so that Gorky, in spite of the enormous financial success of his books, never enjoyed the wealth of his successful Western confrères. It was easy to become a martyr in Russia about 1900 and Gorky was very soon arrested and banished to Nizhni. In 1902 he was elected an honorary member of the Imperial Academy of Science. This was an unprecedented act in regard to a writer of thirty-three. But before Gorky could avail himself of his new rights, his election was annulled by the Government, the new Academician being under "the supervision of the police." Following this incident, Chekhov and Korolenko renounced their membership of the Academy. Gorky played a prominent part in the First Revolution. In January, 1905, he was arrested for taking part in a protest against the "9th of January," and this arrest became the cause for world-wide demonstrations in his favour. After his release he edited a daily newspaper which supported the Bolsheviks and where he published a series of articles in which he denounced all the Russian writers of the twentieth century, including Dostoevsky and Tolstoy, as "petty bourgeois" (*meshchane*). He took a prominent part in the campaign against the Russian foreign loans, and in December he gave active help to the armed rebellion in Moscow.

In 1906 he left Russia for the United States. His journey through Finland and Scandinavia was a triumphal procession. His arrival in New York was equally triumphant. But before long it transpired that the woman Gorky was living with and whom he called his wife had not been wedded to him, and American opinion turned with sudden fury against the writer. He was asked to leave his hotel, and Mark Twain refused to take the chair at a banquet in his honour. It is rather natural that Gorky was deeply hurt by this sudden outburst of Puritanism, so entirely unintelligible to a Russian, and that he gave vent to his resentment in a series of American stories, which appeared under the suggestive title of *The City of the Yellow Devil* (1907). On his return to Europe, he settled in Capri, where he remained till shortly before the War, and where he became immensely popular with the natives. His Italian popularity was increased by the active part he took in the relief work after the terrible Messina catastrophe. In Russia, meanwhile, his popularity in the higher intellectual classes began to sink. All his works since *Na Dne* (1902) were received with comparative indifference, and from being the great national favourite he was in 1900, he sank to the position of the party pet of the Bolsheviks, who were about alone to praise his new works. But, on the other hand, his works began to penetrate into the masses of the working-class and contributed largely to forming that mentality of the Russian workman which has manifested itself since 1917. On his return to Russia, Gorky founded a monthly review (*Letopis*), which did not increase his importance. Even *Childhood* and its sequel which appeared in 1913 and 1915 changed little in the general attitude, and have come into their own only in the light of Gorky's post-Revolutionary work.

When the Great War broke out, Gorky took up a distinctly internationalist and *défaitiste* position, and in 1917 he gave his support to his old friends the Bolsheviks. But this support was not quite unconditional, and though the balance of Gorky's influence was in favour of Lenin and his policy, he did not this time identify himself with the party, but rather tried to assume the rôle of a non-party umpire and a champion of peace and culture. This attitude of fastidious superiority and sympathetic, but critical, aloofness has lasted ever since. The Bolsheviks were not over-enthusiastic about it, but Gorky's personal relations with their leaders on the one hand, and the great weight of his reputation abroad, gave him a unique position: he was in 1918–1921 practically the only independent public force outside the Government in the whole of Soviet Russia. Gorky's attitude of fastidious superiority and "hand-washing" may not arouse much sympathy, but his activity in those dreadful years was extraordinarily useful and salutary. He played the part he pretended to of defender of culture and civilization as well as he could have done. The debt of Russian culture to him is very great. Everything that was done between 1918 and 1921 to save the writers and other higher intellectuals from starvation was due to Gorky. This was chiefly arrived at by a whole system of centralized literary establishments where poets and novelists were set to work at translations. The contrivance was by no means a perfect one, but under the circumstances it was probably the only one possible. It is also true, however, that these "circumstances" had been brought about with the active help of Gorky, and by his nearest political friends. Though in 1919 Gorky published his *Recollections of Tolstoy* which once more made everyone realize that he was, after all, a great writer, his literary influence remained insignificant. His great place in modern Russian letters is entirely due to his personal part in the salvaging of Russian civilization when it was in danger of going down. Politically Gorky is hardly a force, except in so far as his word carries weight abroad. Two of his recent political utterances have attracted attention: his article (1920) on Lenin, whom he praises to the skies as the great rational constructor of an ideal future, whose only fault is that he is too good for the beastly and sluggard Russian people; and his pamphlet (1922) *On the Russian Peasantry*, where he denounces that class with unusual bitterness as the depository of every vice, as having no part in the building of national civilization, and as unworthy of its present Internationalist masters. In 1922 Gorky left Russia and settled in Germany. His health, which has always been weak, is constantly reported as very dangerous. He continues working, and his new books are steadily consolidating his position as a classic. He also edits a non-periodical miscellany, *Beseda*, which is largely given to the popularizing of recent scientific progress. This line of work has taken a large part in Gorky's activity for these last years, for he sees in the spreading of elementary knowledge the principal need of his country. In his naïve and almost religious cult of science and knowledge, Gorky is the Russian counterpart of Mr. H. G. Wells.

Gorky's literary work, apart from his purely political and journalistic writings, may be divided into three distinct periods: the first includes the short stories written from 1892 to 1899, which formed the foundation of his popularity; the second, which lasts from 1899 to 1912, is taken up by his more ambitious "social" novels and dramas; the third period begins in 1913 and consists mainly of autobiography and memoirs. The first and last are more important than the middle period, during which his creative power suffered a partial eclipse.

In all Gorky's early work his Realism is strongly modified by Romanticism, and it was this Romanticism that made for his success in Russia, although it was his Realism that carried it over the frontier. To the Russian reader the novelty of his early stories consisted in their bracing and dare-devil youthfulness; to the foreign public it was the ruthless crudeness with which he described his nether world. Hence the enormous difference between Russian and foreign appreciations of the early Gorky—it comes from a difference of background. Russians saw him against the gloom and depression of Chekhov and the other novelists of the eighties; foreigners, against a screen of conventional and reticent Realism of Victorian times. His very first stories are purely romantic. Such are his first published story, *Makar Chudra*, *The Old Woman Izergil* (1895), and his early poetry, the most popular of which is the *Song of the Falcon* with its burden:

> "We sing the praise
> Of the brave one's folly."

This Romanticism is very theatrical and tawdry, but it was

genuinely infectious and did more to endear Gorky to the Chekhov-fed Russian reader than all the rest of his work. It crystallized in a philosophy which is expressed most crudely and simply in the very early parable of *The Siskin Who Lied and the Truth-loving Woodpecker*, and which may be formulated as a preference of a lie that elevates the soul to a depressing and ignoble truth.

By 1895 Gorky abandons the conventional stock-in-trade of his early gipsy and robber stories and develops a manner which combines realistic form and romantic inspiration. His first story, published in the "big" press, *Chelkash* (1895), is also one of the best. His subject is the contrast between the gay, cynical, and careless smuggler Chelkash and the lad he employs to help him in his dangerous business, a typical peasant, timid and greedy. The story is well constructed, and though the romantic glamour round Chelkash is anything but "realistic," his figure is drawn with convincing vividness. Other stories of the same kind are *Malva* (1897), who is a female Chelkash, and *My Fellow-Traveller* (1896), which from the point of view of character-drawing is perhaps the best of the lot; that primitive immoralist, the Georgian Prince Sharko, with whom the narrator makes on foot the long journey from Odessa to Tiflis, is a truly wonderful creation, which deserves to stand by the side of the best of his recent character sketches. There is not an ounce of idealization in Sharko, though it is quite obvious that the author's "artistic sympathy" is entirely on his side. One of the features of the early Gorky which won him most admirers was his way of "describing nature." A typical instance of this manner is the beginning of *Malva*, with the famous opening paragraph consisting of the two words, *"More smeyalos"* (The sea was laughing). But it must be confessed that the brightness of these descriptions has greatly faded and fails to-day to take us by storm. About 1897 Realism begins to outweigh Romanticism, and in *Ex-People* (*Byvshii lyudi*, 1897; in the English version, *Creatures That Once Were Men*, an arbitrary mistranslation) Realism is dominant, and the heroic gestures of Captain Kuvalda fail to relieve the drab gloom of the setting. In this story and in all other stories of

these years, a feature appears which was to be the undoing of
Gorky: an immoderate love for "philosophical" conversations.
As long as he kept free from it, he gave proof of a great power
of construction, a power which is rare in Russian writers, and
which gives some of his early stories a solidness and cohesion
almost comparable to Chekhov's. But he had not Chekhov's
sense of artistic economy, and though in such stories as *Her
Lover* (in Russian, *Boles*, 1896) and *To Kill Time* (untrans-
lated) the skeleton is firm and strong, the actual texture of the
story has not that inevitableness which is the hall-mark of
Chekhov. Besides (and in this respect Chekhov was no better),
Gorky's Russia is "neutral," the words are mere signs and have
no individual life. If it were not for certain catchwords, they
might have been a translation from any language. The only
one of Gorky's early stories which makes one forget all his
shortcomings (except the mediocrity of his style) is that which
may be considered as closing the period, *Twenty-six Men and
a Girl* (1899). The scene is an underground bakery where
twenty-six men work in a dreadful airless atmosphere for
sixteen hours a day and for a beggar's wages. A young girl
comes every day to them to take some loaves; her fresh and innocent beauty is the only ray of light in their hopeless life. A
soldier who has some much easier work in the same yard bets
he will seduce her, and wins his bet. When the girl appears
after her fall, she is savagely hooted out by the bakers. The
story is cruelly realistic. But it is traversed by such a powerful current of poetry, by such a convincing faith in beauty and
freedom and in the essential nobility of man, and at the same
time it is told with such precision and necessity, that it can
hardly be refused the name of a masterpiece. It places Gorky,
the young Gorky, among the true classics of our literature.
But *Twenty-six Men and a Girl* is alone in its supreme beauty
—and it is the last of Gorky's early good work: for fourteen years he was to be a wanderer in tedious and fruitless
mazes.

Gorky early attempted to transcend the social limits imposed
on him by his early experience. As early as 1897 he wrote
Varenka Olesova (the English translation bears the title *A*

Naughty Girl), where he tried to paint the educated classes, and which is curiously anticipatory of many stories written a few years later by Artsybashev and others. We know from his memoirs that Gorky disliked being merely a writer risen from the people and wanted to become a leader and a teacher. This ambition found expression in the series of novels and plays written by him between 1899 and 1912. They are the least valuable part of his work. Two features are common to the whole series: an entire disappearance of that constructive skill which was so promising in his early work, and an immoderate prolixity in conversations on "the meaning of life" and similar subjects. Gorky never wrote either a good drama or a good novel, and in so far as his works of this period have any merit, they possess it in spite of being dramas or novels. The principal novels of this period are *Foma Gordeev* (1899), *Three of Them* (*Troye*) (1900–1901), *The Mother* (1907), *A Confession* (1908), *Okurov City* (1910), and *Matvey Kozhemyakin* (1911). All of them purport to be vast synthetic pictures of Russian provincial life shown in all its meaningless barbarity, filth, and darkness, relieved only by the efforts of isolated individuals to grasp "the meaning of life," to escape the slough of provincial stagnation, and to show the ignorant and oppressed masses the way. The first two novels are less tendentious and less distinct in their social message. The post-Revolutionary series is more definitely connected with the ideas of the Bolsheviks, though these ideas are reflected in a strangely mystical interpretation. By far the best of the whole series is the first—*Foma Gordeev*. Though like the rest it is disfigured by lack of architecture and by immoderate talking, it has many merits of the first order. The first chapters, containing the story of Ignat Gordeev, Foma's father, the maker of a great fortune, are among the best Gorky ever wrote. Its constructive and masculine spirit gives it a flavour rare in Russian literature. The story of Foma, the son, the "superfluous" man who does not know what to do with his life and wealth, contains pages of excellent, vivid painting, but as a whole it belongs to the ineffective "conversational" style. Gorky's novels almost invariably begin very well, and the first few pages of *Three of Them* and *A Confession* keep the reader spellbound by the straightforward and direct development of the narrative. But then begins that interminable and tiresome "quest" which becomes even more tiresome as it approaches its goal and the hero thinks he finds the social panacea. Of the later novels, *Okurov City* and *A Confession* are better than the others, first of all because they are shorter (about 60,000 words each, *Matvey Kozhemyakin* having over 200,000!). Besides, *Okurov City* contains comparatively little of the "quest for truth" element, and more in the way of vivid action and incident. As for *A Confession*, it is certainly a remarkable work, for in it Gorky gives the most quintessential expression to that strange religion of the people which he professed about 1908 and which is so unlike the real Gorky, the Gorky both of the early and of the later works. This "religion" became known as *bogostroitelstvo* (the building of God), as opposed to *bogoiskatelstvo* (the quest after God). God, according to Gorky, was to be "built" by the people's faith. One of the closing scenes of *A Confession* gives a very realistic, though hardly convincing, illustration of how the thing might be done —a sick person is healed by a miracle, which is wrought apparently by a miraculous image but in reality by the fervent and realistic faith of the assembled crowd. Apart from its religion, *A Confession* is, as far as about the middle, a good story of the adventures of the tramp after truth, with a rapid development of narrative on which there lies a pale and distant (very distant, but unmistakable) reflex of Leskov's narrative masterpiece, *The Enchanted Wanderer*. Gorky's plays are numerous, but most of them are unknown, even by name, to the professional reader. All those written after 1905 fell quite flat and had no kind of success. On the other hand, as I have already said, *The Lower Depths* (1902) was one of the greatest successes of the literary drama for the last thirty or forty years. This does not mean that it is intrinsically much better than the rest: its success was entirely due to irrelevant and unliterary causes, and there is no ground to single it out from the rest for solitary praise. As a dramatist Gorky (in spite of Chekhov's censure of his first play for its "conservatism of form") is nothing but a bad disciple of Chekhov (the word "bad," however, is superfluous, for it is impossible to be a good disciple of that dramatist). His dramatic system is exactly the same, with the same inevitable four acts undivided into scenes; the same absence of all apparent action; the same standardized suicide in the last act. The only thing Gorky did not notice in Chekhov's dramatic art was the only thing that justifies it: its hidden dynamic structure. The only thing he added to it (or rather gave more room to, for Chekhov did not quite abstain from it) were "conversations on the meaning of life," which would be capable of killing even the greatest drama of Shakespeare and the tensest tragedy of Racine. However it may be, Gorky's first two plays met with success. In the case of *Meshchane* (*The Petty Bourgeois*, 1901), this was largely a *succès d'estime*. But his second play, *Na Dne* (*The Lower Depths*) (1902), was a triumph. This was due at home to the wonderful acting of the Stanislavsky cast. Abroad it must be explained by the extreme novelty of this sort of thing: the sensational realism of the setting and the novel pleasure of listening to the profound conversations of philosophical thieves, tramps, and prostitutes—"so Russian!" *The Lower Depths* contributed more than anything else to the silly idea the average European and American "intelligent" has formed for himself of Russia as a country of talkative philosophers occupied with finding their way to what they call "God." Gorky's next two plays—*Suburbans* (1904) and *The Children of the Sun* (1905)—failed to bear out the promise of *The Lower Depths*: they lacked the sensational setting of that play, and proved signal failures. As for those that followed—*The Barbarians* (1906), *Enemies* (1907), *Vassa Zheleznova* (1911), etc.—they remained quite unnoticed.

Concurrently with his plays and novels, Gorky wrote a great many minor works—poems like *The Song of the Petrel* (1901) and the one-time famous *Man* (1903); political satires, for which he had no talent, lacking as he did both the necessary gifts: humour and moral earnestness; journalistic sketches (including the American series, *The City of the Yellow Devil* and *One of the Kings of the Republic*); etc. Towards the end of this period he began publishing short sketches founded on his early recollections (*The Notes of a Passer-by*, (1912), which introduce us to his last, autobiographical period.

The works of this period have, up to the present, formed the contents of five volumes: the three volumes of the autobiographical series, *Childhood* (1913), *Among Strangers* (1915), and *My Universities* (1923); a volume of *Recollections* (of Tolstoy, Korolenko, Chekhov, Andreev, etc.); and *Notes from a Diary* (1924). In these works Gorky has abandoned the form of fiction and all (apparent) literary invention; he has also hidden himself and given up taking any part in his characters' "quest for truth." He is a realist, a great realist finally freed from all the scales of romance, tendency, or dogma. He has finally become an objective writer. This makes his autobiographical series one of the strangest autobiographies ever written. It is about everyone except himself. His person is only the pretext round which to gather a wonderful gallery of portraits. Gorky's most salient feature in these books is his wonderful visual convincingness. The man seems to be all eyes, and the reader sees, as if they were painted, the wonderfully live and vivid figures of the characters. We can never forget such figures as those of the old Kashirins, his grandfather and grandmother; or of the good Bishop Chrysanthus; or of that strange heathen and barbaric orgy of the inhabitants of the little station (*My Universities*). The series invariably produces an impression of hopeless gloom and pessimism on the foreign, and even on the older Russian, reader, but we who have been trained to a less conventional and reticent realism than George Eliot's, fail to share that feeling. Gorky is not a pessimist, and if he is, his pessimism has nothing to do with his representation of Russian life, but rather with the chaotic state of his philosophical views, which he has never succeeded in making serve his optimism, in spite of all his efforts in that direction. As it is, Gorky's autobiographical series represents the world as ugly but not unrelieved—the redeeming points, which may and must save humanity, are enlightenment, beauty, and sympathy. The other two books reveal Gorky

as an even greater writer than does this autobiography.   The
English-speaking public has appreciated the wonderful *Recollections of Tolstoy* (which appeared in the *London Mercury*
soon after their first publication), and in speaking of Tolstoy
I have mentioned them as the most worthwhile pages ever
written about that great man.   And this in spite of the fact
Gorky is most certainly nothing like Tolstoy's intellectual
equal.   It is his eyes that see through, rather than his mind
than understands.   The wonderful thing is that he saw and
noted down things other people were incapable of seeing, or,
if they saw, powerless to record.   Gorky's image of Tolstoy
is rather destructive than constructive: it sacrifices the unity
of legend to the complexity of life.   It deals a death-blow to
the hagiographical image of "St. Leo."   Equally remarkable
are his *Recollections of Andreev*, which contain one of his best
chapters—the one which describes the heavy and joyless drunkenness of the younger writer.   *Notes from a Diary* is a book
of characters.   Nowhere more than here does Gorky reveal
his artist's love for his country, which is after all to him the
best country in the world in spite of all his Internationalism,
of all his scientific dreams, and of all the dirty things he
has seen in her.   "Russia is a wonderful country, where even
fools are original," is the burden of the book.   It is a collection
of portraits, striking characters, and of glimpses of strange
minds.   Originality is the keynote.   Some of the characters
are those of very eminent men: two fragments are devoted to
Alexander Blok.   Memorable Portraits are drawn of the well-
known Old-Believer millionaire Bugrov, who himself used to
cultivate Gorky as an original; and of Anna Schmidt, the
mystical correspondent of Vladimir Soloviev.   Other interesting chapters are those on the morbid attraction exercised on
human beings by fires; and the uncanny things people sometimes do when they are alone and don't expect to be overlooked.
With the exception of *Recollections of Tolstoy*, this last book
is perhaps the best Gorky ever wrote.   Other stories have
appeared in periodicals signed by him which partly continue
the manner of *Notes from a Diary*, partly seem to indicate
a return to more conventional and constructed forms of fic-

tion. This seems dangerous, but Gorky has so often deceived us by his developments that this time our misgivings may again be deceived.

Gorky's last books have met with universal and immediate appreciation. And yet he has not become a living literary influence. His books are read as freshly discovered classics, not as novelties. In spite of his great personal part in the literature of to-day (innumerable young writers look up to him as their sponsor in the literary world), his work is profoundly unlike all the work of the younger generation; first of all, for his complete lack of interest in style, and, secondly, for his very unmodern interest in human psychology. The retrospective character of all his recent work seems to emphasize the impression that it belongs to a world that is no more ours.

3. THE ZNANIE SCHOOL OF FICTION

Soon after his first great success, Gorky founded a publishing-business which received the name—characteristic of its founder—of *Znanie* (knowledge). It became the rallying-ground for all the young school of prose-writers, and for a few years it almost monopolized Russian imaginative prose.* All the most prominent young novelists joined Gorky's group and had their works published by *Znanie*. Three of them grew to be original and significant writers—Kuprin, Bunin, and Andreev. The majority remained minor figures and may be conveniently grouped as the school of Gorky—or the *Znanie* school of novelists. The common characteristic of the school is its open and emphatic tendentiousness—they are the revolutionary school of fiction. Though kept in check by the censorship, they were more outspoken than the old Radical writers, especially in and after 1905. They were also more outspoken in their realism, richly availing themselves of that emancipation from conventions which had been inaugurated by Tolstoy and confirmed by Gorky. The influence of Chek-

* Chekhov's *Cherry Orchard* was originally published in one of the *Znanie* miscellanies.

hov and Gorky is usually apparent, but Chekhov's is seldom
more than superficial, and on the whole the writings of the
school are seldom much more than glorified journalism.

There is no need to give more than a short enumeration of
these writers. Their doyen was Evgeni Nikolaevich Chìrikov
(b. 1864), a mild and moderate representative of the school.
V. Veresayev (pseud. of Vikenti Vikentievich Smidowicz,
b.1867), a doctor by profession, who produced a sensation in
1901 by a book of "revelations," *The Note-book of a Doctor*,
but most of his stories and novels are devoted to the description
of the various moods and developments of the Marxist *intelli-*
gentsia. A. Serafimòvich (pseud. of Alexander Sergeevich
Popòv, b. 1863) is also a "political" writer. He is now a
Communist, and his last novel, *The Iron Stream* (1924), has
received high praise from official Bolshevik writers as the most
strictly Marxist work of fiction written since the Revolution.
Sergey Ivanovich Gùsev-Orenbùrgski (b. 1867) is an unpretentious social realist describing the rural conditions of his
native Orenburg province. His old novel, *The Land of the*
Fathers (1904), has been recently translated into English.
A typical disciple of Gorky is Skitàlets (pseud. of Stepan
Gavrilovich Petròv, b. 1868), whom Chekhov mentions in one
of his letters, saying that he prefers him as a live sparrow to
"the artificial nightingale" Andreev. Skitàlets's stories are
very simple and crudely naïve; they describe the revolutionary
idealism and thirst for enlightenment of the class of men
discovered by Gorky. A somewhat more interesting figure
is Semen Solomonovich Yushkévich (b. 1868), a Jew, who concentrated on the life and manners of his people. His best-
known novel, *The Jews*, describes the life of the Jewish proletariate and introduces a pogrom. *The Adventures of Leon*
Drey is the picaresque history of a light-hearted and cynical
Jewish rogue. He also wrote plays in which he succumbed to
the influence of Hauptmann and the German *Moderne*. Of
these, *Miserere* was produced by Stanislavsky and had a certain success. The younger writers who came into literature
after 1902–1903 were less obsessed by Revolution, and their
work bears the impress of other influences. Only one of them,

Viktor Vasilievich Muyzhel (b. 1880), a clumsy, gloomy, and scarcely readable naturalist, can be counted with the *Znanie* school. He chose peasants' life for his subject. and tried to see how far he could go by the systematic application of black paint. This excessive blackness of colour related him to the pessimist school of Andreev, though his primary preoccupation is with social rather than with metaphysical wrongs.

4. KUPRIN

Alexander Ivanovich Kùprin * also began as a writer of the *Znanie* school, but his literary personality is sufficiently original for him to be treated separately. Born in 1870, he was educated in Moscow in a cadet school and was for several years an officer in the army. Army life is the principal subject of his early stories. He treats it in the orthodox "oppositional" manner, representing the wretched soldier, oppressed by stupid and mechanical sergeant-majors and brutal officers. The central figure is always a young officer who is himself oppressed by the gloomy reality round him and broods on the meaning of his life and life in general.

These stories culminated in a novel, *The Duel*, which appeared in 1905, immediately after the great disasters of Mukden and Tsushima, when all Radical Russia was united in exulting over the defeats of the Imperial Army. *The Duel* had an enormous success and was freely quoted in attacks against the army. For all that, *The Duel* is not really a revolutionary work. Its point of view is rather that of the typical "Chekhovian intelligent." The hero, Second-Lieutenant Romashov, is a very sensitive young man (and a very bad officer), who is constantly wounded by the coarse reality of life. *The Duel* is very "passive" and "morbid," but within its limitations it is a good novel. The character-drawing is excellent and the gallery of types of infantry officers is convincing and varied. The heroine, Shurochka, the wife of a

---

* The pronunciation *Kuprìn* is incorrect.

lieutenant, is one of the best feminine portraits in recent Russian fiction.

The Duel made Kuprin famous and he became a prominent and much discussed figure of literary Petersburg, largely in connexion with his visits to the favourite haunt of the old (pre-poetical) literary Bohemia—the Vienna Restaurant. Between 1905 and the beginning of the War, Kuprin wrote much, but he failed to create an unforgettable and inevitable expression of himself. He was torn between various tendencies. Being essentially a man of no culture, he could not really profit from any literary example; and, possessing very little of artistic tact, he could not distinguish between what was good in his writings from what was bad. He emulated Tolstoy in trying to describe the psychology of animals (a racehorse in *Izumrud*); he fell into incredible bad taste in a would-be Flaubert-like evocation of Solomon's Jerusalem (*Sulamith*), and gained doubtful popularity (in Russia, and again in France when it was translated in 1923) by a journalistically realistic, crude, and sentimental novel from the life of prostitutes (*Yama*) which appeared shortly before the Great War.

Kuprin had in him a valuable germ which remained almost undeveloped: he was attracted towards the "Western" type of story, which unlike the Russian story is a story of action and strong situations, which loves intrigue, and does not shun sensationalism. He was attracted by Kipling and Jack London (in whose praise he wrote with great eloquence), and by that somewhat conventional idea Russians have of England as a land of pipe-smoking, strong and silent, drunken, rowdy, and sentimental sailors. He never succeeded in casting aside his *intelligentsia*-ism and in setting out to write *à la* Jack London. But two or three times he attained something that was not attained by any one of his contemporaries in Russian literature: he wrote several good stories of vigorous and sensational situation with a romantic and heroical keynote. One of the best is *Lieutenant-Captain Rybnikov* (1906), the story of a Japanese spy in Petersburg who with wonderful skill succeeds in aping the appearance and mentality of an average Russian infantry officer, and then betrays himself by crying *Banzai* when asleep in the arms of a harlot (this detail is the hall-mark of the "Gorky" school).   Another good story (and this time free from "Gorkyisms") is *The Bracelet of Garnets* (1911), the romantic and melodramatic story of the love of a poor clerk for a society lady.   For sheer narrative construc-tion it is one of the best stories of its time.

Since *Yama* Kuprin has written little, and nothing of any importance.   He is a decided anti-Bolshevik. and emigrated after the fall of the White Army.   He is now a resident in France.

5. BUNIN

In the opinion of some competent judges, one of whom is Gorky, the greatest of living Russian writers is Ivan Alexeyevich Bùnin.   He is rather difficult to pigeonhole.   For many years he was a faithful member of the *Znanie* group, but intrin-sically he has little in common with that school of revolutionary fiction.   The subjects of some of his most important master-pieces are distinctly social, but his way of approaching these subjects has nothing to do with the distinction of "right" and "left."   He is obviously a greater *artist* than either Gorky or Andreev, or any other writer of his generation outside the Symbolist school.   His literary ancestors are pretty clear—they are Chekhov, Tolstoy, Turgenev, and Goncharov.   His obvious relationship with the two last gives him that "clas-sical" appearance which distinguishes him from his contempo-raries.   To emphasize this difference, Bunin comes of a class which has long lost its leadership in Russian culture and which he was at one time alone to represent in literature.   He was born in 1870, in Voronezh, of an ancient family of country gentry.   The great poet Zhukovsky (1783–1852), the natu-ral son of a squire of the name of Bunin, belonged to the same family.   Bunin grew up in his country home and in the district town of Yelets—and Yelets and its neighbourhod are the almost invariable setting of his most characteristic stories.   From the gymnasium of Yelets he went to the Univer-sity of Moscow, and, while still a student, began publishing

verse in the literary press. His first book of verse appeared
in 1891, in the capital of his native province, Orel. Gradually the antimodernist party began to regard him as the
most promising of young poets. In 1903 the Academy assigned to him the Pushkin prize for literature and in 1909
elected him its honorary member. In the late nineties he joined
the Gorky group and for more than ten years all his works
were published by the *Znanie* publishing-house, but he never
identified himself with the political extremists. His stories
had begun to appear as early as 1892, but he was thought
of as primarily a poet, all the more as his early "stories" are
essentially "lyrical." In 1910 appeared his "novel" (the
Russian sub-title is *poema*, which means "a big poem," "an
epic") *The Village*, which placed him in the very front row of
Russian novelists. *The Village* was followed by the four books
which contain most of his masterpieces: *Sukhodol* (1912),
Ioann the Weeper (1913), *The Cup of Life* (1914), and *The
Gentleman from San Francisco* (1916). In the years preceding
the War, Bunin travelled much in Mediterranean and tropical
countries. Many of his works are dated from Capri; Algeria,
Palestine, the Red Sea, and Ceylon are the frequent background
of his stories and poems. In 1917 Bunin took a very definite
anti-Bolshevik position. In 1918 he left Soviet Russia and after
many wanderings and hardships won Odessa and thence Paris,
where he has lived since 1919, passing most of his summers at
Grasse. He is, together with the Merezhkovskys, one of the
most intransigent of the anti-Bolsheviks. His literary output,
which almost ceased in 1917–1920, has increased since 1921,
but on the whole the stories contained in his last book (*The
Rose of Jericho*, 1924) do not mark any progress, and seldom
attain the level of his earlier work.

In the early years of his literary career Bunin did much
translation from English, and we owe to him complete Russian
versions of the *Song of Hiawatha* and of the mystery plays
of Byron.

As a poet Bunin belongs to the old, pre-Symbolist school.
His technique has remained that of the eighties, but it attains
a higher level, and his verse is less "empty" than Nadson's or

Minsky's. His poetry is mainly objective, and impressions of Nature, Russian and exotic, are its principal subject. Though by no means so important a poet as he is a novelist, he is a genuine poet, the only significant poet of the Symbolist age who was not a Symbolist. His verse up to 1907 is contained in three separate volumes of which the second, 1903–1906, probably contains his best poems, including the powerful and haunting *Sapsan*, a poem of wild Bashkiria, and memorable evocations of the Mohammedan East. After 1907 he discontinued the practice of publishing his verse separately and composed most of his books of prose and verse.

Much of Bunin's prose is more "poetical" and more subjective than his verse. Purely lyrical compositions in prose are to be found in every one of his books, and in his latest (*The Rose of Jericho*) they are again the most prominent feature. This lyrical style was the first aspect of his prose that attracted general attention to his individuality. In his first volumes (1892–1902) they were certainly the most interesting item; the rest consisted of realistically sentimental stories of the conventional type, or of attempts to emulate Chekhov in the representation of the disintegrating "pinpricks" of life (*The Schoolmaster* *). The lyrical stories went back to the tradition of Chekhov (*The Steppe*), of Turgenev (*Forest and Steppe*), and of Goncharov (*Oblomov's Dream*), but Bunin accentuated still further the lyrical element, eliminated all narrative skeleton, and at the same time studiously avoided (except in certain attempts tainted with "modernism") the diction of lyrical prose. His lyrical effects were produced by the poetry of *things*, not of rhythms or words. The most notable of these lyrical poems in prose is *Antonov Apples* (1900), where the smell of a special kind of apples leads him from association to association to reconstruct a poetical picture of the dying life of his class, the middle gentry of Central Russia. The tradition of Goncharov, with his epical manner of painting stagnant life, is especially alive in the lyrical "stories" of Bunin (one of them even bears the title *A Dream of Oblomov's Grandson*). In later years the same

* In the earlier editions, *Tarantella*.

lyrical manner was transferred to other subjects than dying Central Russia, and, for instance, his impressions of Palestine (1908) were written in the same restrained, subdued, and lyrical "minor key."

The Village, which appeared in 1910, presented Bunin under a new aspect. It is one of the sternest, darkest, and bitterest books in Russian literature. It is a "social" novel, and its subject is the poverty, darkness, and barbarity of Russian life. There is almost no development in time, it is almost static like a picture, but, for all that, the construction is masterly and the gradual filling up of the canvas in a deliberately planned succession of strokes produces an impression of inevitable and conscious power. In the centre of the "poem" stand the two brothers Krasov, Tikhon and Kuzma. Tikhon is a successful shopkeeper, Kuzma is unsuccessful in business and a "seeker after truth." The first part is written from Tikhon's, the second from Kuzma's standpoint. Both are ultimately "undone," coming to the conclusion that all their life has been a failure. The background is the Central Russian village—poor, savage, stupid, brutal, lacking in every moral foundation. Gorky in his indictment of the Russian peasant speaks of Bunin as of the only writer who dared say the truth about the *moujik* without idealizing him.

The Village, in spite of its great powerfulness, is hardly a perfect work of art: it is too long and loose and contains too much definitively "publicistic" matter; like Gorky's, the personages of *The Village* talk and meditate at excessive length. But in his next work Bunin overcame this defect. This next work, *Sukhodol*, is one of the greatest masterpieces of modern Russian prose, and more than anything else bears the impress of Bunin's original genius. As in *The Village*, Bunin carries to the utmost the unnarrative ("imperfective," as Miss Harrison has called it) tendency of the Russian novel, and constructs his story athwart all temporal order. It is a perfect work of art, quite *sui generis*, and of which no European literature has a counterpart. It is the story of the "fall of the house" of Khrushchev, of the gradual undoing of a family of squires, told from the point of view of a female servant. Short (it contains only about 25,000 words) and concentrated, and at the same time elastic and ample, it has all the "density" and tightness of poetry, though it never for a moment abandons the calm and level diction of realistic prose. *Sukhodol* is, as it were, a counterpart to *The Village*, and in both "poems" the theme is the cultural poverty, "rootlessness," emptiness, and savagery of Russian life. The same theme is repeated in a series of stories written between 1908 and 1914, many of which stand on the same high level, though hardly any one reaches the absolute perfection of *Sukhodol*. In *The Devil's a Beggar* (1908), *A Night Conversation* (1911), and *A Spring Evening* (1913), the subject is the fundamental callousness of the peasant and his indifference to all but gain. In *The Cup of Life* (1913), it is the joyless and hopeless life of a country town. *A Goodly Life* (1912) is the story told by herself of a heartless (and naïvely self-righteous in her heartlessness) woman of peasant origin who succeeds in life, after being the cause of the death of the rich young man who loved her, and of the ruin of her son. The story is remarkable, among other things, for its language—it is an exact reproduction of the dialect of a petty townswoman of Yelets, with all the phonetic and grammatical peculiarities carefully reproduced. It is remarkable that even in reproducing dialect Bunin succeeds in remaining "classical," in keeping the words subordinate to the whole. This manner is the opposite of Leskov's who is always playing with his language and whose words always protrude to the point of beggaring the story. It is interesting to compare the two writers in the examples of *A Goodly Life* and Leskov's sketch of a somewhat similar character, *The Amazon*. It is like the difference of the same Jesuit style in the hands of a Frenchman and in those of a Mexican. *A Goodly Life* is Bunin's only story told in dialect from beginning to end, but the speech of the Yelets peasants, reproduced with equal precision and equally "unprotruding," reappears in the dialogue of all his rural stories (especially in *A Night Conversation*). Apart from his use of dialect, Bunin's language is "classical," sober, concrete. Its only expressive means is the exact notation of things; it is objective because its effect depends entirely on the "objects" spoken of. Bunin is probably the only modern Russian writer whose language would have been admired by the "classics," by Turgenev and Goncharov.

It is almost an inevitable consequence of this "dependence on object" that when Bunin leaves the familiar and domestic realities of the Yelets district and sets his stories in Ceylon or in Palestine, or even in Odessa, his style loses much of its vigour and aptness. In his exotic stories he is often inadequate, and especially when he is poetical the beauty of his poetry is apt to become mere tinsel. To keep free from this inadequateness when dealing with a foreign (or even with a Russian urban) subject, Bunin must mercilessly keep down his lyrical proclivities. He must be bald and terse at the hazard of becoming cheap. He has achieved this baldness and terseness in a few stories, one of which is by most of his (especially foreign) readers considered his indubitable masterpiece—*The Gentleman from San Francisco* (1915).

This remarkable story is sufficiently well known in English translations to need recalling. It belongs to the progeny of *Ivan Ilyich,* and its "message" is quite in keeping with the teaching of Tolstoy: the vanity of civilization and the presence of death, the only reality. But no direct influence of Tolstoy can be traced in Bunin's story, as it can in the best of Andreev's. It is not a work of analysis, for Bunin is no analyst and no psychologist. It is a "thing of beauty," a solid "object," it has the consistency and hardness of a steel bar. It is a masterpiece of artistic economy and austere, "Doric" expression. Like the two rural "poems" *The Village* and *Sukhodol, The Gentleman from San Francisco* has also its accompanying constellation of foreign and urban stories told in bald outline and with austere matter-of-factness. Among the best are *Kazimir Stanislavovich* (1915) and *Thieves' Ears* (1916), a powerful study of criminal perversity.

Of the more lyrical exotic and urban stories, the most notable are *The Dreams of Chang* (1916) and *Brothers* (1914). In both of them, Bunin's lyrical poetry, torn away from its native soil, loses much of its vitality, and is often unconvincing and conventional. His language also loses its colour and becomes "international." Still, *Brothers* is a powerful work. It is the story of a Singhalese * jinricksha man of Colombo and of his English fare. It avoids the pitfall of sentimentality in a masterly way.

Of Bunin's post-Revolutionary stories, the best is *Passing Away* (*Iskhod*, 1918), which for the density and richness of its texture and the pervasiveness of its atmosphere almost approaches *Sukhodol*. Since 1918 Bunin has not written anything on the same level. Some of his shortest stories (*Gautami, In a Far-off Kingdom*) are admirably concentrated pieces of "objective" lyricism. But most of what he writes is more flaccid and less solid. The lyrical element seems to be growing, and bursting the bonds of that strong restraint which alone makes it powerful.

6. LEONID ANDREEV (1871–1919)

When Gorky's popularity began to diminish, the first place in the public favour passed to Leonid Andreev. This process began before the Revolution of 1905. Soon after that date the revolutionary school of fiction was finally superseded by a new school which may be called the Metaphysical, or the Pessimistic school, for they wrote stories and plays on metaphysical problems, and the solutions they gave to these problems were invariably pessimistic and nihilistic. These writers were in the height of their fame in the years immediately following the defeat of the First Revolution (1907–1911), and the sociological historians of Russian literature have always tried to explain the whole movement by political disillusionment. In the success of the movement with the public, the political motive was certainly important, but the movement itself began earlier, and much of Andreev's best and most characteristic work was written before 1905.

Old-fashioned critics and readers of the older generation of the orthodox Radical (and, still more, of the Conservative) school were scarcely able to distinguish between Andreev and

---

* The English translation makes him a Senegalese!

the Symbolists. Both were to them equally detestable mal-
formations. In reality there is very little in common between
the two, beyond the common tendency away from accepted
standards, and a decided inclination towards the grandiose and
the ultimate. Both the Symbolists and Andreev are always
somewhat stiltedly serious and solemn, and distinctly lack a
sense of humour. But the differences are far more important.
The Symbolists are united by a high degree of conscientious
craftsmanship; Andreev dealt in ready-made clichés and was
simply no craftsman. Secondly, the Symbolists were men of
superior culture and played a principal part in the great cultural renaissance of the Russian *intelligentsia;* Andreev, on the
contrary, lacked culture as much as he despised it. At last,
and this is the most important point, the Symbolists stood on
a foundation of a realistic (in the mediæval sense of the word)
metaphysics, and even if they were pessimists of life they were
optimists of death—that is to say, mystics. Blok alone of
them knew that absolute emptiness which brings him near
Andreev; but Blok's emptiness comes from a sense of *exclusion*
from a superior and real Presence, not from a consciousness of
Universal Void. Andreev (and Artsybashev) proceeded from
a scientific agnosticism and were strangers to all mystical
optimism—theirs was an all-round and absolute pessimism, a
pessimism of death as well as of life. It may be said, in short
(with a degree of simplification), that while the Symbolists
proceed from Dostoevsky, Andreev proceeds from Tolstoy.
The negation of culture and the intense consciousness of the
elemental realities of life—death and sex—are the essence of
Tolstoyism, and reappear in the philosophy of Andreev and of
Artsybashev. As for the purely literary influence of Tolstoy
over these two writers, it can hardly be exaggerated.

Leonid Nikolaevich Andréev was born in Orel in 1871. His
family belonged to the small provincial *intelligentsia.* The
father died early and the Andreevs lived in poverty, but Leonid
received the usual middle-class education at the Gymnasium of
Orel, and in due time (1891) went to the University of Petersburg. At the end of his first term he attempted suicide for
disappointed love, went home, and spent the next few years in

idleness.   Like practically all Russian *intelligentsia* young men
who were not absorbed by revolutionary ideas, Andreev had
no genuine interest in life.   His life was only an effort some-
how to fill up the void of his soul.   This usually led to drunkenness, for they needed some sort of intoxication to keep them
running.   So it was in the case of Andreev.   He was by no
means gloomy or solitary; he had many friends and was rather
gay and sociable than otherwise.   But his gaiety was artificial
and fictitious, and at the bottom of it was a vague, undirected
restlessness.   A characteristic episode of Andreev's youth was
how he lay down on the railway between the rails under a train,
which passed over him without injuring him.   He liked to play
with terror and in later life Edgar Allan Poe's tales were his
favourite reading.   In 1893 Andreev went again to the university, this time in Moscow, and in due time took his degree in
law and was admitted to the bar (1897).   But before that he
had already begun his literary career.   His first printed works
were reports from the law courts and short stories printed in
the Orel papers.   His legal practice did not last long, for he
was soon received into the literary press, and in 1898 his
stories began to attract the attention of critics and fellow-
writers.   One of the first men to encourage him was Gorky.
The two contracted a friendship which lasted till after 1905.
By 1900 the distinctly Andreev note appears, and in 1901 he
published *Once Upon a Time There Lived* . . . (*Zhili-byli*),
which remains one of his best stories.   It was just that he
should be greeted as the rising hope of the New Realism and
the worthy younger brother of Gorky.   When his stories appeared in book form their success was very great.   These were
the happiest years of Andreev's life.   He had just been happily
married; he was surrounded by admiring friends, largely young
novelists who looked up to him as to a *maître;* his fame was
growing; he was gaining money.   And it was at the height of
this happiness that he finally found the note of hopeless despair
which is peculiarly his.

In 1902 appeared two stories, *The Abyss* and *In the Fog*, in
which sexual subjects were treated with more than ordinary
realism and audacity.   In spite of the obvious earnestness, al-

most moralism, of the two stories, they were received with an angry uproar in the Conservative and old-fashioned Radical press, and the Countess S. A. Tolstoy wrote an indignant letter to the papers, protesting against such dirt in literature.   She must have recognized in *In the Fog* traces of her husband's influence.   Since then Andreev became the most debated author in Russia, and a large section of the press treated him with more than usual lack of courtesy.   But his success with the public only grew, and from 1902 to at least 1908 every new story by him was a literary event and brought him new fame and new money.   He became rich.   In 1906 he lost his first wife, and though he married again, he never regained his early happiness, and gloom and emptiness became dominant forces in his life as well as in his work.   He lived in Kuokkala in Finland, where he had built a pretentious house in "modern style."   His dress was as pretentious as his house.   He required constant intoxication to keep going.   He never ceased drinking, but the principal form this need for stimulants took was a constant succession of fads to which he gave himself away for short periods of time with pathetic whole-heartedness: now he was a sailor, now a painter; everything he did he did in grand style; he was as fond of bigness in life as he was in literature.   His way of working was in bearing with all his style; he worked by fits and starts, dictating for whole nights at a time and finishing his stories and plays in extraordinarily short spaces.   Then for months he would remain idle.   When he dictated, the words poured out of his mouth in an uninterrupted flow of monotonous rhythmical prose with such speed that his typist had all the trouble in the world to keep pace with him.

After 1908 Andreev's popularity began to wane.   He had now against him not only the old generation, but also a more dangerous enemy in the form of the young literary schools whose influence was rapidly growing, who never regarded him as anything but a literary bubble.   His talent also declined.   After *The Seven That Were Hanged* (1908), he wrote nothing that can be compared with his best work.   By 1914 he was little more than the ghost of his literary self.

The Great War woke him to new life. It was a new stimulant. He plunged head over heels into patriotism and anti-Germanism. He began writing frankly propaganda books, and in 1916 accepted the editorship of a newly founded large pro-War daily. In 1917 he naturally took up a decidedly anti-Bolshevik attitude, and during the civil war, the sounds of which he could hear from his villa at Kuokkala, he contributed freely to anti-Bolshevik propaganda. His last work was a passionate appeal to the Allies to save Russia from Bolshevik tyranny, entitled *S O S*. He died in September, 1919, to the sounds of the Red guns of Petrograd holding back the last offensive of the White Army.

The personality of Leonid Andreev has already become the theme of numerous memoirs. The most interesting are those by Gorky and by Chukovsky.

Andreev began as a naïve and unpretending, rather sentimental realist in the old "philanthropic" tradition in the manner of Korolenko, rather than of Gorky, and it was by stories of this kind that he first attracted attention (*Bergamot* and *Garaska, The Little Angel*). But before long he developed a style of his own—or, to be more precise, two styles, neither of which was quite his own. One of these two styles, and by far the better, was learned from Tolstoy's problem stories, *The Death of Ivan Ilyich* and *The Kreutzer Sonata.* The other is a "modernist" concoction of reminiscences from Poe, Maeterlinck, German, Polish, and Scandinavian modernists. The first of these two manners is sober and discreet; the second is shrill, rhetorical, and, to our present taste, ineffective and unpalatable. But it was a novelty in Russian literature, and as Andreev's subjects were intelligible and interesting to the general reader, it had its moment of tremendous success. These two styles may almost seem to belong to two different writers, but the "message" conveyed by the one and the other is the same. It is a message of thorough nihilism and negation— human life, society, morals, culture are all lies—the only reality is death and annihilation, and the only feelings that express human understanding of the truth are "madness and horror"— the opening words of *The Red Laugh*. Whether this is expressed with rhetorical emphasis or with soberly concentrated force, the substance is the same. It is the necessary outcome of all the history of the *intelligentsia:* the moment the "intelligent" ceased to be inspired by revolutionary faith, the universe became to him a meaningless and terrible void.

If Andreev had left unwritten the greater part of his works, and we knew only his three best stories, we should think more highly of him as a writer, and his place as a classic would be less in jeopardy. The three stories I allude to are *Once upon a Time There Lived* . . . (1901), *In the Fog* (1902), and *The Governor* (1906). They are all in the "Tolstoyan" manner. The first and the last proceed from *The Death of Ivan Ilyich*, the second from *The Kreutzer Sonata*. The manner of Tolstoy is assimilated thoroughly and at the same time creatively. *Once upon a Time* is the story of a provincial merchant dying in a university clinic; *The Governor*, written during the revolutionary excitement, describes the governor of a province who, after ordering the troops to fire at a meeting of workingpeople, receives the intimation that he will be assassinated by the revolutionaries. His expectation of death is the subject of the story. In both stories the growth of death in the consciousness of the man to die is traced with a strong and steady hand. It is all the more effective because the author never raises the tone of his voice and carefully avoids emphasis. *The Governor* ends on a note of disinterested submission to the inevitable, which is very distant from the religious rebirth in *The Death of Ivan Ilyich*. *In the Fog* is the powerful and cruel story of a young boy who discovers the results of his early-begun sexual relations, and ends by the murder of a prostitute and suicide. The story, though denounced on its appearance as pornography, is really quite as moral and "cautionary" as Tolstoy's *Sonata*. It is full of genuine tragedy, and the conversation between the boy and the father who lectures him on the danger of early sexual relations without knowing of his son's illness is a fine piece of dramatic irony. Andreev, though incapable of genuine humour, had an unmistakable gift of irony. A fair example of this irony may be seen in his sketch *Christians*, where a prostitute refuses to take the oath in a law court on the ground that she cannot consider herself a Christian. The dialogue, which verges on the grotesquely impossible, ridicules the judges and officers of law in the true Tolstoyan spirit.

But long before *The Governor* was written, Andreev had already committed misconduct with the siren of Modernism. *The Wall*, his first metaphysical story in the rhetorical "modern" style, was written as early as 1901. This was followed by a succession of "metaphysical" problem stories, most of which are in the same intensely rhetorical style. At first Andreev kept to the familiar moulds of realism, but later on he preferred conventional settings, which become predominant beginning with *The Red Laugh* (1904). The principal of these problem stories are: *Thought* (1902)—a doctor who goes mad from the hypertrophy of pure thought working in the void; *The Life of Vasili Fiveysky* (1903)—a priest who goes mad after losing his faith; *The Red Laugh* (1904)—the "madness and horror" of war (this is the most crudely rhetorical of all Andreev's writings); *And So it Was* (1906)—the eternal vanity of political revolutions; *Judas Iscariot* (1907)—the problem of free will and necessity; *Eleazar* (1907)—Lazarus returned to life after tasting of death; *Darkness* (1908)—the "right to be good"; *The Curse of the Beast* (1908)—the horror of big cities; *My Memoirs* (1908)—the memoirs of a man sentenced to solitary imprisonment for life—the vanity of freedom. Vanity of vanities, the meaninglessness, falseness, hollowness of all human conventions and creations, the relativity of moral standards, the voidness of all earthly desires, the insuperable isolation of man from man, are the subject of all these stories, and above them the one great reality—death. Two stories of this period only stand out for their merits: both of them have revolutionaries for their heroes—*Darkness* (1907) and *The Seven That Were Hanged* (1908). In *Darkness* a tracked terrorist seeks refuge in a brothel (I must apologize for these ever-recurring details, but it is impossible to avoid them in writing of this school of writers). The prostitute who receives him is offended by his chastity and flings into his face the very Andreevian question, "What right have you to be good if I am bad?" *Darkness* offended the Left, and Andreev, to exculpate himself from the charge of disrespect for the terrorists, wrote *The Seven That Were Hanged.* This is the story of five terrorists and two common murderers who are sentenced to death, from the sentence to the execution. Though it deals with Andreev's favourite theme of death, its principal subject is not the horror of death, but the heroism and purity of the terrorists. It is not a protest against violent death, but a tribute to the Russian revolutionaries. In this respect it stands apart from the rest of Andreev's work. It also stands apart from what he wrote about the same time, for the elegant simplicity and reserve with which it is written. It is characteristic of the atmosphere of Russian public life that though Andreev was quite non-political, he is firmly convinced of the sanctity of the terrorists. Even the prostitute has no doubt that the acme of goodness is to be a political assassin. *The Seven That Were Hanged* is as devout as anything in the Acts of the Martyrs. After 1908 Andreev wrote more plays than stories. His last and longest novel, *Sashka Zhegulev* (1912), appeared when he was on the wane and attracted comparatively little attention.

Andreev wrote his first drama (*Towards the Stars*) in 1906, and after that date about a dozen other plays, some of which have become very famous, but none of which is comparable to the best of his stories. These plays are of two kinds: realistic plays of Russian life in which he continued the tradition of Chekhov and Gorky, bringing it still lower down and finally stullifying it (*Days of Our Life,* 1908; *Anfisa,* 1910; *Gaudeamus,* etc.); and symbolical dramas in a conventional setting (*The Life of Man,* 1907; *King Hunger,* 1908; *Black Masks,* 1909; *Anathema,* 1910; *He Who Gets Slapped,* 1914). Of these, *The Life of Man* and *He Who Gets Slapped* had a considerable success. In all of them he studiously avoids every suspicion of real life and live colour. They are perfectly abstract and rhetorical. They are the distant descendants, through various, mainly Teutonic intermediaries, of the mystery plays of Byron. They are written in an intensely stilted, rhetorical, "international" prose, and their colouring is gaudily black and red, without any shades. *The Life of Man* is, after all, the best, for it does produce a certain cumulative effect by the monotonous chant of the unreal personages, and its success was not entirely unmerited. Still, it is impossible to re-read it. As for the philosophy of these plays, it is always the same—death and nonentity, and the vanity and falsity of everything human. In his last plays, both of the realistic and of the symbolical type, there is a notable growth of the element of melodrama. This makes them more theatrical and actable. A characteristic example of this later manner of Andreev's is *He Who Gets Slapped*, which has recently been turned into a movie drama in America. It loses nothing for being stripped of its literary garb and it bids well to become a success in this new form. The combination it offers of tantalizingly obscure symbolism, of allegorically interpreted farce, and of the most orthodox sentimental melodrama, is precisely the combination which must make it a "paramount picture" of the would-be highbrow type. Andreev also tried his hand at "humorous" plays (*The Beautiful Sabine Women*, etc.), but his heavy, joyless, and stilted fun is even worse than his gloomy rhetoric.

Andreev as a writer (with the exception of the few stories mentioned above) is almost dead. It is impossible to revive in the Russian reader of to-day the naïve mentality which was moved by the rhetoric of *The Red Laugh* and *The Life of Man*. The Andreev feeling of the emptiness of the world has been (happily enough) lost by us, so we can appreciate him only in so far as he infects us æsthetically. But his rhetorical style is a mass of clichés; his words have no individual life; they are melted together into formless masses of verbal concrete. "Andreev says 'boo' and I am not afraid" was Tolstoy's appreciation of one of his early stories, and though our taste may be different from Tolstoy's, we shall never again be frightened by the great majority of Andreev's writings. Andreev was a genuine and sincere writer. But sincerity counts for very little unless it has at its service the power of inevitable expression, that is to say, superior craftsmanship. Andreev was a dilettante of form who had great pretensions and no tact. He will remain in the history of Russian civ-

ilization as a very interesting and representative figure: the
most representative man of a dark and tragic phase in the
evolution of the *intelligentsia*, when, losing faith in its naïve
revolutionary optimism, it suddenly found itself in the universal
void—naked men, solitary and empty, on a meaningless earth
under a cold and empty sky. This stage has most certainly
been passed, and if we ever return to the experience that produced it, we shall have to find some new expression for our
feelings; for Andreev does not make us afraid. All this refers to that Andreev who, intoxicated by success and self-
importance, and unguided by culture and taste, embarked on
the dark seas of Modernism. The other Andreev, who was a
modest and intelligent follower of the great example of Tolstoy,
and who wrote *Once upon a Time There Lived* . . . , *In the
Fog*, and *The Governor*, has his secure, if modest, place in the
pantheon of Russian authors.

7. ARTSYBASHEV

Soon after the First Revolution, Andreev's popularity was
almost eclipsed by the great vogue of the author of *Sanin*,
Michael Petrovich Artsybàshev. Born in 1878, Artsybashev
made his first appearance in literature in 1902. In 1904 he
attracted attention and roused hopes by *The Death of Lande*,
the story of a life of quest followed by a tragically meaningless death. In 1905–1906 he pleased the Radical public by
a series of stories of the Revolution. But the Revolution was
defeated, the intoxication passed, and a wave of disillusionment
in public ideals swept the *intelligentsia*. Personal enjoyment
and freedom from morality became the order of the day, and
sexual licence, often on a definitely pathological foundation,
spread like an epidemic. This epidemic was both reflected
and further favoured by Artsybashev's famous novel which
appeared in 1907. Its success was instant and tremendous.
The old-fashioned critics cried out against its immorality, and
the modernists pointed out the absence in it of all literary
merit. But it was a sensation and everyone had to read it.
It became for a few years the Bible of every schoolboy and

schoolgirl in Russia. It would be wrong to suppose that Artsybashev consciously sought either to corrupt schoolgirls or to gain money by pandering to animal instincts—Russian literature has never been openly meretricious; and he had from the very beginning shown symptoms of that Andreevian nihilism which was the brand-mark of the generation. Still, the effect was certainly serious, and the author of *Sanin* cannot be exculpated from having contributed to that moral deterioration of Russian society, especially of provincial schoolgirls. The didactic character of Russian literature (or at least the didactic spirit in which it had always been approached) was the cause of the strangely serious reception given to *Sanin*— it was not read as light literature, but as a revelation and a doctrine. The book is indeed didactic; it is a heavy, professorial sermon on the text: Be true to yourselves and follow your natural inclinations. These inclinations, Artsybashev preaches, can all be reduced to a carnal desire for the other sex—that man is good who obeys them, and that man bad who tries to hoodwink them. There is no such thing as love—it is a mere invention of artificial culture—the only reality is desire. Artsybashev's preaching proceeds direct from Tolstoy— only it is Tolstoy the other way round, and Tolstoy without genius. But the common ground is unmistakable—it is contempt for human conventions and culture, and the negation of all but the primitive realities. As literature *Sanin* is very mediocre. It is long, tedious, overloaded with "philosophical" conversations. Artsybashev avoids the modernist pitfalls of Andreev, but his psychology is puerile: it can all be reduced to one pattern, borrowed from Tolstoy; he (or she) thought he wished this and that, but in reality he only wished quite another thing—that is, to quell his sexual desire, which is the only human reality.

The other reality of Artsybashev's world is death; and to death is devoted his second big novel, *At the Brink* (in the English translation, *Breaking-Point*) (1911–1912). It is also heavily didactic—its subject is an epidemic of suicides in a provincial town, which destroyed all its intellectual élite. All Artsybashev's stories, long or short, are stories with a purpose, and the purpose is always to show the inanity of human life, the unreality of artificial civilization, and the reality of only two things—sex and death. In long stories and in little parable-like sketches, it is always the same over again. With painstaking and conscientious monotony, the sermon is hammered into the reader—as long as he agrees to submit to this dreary lecturing.

After *At the Brink*, Artsybashev devoted himself to the stage. His plays (*Jealousy*, *War*, etc.) are also purpose plays, and the "message" is always the same. They are constructed with simple straightforwardness, and this is not out of place in the drama. It is precisely owing to this organizing force of the "purpose" that they have, unlike most Russian plays, a genuine dramatic skeleton. They are quite actable, and with good actors have had deserved successes.

The Bolsheviks treated Artsybashev very harshly, and included *Sanin* and other of his works in their index of forbidden books, and finally expelled him from Russia (in 1923). So it is not surprising that he has adopted a very intransigent anti-Bolshevik attitude. He has devoted himself to political journalism in the Russian press of Warsaw. His reputation in Russia (including emigrated Russia) has suffered a complete eclipse. It is significant that *Sanin* has not been reprinted even outside of Russia. At present no one regards him as a significant writer, but only as a curious and, on the whole, regrettable episode in the history of Russian literature.

8. SERGEYEV-TSENSKY

Sergeyev-Tsensky never attained to those giddy heights of popularity that were the lot of Andreev and Artsybashev, and outside Russia—where his most successful contemporaries have become international celebrities—his name is practically unknown. But now, when Andreev's fame has faded and Artsybashev's gone, he emerges a much more significant figure, and his recent work seems to be full of unexpected promise. Sergey Nikolaevich Sergéyev-Tsénsky (born 1876) began his literary career in 1904. His stories soon attracted general attention, were warmly welcomed by many critics, but generally censured for an exclusive exuberance and elaboration of style. His most important works of this early period are *The Forest Quagmire* (1907), *Babayev* (1907), *The Sadness of the Fields* (1909), and *Movements* (1910). In 1914 appeared *The Oblique Elena*, which was unexpectedly free from all his previous exuberance. Then he became silent for many years. During all this time he lived in the Crimea, writing *Transfiguration*, a novel of extraordinary vastness which is to be the history of the Russian *intelligentsia* mentality from before the War to after the Revolution. The first part of this novel appeared in 1923. Unfortunately it was published in the Crimea and the difficulties of communication in the Soviet Union are so great that only an insignificant number of copies have reached Moscow, and outside Russia the book is inaccessible. So until it is reprinted in Moscow or Petersburg, we can judge of it only by hearsay. Gorky is reported to have pronounced it the most significant Russian book since the beginning of the century. One can almost believe it, for the little that has reached us of Sergeyev-Tsensky's post-Revolutionary work is certainly on a very high level of concentrated excellence.

Sergeyev-Tsensky's early work acquired a reputation for exaggerated exuberance and elaboration of style. It is loaded with imagery, with comparisons, often far-fetched, and bold metaphor. Alone of all his literary group, he had a feeling for words, for the actual verbal texture of his writings. His early style vibrates with expressiveness and life. It is "ornamental" prose very much akin to that which has been cultivated by the disciples of Remizov and Bely, but his starting-point is different and there is no actual connexion between him and the modern school. One of the most striking merits of his early work is the wonderful vividness of the speech of his characters. He freely uses dialect and broken language and slang—and uses it with knowledge and precision. The conversation of Anton Antonovich, a Russianized Austrian Pole, the hero of *Movements*, is a masterpiece of exact notation and at the same time of phonetic effectiveness: the exuberant and unconquerable energy of the self-made man vibrates in every syllable and intonation of it. Tsensky is equally precise in everything: he knows everything he writes about, he revels in technical terms, and, for instance, in *The Sadness of the Fields,* make his characters indulge in long technical conversations about the house they are building, and, an extraordinary thing, these conversations are never boring, so intensely alive are they. He is also one of the few writers who know and feel the geography of Russia and the individuality of its parts. In *The Oblique Elena* (the strange title is the name of a coalshaft in the Donets district), his style suddenly settles down, and he seems of set purpose to avoid all distracting ornament—a heroic development in an author with such personal style. In his post-Revolutionary *The Professor's Narrative* (1924), he continues to shun all imagery and ornament, but revives his art of making you hear his characters speaking: the story is a narrative in a narrative, and the contained narrative is told by a Red Army officer in a language as characteristic and alive as Anton Antonovich's in *Movements.*

Apart from his style, Sergeyev-Tsensky is of the same school as Andreev and Artsybashev—his principal themes are death, the tyranny of fate, and the insuperable solitude of man; morbid psychological states, and the lure of crime. *The Forest Quagmire* (one of his most elaborately written works) is the story of a peasant girl who becomes an idiot subsequent to a violent fit of terror in the haunted wood, and after an irresponsible life dies a tragic and hideous death. *The Sadness of the Fields* is the life of a woman whose children all die before their birth and who lives in constant terror of the mysterious forces of destruction in her womb. *Babayev* is a young, neurasthenic officer morbidly attracted by the desire of crime, and who finds an outlet to it (and ultimately his own death) in his work during the suppression of the Revolution. It is noteworthy that Tsensky succeeds in making the politically attractive subject quite unpolitical. *Movements* is the undoing of a man, the energetic and exuberant Anton Antonovich, by a succession of strokes of fate, is brought to disgrace (he is convicted of arson), indifference, and death. The last chapters of the novel belong to the great family of *Ivan Ilyich*. There is a note of noble and manly resignation in them, which grows in *The Oblique Elena* (the history of how an engineer decided to commit suicide and how and why he did not) into a more active acceptance of life. The same return from an "everlasting no" to an "everlasting yea" seems to be the subject of *Transfiguration*. *The Professor's Narrative*, however, is outside this development: it is a steady objective study of the making of a murderer, of a man who can coolly and simply kill another man. The story is told to the Professor by the murderer himself (a Red Army commander, formerly an officer of the Old Army) with a directness and simplicity that makes one's flesh creep. It is a masterpiece of straightforward and concentrated narrative, and makes one expect still better things from its author.

9. MINOR NOVELISTS

Between the First Revolution and the Great War a great quantity of fiction was written in Russia and most of it came from writers more or less connected with the same publishing-houses as Andreev and Artsybashev. By the side of Artsybashev may be mentioned Anatoli Kaménsky (b. 1877), whose book of stories published in 1907 used to be quoted next to *Sanin* as a sign of the growing depravation: one of the stories relates of a lady who received her guests in nothing but a pair of slippers; another, of a lieutenant who seduced four girls in a few hours. It is hardly literature. The "philosophical" side of Artsybashev is reflected in the numerous novels and dramas of V. Vinnichénko, the leader of the Ukrainian S.D. party and for a few months the head of a semi-Bolshevik Ukrainian Government. His novels were a degree more successful than his political career. The short stories of Osip Dỳmov (pseud. of O. I. Perelman, b. 1878) are sustained in the mincing "modern" style imitated from the Viennese modernist Altenberg. His novels of Jewish life are drearily realistic, with psychological and ideological pretensions. A more simple realism continued to flourish and to find favour with the public. It still continues to exist, though it belongs more or less to the "basement" of literature. Among the simpler realists of the generation, one may name K. Trenev, who has recently published a big "popular drama" about the eighteenth century, "Bolshevik" Pugachev, and George Grebenshchikov, a Siberian, whose exceedingly mediocre stories have attracted attention since he emigrated, owing to the interest of the Siberian *milieu* depicted in them.

A more interesting and significant writer is Ivan Sergeevich Shmelév (b. 1875), who first attracted attention in 1910 by his powerful and well-written novel, *The Waiter* (*The Man from the Restaurant*). Quite recently he has written a work of outstanding interest, *That Which Was* (1923; there exists an English translation): in a military lunatic asylum near the front, the patients rebel against their guardians, and a mad colonel sets up his rule in it. The story, sometimes unduly hysterical and prolix, is powerfully written and conveys with great force an atmosphere of madness in which the clinical madness of the lunatic colonel and the moral madness of War become indistinguishable.

Another interesting author is Boris Sàvinkov (b. 1879), whose life, however, is even more interesting than his works. He was one of the heads of the terrorist organization of the S.R. party. He organized the assassination of the Grand Duke Sergius (February, 1905). He was arrested, sentenced to death, and escaped from prison in the most sensational way. From 1906 to 1917 he lived abroad, where he came in contact with the Merezhkovskys and, largely under the influence of Mme. Merezhkovsky, wrote *The Pale Horse* (1909)—the confession of a terrorist, who arrives at questioning his right to kill. The book appeared under the pseudonym of V. Ropshin and created a sensation, which was enhanced by the fact that after the revelations of Azef political terror had become a problem of the day and had lost much of its glamour and prestige. This was followed in 1913 by another terrorist novel, *That Which Never Happened*. In 1914 Savinkov joined that section of the Socialists which advocated war to the end in the name of liberty and democracy. In 1917 he became the loudest mouthpiece of patriotic Socialism and the greatest enemy of the Bolsheviks and other *défaitistes*. He was at one time Acting Minister of War, and in this capacity reintroduced capital punishment for deserters. After the Bolshevik Revolution he joined the White Movement, put up his head-quarters in Poland, and acted in concert with the Poles against Soviet Russia. His "partisans" were notorious for their cruelty and lack of discipline. After the peace of Riga he remained in Poland, continuing to intrigue and to conspire against the Soviet Government. In 1923 he published *The Black Horse*, a story of the White movement, which, like its predecessor, finished with a doubt about the right to promote civil war. A few months later he emerged in Moscow, where he was "arrested" by the Bolshevik police under mysterious circumstances, and made sensational revelations of the White Movement. As a writer, Savinkov-Ropshin is not very significant: *That Which Never Happened* is a pale reflection of Tolstoy's methods; *The Black Horse* is little more than "impressionistic" journalism; *The Pale Horse* will survive, but rather as a human document, a first-hand account of the terrorist mentality, than as a work of literature.

The lyrical style of short story which proceeds from Turgenev and was cultivated by Bunin (and discerned by many readers of the period in Chekhov), was imitated by many minor writers of the period, and has degenerated since into the lowest journalism. Only one writer gave it a personal impress and developed it along his own lines. That was Boris Konstantinovich Zàytsev (b. 1881), whose first book of stories appeared in 1906 and who is at present one of the most prominent *émigré* men of letters. His short stories and novels of Russian life are made of nothing but atmosphere. The lyrical mellowness, of a softer and weaker kind than Bunin's, is almost nauseously sweet. They have no skeleton—they are flabby, like oysters. Still, he succeeds in creating an atmosphere in which pink and grey tones dominate. What makes Zaytsev different from the other writers dealt with in this chapter is his profound and sincere religious feeling—Christian in ap-

pearance but pantheistic in substance. In the years preceding
the War, Zaytsev passed much of his time in Italy. His Italian impressions, are collected in a volume of short sketches recently published, *Italy* (1923). Italy is also the background
of some of his latest short stories, if stories they may be called
(*Raphael,* and other stories, 1924). These Italian writings
are also skeletonless and purely atmospheric, but there is in
them a genuine feeling for Italian soil and for Italian humanity.

10. OUTSIDE THE LITERARY GROUPS

For all their popularity, the works of Gorky, Andreev, or
Artsybashev did not slake the public thrist for ficton. In fact
they scarcely answered it. Russian novelists have always
neglected the element of narrative interest, and a consequence
of this has always been that the public looked elsewhere for
readable novels: hence the enormous consumption in Russia of
translated fiction, and hence the importance of non-literary
novels. It is difficult to convey to the English reader the extent to which Russian readers read foreign fiction. The tastes
changed but the fact remained: towards 1900 the favourite
writers were Zola and Maupassant. In the early years of the
twentieth century Sir A. Conan Doyle was the general favourite. It is no exaggeration to say that about 1914 Jack
London was the most popular of Russian writers.

Of the non-literary Russian novelists, the most famous is
Mme. A. A. Verbítsky (b. 1861), whose endless novel, *The
Keys of Happiness* (1909–1912), appeared in the reports of
every library at the head of the list of books demanded. It
is the orthodox concoction of snobbishness, melodrama, and
sentimentalism, sprinkled with a native spice of vulgar Nietzscheism, revolutionary phrases, and "sexual problems" *à la
Sanin.*

On a higher literary level stand the novels of another woman
author, Mme. E. A. Nagródsky, whose first novel, *The Wrath
of Dionysus* (1910), had a large sale but was also welcomed
by some very refined critics. These and her subsequent books
are typical novels "for adults" where the thrill has a mainly

sexual foundation, and the technique is an intelligent imitation of the French school. It is characteristic that Mme. Nagrodsky is a well-to-do dilettante, who never wrote for a living and had nothing to do with literary circles.

The detective story did not thrive on Russian soil: Sherlock Holmes degenerated into something extraordinarily crude and illiterate in the Russian-made stories about the detective Nat Pinkerton: millions of copies of these penny productions were sold in the years 1907 and following. Schoolboys of twelve and aged senators spent sleepless nights over these absorbing, if illiterate, shockers.

As to the story of adventure, it found at least one literary adept in the person of Alexander Grin, who, though a writer of considerable talent, received no encouragement from the critics and could not compete with the foreign masters. His very name (pronounced *Green*) sounded foreign and Anglo-Saxon, and seemed to exclude him from the family of Russian writers. His stories are laid out in more or less conventionally exotic countries, and the characters are vaguely English, or American, or Dutch. But Grin is too much a writer of his country and generation to be able to avoid the psychological virus. So he looks much more like a miniature Conrad (whom he probably did not know at the time) than like a genuine writer of maritime adventure. Recently he has again appeared in print, and the turning tide of literary taste bids fair to bring him into greater prominence.

11. FEUILLETONISTS AND HUMORISTS

A notable feature of Russian literary life at the end of the nineteenth and beginning of the twentieth century was the growth of the daily press. The large publishers did all they could to raise the literary standards of their publications. Some went so far as to give much place to genuine literature (especially the Cadet paper *Rech* in 1906–1917), but a special style of journalese semi-literature was also developed which found its home in Suvorin's *Novoe Vremya* and in the capitalistic and Liberal *Russkoe Slovo*. This semi-literature was printed, as is the custom in French dailies, in the lower half of the middle pages, which is known by the French name *feuilleton*. The most brilliant and popular of the writers of these *feuilletons* was V. Doroshévich (b. 1864), who worked on the *Russkoe Slovo*. He evolved a peculiar staccato style which was imitated by countless good, bad, and mediocre feuilletonists. Tolstoy at one time (about 1900) expressed the opinion that of living writers Doroshevich was second only to Chekhov.

The "days of freedom" of 1905–1906 brought a great harvest of satirical journals, which, however, were very short-lived, being very soon suppressed by the Government. But a result of their appearance was to refresh the stale atmosphere of the old humorous papers, and to give birth to a humorous paper of a somewhat more literary type—the *Satyricon*. This paper flourished from 1906 to 1917 and harboured a whole school of humorists. Of these writers of short stories, the most noteworthy are Teffy (pseud. of Mme. N. A. Buchinsky, sister of the poetess Lokhvitsky) and Arkadi Avérchenko. Teffy combines the good old traditions of Russian literary humour. Her humour is delicate and founded on the careful choice of suggestive detail. There is nothing crude or coarse in her: she is a disciple of Chekhov. Averchenko, on the other hand, is a pupil of the Anglo-American school of comic writing. His stories are full of crude buffoonery and extravagantly funny situations. He is as international and plebeian as Teffy is refined and Russian.

The *Satyricon* also had its poets, of whom the most celebrated is Sasha Chérny (pseud. of A. Glikberg). He wrote very creditable satirical verse and was the only unpoetical poet of any worth during the rule of Symbolism. His example had a certain effect on the development of Mayakovsky, who was also for a short time (1915–1916) a contributor to the *Satyricon*.

Another notable humorist was the feuilletonist of the *Novoe Vremya*, Yuri Belyaev. His style is a somewhat affected mixture of sentimental poetry and whimsical humour. His sentimentally comic vaudevilles of old Petersburg had a considerable success. His best-known book is *The Misses Schneider* (1912), the scandalous and pathetic story of two young girls, of a respectable family, gone wrong.

CHAPTER IV

1. THE NEW MOVEMENTS OF THE NINETIES

IN spite of the great difference between the two parties of *intelligentsia* Radicalism—the old Populists and the new Marxists—they had in common certain immovable tenets, among which were agnosticism and the subordination of all human values to the ends of social progress and political revolution. Among the Conservative and Slavophil sections of the educated classes, the supremacy of political and social over all other values was also the rule, and Christian Orthodoxy was valued as a justification of political theories rather than for its own sake. Between atheism and progress, on the one hand, and religion and political reaction, on the other, the alliance was complete. To dissolve these alliances, and to undermine the supremacy of political over cultural and individual values, was the task of the generation of intellectuals who came of age in the last decade of the nineteenth century. The first of these two developments culminated in the theories of the Christian Liberals who edited the *Landmarks* (1909) and in the various forms of mystical revolutionism—from the "Christian" revolutionism of Merezhkovsky to the Socialist Messianism of Ivanov-Razumnik. All these movements, however, retain the other salient feature of the old *intelligentsia*-ism: they tend to identify (perhaps a little less crudely than their predecessors) moral good with public utility, with a marked predominance of the latter over the former.

But simultaneously with the growth of this new "civic" idealism, a more subversive attack was launched against the very foundations of Radical *intelligentsia*-ism and of civic morality. Æstheticism substituted beauty for duty, and individualism emancipated the individual from all social obligations. The two tendencies, which went hand in hand, proved a great civ-

151

ilizing force and changed the whole face of Russian civilization between 1900 and 1910, bringing about the great renascence of Russian art and poetry which marked that decade. In literature the principal creative expression of the new movement is the poetry of the Symbolists, but before we come to them, it is necessary to give an account of the new movements outside the domain of strictly imaginative literature.

The various currents of thought which combined to change the face of Russian culture and to overthrow the exclusive rule of the old *intelligentsia* outlook have so little in common that no general definition is possible, except it be some anodyne and inexpressive adjective, such as "modern" or "new." Yet it is evident that they belong to one historical stratum, and that together they form one movement of revolt against the agnostic idealism of the old *intelligentsia*, and of intellectual and cultural expansion. Perhaps the Marxists are not far from the truth in their explanation of the facts: the new movements, according to them, were the symptoms of a social transformation, of the birth of a bourgeoisie, of an educated class with a place in civilized life.

What distinguishes these writers from the other literary groups of the time, from the Marxists, for instance, and from the Gorky-Andreev "school," is a distinctly superior cultural level. The Marxists and the Gorky-Andreev realists, however great may have been their personal (for instance, Gorky's) superiority to the average man and even to the superior man, remained on the *cultural* level of the average Russian "intelligent" of about 1890. The æsthetes, the mystics, and the religious philosophers, whatever their personal value, worked for the enrichment and greater complexity of Russian culture. At the risk of scaring some of my prospective American readers from the whole lot of them, I will sum it up in one word by saying that they were all *highbrows*.

In accordance with the general plan of this book, I am not going to give any detailed analysis of their *ideas*, but shall treat their work as literature. Consequently I will give most of this chapter to men who are either like Rozanov and Shestov, not only great thinkers but also great writers, or like Merezhkovsky, who, though intrinsically belonging to the second order, played a principal part in the literary evolution of the times. On the contrary, a writer like Berdyaev, who would have to have a prominent place in the history of Russian thought, will receive little more than a brief notice.

The "sources" of the new movements are as various as their currents. They are partly of Russian and partly of foreign origin. Of Russian writers, the greatest influence was exercised by Dostoevsky—in both his aspects, as Christian and individualist, and by Soloviev. Of foreign influences, the greatest was that of Nietzsche. The name of Nietzsche might well open the chapter, for the first symptom of a new movement to be noticed by the press and public was the appearance of Nietzscheism. Afterwards Nietzscheism took all the forms possible in Russian literature, from the zoological immoralism of *Sanin* to the mythopoetic theories of Vyacheslav Ivanov. In the beginning, Nietzsche was first of all a powerful emancipator from the fetters of "civic duty." In this aspect he appears for the first time in *By the Light of Conscience*, by Minsky (1890). Minsky, who has already been mentioned in a preceding chapter as a "civic" poet, was regarded in the nineties as a principal leader of the new movement, together with Volynsky and Merezhkovsky. But his work is intrinsically insignificant, and demands little attention. Not much more remarkable is A. Volynsky (pseud. A. L. Flekser, b. 1865), a critic who attacked the accepted Radical authority in the name of a rather vague philosophical idealism. This required courage, and Volynsky got some severe blows in the fight. Mikhaylovsky proposed to "expel him from literature" and for many years he was under the boycott of the "civic" press. So, though his work is unimportant, he must be gratefully remembered as a "martyr" in the cause of emancipation. But the principal work of emancipation centred round Diaghilev and his magazine *Mir Iskustva*, and Merezhkovsky.

2. THE ÆSTHETIC REVIVAL

The æsthetic revival is one of the most important aspects of the great revolt. In poetry it became one of the constituent elements of the Symbolist movement, but its purest expression is found in art, especially in painting, and in art criticism. Appreciation of art and beauty was not, of course, an entirely new thing in Russian society. In the early days of *intelligentsia* Radicalism, when it had not yet severed the ties which attached it to German Idealism and French Romanticism, the Good, the True, and the Beautiful had been an inseparable trinity. By the end of the century this trinity was still dragging on a precarious and hectic existence, and we have seen that the eighties had witnessed a sort of half-hearted and timid revival of artistic values. But, after all, Beauty was always the Cinderella of the family and was strictly subjected to her two elder sisters, nowhere more severely than in the idealist philosophy of Soloviev. Taste was deplorably low and narrow. There was among the *intelligentsia* no active feeling for form, no artistic culture. There was a small number of æsthetically civilized people, but these were hopelessly conservative. They were watertight to every novel impression and capable only of chewing the old cud of idealist æstheticism.

The æsthetic pioneers of the nineties, on the contrary, were both genuinely cultured and frankly revolutionary. They had two tasks to fulfil—to re-establish a direct contact with *old* art, and to promote and encourage *modern* art. In literature these tasks fell to the lot of the Symbolists—in the plastic arts, to that of the brilliant group of painters and connoisseurs who are now known by the name of *Mir-Iskustva* men. *Mir Iskustva* (*The World of Art*), an art periodical founded in 1898 by Sergey Pavlovich Diaghilev (Dyagilev), became for several years the centre of the new movement. It was devoted primarily to art, to the revival of Russian eighteenth-century painting and architecture, to the propaganda of modern French painting, to the popularizing of such Russian artists as Vrubel, Somov, Levitan, Serov. But it also generously opened its columns to such independent critics as Rozanov and Shestov. Until the Symbolists founded their own organ in 1904, *Mir Iskustva* was not only the only art magazine in Russia, but also the only literary magazine of the new movement. The civilizing work of Diaghilev and his friends cannot be overestimated. We may have lost all taste for such a favourite of theirs as Aubrey Beardsley, but it is only owing to them and their successors that we have rediscovered our own prenaturalist painters, and classical architects, and our wonderful pre-Petrine art. It is owing to them that Russians know anything at all about the history of art and are capable of seeing anything in Florence or in Venice, in Velazquez or in Poussin. In 1890 the sole function of art in Russia was to "express ideas"; in 1915 Russian society was æsthetically one of the most cultivated and experienced in Europe. Of the men to whom we owe all this, the principal names are, besides that of Diaghilev himself, Alexander Benois, Igor Grabar, and P. P. Muratov. Grabar, who organized the rediscovery of Russian art, is not important as a writer; Muratov, who belongs to a younger generation, will be mentioned in a later chapter, but Benois cannot be passed over in silence in this chapter, for quite apart from his importance in the revival of artistic culture, he is one of the most brilliant essayists of modern Russian literature.

Alexander Nikolaevich Benois (in Russian, Benuà) was born in Petersburg of a family of French extraction, which has produced several artists of note. He is himself one of the most gifted and exquisite painters of the *Mir Iskustva* school, and his place of birth and his extraction are abundantly reflected in his writings. He is the greatest European of modern Russia, the best expression of the Western and Latin spirit. He was also the principal influence in reviving the cult of the northern metropolis and in rediscovering its architectural beauty, so long concealed by generations of artistic barbarity. Benois is one of the most cultured Russians alive. His knowledge of Western art is enormous. He is saturated with the spirit of the seventeenth and eighteenth centuries. Long before the famous Florentine Exhibition of Seicento painting, he had discovered the neglected charm of the great *barocco* painters of Italy. But he was never blind to Russian art, and in his work, as in that of the *Mir Iskustva* men in general, Westernism and Slavophilism were more than ever the two heads of a single-hearted Janus.. His essays, chiefly dealing with art criticism, reveal a very personal literary temperament. He is one of the best prose-writers of his generation, and admirably adapts his style to the subtleties and refinements of his judgment. It is an easy, colloquial, man-of-the-world prose, equally removed from the pedantry of the scholar and from the slipshodness of the journalist. His principal work is the *History of Painting* (begun in 1911 and, owing to difficulties of printing, left unfinished in 1917); it is a work of more than local importance and deserves to be translated into every civilized language. For it combines the charm of a personal and eminently readable manner with an extraordinary wealth of first-hand information and acute critical judgment. Benois is not only a painter and an art critic—he is also an important figure in the history of the Russian stage as the author of several ballets, for which he both painted the decorations and wrote the scenarios. The most important of these is *Petrushka*, the music of which by Stravinsky has made it widely known. The idea belongs to Benois, and once more he revealed in it his great love for his native town of Petersburg in all its aspects, classical and popular.

3. MEREZHKOVSKY

The principal figure of the "modern" movement in literature during its first stages was Dmitri Sergeevich Merezhkòvsky. Born in 1866 in Petersburg (his father was the steward of one of the minor Imperial palaces), he studied at the university of that city, and began his literary career very early. So soon as 1883, verse over his signature began to appear in the Liberal magazines, and before long he was universally recognized as the most promising of the younger "civic" poets. When Nadson died (1887), Merezhkovsky became his lawful successor. His early verse (collected in book form in 1888) is not strikingly above the level of its day, which was a very low one, but it shows a greater carefulness for form and diction, it is tidier and more elegant than that of his contemporaries. His reputation as the most promising poet of the younger generation was further enhanced by his narrative poem *Vera* (1890), written in a style which is the distant descendant of Byron's *Don Juan*, but had been sentimentalized and idealized out of recognition by two generations of Russian poets. It is a story of self-disbelieving love, and it ends on a vaguely religious note. It was admirably adapted to suit the taste of the time, and had a greater success than any narrative poem had had for several decades. About the same time, Merezhkovsky married Zinaida Nikolaevna Hippius, a young poetess of outstanding talent, who became a little later one of the principal poets and critics of the Symbolist movement.

New ideas were in the air, and their first swallow had appeared in 1890 in the shape of Minsky's "Nietzschean" book. *By the Light of Conscience.* Merezhkovsky soon followed suit, and abandoned the colours of civic idealism. In 1893 he published a collection of essays, *On the Causes of the Present Decline and the New Currents of Contemporary Russian Literature,* and a book of poems under the aggressive and modern title *Symbols.* Together with his wife, with Minsky, and Volynsky, he became one of the staff of the *Northern Messenger,* which came forth as the champion of "new ideas." These "new ideas" were on the whole a rather vague revolt against the positivism and utilitarianism of orthodox Radicalism. In *Symbols* and in *On the Causes,* Merezhkovsky is as vague as Volynsky, but soon his "new ideas" began to take definite shape and to form themselves into a religion of Greek antiquity. Henceforward he developed that taste for antithetic thinking which finished by ruining both himself and his style. This antithetic tendency found its first striking expression in his conception of *Christ and Antichrist,* a trilogy of historical novels, the first of which, *Julian the Apostate, or The Death of the Gods,* appeared in 1896. It was followed in 1902 by *Leonardo da Vinci, or The Gods Reborn,* and in 1905 by *Peter and Alexis.* The last of these belongs already to another period of Merezhkovsky's evolution, but the first two are characteristic of that stage of his activity which was parallel to the Westernizing action of Diaghilev and Benois. *Julian* and

Leonardo are animated by a pagan "Hellenic" feeling, and the same spirit animates all he wrote between 1894 and 1900. This includes a series of *Italian Novellas*, translations of *Daphnis and Chloe*, and of the Greek tragic poets, and *Eternal Companions* (1897), a collection of essays on the Acropolis, *Daphnis and Chloe*, Marcus Aurelius, Montaigne, Flaubert, Ibsen, and Pushkin.   All these writings are centred round one central idea—the "polar" opposition of the Greek conception of the sanctity of the flesh, and of the Christian conception of the sanctity of the spirit, and the necessity of uniting them in one supreme synthesis.   This central antithesis dominates a number of minor antitheses (such as the Nietzschean antithesis of Apollo and Dionysos), so that the general impression of his work as a whole is one of significant contrasts and relations.   The identity of opposites and the synthesis of contrasts dominate all this world of interconnected poles.   Every idea is a "pole," an "abyss" and a "mystery."   "Mystery," "polar," and "synthesis" are his favourite words.   Οὐρανὸς ἄνω, οὐρανὸς κάτω is his favourite maxim, and its symbol the starry sky reflected in the sea.   This new world of his, with its mysterious connecting-strings and mutually reflected poles, attracted the tastes of a public which had been for generations fed on the small beer of idealistically coloured positivism. Merezhkovsky's popularity became very great among the advanced and the young, and for about a decade he was the central figure of the whole "modern" movement.   At present all this symbolism seems to us rather puerile and shallow, lacking in those qualities which make the work of the genuine Symbolists more than a mere chequer-board of intersecting straight lines.   He has neither the subtlety and saturated culturedness of Ivanov nor the intense personal earnestness of Blok nor the immaterial Ariel-like quality of Bely.   His style also lacks charm.   Even more obviously than his philosophy, Merezhkovsky's prose is nothing more than a network of mechanical antitheses.   But in spite of this, all his work is historically important and was for its time beneficent.   It introduced to the Russian reader a whole unknown world of cultural values; it made familiar and significant to him figures and epochs that had been only names in text-books; it gave a life to objects and buildings, to all the material side of bygone civilizations, which is loaded with such portentous symbolism in Merezhkovsky's novels. This shallow symbolism is dead, but it has done good educational service. After Merezhkovsky, Florence and Athens became something more than mere names to the Russian intellectual, and if they are now living entities he owes it very largely to the sophistications of *Julian* and *Leonardo*.

In 1901 Merezhkovsky began publishing (in monthly instalments in *Mir Iskustva*) his most important work, *Tolstoy and Dostoevsky*. The first two of its three parts—*Life*, *Writings*, and *Religion*—are the most intelligent and readable thing he ever wrote. His interpretation of the personalities of Tolstoy and Dostoevsky dominated Russian literature for many years, and still dominates all German works on the subject. Like all his conceptions, it is a more or less cleverly constructed antithesis, which is developed in the most thoroughgoing way to explain and bring into order the minutest details of the life, work, and religion of the two great writers. Tolstoy, in Merezhkovsky's interpretation, is the great Pagan and Pantheist, the "seer of the flesh" (*taynovidets ploti*)—a half-truth there was some merit in discovering in 1900. Dostoevsky is the great Christian, "the seer of the spirit" (*taynovidets dukha*)—another half-truth which it was less difficult to discover. The book may still be read with interest and profit, but the simple-minded reader who is uninitiated into the mazes of Merezhkovsky's mentality will either be repelled by its geometrical see-saw of contrasts or fall too easily into the carefully woven nets of his sophistry. *Tolstoy and Dostoevsky* marks the transition of Merezhkovsky from West to East, from Europe to Russia, from the Greek to the Christian ideal. The "great Pagan" Tolstoy is consistently belittled before the "great Christian" Dostoevsky, and the Messianic mission of Russia is everywhere emphasized. *Peter and Alexis* (the third part of *Christ and Antichrist*), written immediately after *Tolstoy and Dostoevsky* and published in 1905, is a further vindication of the "Russian" and "Christian" cause against the Western and Pagan spirit of "Anti-christ" embodied in Peter the Great.

In 1903 "the Merezhkovskys" (a term which, besides him and his wife, includes also their friend D. V. Filosofov) became the centre of the "religious-philosophical" movement. They founded the excellent monthly review *Novy Put* (*The New Way*), which opened its columns to the Symbolists and to all the new movements (Blok and Bely first made their appearance in it), and they became the soul of the "religious-philosophical meetings," the primary aim of which was to bring together the cultured part of the Orthodox clergy and the religious part of the *intelligentsia*. These meetings attracted great interest and considerable attendance. Questions of the greatest religious and philosophical importance were discussed there, and they contributed greatly to that change of atmosphere in Russian intellectual life which is the subject of the present chapter.

At this time the Merezhkovskys were at the height of their Slavophilism and Orthodoxy—for a moment, even inclined towards a religious acceptation of autocracy. But the current of Revolution carried them to the Left, and in 1905 they took a definitely revolutionary attitude. After the failure of the revolution they emigrated to Paris, where they published in French a violent collection of pamphlets, *Le Tzar et la Révolution*.

Merezhkovsky's importance began to decline. His accession to revolutionary doctrines did not give him much influence among the revolutionaries—and Russian radicalism, even in so far as it has become mystical, has been little affected by his verbal constructions. One of the few men who came under the influence of the Merezhkovskys was the terrorist Savinkov (see chap. iii), in whose sensational "confession," *The Pale Horse*, unmistakable traces were discerned not of Merezhkovsky's but of Mme. Merezhkovsky's influence.

In 1914 the Merezhkovskys, together with the majority of Russian radicals, adopted an anti-War attitude, but did not join the extreme *défaitistes*, and in 1917 assumed an attitude of decided opposition to Lenin and Bolshevism. After the

Bolshevik *coup d'état*, they still continued to lay all their hopes on the Constituent Assembly, and only after the dispersion of that assembly did they lose all hope in the triumph of "religious" Revolution. The years 1918 and 1919 they lived in Petersburg, where Mme. Merezhkovsky published a book of violently anti-Bolshevik verse (those were days of lenient or inefficient censorship) and wrote her *Petersburg Diary*. Towards the end of 1919 the Merezhkovskys succeeded in escaping from Soviet Russia and came at first to Warsaw, where they joined hands with Savinkov and supported that notorious adventurer in his policy of fighting the Bolsheviks in alliance with Poland. However, they soon were disgusted with the treacherous duplicity of the Poles and retired to Paris, where they published *The Reign of Antichrist*, one of the most violent (and hysterical) books written against Bolshevism. There they still live, maintaining an attitude of intransigent anti-Bolshevism. Merezhkovsky has devoted himself to Egyptian studies, and, besides a series of "aphorisms," has written a novel of Egyptian life, *The Birth of the Gods, or Tutankhamen in Crete*, all of which are even more unreadable than his previous writings.

There is no need to deal in any detail with Merezhkovsky's numerous books of "philosophical" prose published after *Tolstoy and Dostoevsky* (*Gogol and the Devil, The Prophet of the Russian Revolution, Not Peace but a Sword, Sick Russia*, essays on Lermontov, on Tyutchev and Nekrasov, etc., etc.). In them he retains and even exaggerates the fundamental characteristic of his style—an immoderate love of antithesis. But whereas his early works are written in a reasonable and "tidy" manner, from about 1905 he developed a sort of verbal hysteria which has made all he wrote after that date utterly unreadable. Every one of his books and essays is a see-saw of mechanical antithesis sustained from beginning to end in the shrillest of hysterical falsettos. This style developed when he grew conscious of himself as a great philosopher and prophet, and its appearance is roughly simultaneous with the time his teaching took its final form. This teaching styles itself Third Testament Christianity. It insists on the imminence of a new revelation and on the approach of a new religious era. But his mysticism is not concretely personal like Soloviev's: it represents the universe as a system of variously interconnected ideas reflected in individual and material symbols. His Christ is an abstraction, not a Person. His religion is not based on personal religious experience, but on the speculations of his symmetry-loving brain. Judged by religious standards, his writings are mere literature. Judged by literary standards, they are bad literature.

Merezhkovsky's fame outside Russia is mainly based on his novels. The first of these, *The Death of the Gods* (*Julian the Apostate*, 1896), is also the best. Not that it is in any sense a great novel, or even a novel at all in any true sense of the word. It is entirely lacking in creative power. But it is a good work of popularization, an excellent "home university" book which has probably interested more Russian readers in antiquity than any other single book ever did. The same may be said of *Leonardo da Vinci*, but this time with some reservation. In *Julian* the material is kept in hand and the "encyclopædia" side is not allowed to grow beyond all measure; *Leonardo* is already in danger of being stifled by quotations from sources, and by the historical bric-à-brac which is there only because Merezhkovsky happens to know it. Besides, both these novels are disfigured by the artificiality of the ideas that preside over them, which are of his ordinary crudely antithetic kind. Both *Julian* and *Leonardo* are inferior to Bryusov's *Fire Angel*. Merezhkovsky's novels on Russian subjects (*Peter and Alexis, Alexander I, December the Fourteenth*), as well as his plays *Paul I* and *The Romanticists*, are on a much lower level of literary merit. They are formless masses of raw (sometimes badly understood, always wrongly interpreted) material, written from beginning to end in an intolerable hysterical falsetto, and saturated *ad nauseam* with his artificial, homuncular "religious" ideas. Merezhkovsky is a victim of ideas. If he had never tried to have any, he might have developed into a good novelist for boys, for even in his worst and latest novels, there is always a page or two which reveals him as a creditable and vivid describer of events. Thus, in the

dreary *December the Fourteenth*, the scene where a mutinous
battalion of the guards appears rushing down the street with
bayonets lowered and its officers brandishing their swords
breathless with running and revolutionary excitement might
have been quite in its place in a less sophisticated narrative.

To sum up, Merezhkovsky's place in literary history is very
considerable, for he was the representative man of a very important movement for more than a decade (1893–1905). But
as a writer he scarcely survives, and the first part of *Tolstoy
and Dostoevsky* remains his only work that will still be read in
the next generation.

4. ROZANOV (1856–1919)

The name of Merezhkovsky is usually associated with those
of Rozanov and Shestov. But beyond the fact that they were
contemporaries, that they also wrote on questions of "religious
philosophy," and that some of their most remarkable works
take the form of commentaries on Dostoevsky, there is practically nothing in common between Merezhkovsky and these two
writers. Though neither Rozanov nor Shestov ever played
such a central part in the literary movement as Merezhkovsky
did, they are much more important figures in the history of
Russian literature, not only for the significance and genuineness of their religious ideas, but also as *writers* of the first
order, and of exceptional originality.

Vasili Vasilievich Ròzanov was born in 1856 in Vetluga
(province of Kostroma), and spent most of his early life in the
capital of that province. He came of a poor middle-class family. He received the usual middle-class education at a
gymnasium, whence he went to the University of Moscow,
where he studied history. After taking his degree, he was for
many years a teacher of history and geography in the secondary schools of various provincial towns (Bryansk, Yelets,
Bely). He never took any interest in his subjects and he had
no pedagogic vocation. About 1880 he married Apollinaria
Suslov, a woman of about forty, who had been in her first youth
in intimate relations with Dostoevsky. The marriage proved

singularly unhappy. Apollinaria was a cold and proud, "infernal" woman, with unknown depths of cruelty and sensuality, which seem to have been a revelation to Dostoevsky (it was immediately after his voyage with her that he wrote *Memoirs from Underground*). She lived with Rozanov for some three years and then left him with another. They retained for each other a lifelong hatred. Apollinaria refused to grant Rozanov a divorce.* Several years after his rupture with Apollinaria, Rozanov met, in Yelets, Varvara Dmitrievna Rudneva, who became his unofficial wife. He could not marry her because of his first wife's intractability, and this largely explains his bitterness in all his writings on the question of divorce. This second, "unofficial" marriage was as happy as his first and official marriage was unhappy.

In 1886 Rozanov published a book *On Understanding*, which he later described as "a continuous polemic against the University of Moscow," that is, against positivism and official agnosticism. It had no success, but it attracted the attention of Strakhov, who entered on a correspondence with Rozanov, introduced him into the Conservative literary press, and finally arranged him an official appointment in Petersburg. This, however, did not much help Rozanov, and he remained in very straitened circumstances until the time he was invited by Suvorin (1899) to write for the *Novoe Vremya*, the only conservative paper that could pay its contributors well. Rozanov's early writings lack the wonderful originality of his developed style, but some of them are of great importance. Foremost among them is *The Legend of the Great Inquisitor* (1890), a commentary on the well-known episode in *The Brothers Karamazov*. It is the first of that long succession of Dostoevskian commentaries (continued by Shestov and Merezhkovsky) which form such an important feature of modern Russian literature. It was the first attempt to delve deep

---

* The expression "to grant a divorce" is of course not legal, but in colloquial language it has become technical. Divorces, under the old Russian law, were practically impossible without, but very easy with, the collusion of the parties.

into the mind of Dostoevsky and to discover the mainsprings of his individuality. The fact that Rozanov through his first wife had "first-hand" knowledge of certain hidden aspects of Dostoevsky is of particular importance. It is interesting in this connexion to note that Rozanov lays great stress on the *Memoirs from Underground* as the central point in the work of Dostoevsky. He feels with wonderful acuteness, as no one before him had done, Dostoevsky's passionate and morbid striving towards absolute freedom, including the freedom of not desiring happiness. Among other things, the book contains a wonderful chapter on Gogol; Rozanov was the first to discover a thing that to-day seems a truism, that Gogol was not a realist and that Russian literature in its entirety is not a continuation but a reaction against Gogol. *The Legend* would suffice to make Rozanov a great writer, but the mature Rozanov has other qualities of a still higher order.

In the nineties Rozanov lived in Petersburg, in active intellectual intercourse with a few men who could lend him an understanding ear. This circle included all there was of independent conservative thought in Russia. It included I. F. Romanov, an original writer who wrote under the pseudonym of Rtsy, and Fedor Shperk (1872-1897), a philosopher who died young and whom Rozanov always recognized as the greatest man of genius he ever met. Shperk and Rtsy, according to Rozanov's own opinion, had an important influence on the formation of his style. Towards the end of the nineties Rozanov came into contact with the Modernists, but though they gave him more unstinted recognition than any other party, he never became very intimate with them. In his writings Rozanov always had one curious defect, especially when he wrote on subjects that did not very deeply affect him—a certain lack of inhibition which made him go to lengths of paradox which he did not seriously mean and which exasperated the more conventional. This cost him a biting and witty attack from Soloviev, who nicknamed him Porfiri Golovlev—the name of the hypocrite in Saltykov's *The Golovlev Family*, who had the same lack of inhibition in his interminable and nauseously unctious speeches. Another disagreeable incident for Rozanov was Mikhaylovsky's proposal to "expel him from literature" for an insufficiently respectful article on Tolstoy.

In 1899 Rozanov became a permanent contributor to the *Novoe Vremya*, and this at last gave him a comfortable income. Suvorin gave him a free hand to write whatever he liked and as often as he liked, so long as he was brief and did not take up too much place in one number. This freedom and this obligation were largely active in developing Rozanov's peculiar fragmentary and seemingly formless mode of expression. About this time Rozanov's interest became concentrated on questions of marriage, divorce, and family life. He waged a determined campaign against the abnormal state of family life in Russia and in Christendom in general. He saw in the existence of illegitimate children the shame of Christianity. A child, he thought, should become legitimate by its very birth. He also dwelt with bitterness on facts from life displaying the abnormal state of things conditioned by the difficulty of divorce.* All this criticism converges in an attack on Christianity as an essentially ascetic religion which in its heart considers every sexual relation an abomination and only half-heartedly gives its blessing to marriages. At the same time he was irresistibly attracted by it, and especially by what he called its "dark rays," those less apparent but really more fundamental features without which Christianity is not itself. The essential thing in Christianity, according to Rozanov, is sadness and tears, a concentration on death and "after death," and a renunciation of the world. A merry Christian, he said, was a contradiction in terms. To the religion of Christ he opposed the religion of God the Father, which he thought was the natural religion, the religion of growth and generation. This primitive naturalistic religion he found in the Old Testament, in the sexual piety of mediæval Judaism, and in the religion of the Ancient Egyptians. His ideas on the philosophy of Christianity and of his own "natural" (in fact phallic) religion

* His writings on the question were collected in *The Family Problem in Russia* (2 vols., 1903).

are contained in a series of books—*In the Realm of Riddle and Mystery* (2 vols., 1901), *In the Shade of Church Walls* (1906), *The Russian Church* (1906), *The Dark Face* (*A Metaphysic of Christianity*, 1911), and *Moonlight Men* (1913). His meditations on Egyptian religion appeared as a series of pamphlets during the last years of his life (*From Oriental Motives*). In politics Rozanov remained a Conservative. And though at bottom he was completely non-political, there were reasons for his being so. As a profoundly mystical and religious mind, he was repulsed by the agnosticism of the Radicals. As an exceptionally independent thinker, he hated their obligatory sameness. As an immoralist, he despised their drab moral respectability. He was also a born Slavophil—mankind existed for him only in so far as it was Russian (or Jewish, but his attitude to the Jews was ambiguous)—and the cosmopolitanism of the *intelligentsia* revolted him as much as did their agnosticism. Besides, for many years anything like recognition and support came to him only from the Right, from Strakhov, and from Suvorin, afterwards from the Decadents. The Radicals ceased to consider him a despicable reactionary only after 1905. The events of 1905, however, somewhat disconcerted Rozanov, and for a time he was attracted by the Revolution, most of all by the buoyant youth of its young people. He even wrote a book (*When the Authorities Were Away*) full of praise of the Revolutionary movement. At the same time, however, he continued writing in his usual conservative spirit. At one time he wrote conservative articles in the *Novoe Vremya* over his full name, and Radical articles over the pseudonym V. Varvarin in the progressive *Russkoe Slovo*. He did not regard this inconsistency as anything outrageous. Politics were to him a very minor business that could not be brought *sub speciem æternitatis*. What interested him in both parties were only the various individualities that went to form them, their "taste," their "flavour," their atmosphere. This point of view was not shared by the majority of the Republic of Letters, and Rozanov was charged with moral insanity by Peter Struve, and again threatened with boycott.

Meanwhile the genius of Rozanov had reached its full maturity and found its own characteristic form of expression. In 1912 appeared *Solitary Thoughts, Printed Almost Privately* (*Uedinennoe, pochti na pravakh rukopisi*). The book is described in the catalogue of the British Museum as consisting of "maxims and short essays." But these terms give no idea of the extraordinary originality of its form. The little fragments which form it ring with the sound of a live voice, for they are constructed not along the lines of conventional grammar, but with the freedom and variety of intonation of living speech; the voice often falls to a hardly audible, interrupted whisper. But at times in its unconventional and unfettered freedom it attains real eloquence and a powerful emotional rhythm. This book was followed by *Fallen Leaves* (1913) and *Fallen Leaves, a Second Basketful* (1915), which are a continuation of the same manner. The capricious and, as he called it, "anti-Gutenberg" nature of Rozanov finds a curious expression in the fact that, apart from these books, his most remarkable utterances are to be found where one would least expect them—for instance, in footnotes to other people's letters. Thus, one of his greatest books is his edition of Strakhov's letters (*Literary Exiles*, 1913) to himself: the footnotes contain passages of unsurpassed genius and originality.

The Revolution of 1917 was a cruel blow to Rozanov. At first he felt the passing enthusiasm he had felt in 1905, but soon he fell into a state of nervous anxiety which lasted till his death. He left Petersburg and settled at Troitsa (the Trinity Monastery near Moscow). He continued writing, but under the new conditions he could make no money out of his books. His last work, *The Apocalypse of the Russian Revolution*, appeared in little pamphlets at Troitsa in a very small number of copies and has become extremely rare.

His last two years were spent in poverty and misery. On his deathbed he became finally reconciled with Christ, and died comforted by the sacraments of the Church on February 5 (N.S.), 1919. So his words (in *Fallen Leaves*) came true:

But of course when I die I shall die *in the Church,* of course I need the Church *incomparably more than I do* literature (don't need that at all), and *our clergy, after all, are dearer to me than all* [classes].

The principal thing in Rozanov was his religion: his naturalistic religion of sex and procreation. It was primarily a religion of marriage and of the family. It was strictly monogamous, and the child's part in it is at least as great as the wife's. Rozanov was fully saturated with a profound piety for the associations of the Russian Church—with its services, its holy images, its poetry, and its clergy. He had an infinitely sympathetic insight into the very essence of Christianity and of its essentially ascetic and puritan ideal. But what was at the bottom of his heart was a religion that included both Christianity and natural religion. It was the primary element of religion—the feeling of a common life with the universe—a *religio*, a *pietas*. Christianity attracted him as a religion and at the same time repelled him as the enemy of another religion—the religion of life. What is particularly original in Rozanov, and what makes him so much akin to Dostoevsky, is his peculiar attitude to morality. He was a profound immoralist, and at the same time he valued above all things sympathy, pity, and kindness. Moral good existed for him only in the form of natural, spontaneous, indestructible *kindness*. He had no use for systems, as he had no use for logic. He was altogether intuitive, and for depth of intuition he has no equals among the writers of the world, not even Dostoevsky. This gift is displayed in every page of his writings, from *The Legend of the Great Inquisitor* to *The Apocalypse of the Russian Revolution*, but most of all where he speaks of religion and of living personalities. The human personality was to him a supreme value, the only thing on a level with religion. And the pages he devotes to the characters of living persons are inimitable. As fair examples of his intuition and his style, I may mention two passages (they are too long to quote)—the last three pages of *A World of Things Indistinct and Undecided*, where he speaks of the difference of the attitude of the Church to the six New Testament sacraments and the only old sacrament—marriage—and the passage on Vladimir Soloviev (from the point of view of style, one of the greatest achievements in Russian prose since Avvakum), characteristically contained in a footnote to one of Strakhov's letters to him (*Literary Exiles*, pp. 141–144).

Rozanov's style is of course, more than any other style, untranslatable. In it, it is the *intonation* that matters. He uses various typographical devices to bring it out—inverted commas and brackets—but the effect is changed and lost in another language: so rich is it in emotional shades and overtones, so saturated with the spirit of Russia, and so peculiarly Russian are the intonations. I can do no more than present a few rude woodcuts of great paintings.

Here is Rozanov on himself and the universe (from a footnote to one of Strakhov's letters; I preserve all the brackets and inverted commas of the original):

There is in me (probably) some enmity against free air and I do not remember myself ever "going out for a walk" or "having an airing" or "having a breath of fresh air." Even in a wood I always tried to get into some nook ("away from other people's eyes" and "away from the beaten track"), that I might lie down and begin sniffing the moss or (better still) some chance mushroom, or gaze at the sky past the tops of the trees. Once as a schoolboy I remember lying down on a bench (in the town park): I screwed myself so fixedly to the stars ("always deeper and deeper," "always further and further") that soon I became only vaguely conscious that I was "a schoolboy" and in "Nizhni"—I began to ask myself, touching the button of my coat: "What's the truth, then? Is it that I am a *schoolboy and buy tobacco at the shop over there,* or is it that this dreadful *impossibility,* schoolboys, etc., tobacco and the rest of it, simply DOES NOT EXIST, and it is only our DREAM, an unhappy dream of erring mankind, and what exists are . . . WHAT? WORLDS, immensities, orbits, eternities!! ETERNITY and I are incompatible, but ETERNITY— I see it, and as for me, *I* am a mere phantom."—And so on, in the same strain.

On his friend Shperk and immortality (from *Fallen Leaves*):

To say that Shperk *is now nowhere in this world,* is impossible. Maybe "the soul's immortality," in some Platonic sense, is an error;

but when it comes to my friends, it cannot possibly be an error.

Not that "the soul of Shperk is immortal," but his little red beard cannot have died, his Byzov (he had a friend of that name) is waiting at the house-door, and he himself is in the tram on his way to my rooms in Pavlovski street. All as it was. As for his soul, whether it is immortal, I neither know nor want to know.

All is immortal. Eternal and living. To the hole in his boot, which neither grows nor is mended since the time it was. This is better than "the immortality of the soul," which is dry and abstract.

I want to come "into the next life" with my pocket handkerchief. I won't have less.

On God and the world order (from *Fallen Leaves*) :

What will I say to God (in the n. w.) about what he sent me to see down here? Will I say the world he made is beautiful? No. What then will I say? G. will see me cry in silence and my face smiling at times. But he will not hear a word from me.

On nationality (from *Uedinennoe*) :

You look at a Russian with a shrewd eye. . . . He looks at you with a shrewd eye. . . . And all is said. And no words wanted. This is just the thing that is impossible with a foreigner.

This last quotation will remind the reader how difficult, how impossible, it is to convey to him the flavour, the taste, the smell of a man like Rozanov. Nor is it, perhaps, after all very desirable (from the Russian patriot's point of view) to make propaganda for him among foreigners. There are people who hate, actively hate, Rozanov, and who think him abominable and disgusting. Strictly Orthodox priests are united in this feeling with men of a very different orthodoxy, like Trotsky. Rozanov is the antipodes of Classicism, of discipline, of everything that is line and will. His genius is feminine; it is naked intuition without a trace of "architecture" in it. It is the apotheosis of "Natural Man," the negation of effort and of discipline. André Suarès has said of Dostoevsky that he presented the scandal of nakedness (*le scandale de la nudité*). But Dostoevsky is quite decently draped in comparison with

Rozanov. And the nakedness of Rozanov is not always beautiful. For all that, Rozanov was the greatest writer of his generation. The Russian genius cannot be gauged without taking him into account, and whatever way they turn out, we must take the responsibility for our great men.

5. SHESTOV

Shestov has some points in common with Rozanov. Both are irrationalists and immoralists. Both value the human personality above all ideas and systems. Both found their first starting-point in Dostoevsky, and later on a kindred spirit in the Old Testament. Both are mystics—but Rozanov is a biological mystic, a mystic of the flesh. Shestov is a pure spiritualist. Rozanov is an irrationalist in practice as well as in theory: he is no logician, and the only arguments he was capable of were emotional and "intuitive" arguments. Shestov fights Reason with her own arms—in his confutation of logic, he has proved himself a consummate logician. Rozanov is deeply rooted in the Russian and "Slavophil" soil, and even in Judaism what attracts him is its soil, its procreative roots. Shestov has no roots in any soil: his thought is international, or rather supra-national, and in this respect more akin to Tolstoy than to Dostoevsky. The real name of Leo Shestòv is Leo Issakovich Schwarzmann. He was born in Kiev in 1866 of a family of wealthy Jewish merchants. He studied for the bar and was attracted towards philosophy and literature only rather late in life. His first book, *Shakespeare and His Critic Brandes*, appeared in 1898; in it he attacked the positivism and rationalism of that greatly overrated Danish critic, in the name of a rather vague idealism which found its hero in the character of Brutus. This book reveals some of Shestov's best literary qualities, but it stands apart from his later work in its attitude to idealism. For war against idealism in all its forms is the principal object of all Shestov's later books, beginning with *The Good in the Teaching of Tolstoy and of Nietzsche* (1900) and *Dostoevsky and Nietzsche: The Philosophy of Tragedy* (1901). These two books form the introduction to

Shestov's work, and contain the whole force of his destructive criticism. These were followed by a book of fragmentary maxims, *The Apotheosis of Soillessness* (1905)—the very inadequate English translation has for title *All Things Are Possible*—and by a series of essays on individual writers (Ibsen, Chekhov, Berdyaev). Then for many years Shestov was silent; he lived abroad, studying the history of philosophy and mysticism. His next work, *Potestas Clavium* (1916), ushers in a new stage of his work in which, without in any way changing the main point of his outlook, he passes from modern individualists to the accepted religious leaders and mystics of the past—Luther, St. Augustine, Plotinus, St. Paul, and the Bible, and discovers in them the same truth he had found in Nietzsche and in Dostoevsky. In 1917 Shestov (to the great disappointment of some of his admirers, who thought that his destructive spirit would sympathize with the destructive work of the Bolsheviks) assumed a distinctly anti-Bolshevik position. He left Russia and has settled in Paris, where he has attracted considerable attention on the part of the intellectual French élite. His last book (*The Night of Gethsemane*, a study of Pascal) first appeared in French.

Shestov is a man of one idea, and in all his books he says the same thing over and over again. The keynote of all his writings is found in the closing lines of *Tolstoy and Nietzsche:* "Good—we now know it from the experience of Nietzsche—is not God. 'Woe to those who live, and know no love better than pity.' Nietzsche has shown us the way. We must seek for that, which is *above* pity, *above* Good. We must seek for God." The identification of Good and Reason with God has ever since Socrates been the foundation-stone of our civilization. To confute this identification is the object of Shestov. He opposes to it the religious experience of the great mystics, revealed to him by Nietzsche and Dostoevsky, and afterwards confirmed by Pascal, by St. Paul, by Plotinus, and in the Old Testament—that God, the supreme and only value, transcends the human standards of morality and logic, and the seeking of this irrational and immoral God is the only thing worth doing. With particular relish Shestov quotes the most paradoxical and pointed statements of this doctrine which he finds in Tertullian and in Luther and in other authoritative authors, and insists on the identity of experience of all the great mystics and on the essential incompatibility of their "biblical" mentality with the Greek mentality. To transcend and reject morality and logic is the only way to approach God. And this is attained only in those moments of insurmountable crisis—of ultimate tragedy—which make a man dead to life. Only when he is thus dead does he become alive to the real reality—God. "The philosophy of tragedy" which reveals to man the real entity, is the only philosophy Shestov has anything to do with. For the idealistic speculations of the accepted masters of philosophy, from Socrates and the Stoics to Spinoza and Kant, he has nothing but contempt and sarcasm. To a superficial observer Shestov has all the appearance of a Nihilist and a Sceptic. And this is to a certain extent true, for though the inner kernel of his philosophy is profoundly religious and pious, it has and can have no practical bearing. The Symbolist's mentality is entirely alien to him— the things of this world are an inferior reality, whch have no relation to the one real reality. They are indifferent, *adiaphora*, and religious standards can in no way be brought down to measure them. Truth to Shestov is a mathematical point of no dimensions, which can have no action in the external world. The external world is as it may be and remains unaffected by it. As soon as Shestov has to do with the world of ordinary experiences, with the conduct of men and the facts of history, his religious immoralism and irrationalism become inapplicable and unnecessary, and he falls back on the most ordinary common sense. It was from the point of view of common sense that he condemned Bolshevism, not from that of his religion. But it must be granted that Shestov's method of writing on philosophical and religious subjects has forged a weapon which is most suitably used in the service of common sense: his style is the best and finest and aptest polemical style ever used in Russian. Of the many readers of Shestov, only a minority are in tune with his central idea; the majority like in him the great ironist, the master

of sarcasm and argument.   Though Socrates and the moralist
Tolstoy (as distinguished from Tolstoy the mystic of *Memoirs
of a Madman* and of *Master and Man*) are his worst enemies
and have suffered more than anyone else from his destructive
criticism, as a writer and a dialectician he proceeds from
Socrates and Tolstoy more than from anyone else.   He uses
the arms of logic and reason with admirable skill to the undoing
of logic and reason.   His prose is at the opposite pole to
Rozanov's, it is the tidiest, the most elegant, the most concentrated, in short, the most classical prose in the whole of
modern Russian literature.

6. OTHER "RELIGIOUS PHILOSOPHERS"

Whether we consider them as thinkers or as writers,
Rozanov and Shestov are intrinsically the most important
figures of the "religious-philosophical" movement of 1900–
1910.   But the main line of development was little affected
by their influence.   It proceeds from Vladimir Soloviev.   His
friends the brothers Troubetzkòy, Prince Serge (1856–1905)
and Prince Eugene (1862–1920), continued his tradition of
political Liberalism that was free from Messianic nationalism,
and rooted in a Catholic Christianity firmly based in philosophical idealism.   Eugene Troubetzkoy was a brilliant political pamphleteer, and his writings may be regarded as the
"voice of conscience" guiding Russian political life.

The most remarkable group of "religious philosophers" who
tried to Christianize politics, were two men who began their
career in the nineties as Marxists, and by a gradual evolution
ultimately came to a more or less strict Orthodoxy.   These
were Sergey Nikolaevich Bulgàkov (b. 1871 in Livny) and
Nikolay Aleksandrovich Berdyàev (b. 1874 in Kiev).   This
evolution from Socialism to Orthodoxy and National Liberalism is typical of a great number of Russian intellectuals between 1900 and 1910.   In its more political aspect, it appears
in the writings of Peter Struve.   Bulgakov and Berdyaev
belong to the history of ideas rather than to that of literature.
They are not powerful literary personalities.   They are largely

responsible (especially Berdyaev) for the heavy and pedantic philosophical jargon which is now used by most modern writers on religious and philosophical subjects and which is so different from the examples of Tolstoy, Shestov, Rozanov, even of Soloviev. Of the two, Bulgakov is by training an economist, and even after he took holy orders (during the war) he occupied the chair of economics at the Crimean University. His theology is closely connected with Soloviev's, and the conception of the Church as a living body occupies in it a central place. His economic training has not remained without its reflection in his theology, and one of his books is on *The Philosophy of Economics.* He is now one of the most prominent intellectual influences in the Russian Church, but some critics consider his teaching Gnostical rather than Orthodox. Of recent years, imitating Soloviev, he has chosen the dialogue as his favourite form (*At the Feast of the Gods,* 1918, has been translated into English), but his dialogues lack the wit and liveliness of *The Three Conversations.*

Berdyaev is not very much better than Bulgakov as a writer of prose, but he has a more original personal temperament, and his writings are more interesting and stimulating apart from their theological and philosophical contents. He is the typical "seeker after God" (*bogoiskatel,* a term very much in vogue twenty years ago); religion to him is a constant quest and evolution. His books form a sort of philosophical diary of his evolution "from Marxism to Idealism" (the title of one of his books) and thence to Orthodox or quasi-Orthodox mysticism. He is full of apocalyptic and eschatological presentiments, and, like Soloviev and Dostoevsky, has a keen sense of the symbolical and supra-human meaning of history. His most interesting book is *The Meaning of Creativeness* (1916), a sort of transposition of Bergsonism in terms of Orthodox Spiritualism. His books written since the Revolution (*The Philosophy of Inequality* and *The New Middle Ages*) are full of a feeling of the end of European civilization. In them, his National Liberalism of ten and fifteen years ago gives way to a violent anti-democratic craving for a new Dark Age. He has become the spokesman of that part of the intellectual genera-

tion which hopes no more for worldly goods and worldly progress for Russia, but lays all its hope in the coming of a new
age of intense religious enthusiasm akin to the days of the
primitive Church.

A more solitary and curious figure is Paul Florénsky.   Before he became a priest, he received a brilliant mathematical
education, and to-day after many years of priesthood and
theological studies he has once more returned to higher mathematics, and lectures at Moscow on *Imaginary Quantities in
Geometry*.   His reputation as a writer and a philosopher is
founded on *The Pillar and Foundation of Truth* (1913),
which, as the sub-title has it, is an *Essay towards an Orthodox
Theodicy*.   Unlike Berdyaev, Florensky's thirst is not for
eternal quest, but for eternal peace and calm; he accepts the
dogmas of Orthodoxy in their most rigid Byzantine form and
adds to this rigidity the rigidity of his own mathematically
trained intellect—which develops into a hard and unbending
scholasticism.   His thought is extraordinarily subtle and
sophisticated: he delights in accepting the most un-modern
interpretations and fulminates against heresy with the fire of
a mediæval Schoolman.   And yet the moment he gives free
rein to his own speculative thought, it becomes apparent that
the core of his thought is quite unorthodox.   The doctrine
of St. Sophia, the feminine hypostasis of the Deity, is dearer
to him than the truly Orthodox dogmas of the Church.   Under
the rich splendour of his style, erudition, and dialectic, there
is unmistakably apparent a soul full of strife, pride, and
boundless spiritual desire.   The most memorable passages in
his book are those in which he describes the racking torments
of doubt, which he identifies with the torments of hell.   Florensky is, after all, an æsthete for whom the Orthodox dogma is
a beautiful intellectual world, full of adventure and danger.
He accepts it to quell the torments of his doubt, but he handles
it as an artist would handle some rich and sumptuous material.
His style is precious and ornate, and the whole book is
strangely reminiscent of certain English writings of the seventeenth century, with their precious and ornate diction,
their rigid and hard scholasticism, and the constant feeling

of unknown forces of intellectual passion burning under the austere and repelling surface.

Though a return to Orthodoxy was the ultimate form of the intellectual evolution of the early twentieth century, not all the "seekers after God" reached it. Some of them stopped at various intermediate stages on the march away from agnosticism and positivism. Of these, one of the most significant is Michael Osipovich Gershenzòn (b. 1869), a Jew, whose biographical and historical studies have contributed so much to our acquaintance with the Russian Idealists of the thirties and the forties of the nineteenth century. His metaphysics is closely akin to that of the Symbolists: it is a mysticism of impersonal forces which he has associated with the dynamic philosophy of Heraclitus the Dark. His historical studies have in late years led him to Pushkin. They are contained in *The Wisdom of Pushkin* (1918), where he reveals both a wonderfully acute insight into certain details of Pushkinian problems and an equally remarkable lack of sympathy with the essential core of the great poet's personality. Gershenzon was one of those Russian intellectuals who welcomed the Communist Revolution as a great devastating storm which would free the modern soul from the oppressive scales of excessive culture and knowledge, and open the way towards a "naked man on the naked earth." This new Rousseauist nihilism of Gershenzon has found a poignantly sincere expression in his part of that remarkable dialogue of letters in which he took part with Vyacheslav Ivanov when the two were lying in 1920 in a nursing-home near Moscow (see Chapter V, 7).

7. "THE LANDMARKS" AND AFTER

In 1909 a group of Liberal intellectuals published a book containing essays by seven authors and entitled *The Landmarks*. It included, among others, contributions by Bulgakov, Berdyaev, Gershenzon, and Peter Struve. The book was an indictment of the whole spirit of the Russian *intelligentsia*: the *intelligentsia* was denounced as anti-religious, anti-philosophical, anti-statesmanlike, and anti-national. *The*

Landmarks laid the foundation of a new National Liberalism which rapidly spread among the more cultured strata of the *intelligentsia* and contributed very much towards the kindling of a patriotic war-spirit in 1914 and towards the success of the White Army movement in 1918. The philosophical side of the movement is best reflected in the work of Bulgakov and Berdyaev; its political aspect found its principal reflection in Peter Struve (see Interchapter I), for more than twenty years a central figure in the evolution of the *intelligentsia* mind. A leader in the nineties of "legal" Marxism, in 1903–1904 of revolutionary Liberalism, he became after 1905 the head of that section of the Liberal *intelligentsia* which was primarily patriotic and Russian and tended towards an acceptance of the imperialism that had been the tradition of imperial Russia since Peter the Great, rejecting at the same time the decadent and exclusive nationalism of the successors of Alexander II. After 1917 he has been the principal political brain of anti-Bolshevism, and is now the most significant political writer among the *émigrés*. Saturated with a deep feeling and profound understanding of Russian history, he is certainly one of the most brilliant political writers of our times, and his short articles are sometimes masterpieces of concentrated thought and direct expression. Though, being a live and strong political force, he is intensely hated by large sections of public opinion, including even his nearest neighbours to the left (Milyukov and the old-fashioned positivist Radicals), when party feeling grows less acute he will be recognized as one of the classics of Russian political thought and political literature.

Struve's influence on political and historical thought has been great. Some of the writers who proceed from him will find a place in the next interchapter. Here I will only mention Dmitri Vasilievich Bóldyrev, a writer of very great promise, who died in 1920 in Siberia in a Bolshevik prison. Those who knew him consider him a man of exceptional moral and spiritual purity. He was a philosopher by training, and his *opus magnum* was to have been a work on psychology. It remained unfinished. As a writer he has to be remembered almost exclusively for the few articles he published in 1917 in Struve's *Russian Freedom* and directed against the *défaitisme* of the Socialists. In them he reveals a quite exceptional polemical gift and a literary temperament of great originality. His pungent, racy, pointed, and vivid style places him in the very front rank of Russian prose-writers.

CHAPTER V

1. THE SYMBOLISTS

THE complex and many-sided movement of ideas described in the preceding chapter is closely connected with the movement in imaginative literature known as Symbolism. Russian Symbolism is part of the general cultural upheaval which changed the face of Russian civilization between 1890 and 1910. It was at once an æsthetic and a mystical movement: it raised the level of poetical craftsmanship, and it was united by a mystical attitude towards the world, which is expressed in the very name of Symbolism. The name was, of course, borrowed from the French school of that name. But the importance of French influence must not be exaggerated. Only very few of the Russian Symbolists had any considerable first-hand acquaintance with the work of their French godfathers, and Edgar Allan Poe had certainly a wider and deeper influence than any single French poet. But the principal difference between French and Russian Symbolism was that while, for the French, Symbolism was merely a new form of poetical expression, the Russians made it also a philosophy. They actually saw the universe as a system of symbols. Everything was significant to them not by itself only, but as the reflection of something else. Baudelaire's famous sonnet *Correspondances* (where occur the words *"des forêts de symboles"*) was used as the completest expression of this metaphysical attitude, and the line *"les parfums, les couleurs et les sons se répondent"* became a favourite slogan· Another favourite text were two lines from the last scene of *Faust:*

Alles Vergängliche
Ist nur ein Gleichniss.
181

This vision of the world as "a forest of symbols" is an essential feature in the work of every Russian Symbolist, and gives the whole school a distinctly metaphysical and mystic character. The only difference between the individual poets is the importance they attached to this mystical philosophy: to some, like Bryusov, Symbolism was primarily a form of art, and the "forest of symbols" was only the material of which to build. But others, and among them the most original and characteristic poets of the school—Ivanov, Blok, and Bely— wanted to make Symbolism, above all, a metaphysical and mystical philosophy, and poetry subservient to the higher ends of "theurgy." This difference of interpretation became especially acute about 1910 and was one of the causes which led to the dissolution of the unity of the school.

There is much variety in the style of the individual Symbolists, but they have also much in common. First of all, they are always intensely serious and solemn. Whatever the subject-matter of the Russian Symbolist, he always treats it *sub specie æternitatis*. The poet appears before the profane as the priest of an esoteric cult. All his life is ritualized. In Sologub and in Blok this ritual solemnity is relieved by a keen and bitter feeling of "metaphysical irony," but only in Bely does it give way to a genuine and irrepressible gift of humour. Solemnity produces a partiality for "big" words: "mystery" and "abyss," familiar to us already in Merezhkovsky, are among the most common in the Symbolist vocabulary. Another feature common to all the Symbolist poets is the great stress laid on the emotional value of mere sounds. Like Mallarmé, they tried to bring the art of poetry nearer to the twin art of music. In their writings the logical value of words is partly obliterated, and words, and especially epithets, are used not so much for their exact meaning as for the emotional value of their form and sound: they cease to be signs, and become, to use the phrase of a Russian critic, "phonetic gestures." This partial subordination of sense to sound, together with the symbolical use of words which gives every word and image so many meanings, combined to produce the general impression of obscurity which for a long time the general public considered the inevitable characteristic of "decadent" poetry.

In its initial stages Symbolism was distinctly Western, for its principal task of raising the standards of poetical workmanship and of introducing new forms of poetical expression was most easily achieved by learning from foreign example. This "foreign" strain for ever remained one of the constituent elements of Symbolism, but it had also a "Slavophil" soul. And the general trend of its evolution was from foreign models back to national tradition. Dostoevsky was a principal influence in this evolution: the Symbolists had a full share in the general Dostoevskianism of the time. Almost every Symbolist was more or less powerfully affected by the individualism and tragic conception of life of the great novelist. But, apart from this, the Symbolists played the same part in the "rediscovery" and revaluation of Russian literature as Diaghilev and Benois in that of Russian art. They revived the work of many forgotten, or half-forgotten, or undervalued writers, but they also introduced fresh blood into the understanding of the national classics. They freed them from the accumulated varnish of text-book criticism and *intelligentsia* commonplace, and though they sometimes obscured them by the lacquer of their own mystical interpretation, they did splendid work in presenting the past of Russian literature in a new and fresh aspect.

Apart from everything else, in spite of their limitations and mannerisms, the Symbolists combined great talent with conscious craftsmanship, and this makes their place so big in Russian literary history. One may dislike their style, but one cannot fail to recognize that they revived Russian poetry from a hopeless state of prostration, and that their age was a second golden age of verse inferior only to the first golden age of Russian poetry—the age of Pushkin.

The first faint symptoms of the new movement appeared about 1890 in the work of the men who had begun as common-and-garden "civic" poets—Minsky and Merezhkovsky. But apart from a greater interest in metaphysical problems, a taste for metaphor, and (in the case of Merezhkovsky) a slightly higher level of technique, this poetry differs both from the general run of the "eighties" poets and has little intrinsic value. The real beginners were Balmont and Bryusov, who were for many years the battering-rams of the new movement against the skulls of the Philistine, and when the battle was won were recognized by the same Philistine as the greatest poets of their age. They both made their first appearance in the same year—Balmont's *Under Northern Skies*, and *The Russian Symbolists*, a miscellany containing the first poems of Bryusov, both appeared in 1894, the last year of Alexander III's reign.

2. BALMONT

Constantine Dmitrievich Balmònt was born in 1867, on his father's estate not far from Ivanovo-Voznesensk, the "Russian Manchester." He believes his family to be of Scottish extraction. He was expelled from school on political grounds, and the same thing happened to him when he went to Moscow University. But he succeeded in taking a degree at the College of Law at Yaroslav. There he printed in 1890 a first book of verses, which, however, is quite insignificant and attracted no attention. His literary career begins in earnest with the publication in 1894 of *Under Northern Skies*. In the nineties Balmont was considered the most promising of "decadent" poets and was given a good reception by those magazines which piqued themselves on being reasonably modern. He continued publishing books of poetry, of which *Buildings on Fire* (1900) and *Let Us Be as the Sun* (1903) contain his best poems. After that commenced a precipitous decline of his talent, and though he has ever since published about a volume a year, all those that appeared after 1905 are worthless. In the nineties he had forgotten his schoolboyish revolutionism and was notorious (like the other Symbolists) for his "uncivic" attitude, but in 1905 he joined the S.D. party and published *Songs of an Avenger*, a collection of remarkably crude and violent party verse. In 1917, however, he took a firmly anti-Bolshevik position, and eventually emigrated. He now lives in France. In the course of his life he has travelled much and seen many exotic countries, including Mexico and the South Sea Islands.

Balmont's work is very voluminous. But by far the greater part of it may be swept aside as quite worthless. This part will include all his original verse since 1905, most of his numerous translations (the complete metrical version of Shelley is especially bad; on the contrary, his translations of Edgar Allan Poe are quite acceptable), and all his prose without exception, which is the most insipid, turgid, and meaningless prose in the language. In so far as a place is reserved for him in the pantheon of genuine poets, he will be remembered for the six books of verse published from 1894 to 1904. Even in these books he is very uneven, for though he had at that time a genuine gift of song, he was always incapable of *working* at his verse, he could only sing like a bird in the bush. But he had a keen sense of form, and his poetry is pre-eminently formal; sound and tune are the most important things in his verse. In the nineties and early 1900's, he struck the ear of the public with a richness of rhythm and vocal design which seemed even excessive, disconcerting, and, to the stauncher of the Radical puritans, wicked. This pageant of sound was a new thing in Russian poetry; its elements are borrowed (without any slavish imitation) from Edgar Allan Poe and from the Shelley who wrote *The Cloud*, *The Indian Serenade*, and *To Night*. Only Balmont is less precise and mathematical than Poe and infinitely less subtle than Shelley. These achievements went to his head, and *Let Us Be as the Sun* is full of assertions of this kind: "Who is equal to me in the power of song? No one! No one!" and "I am the refinement of Russian speech." These immodesties are not entirely unfounded, for in this peculiar quality Balmont has no rival among Russian poets. But of refinement there is precisely very little in his verse. It is curiously devoid of the "finer touch" and of the finer shades. He has a sufficiently wide scale of emotion to express, from the brave *fortissimo* of the most characteristic poems of the last-named book to the sweet, subdued undertone of *Wayside Grasses* or *Belladonna*, but in every single case the expression is simple, monotonous, all in one note. Another serious shortcoming, which he shares with Bryusov, and which is explained by the necessarily Western character of his poetry, is his complete lack of feeling for the Russian language. His verse has a foreign appearance. Even at its best, it sounds like a translation. A certain number of his poems have been translated into English (he is easy to translate). Mr. P. Selver's versions in *Modern Russian Poets* are especially good. No better idea can be had of his style than from one of these, a version of the well-known, very familiar (to Russians, almost nauseously familiar) *Reeds*. The purely "phonetic" character of his style has been excellently conveyed by Mr. Selver.

The Reeds

When midnight has come on the desolate slough,
Scarce heard are the reeds, so softly they sough.
Of what do they whisper and talk to and fro?
For what are the flamelets amongst them aglow?
They shimmer, they glimmer, and once more they wane,
Then the wandering light is enkindled again.
When midnight has come, then the reeds are aquake,
They harbour the toad and the hiss of the snake.
In the slough is aquiver a perishing gaze:
'Tis the purple-hued moon that forlornly decays.
There is odour of slime. And the soddenness crawls.
The marsh will allure and engulf as it mauls.
"But whom? And for what," say the reeds to and fro,
"For what are the flamelets amongst us aglow?"
But the moon that forlornly and mutely decays
Cannot tell. But yet lower she settles her gaze.
'Tis the sigh of a perishing spirit that now
The reeds softly raise as they mournfully sough.

3. BRYUSOV (1873–1924)

Valery Yakovlevich Bryùsov was born in 1873, in a merchant family. He received a good education and in later life, by studious reading and constant work, he became perhaps the most widely informed man of his generation. In 1894, together with A. L. Miropolsky, he published *Russian Symbolists*, which had the success of a scandal. This and the books that followed it were for a whole decade the favourite laughing-stock of the whole press. Bryusov's name became the synonym of a literary mountebank, and while other Symbolists, like Balmont, Sologub, and Hippius, were more or less welcome guests in the literary press, Bryusov was forbidden its doors until at least 1905. Bryusov hardly answered to his first reputation: far from being the mountebank he was imagined to be, he is one of the most solemn and dead-serious figures in the whole of Russian literature. But his early poetry was so unlike the usual run of Russian magazine verse that the blockheads of criticism could account for it only as insolent tomfoolery. In reality it is only a rather youthful, immature imitation of the French poets of the day. For many years every new book by Bryusov was received with indignation or ridicule. But Bryusov persevered. His style matured. His following grew. By 1903 he was the recognized head of a numerous and energetic literary school; by 1906 his school had won its struggle; Symbolism was recognized as the whole of Russian poetry, and Bryusov as the first Russian poet. *Stephanos*, which appeared in 1906 at the height of the revolutionary excitement, was greeted with enthusiasm by the same critics who had ridiculed his early work. Its success is perhaps the most significant date in the history of the Symbolist march toward supremacy.

In 1900 Bryusov became the *de facto* head of a publishing-business which united the forces of the new movement. In 1904 it started a review, *Vesy* (*The Scales*), which lasted till 1909 and was without doubt the most civilized and European publication of its time. From 1900 to 1906 Bryusov was the head of a compact and vigorous party on its march to success; after 1906 his position became even more influential. But his talent began to decline. *All My Melodies* (1909) marked no progress as compared with *Stephanos;* the books that followed betrayed a steady and accelerating decline. Ever since the nineties Bryusov has worked with wonderful energy in the most various literary fields; in point of volume, his original poetry is only a small part of his whole output: he translated poetry with signal success; he wrote prose stories and plays; he reviewed almost every book of new verse; he edited classics; he worked in the archives, preparing material for the lives of Pushkin, Tyutchev, and others; he read enormously and was all the time the *de facto* editor of a magazine. At the same time he was by no means an ascetic—his abundant love poetry has a solid foundation in fact, and he explored the "artificial paradises" of opium and cocaine. This never impaired his working capacity. A fair example of this is his work on Armenian poetry; in 1915 a committee of Armenian patriots asked Bryusov to edit a selection from the Armenian poets in Russian. In less than a year he learned the language, read all there was to read of books on the subject, and did the greater part of the translations for the enormous quarto volume *Armenian Poetry*, which appeared in 1916. The book is a wonderful monument of human industry and the best there is of its kind.

Bryusov was always essentially unpolitical. His attitude to politics was purely æsthetic. It is well expressed in his lines (written in 1905): "Beautiful in the splendour of his power is the Oriental King Assarhaddon, and beautiful the ocean of a people's wrath beating to pieces a tottering throne. But hateful—are half-measures."

Till 1917 he took no part in politics, but after the Bolshevik triumph he became a Communist. This adhesion was caused not by any political conviction, but rather, on the contrary, by the lack in him of those political and moral inhibitions which prevented more "civic-minded" men from taking that step. Another reason may have been the feeling that he had lost touch with the times, that he was no longer a leader, and the hope once more to become advanced and modern by joining the most advanced of political parties. Again the Revolution of 1917 answered very well to his æsthetic ideal of an "ocean of a people's wrath," and he distinctly sympathized with the mechanical schemes of Lenin.

He received at first a sinecure, then a more responsible post at the head of the censorship, but failed in the long run to adapt himself to the orthodox Communists, and was replaced

by a more trustworthy party man (the novelist Serafimovich).
He also failed to gain the recognition of the "left front" of
poets whose favour he had courted ever since the first appearance of Futurism. His last years were lonely and he suffered
acutely from being out of the movement. His only consolation
was his work with the young proletarian poets, to whom he
gave regular instruction in the art of poetry. He died in
October, 1924, only fifty-one years old, but having outlived
by about fifteen years the high-water mark of his fame.

Bryusov's poetry shares with Balmont's a general "foreign"
air, the result of a more intimate connexion with French and
Latin than with Russian poetical tradition. It has also in
common with Balmont's a certain lack of refinement, of the
"finer touch" and the finer shades. At its best it is gorgeous—
all gold and purple—at its worst, gaudy. Like that of most
Russian Symbolists, it is continuously solemn and hieratic,
and big words are his stock material. In his early poetry
(1894–1896) he tried to naturalize in Russia the "singing"
accent of Verlaine and the early French Symbolists, and to
revive and modernize the "melodies" of Fet. But, on the
whole, Bryusov is not a "musical" poet, though, like all the
Russian Symbolists, he often uses his words as emotional
gestures rather than as signs with a precise meaning. Though
his verse is saturated with the culture of ages, Bryusov is not
a "philosophical" or thinking poet. At one time, under the
influence of Ivan Konevskoy, he devoted himself to writing
metaphysical poetry; some of it makes excellent rhetoric, but
there is very little philosophy in it, only a succession of
pathetic exclamations and juxtapositions. Bryusov's diction
is terser and more compact than Balmont's, and at times he
achieves excellent feats of poetical compression and expressiveness, but it lacks precision, and his words, often splendid, are
never "curiously felicitous." His favourite subjects are meditations on the past and future of humanity, the representation
of carnal love as a mystical ritual, and—in a favourite catchword of twenty years ago—the "mysticism of every day,"
that is to say, evocations of the modern big towns as a forest
of mysteries and symbols. His best work is contained in

Urbi et Orbi (1903) and *Stephanos* (1906). The latter includes *Eternal Truth of Idols*, a series of magnificent variations of the eternal subjects of the Greek fable. Such poems as *Achilles at the Altar* (awaiting his fatal betrothal with Polyxene), *Orpheus and Eurydice*, and *Theseus to Ariadne* are the best achievement of the "classical" aspect of Russian Symbolism, which aimed at hieratic majesty and symbolical pregnancy.

Bryusov's prose is, on the whole, of a piece with his verse: it is solemn, hieratic, and academic. Its subjects are the same—pictures of the past and future, and the mysterious "abysses" of love, very often in its most perverse and abnormal aspects. Like his verse, it has a distinctly "translated" air. Bryusov felt this and often modelled it according to some definite foreign model of the past ages. One of his best short stories, *In an Underground Prison*, is in the style of a *novella* of the Italian Renaissance. His best novel, *The Fire Angel* (1907), is the narrative of a German mercenary of the age of Luther. This helped to save his prose from the dangers of "poeticalness" and of impressionism. On the whole, it is straightforward and manly, and free from mannerisms. The subject-matter and the construction of his stories were much influenced by Edgar Allan Poe. Both the detailed and documented presentation of the future of civilization in *The Republic of the South Cross*, and the cold-blooded study of pathological states of mind in a story like *Now That I Am Again Awake*, bear the unmistakable impress of the great Southerner. There is coldness and cruelty in all Bryusov's prose, no sympathy, no pity, only a cold flame of sensual exaltation, and a desire to penetrate into the farthest recesses of human perversity. But Bryusov is no psychologist, and his visions of sensuality and of cruelty are only pageants of loud colour. His principal work in prose is *The Fire Angel*, which is perhaps the best Russian novel on a foreign subject. The story turns on witchcraft and the trial of a witch. Dr. Faustus appears, and Agrippa of Nettesheim. It is saturated with a genuine feeling for the epoch, and is as full of erudition as any of Merezhkovsky's novels, but it is free from that writer's puerile sophistications, and as a narrative it is incomparably better. In fact it is a very good and ably constructed romance. The *Lanzknecht's* leisurely manner of narrating the thrilling and mysterious events of which he was a witness, only adds to the tension of the reader's interest. Bryusov's second novel, *The Altar of Victory* (1913), a romance of fourth-century Rome, marks a definite decline: the book is long and tedious, and lacks every creative element.

4. METAPHYSICAL POETS: ZINAIDA HIPPIUS

Bryusov and Balmont were the Westernizers, the miniature "Peter the Greats," of Russian Symbolism. Their work is not philosophical or intimate, it is loud and rhetorical. Both these poets sought to find a new language for the expression of "great poetry." Both of them were æsthetes and their ideal of beauty was sufficiently near to the popular idea for them eventually to become popular poets. Other poets appeared who may be called the Slavophils of Symbolism. For them the principal thing was not to make things of beauty, but to grasp the meaning of things. They brought with them an intense will to know, and to make their poetry its instrument. They did not seek for striking and eloquent expression, but tried to make their language adequate to their often complicated and abstruse ideas. They may be termed metaphysical poets.

Such was Ivan Konevskòy (1877–1901—pseud. of I. I. Oraeus, a name of Swedish origin), a young man of extraordinary promise and powerful personal attraction, who was drowned at twenty-four when bathing in a river. He was a mystical pantheist, with a passionate desire to grasp and comprehend the universe in all its multiplicity. He was on the way towards creating a vigorous and terse manner of expression which would be adequate to all the complexity of his ideas. He used to say that "poetry must be a bit *rugged.*" His is decidedly so, but it is the ruggedness of Michael Angelo struggling with the resistant marble. He had a wonderfully keen sense of the value of Russian words, which appeared to him in their naked aspect, stripped of their literary associations. In this respect he was a precursor of Khlebnikov. There is no banality and no cheap prettiness in his poetry. His best poems are powerful evocations of Nature—of the forest (*The Wilderness*), of rain (*A Hymn to Rain*), of waterfalls (*Eruptions of Waters*), and of wind (*A Vision of Struggle*).

Another remarkable man of the period was Alexander Mikhaylovich Dobrolyùbov. Born in 1876, he appeared in the modernist coterie of the nineties, producing the impression of a madman on most, of a saint on a few. He published two little pamphlets of verse, and disappeared. He went "into the people," where he became the founder of a mystical and anarchist sect. He became so completely assimilated to the peasants that when he came to Yasnaya Polyana, Tolstoy, after a two hours' talk with him, was firmly convinced he had been talking to a genuine peasant and refused to believe that he was a "decadent" poet. In 1905 Bryusov published a book of mystical writings by Dobrolyubov (*From the Book Invisible*). But Dobrolyubov himself disappeared and has not been heard from since. He may be still alive, wandering homelessly over Russia. His early poetry is aggressively original and obscure, but it is the obscurity of a man struggling to express new and unexpressed feelings in a new form, like Konevskoy's. His poetry is singularly free from banality and prettiness. *From the Book Invisible* consists of fragmentary notations in prose of his spiritual states, especially of his communion with Nature. The prose is interspersed with poems of extraordinary freshness and originality—mystical, biblical, and nature hymns which proceed to a certain extent from the hymns of Russian Protestant sects, but have in them the nervous throb of life of an intensely personal poet.

The most remarkable of these early metaphysical Symbolists is Zinaida Hippius. Like Konevskoy and Dobrolyubov, she avoids rhetoric and prettiness. She considers her matter more important than her manner, and she works at her form only to make it more flexible and adequate to the expression of her ideas. She is a Slavophil also, inasmuch as she proceeds

not from any French example, but from the Russian traditions—from Baratynsky, Tyutchev, and Dostoevsky. Zinaida
Nikolaevna Hippius (b. 1867), who is better known in letters
by this, her maiden name, is the wife of D. S. Merezhkovsky, and
what it is necessary to know of her life has been told in a preceding chapter. Though almost unknown abroad, she is regarded by all competent Russians as a more original and
significant writer than her somewhat overrated husband. Her
activity is almost as many-sided as his; she has written short
stories and longer novels, plays, critical and political articles—
and poetry. The most salient feature in all her writings is
intellectual power and wit, things rare in a woman. In fact
there is very little that is feminine in Mme. Hippius, except
a tendency to be over-subtle and a certain wilfulness—the ca-
priciousness of a brilliant and spoilt coquette. This last
quality gives a peculiarly piquant flavour to her work, which
is, on the whole, intense and serious. Like Dostoevsky, she
"feels ideas" as living entities, and all her literary life is a life
"among ideas." Her imaginative prose is voluminous—but
inferior in quality to her verse. It consists of several volumes
of short stories, two longer novels, and one or two plays.
All these are with a "purpose," to give expression to some idea
or to some subtle psychological observation. The ideas are
the real characters in her stories, but she does not possess
Dostoevsky's power of giving them an individual and complete
existence. Her characters are abstractions. Her most ambitious works, the two novels *The Devil's Doll* (1911) and
Roman-Tsarevich (1914), are weakly offshoots of a great
trunk—Dostoevsky's *The Possessed;* they are mystical studies
in political psychology. A fair example of her manner may
be had in her play *The Green Ring* (1914), which is her only
work available in English.

Her poetry is much more important. Some of it is also
abstract and merely intellectual. But from the very beginning
she made her verse a wonderfully refined and well-tempered instrument for the expression of her thought. She went on re-
fining it, and making it more obedient to every twist and turn
of her subtle musings. Like Dostoevsky's people, Mme. Hip-

pius oscillates between the two poles of spirituality and earth-liness, between burning faith and apathetic scepticism, and it cannot be denied that her sceptical and nihilistic moods have found more memorable expression than her moments of faith. She has an intensely acute feeling of the "stickiness," of the slime and ooze, of everyday life, and feels her most intimate self in thrall to it. Mr. Selver has translated what is perhaps her most characteristic poem in this order of ideas (*Psyche*). In *Crime and Punishment*, Svidrigailov wonders if eternity is not but a "Russian bath-house with cobwebs in every corner." Mme. Hippius has taken up the idea and perhaps her best poems are variations of this theme. She has created for them a sort of quaint mythology, of filthy, "sticky," and quite mor-bidly attractive little demons. Here is an example of this kind of poems. I must apologize for my prose translation. In the original the effect is greatly enhanced by the languid drawling metre. It is called *What Next?*

Angels do not converse with me.

A dark little earth-spirit comes to me.
He is fond of sweet things, modest and big-eyed.
But what of that, that he is dark?
Are we so very much better?

Shyly the earth-spirit crawls up.

I question him on the hour of death.
My tiny one, though modest, knows things.
He knows all about these things.
What, I ask him, do you know about us?

What manner of thing is the hour of death?

The dark creature sucks with zest a caramel.
He whispers joyfully: All of them have lived.
The hour of death came—and they were crushed.
They just came and squeaked—and there was an end of it.

Just hand me another caramel.

You were born an earthworm.
You won't be left alone long on the path.

You may crawl about, and then you will be squashed.
Every one of you, in the hour of death, will ooze out

Like a worm on the path, trodden on by a boot.

There is a variety of boots.
But the way they squash is very much the same always,
And your case will not be different.
You won't escape one foot or another.

There is a variety of boots in the world.

.   .   .   .

In silence I understood all about the hour of death.
I fondle my guest as if he were my own,
I give him sweets and question him again:
"I see you know a lot about us.

I have understood all that, about the hour of death,

But when I am squashed—what next?
Tell me, do!   Take another caramel.
Suck it, my little dead baby."
But he did not take one.   He looked askance at me:

"I'd rather not tell you what next."

In 1905 Zinaida Hippius, like her husband, became an ardent revolutionary.   Since then she has written much political verse, which is certainly the best of its kind, unrhetorical, unexpected, fresh, and often biting.   She excels in sarcasm: a splendid example is *Petrograd*, a satire on the renaming of St. Petersburg.   In 1917, like Merezhkovsky, she took a violently anti-Bolshevik attitude.   Her later political verse is often as good as the earlier.   But in her recent prose writings she does not show up very attractively.   Her *Petersburg Diary*, describing life in 1918–1919, is inspired by spiteful hatred rather than by noble indignation.   However, her prose must not be judged by such examples.   She is a brilliant literary critic, the master of a wonderfully flexible, expressive, and unconventional style (her critiques appeared over the signature of Anton Krayni—Anton Extremist).   Her judgment is swift and sure, and her sarcasm had a glorious time of it when she dealt with the swollen reputations of fifteen and twenty years ago.   Her criticism is frankly subjective, almost capricious, and is more valuable for its manner than for its matter.   She has recently published—a sign of approaching age—interesting fragments of reminiscences of literary life.

5. SOLOGUB

All the writers hitherto mentioned in this chapter came from civilized upper-middle-class families of one of the two capitals; but the greatest and most refined poet of the first generation of Symbolists rose from the lower orders, and his strange genius grew under the most unpropitious circumstances. Fedor Sologùb, whose real name is Fedor Kuzmich Tetérnikov, was born in Petersburg in 1863.   His father was a shoemaker, and when he died his mother became a domestic servant.   With the help of her employer, Sologub received a comparatively good education at a "teachers' institute."   On terminating his studies, he got an appointment as schoolmaster in a small out-of-the-way provincial town.   In time he was made district inspector of elementary schools, and at last, in the nineties, was transferred to Petersburg.   Only after the great success of his famous novel *Melki Bes* was he able to leave his pedagogical work and rely on his literary income.   Like the other Symbolists, he was fundamentally unpolitical, and though in 1905 he took up a distinctly revolutionary attitude, he remained coldly aloof in 1917 and since.   In 1921 he lost his wife, who was known in literature as Anastasia Chebotarevsky, under tragical and mysterious circumstances, but apart from this there is little else to be divulged of Sologub's personal life, and his biography is the history of his work.

He began writing early in the eighties, but until about ten years later did not come into contact with the world of letters. His first books appeared in 1896, when he published three at once—a volume of verse, a volume of short stories, and a novel, *Bad Dreams*, at which he had worked for more than ten years. His next book of verse and next book of short stories appeared

only in 1904. His great novel *Melki Bes*, at which he had
worked from 1892 to 1902, could not find a publisher for several years. It began appearing in instalments in a magazine
in 1905, but the magazine came to an end. Only in 1907 was
it at last published in book form, and met with an enormous
success. *Melki Bes* brought Sologub universal recognition and
an all-Russian reputation. But his later work, in which he
gave freer rein to his idiosyncrasies, did not meet with the same
success, and after 1910 people began to discern in him signs
of diminishing power. *The Created Legend* (1908–1912), a
remarkable and strangely original book, met with an indifferent
reception. His last novel, *The Charmer of Snakes*, is decidedly weak, but his poetry, the output of which continues
steadily and unceasingly, is always on the same high level,
though its relative monotony will hardly satisfy the lover of
novelties and sensations.

Two aspects of Sologub's work must be distinguished, for
they are not necessarily inseparable, nor do they seem to be
interdependent: his Manichæan Idealism, and the peculiar
"complex" which is the result of a perverse and long-suppressed
libido. There can be no doubt that many of his writings,
especially in his later period, have no other *raison d'être* than
to satisfy, by exteriorizing it, this "complex." It is not for
the literary historian, but rather for the specially trained
psychoanalyst, to study it in detail. Delight in cruelty and
in the humiliation of beauty are among its prominent features.
A minor but ever recurrent detail is the "obsession" of *bare
feet*. A heroine who walks barefoot is like his sign-manual in
almost every one of Sologub's novels and short stories. His
Manichæan philosophy, on the contrary, is purely idealistic
in the Platonic sense of the word. There is a world of Good,
which is that of Unity, Calm, and Beauty, and a world of Evil,
which is that of Diversity, Desire, and Vulgarity. This world
of ours is a creation of Evil. Only inside oneself can one find
the other world of Unity and Calm. To free oneself from the
evil fetters of matter and to become a self-satisfied deity is the
aim of man. But man projects into the outer world his dreams
of heaven—and this produces the essential "romantic" irony

of life.   Sologub symbolizes this irony in two names borrowed from *Don Quixote*—Dulcinea and Aldonsa.   What we believe to be the ideal Dulcinea, turns out in fact to be the vulgar Aldonsa.   Matter and desire are the main expression of evil, and the only incarnation of the higher world of ideals in real life is Beauty, the ideal beauty of the nude human figure.   This is the point of meeting of Sologub's idealism and of his sensuality.   His attitude towards fleshly beauty is always twofold— it is at once platonically ideal and perversely sensual.   The flavour of Sologub's sensuality is so repellent to many readers that it becomes an insurmountable obstacle to the enjoyment of his work.   But even apart from this perversity his philosophy itself inclines towards a nihilism akin to Satanism. Peace and Beauty become identified with Death, and the sun, the source of all life and activity, becomes the symbol of the evil power.   And in his attitude to our existing religion—he takes a course opposite to that of his mediæval predecessors the Albigenses—he identifies God with the evil creator of the evil world—and Satan becomes the king of the cool and calm realm of beauty and death.

Sologub's poetry developed along different lines from that of the other Symbolists.   His vocabulary, his diction, and his images are closely akin to those of the eclectic poetry of the "Victorians."   His metres are simple and ordinary, but refined to the utmost degree of perfection.   His vocabulary is almost as small as Racine's, but he uses it with almost equal precision and felicity.   He is a Symbolist in that his words are *symbols*, with a double meaning, and are used in their secondary, not in their ordinary sense.   But the completeness of his philosophy allows him to use them with an exactness that is almost classical.   This, however, refers only to that part of his poetry which reflects his ideal heaven, or his yearning for it.   There is another series of poems which are, as his *Inferno*, dark and cruel evocations of the evil diversity of the world, and in them his language becomes cruder and richer and more racy.   This *Inferno* includes a curious cycle of poems, *Masks of Other Existences*—reminiscences of the various forms his soul has assumed in its previous incarnations.   One of these is the lament of a dog whining at the moon; it is certainly one of his best and most original poems. As for his idealistic lyrics, which are, after all, his greatest achievement, it is useless, except one be a master of English verse, to attempt any translation of them. Their beauty is classical; it depends on the imponderables of rhythm and meaning. As in all classic poetry, the poet's silences are as important as his words, that which is left unsaid as that which he says. It is the most refined and most delicate of all modern Russian poetry.

Although his verse is the most perfect and rarest flower of Sologub's genius, his fame at home, and especially abroad, is based on his novels rather than on his poetry. The first of these, *Bad Dreams*, is autobiographical and lyrical. The hero, Login, a schoolmaster in an out-of-the-way provincial town, has the same perverse obsessions and the same ideal visions as haunt Sologub's own poetry. The novel is the history of the man capable of reaching the ideal, in the thick of a world of vulgarity, cruelty, selfishness, stupidity, and lewdness. Russian provincial society is portrayed with incisive cruelty, a cruelty reminiscent of Gogol. But it is not realism in the good old Russian sense of the word, for it is all meant as a symbol of more than Russian vastness. Sologub's second novel, *Melki Bes* (the English rendering of the name, *The Little Demon*, is inadequate; the French title, *Le Démon Mesquin*, is better), is the most famous of all his writings, and it may be recognized as the most perfect Russian novel since the death of Dostoevsky. Like *Bad Dreams*, it is apparently realistic, but internally symbolical. It transcends realism not because Sologub introduces the mysterious demon *Nedotykomka*, which, after all, may be explained away as a hallucination of Peredonov's, but because his aim is not to paint the life of a Russian provincial town, but life, the evil creation of God, as a whole. The satirical drawing is admirable, a touch more grotesque, and consequently more poetical, than in the earlier novel, but the town is only a microcosm of all life. The novel has two planes: the life of Peredonov, the incarnation of the joyless evils of life, and the idyllic loves of the boy Sasha Pylnikov and Ludmila Rutilova. These two are the emanation of Beauty, but their beauty is not pure, it has been polluted by the evil touch of life. The Sasha and Ludmila episode has a subtle sensual flavour, and is introduced not only for its symbolical and constructive value, but also to answer the demands of the poet's *libido*. Peredonov has become a famous figure, in fact the most famous and memorable character of Russian fiction since *The Brothers Karamazov*, and his name is now a word of the literary language. It stands for the incarnation of sullen evil, which knows no joy and resents others' knowing it; one of the most terrible figures ever created by a poet. He lives in constant hatred and believes that all live in constant hatred of him. He loves to inflict cruelty, and to dash to the ground the joys of others. He finally succumbs to a mania of persecution and commits murder in a state of insanity.

Sologub's third novel, *The Created Legend* (or rather, as Mr. Cournos, the English translator of the first part of it, justly remarks, *The Legend in Process of Creation—Tvorimaya Legenda*), is his longest. It consists of three parts, each of which is a self-contained novel. In the first part the scene is laid in Russia in 1905. The hero is Trirodov, a Satanist after the heart of Sologub. He is also a revolutionary, though only a contemplative one. Sologub's political attitude was then strongly revolutionary: it is natural that with his philosophy the existing order of things, the forces of reaction and conservatism, should appear as the fullest expression of evil life. The volume is full of scenes of horror and cruelty in the suppression of the revolutionary movement: hence its title, *Drops of Blood*. Trirodov is the ideal man who has nearest approached the serenity of death, and sheds around himself a cool and calm atmosphere, symbolized in his colony of "quiet boys"—a weird vision of Sologub's perverse imagination. In the second and third parts (*Queen Ortruda* and *Smoke and Ashes*) the scene is shifted to the Kingdom of the United Islands, an imaginary volcanic group in the Mediterranean. These volumes have a powerful and subtle, if suspicious, charm. Unlike most Russian novels, they may be read for the interest of the story. It is a very complicated story of love and political intrigue. It is all dominated by the ever present danger, the volcano, and in the third part the eruption occurs. The story is symbolical, but, as I have said, contains quite sufficient charm apart from its symbolism. The trilogy ends by the Republic of the United Islands electing Trirodov their king!

Sologub's stort stories are a link between his poetry and his novels. Some of them are shorter sketches in the style of *Bad Dreams* and *Melki Bes*. Others, especially after 1905, are frankly fantastic and symbolical. In these more than anywhere else Sologub gave free reign to his morbid sensual demands. *The Dear Page* and, of those stories that have been translated into English, *The Lady in Fetters* are typical examples of this kind. *The Miracle of the Boy Linus*, a revolutionary story in a conventional poetical setting, is one of the most beautiful pieces of modern Russian prose. In general, Sologub's prose is beautiful: limpid, clear, balanced, poetical, but with a keen sense of measure. In his later writings it is marred by certain irritating mannerisms. Apart from his other prose writings stand his *Political Fables* (1905), admirable both for the scathing point of their satire, and for their remarkably elaborate popular language, rich in verbal effects (as all popular speech is) and reminiscent of the grotesque manner of Leskov.

His plays are not on a level with his other writings. Of peculiar dramatic merit they have but little. Such as *The Sting of Death* and *The Gift of the Wise Bees* are academic pageants symbolizing the concepts of his philosophy. They are less genuine than his poetry and constantly fall into the false beautiful. More interesting is *Vanka the Butler and the Page Jehan*, an amusing piece of irony: the familiar history of the young servant who seduces the lady of the house is developed in two parallel variations: in mediæval France and in Muscovite Russia. It is a satire on Russian civilization, with its crudeness and poverty of forms, and is at the same time a symbol of the essential sameness of the evil diversity of life all over the world and throughout the ages.

6. ANNENSKY (1856–1909)

Still older than Sologub, still more eccentric to the general movement, and still later to be recognized, was Innokenti Fedorovich Ànnensky. Born in 1856, in Omsk (Western Siberia), he was the son of an important official, and was educated at Petersburg. He took a degree in classics at the university of that capital, and was invited to prepare for a chair. But he found himself incapable of concentrating on his thesis and instead became a teacher of the ancient languages. He rose to be head master of the Gymnasium of Tsarskoe Selo, and afterwards Director of Schools—that is, an official who has the supervision of the secondary schools of a large district. His educational career was all on a higher level than Sologub's. He was an eminent classical scholar and contributed articles and reviews to the philological reviews. He devoted himself to a complete Russian version of Euripides. In 1894 he published *Bacchæ* and in time the rest. It was not for nothing that he chose Euripides—the most journalistic and least religious of the tragic poets. Annensky's mind was eminently unclassical and he did his best to modernize and vulgarize the Greek poet. But all this would give him but a small place in Russian literature were it not for his poetry. In 1904 he published a book of lyrics (half of which was occupied by translations from French poets and from Horace) entitled *Quiet Songs* and under the whimsical pseudonym of *Nik. T-O*. This is at once an anagram of part of his name, and may be read as *Nikto* (nobody). He means it to be an allusion to the Polyphemus episode in the *Odyssey* where Ulysses gives his name as *Outis*. This far-fetched and elaborate allusion is typical of Annensky. *Quiet Songs* passed unnoticed, even by the Symbolists. Poetry over his name continued to appear from time to time in the magazines, and he brought out two books of critical essays, which are remarkable both for the subtlety and penetration of his criticism and for the perverse pretensions of his style. In 1909 a few people began to realize that Annensky was an uncommonly original and interesting poet. He was "taken up" by the Petersburg Symbolists and introduced to their poetical circles, where he at once became a central figure. He was by way of becoming a principal influence in literature when he suddenly died of heart failure at the railway station in Petersburg on his way home to Tsarskoe, November, 1909. He had prepared for the press a second book of verse—*The Cypress Chest*—which was published the following year, and was recognized in the inner circle of Russian poets as a classic.

Annensky's poetry is in many ways different from that of all his contemporaries. It is not metaphysical, but purely emotional, or perhaps rather nervous. He had no Russian masters. In so far as he had any masters at all, they were Baudelaire, Verlaine, and Mallarmé. But on the whole his lyrical gift is remarkably original. It is a rare case of a very late development. Nor did he at once attain to perfection. *Quiet Songs* is distinctly immature (though written at forty-eight). But in *The Cypress Chest* the majority of the poems are flawlessly perfect jewels. Annensky is a Symbolist, in so far as his poetry is based on a system of "correspondences." But they are purely emotional correspondences. His poems are developed in two interconnected planes—the human soul and the outer world; each of them is an elaborate parallel between a state of mind and the external world. Annensky is akin to Chekhov, for his material is also the pinpricks and infinitesimals of life. His poetry is essentially human and its appeal would be universal, for it deals with the common stuff of humanity. They are constructed with disconcerting and baffling subtleness and precision. They are compressed and laconic—much of the structure has been pulled away and only the essential points remain for the reader to reverse the process and grasp the unity of the poem. Few readers, however, feel themselves capable of the creative effort required. But the work is worth the while. Those who have mastered him usually prefer him to all other poets. For he is unique and always fresh. The extent of his poetry is small, his two books do not contain more than a hundred lyrics all told, and most of them are not over twenty lines long. This makes it comparatively easy to study. He is not really very difficult to translate, as the essential thing in his poems is their structural logic.   As no attempt has ever been made to do him into English, I will run the risk of presenting two very inadequate prose versions of my own.

Poppies

The gay day is ablaze. . . . Among the languid grasses,
Blots of poppies—like avid impotence,
Like lips full of lust and poison,
Like the spread wings of scarlet butterflies.

The gay day is ablaze. . . . But the garden is empty.
It has long since done with lust and feasting,
The withered poppies are like the heads of hags,
And over them is spread the radiant chalice of heaven.

An October Myth

It's too much for me.   I can bear it no longer.
I hear the steps of the blind man
The whole night above my head—
He continues stumbling over the roof.

And are they mine (I cannot tell),
The tears that burn my heart, or is it
Those which trickle and fall
From the blind man's eyes—unanswered?

That fall from his dim eyes,
Down his withered cheeks,
And in this lone midnight hour
Trickle down the window-panes.

It must be added that Annensky's diction is studiously common and trivial.   It is the unbeautiful language of every day—but his poetical alchemy transforms the ugly dross of vulgarity into the purest poetical gold.

Annensky's tragedies written in imitation of Euripides are not on the level of his lyrics.   The most interesting is the posthumous *Thamiras Cytharede*.   The subject is the Apollonian myth of the proud harpist who challenged the god to a contest in music and expiated his arrogance by the loss of his

eyes. There is much poignant poetry in the tragedy, but it
is eminently unclassical. Still less classical are his most
curious translations from Horace. Altogether, considering his
lifelong connexion with the ancients, Annensky is quite dis-
concertingly free from any kinship with antiquity.

7. VYACHESLAV IVANOV

The marriage of Russian Symbolism and Greek tradition
took place in the work of another scholar-poet, Vyacheslav
Ivanovich Ivànov. He was born in Moscow in 1866, and was
the son of a minor civil servant. He studied the classics and
ancient history partly under the guidance of Mommsen, and
published a thesis on the tax-farming companies of ancient
Rome. For a long time he lived abroad, away from any contact with Russian literary life. The only modern writers who
influenced him were Nietzsche and Soloviev. But he lived in
the closest intimacy with the great poets of antiquity, with
Dante and Goethe, and with the mystics and philosophers of
all times. He was especially attracted by the mystic religions
of Greece, and later on (1903–1904) he published an important study on the religion of Dionysos. He early began writing verse, but it remained unpublished for years and he was
free to develop a style entirely his own, hieratic and archaic,
rich in expressive diction and majestic harmony, and quite
unlike the poetry of his contemporaries. In 1903 he published a book of poems entitled *Pilot Stars*, the fruit of this
isolated development. In spite of its unfamiliar appearance,
the Symbolists at once discerned in him one of themselves,
and recognized him as a great poet. He entered the Symbolist circles and even came under the influence of Merezhkovsky,
but on the whole he gave more than he received. His tower-
ing scholarship and powerful personal magnetism soon made
him a master and a leader. In 1905, like the other Symbolists,
he did homage to the Revolution, and, in common with the
young poet and revolutionary George Chulkov (born 1879),
became the prophet of a new revolutionary philosophy, which
received the name of Mystical Anarchism. It preached the

"non-acceptance of the world" * and the revolt against all external conditions, towards a complete freedom of the spirit. This Mystical Anarchism proved ephemeral, but the ascendancy of Ivanov over the modernist circles of Petersburg became unquestioned and lasted for six or seven years. Ivanov became the master of the Petersburg Symbolists as opposed to those of Moscow led by Bryusov. It is impossible to dwell on these quarrels in any detail. The essence of Ivanov's creed was that art was a mystical religious activity, an aspect of the complete syncretic human activity, and was to be dominated by mystical values and to be judged by religious standards. But his religion was syncretic, and included all the religions of the world. The identification of Christ and Dionysos was one of its characteristic tenets. All was one—Christianity and Paganism—sanctity and Luciferian pride—ascetic purity and sexual ecstasy—and all was religious and holy. The Muscovites opposed Ivanov partly because, like Bryusov, they wanted to preserve the autonomy of art against religion and philosophy, partly because, like Bely, they desired a better-defined and less inclusive religion, which would not be seeking for the "synthesis of good and evil, of Christ and Lucifer." From 1905 to 1911 Ivanov remained the uncrowned king of Petersburg poets. His flat on the sixth floor of a house overlooking the Duma building and the Taurida Park was known as "the Tower." Every Wednesday all poetic and modern Petersburg met there, and the more intimate adepts stayed there, in mystical conversation and literary readings, till eight or nine on Thursday morning. In 1907 Ivanov lost his wife (who was known in literature by the name of Lydia Zinovieva-Annibal), but this did not break up the "Wednesdays." Only in 1912 did a succession of grievous incidents lead to Ivanov's estrangement from his most intimate friends. He left "the Tower" and went abroad; when he returned, he did not settle in Petersburg, but in Moscow. At the same time the disintegration of Symbolism as a literary school brought an end to the intellectual hegemony of Ivanov, and he was hence-

* The phrase alludes to the words of Ivan Karamazov: "I accept God but I do not accept His world,"

forward "one of the many." The period of "the Tower" was the golden age of Ivanov's poetical work, which is contained in *Cor Ardens* (two volumes, 1911). The Second Revolution did not kindle Ivanov to the same enthusiasm as the first. He lived in and near Moscow, experiencing, like almost all Russian intellectuals, terrible hardships and privation— cold and hunger. In 1920 he wrote the beautiful *Winter Sonnets* and, together with Gershenzon, the *Correspondence between Two Corners*, both of which are among the most important monuments of the time. In 1921 he was appointed Professor of Greek in the State University of Azorbeijan, in Baku, where for three years he lectured to young Tartars on Homer and Æschylus. In 1924 he returned to Moscow, where he is said to be on excellent terms with the Bolshevik leaders.

Shestov, who is a master of pointed epigram, has given Ivanov the nickname of Vyacheslav the Magnificent, and "magnificent" is the best definition one can think of for his style. In his first book there was still a certain primitivism, a "ruggedness," which gave it a certain freshness that is absent from his mature work. But *Cor Ardens* is the high-water mark of the ornate style in Russian poetry. His verse is saturated with beauty and expressiveness; it is all aglow with jewels and precious metals, it is like a rich Byzantine garment. "Byzantine" and "Alexandrian" are two very suitable epithets for his poetry, for it is all full of the product of past ages, very scholarly, conscious, and quite unspontaneous. Ivanov is the nearest approach in Russian poetry to the conscious and studied splendours of Milton. In his verse every image, every word, every sound, every cadence are part of one admirably planned whole. Everything is carefully weighed and used with elaborate discrimination to the best effect. His language is archaic, and he likes to introduce Greek idioms. This is in the great tradition of ecclesiastic Russian and adds powerfully to the majesty of his numbers. Most of his poems are metaphysical; he has also written many love lyrics and political poems, but love and politics are always treated *sub specie æternitatis*. His poetry is of course difficult, and hardly accessible to the man in the street, but, for those who can move in his sphere of ideas, there is in his heady and spiced wine an attractively troubling flavour. In his magnificence and his scholarship is hidden the sting of a refined and ecstatic sensuality—the sting of Astarte—rather than that of Dionysos. His poetry may be exclusive, Alexandrian, derivative (in so far as our culture is derivative), but that it is genuine, perhaps great poetry, there can be no doubt. The only objection that can be advanced against it is that it is too much of a good thing. Somewhat apart from the rest of his work stand *The Winter Sonnets* (1920); they are simpler, more human, less metaphysical. Their subject is the survival of the undying intellectual flame in the presence of elemental enemies—cold and starvation. Like so many Symbolists, Ivanov was also a translator, and his versions of Pindar, Sappho, Alcæus, Novalis, and especially the unpublished version of *Agamemnon*, are among the greatest achievements of Russian translated verse.

Ivanov's prose is as magnificent as his verse—it is the most elaborate and majestic ornate prose in the language. His earlier essays are contained in two volumes—*By the Stars* (1909) and *Furrows and Boundaries* (1916). In them he develops the same ideas as in his poetry. He believed that our times were capable of reviving the mythological creation of religious ages. He discovered in Dostoevsky a great creator of myths, and he believed that the modern theatre might become religious and choric like the Dionysian theatre of Athens. His most remarkable prose work is the dialogue of letters which he carried on with Gershenzon, when the two philosophers lay convalescent in two corners of the same hospital ward in the worst days of Bolshevik destruction (*A Correspondence between Two Corners*, 1920). In it Gershenzon aspires, Rousseau-like, after a new and complete liberty, after a naked man on a new earth, free from the yoke of centuries of culture. Ivanov takes up the defence of cultural values, and speaks with pointed force and noble enthusiasm for the great past of human achievement against his nihilistic opponent. The six letters, which form his part of the dialogue, are a noble and proud defence of culture, all the more impressive from the circumstances in which they were written.

8. VOLOSHIN

Maximilian Aleksandrovich Volòshin might almost be counted among the minor poets were it not for his last poems on the Revolution, but these are so interesting as to require more than a mere mention. Born in 1877 in South Russia, he travelled much in Central Asia and on the Mediterranean, and lived for many years in Paris, where he studied painting. Afterwards he settled down at Koktebel, near Theodosia, in south-eastern Crimea. In 1906–1910 he was one of the intimates of "the Tower." In his early work, Voloshin was a typical westernizer. His real spiritual home was Paris. He translated French writers, introducing to the Russian public such men as Barbey d'Aurevilly, Henri de Régnier, Paul de Saint-Victor, and Paul Claudel. His poetry is somewhat metallic and coldly splendid. It is like a brilliant pageant of jewels, or of stained glass: one of his longest poems is on the stained glass of the Cathedral of Rouen. He was strongly affected by Catholic mysticism, by the occult sciences, by Ægean and archaic Greece, and by the Mediterranean landscape. Among his best poems are splendid evocations of the Greek summer, full of the aroma of dry lavender, and *Cimmerian Darkness*, a cycle of sonnets on the Crimean winter. His poetry before 1917 was purely decorative and academic, splendid and cold. The great Revolution called from him a series of remarkable "historical" poems on the destinies of Russia. Their burden is the conception of "Holy Russia," the country of pure Christian mysticism, oppressed by the State, which, acording to Voloshin, is an alien growth in Russia: 1917 was an elemental effort of Russia to free herself from its outlandish fetters. "Holy Russia" (in the poem of the same name) refused to be a princess in the czar's chamber, she wanted to be free, so she lent her ear to evil advice, "delivered herself to the robber and to the felon, set fire to her farms and crops, destroyed her ancient abode, and went out into the world humiliated and a beggar, and the slave of the vilest slave. But," says Voloshin, "shall I dare cast a stone at thee? . . . Shall I not go on my knees before thee in the mire? blessing the trace of thy bare foot, thou wretched, homeless, drunken Russia—thou fool in Christ?" In another poem (*Transubstantiation*) he draws a picture of Rome in the sixth century, when the last flicker of imperial Rome went out and Papal Rome, "a new Rome, was born, great and primitive like the elements. Thus the grain of wheat, that it may grow, must dissolve. Dissolve, Russia, and come to new life as the Kingdom of the Spirit!"

Thus the most Western and cosmopolitan of Russian poets has constructed a theory of super-Slavophil quietism. These poems (collected in *Demons Deaf and Dumb*, 1918) have become enormously popular among the *émigrés*, many of whom consider Voloshin the greatest living poet. But this anarchistic quietism does not prevent their author from being on the best of terms with the Communists. His teaching is that all Russians should make peace and forgive each other. If they refuse to do so, he does it for them. His last book (*Poems of the Terror*, 1924) is a denunciation of the civil war in this spirit of reconciliation. In spite of the burning actuality of these poems, one cannot fail to discern that, after all, they are as cold and academic as his early ones. Russia and Revolution, Christ and Lucifer, the Church and the International, are to him purely æsthetic entities absorbingly interesting in their combinations, and as significant as the stained glass of Rouen, or as the myth of Atlantis, but in no way connected with practical and immediate issues.

9. BLOK (1880–1921)

The greatest of all the Symbolists was Alexander Alexandrovich Blok. His work is at once very typical of the whole school—for no one carried farther the realistic mysticism of Russian symbolism—and very peculiar, for he has a definite air of kinship with the great poets of the Romantic Age. His poetry is more spontaneous and inspired than that of his contemporaries. His very appearance was that of a poet. There was in him the innate majesty of a fallen angel. All who knew him felt in him the presence of a superior being. Very handsome, he was a splendid specimen of what it has become the fashion to call the Nordic race. He was the meeting-point of several lines of traditions—he was both very Russian and very European. And to emphasize the fact, he was of mixed descent.

His father's family came over with Peter III from Holstein in the eighteenth century, but his father, A. L. Blok, Professor of Public Law at the University of Warsaw, was already more than half Russian by blood, and an extreme Slavophil in his ideas. He was an unhappy and self-tormented egoist, very attractive, but impossible to live with. His first wife, the poet's mother, discovered this very soon after her marriage; they separated immediately after the birth of their son, and were subsequently divorced. Both of them remarried. The poet's mother was the daughter of Professor Beketov, an eminent scientist and for many years Rector of the University of St. Petersburg.

The poet was born in 1880 in his grandfather's apartment in the university building. After the separation of his parents, he remained with his mother. He saw his father only at rare intervals. In the Beketov family, life was cultivated and idyllic. The winters were spent in the university, the summers at Shakhmatovo, a little estate near Moscow. The people with whom the Beketovs used to mix belonged to the best intellectual élite of the country—they included the family of the great chemist Mendeléeff (whose daughter Blok married in 1903) and that of M. S. Soloviev, the famous writer's brother and "better self."

In 1898 Blok went to the university, where he remained rather a long time, for he passed from the faculty of law to that of philology, and took his degree only in 1906, when he had become a well-known poet. He began writing verse very early. By 1900 he was already an original poet, both in style and in substance. His poetry at first remained unpublished. Only in 1903 a few poems of his were published in the Merezkhovskys' review, *The New Way*. In 1904 they appeared in book form under the title of *Verses about the Beautiful Lady*. Blok always insisted that his poetry can be really understood and appreciated only by those who are in sympathy with his mystical experience. This assertion is especially true in regard to his first book. Unless one understands the mystical "setting," one is apt to take it for mere verbal music. To be understood, it must be interpreted. This, however, is no very difficult task, with the help of Blok's own article *On the Present State of Russian Symbolism* (1910), which is a very important self-revelation, and of Bely's detailed commentary contained in his remarkable *Recollections of Blok*. *The Verses about the Beautiful Lady* is the history of a mystical "love affair" with a Person whom Blok identified with the subject of Soloviev's *Three Visions*—Sophia, the Divine Wisdom, a feminine hypostasis of the Deity. After Blok's own and Bely's commentary, it is no longer difficult to understand these lyrics. Blok's mystical friends and himself always insisted that these *Verses* are the most important part of his work, and though the ordinary poetry-reader may be inclined to prefer the mighty numbers of the third volume, these early *Verses* are certainly very interesting and biographically important. In spite of the influence of Soloviev (in the matter) and of Zinaida Hippius (in metrical form), they are quite original and their style is strangely mature for a young man of twenty to twenty-two. The principal feature of this poetry is its complete freedom from everything sensual or concrete. It is a nebula of words, and affects the uninitiated reader as mere verbal melody. It answers better than any other poetry to Verlaine's rule *"de la musique avant toute chose."* Nothing can be *"plus vague et plus soluble dans l'air"* than this poetry. Afterwards, in his play *The Stranger*, Blok makes a poet (who is obviously a parody of himself) read out his verse to a waiter in a public house, and the waiter's verdict is: "Incomprehensible, but exceedingly refined, sir." Apart from the few initiated, the attitude of Blok's early admirers was much the same as the waiter's.

The subsequent popularity of his early poetry (which

formed the first volume of the collected Poems) was precisely
due to a craze for poetry that would be as pure and as free of
meaning as music.

Blok's poetry was at first appreciated only by the few. The
critics either left it unnoticed, or treated it with the ridicule
and the indignation which were the common lot of the Symbolists. The public began to read it only much later. But the
inner literary circles at once realized the importance of the
new poet: Bryusov and the Merezhkovskys gave him a warm
reception. The younger Symbolists went still further in their
enthusiasm: two young Muscovites, Andrey Bely and Sergey,
the son of M. S. Soloviev, discovered in it a message that was
akin to their own spiritual experience, and Blok became to
them a prophet and a seer, almost the founder of a new religion. These young mystics with fervent and strangely
realistic faith awaited the coming of a new religious revelation, and Blok's ethereal poetry seemed to them the Annun-
ciation of this new era. In his *Recollections* Bely has
described the tense atmosphere of mystical expectation in
which the young Bloks (Blok had married Miss Mendeléeff
in 1903), himself, and Sergey Soloviev moved in the years
1903–1904.

But this did not last. *Verses about the Beautiful Lady* was
still in the press, and the Blokists were at the height of their
ecstasies, when a change come over Blok's visionary world.
"The Beautiful Lady" refused herself to her lover. The
world became empty to him, and the heavens clouded in darkness. Repelled by his mystical Mistress, he turned towards the
earth. This change made Blok certainly more unhappy and
probably a worse man than he had been, but a greater poet.
Only now his poetry begins to acquire human interest and
becomes comprehensible to others than the elect few. It becomes more earthly, but at first his earth is not a material
earth. His heaven-bred style succeeds in dematerializing the
world of common experience when it first comes in contact
with it. His world of 1904–1906 is a drapery of fata-
morganas, thrown over the more real but invisible heaven.
His immaterial and purely musical style was admirably suited

to evoke the mists and mirages of Petersburg, the illusionary city which had haunted the imagination of Gogol, of Grigoriev, and of Dostoevsky. This romantic Petersburg, the dream city arising in the unreal misty atmosphere of the North on the uncertain quagmire of the Neva delta, becomes the background of Blok's poetry ever since he touched the earth after his first mystical flights. "The Beautiful Lady" disappears from his poetry. She is replaced by the Stranger (the Strange Woman—*Neznakomka*), an immaterial but passionately present obsession that haunts the poems of the second volume of this collected verse (1904–1908). She appears with particular vividness in a very famous poem (perhaps, next to *The Twelve*, the most widely popular of all Blok's poems) written in 1906, which is characteristic for its combination of realistic irony with romantic lyricism. The poem begins with a grotesquely ironic picture of a pleasure resort near Petersburg. In this seething den of vulgarity where "experienced wits" go out for walks with ladies, and "rabbit-eyed drunkards screech: *In Vino Veritas*" appears the Stranger.

> And every evening, at the appointed hour
> (Or is it only a dream of mine?),
> A maidenly figure, caught in tight silks,
> Moves in the hazy window.

> And slowly, passing between the drunkards,
> Always without company and alone,
> Exhaling perfumes and mists,
> She takes a seat beside the window.

> And full of ancient legends
> Are her elastic silks,
> And her sable-feathered hat,
> And her narrow hand, covered with rings.

> And fascinated by this strange presence,
> I look through the dark veil,
> And see an enchanted shore
> And an enchanted horizon.

Mysterious secrets have been confided to me,
Someone's Sun is in my keeping,
And all the sinuosities of my soul
Are transpierced with the rough wine.

And the ostrich feathers, inclining,
Sway to and fro in my brain,
And eyes, blue, and unfathomable,
Blossom on a far-off shore.

In my soul lies a treasure,
And the key is confided to me alone.
You are right, drunken monster,
I know it: Truth is in wine!

Of course this translation can give only a very inadequate idea of the original:—Blok's effects are to a very great extent dependent on sound, on vowel harmony, on the emotional and musical colouring of what may otherwise appear vague and loose diction. Still I have preferred to give a prose version rather than use Mr. Yarmolinsky's version, in the metre of the original. This metre (which is octosyllabics with alternately treble and single rhymes) produces in Russian an effect very different from that in English. In Russian, treble rhymes are particularly well suited for immaterial and dreamy music; in English, they are always rather a *tour de force* and dangerously suggestive of limericks.

To the same period belongs a series of exquisite poems where, for once, Blok displays an unexpected gift of homely and whimsical humour. The series is entitled, in a phrase from *Macbeth*, "the Earth's Bubbles." It is about the homely and mischievous spirits that live in the woods and fields. Few poems have won more popular feeling for Blok than the *Little Priest of the Bogs*, a mysterious, impish, and good-natured creation of his fancy, who, standing finger-high amid the mounds,

> "prays, lifting his hat,
> for the reed that bends,
> for the ailing paw of a frog,
> and for the Pope of Rome."

Like most of the Symbolists, Blok welcomed the Revolution of 1905. He joined the Mystical Anarchists. On one occasion he even carried a red flag. The defeat of the Revolution, which followed in 1906–1907, added to his despair and pessimism and emphasized the growing gloom of his soul. His poetry becomes, once for all, the expression of that "fatal emptiness" (of which he speaks in a poem of 1912) which was familiar to many men of his generation. This "emptiness" has much in common with Andreev's. The difference is that Blok was a greater genius, and a man of greater culture—and that he *had* known a state of mystical bliss of which Andreev could have no suspicion. An impotent desire to return into the Radiant Presence he had been expelled from, and a bitter resentment of the way he had been treated by "the Beautiful Lady," form the subject of his "lyrical dramas" written in 1906–1907—*Balaganchik* (*The Puppet Show*) and *Neznakomka* (*The Stranger*), which are among his earliest and most charming masterpieces. *Balaganchik* is a "pierrotic" comedy. It was produced in 1907 and had a fairly long run. On those who saw it, it has produced an unforgetable impression. It contains much of Blok's very best lyrical matter, but it is in essence a satire, a parody, and a piece of grim blasphemy. It is a parody on Blok's own mystical experience, and a satire on his own mystical hopes and aspirations. His friends Bely and S. Soloviev took it as an insult not to themselves only, but to their common faith in Sophia the Divine Wisdom. This led to an estrangement between Blok and his Moscow friends, and the next period passed for Blok in grim solitude. The lyrical charm and capricious symbolism of *Balaganchik* may obscure from most readers its terrible pessimism. But it is in essence one of the most blasphemous and gloomiest things ever written by a poet.

The Stranger is a dreamy and romantic visionary drama developing the subject of the poem of the same name. It has less lyrical charm than *Balaganchik* but it shows at its best Blok's ironic and grotesque realism, which only serves to enhance the visionary romanticism of the main theme. The first scene is laid in a public house where the Poet, who is in love with the mysterious Stranger, engages in conversation with the waiter and is finally kicked out for getting too drunk. The second scene is a field on the outskirts of Petersburg; enter the Poet, dragged by two policemen and in a state of complete drunkenness. At the same time a star falls from heaven, and becomes the very Stranger for whom the Poet is yearning. But in his drunkenness he is unable to recognize her, and she is led away by a vulgar young man who promises to quell her thirst for earthly love. The third scene is a vulgarly elegant drawing-room; the Poet and an Astronomer, who is upset by this unexpected fall of a star of the first magnitude, are there. Suddenly the Stranger appears, following the young man who took her with him. The Poet seems to recognize her and yet cannot. Unrecognized, she disappears, and the fallen star is again shining in the winter sky. Even those who will not sympathize with the romanticism of this play, will yet appreciate the unique mastery of the prose dialogues and the skilful structure of the first and third scenes, which are built along parallel lines, so that the conversation in the drawing-room every moment reminds the spectator in a startling and uncanny way of the conversation in the public house. Public houses henceforward become the frequent setting of Blok's poetry. It becomes full of wine, women, and gipsy song, and all this against a background of passionate despair and hopeless yearning after the irretrievably lost vision of "the Beautiful Lady." This state of passionate and hopeless disillusion is the atmosphere of all Blok's subsequent poetry. Only at rare moments is he seized and carried away from his slough of despond by the whirlwind of earthly passion. Such a whirlwind is reflected in *The Snow Mask*, an ecstatic lyrical fugue written in the first days of the year 1907.

Blok's genius reaches its maturity about 1908. The lyrics written between that date and 1916 are contained in the third volume of his collected poems, which is, together with *The Twelve*, certainly the greatest body of poetry written by a

Russian poet within the last eighty years. He was a man neither of great brains nor of great moral strength. Nor was he really a great craftsman. His art is passive and involuntary. He is a recorder of poetical experience rather than a builder of poetical edifices. What makes him great is the greatness of the poetical spirit that fills him, coming, as it were, from other worlds. He has himself described his creative process in one of his most remarkable poems, *The Artist* (1913), as a purely passive process very much akin to mystical ecstasy as it is described by the great Western (Spanish and German) mystics. The ecstasy is preceded by a state of boredom and prostration; then comes the unutterable bliss of a wind from other spheres, to which the poet abandons himself, will-lessly and obediently. But the rapture is interfered with by "creative reason," which forces into the fetters of form the "light-winged, benevolent, free bird" of inspiration; and when the work of art is ready, it is dead to the poet, who subsides into his previous state of empty boredom.

In the third volume Blok's style pulsates with a more intense and nervous life than in his earlier work. It is more tense and full-blooded. But, as in his earlier work, it depends to such an extent on the "imponderables" of diction, sound and association, that all translation is hopeless. The more purely lyrical poems can be read only in the original. But another group of poems, more ironical and consequently more realistic, are less completely untranslatable. Of one of them I will attempt a prose version.

Danse Macabre

How hard it is for a corpse among living men
To pretend to be alive and passionate!
But he must, he must squeeze himself into society,
Dissimulating, in the interests of advancement, the rattle of his
    bones.

The living are asleep. The dead man gets up from his grave,
And goes to the bank, to the courts of justice, to the senate;
The whiter the night, the blacker his feelings,
And the pens creak triumphantly.

All the day the dead man works at a memorandum.
Office time is over.   And lo!
Wagging his hind parts, he whispers
An obscene anecdote into the ear of a senator.

Evening.   A drizzling rain has covered with dirt
The passers-by, the houses, and all the other rubbish.
But the dead man—towards other obscenities
He is whirled away in a rickety taxi.

Into a crowded and columned ball-room
He hastens.   He wears a well-made evening suit.
He is greeted with a graceful smile
By the hostess who is a fool and her husband who is another.

He is worn out by a day of official boredom.
But the rattle of his bones is covered by the music.
He gives hearty shakes to friendly hands,
Alive, alive, he must pretend to be.

Only at a distant column his eyes will meet with those
Of his companion—like him, she is dead.
Behind their conventional small talk
You hear the real words:

"Weary friend, I feel strange in this ball-room.
Weary friend, the grave is cold.
'Tis midnight."—"Yes, but you have not yet engaged
N. N. for a waltz.   She is in love with you."

And over there N. N. is passionately waiting
For him, for him, with all her blood ablaze.
Her face, maidenly beautiful,
Displays the idiotic ecstasy of live love.

He whispers to her insignificant things,
Words that are charming to the living,
And he looks, how rosy her shoulders are,
How her head has inclined to her shoulder.

With more than human malice he pours out to her
    The witty poison of ordinary society malice.
"How clever he is!   How in love with me!"
In her ears, an uncanny, strange noise.
—It is bones rattling against bones.

The gloom and despair expressed in this *Danse Macabre* are characteristic of most of Blok's poetry since 1907. Yet for a while, and intermittently, Blok seems to have discovered a ray of hope, which was to replace "the Beautiful Lady"; this was his love for Russia. It was a strange love, intensely aware of all that was base and vile in the beloved one, and yet reaching sometimes to veritable paroxysms of passion. The image of Russia identified itself in his mind with the Stranger—the mysterious woman of his dreams—and with the passionate and ambiguous women of Dostoevsky, Nastasia Fili-povna (*The Idiot*) and Grushenka (*The Brothers Karama-zov*). Another symbol and mystical counterpart of Russia became the snow-storm and the blizzard, which in *The Snow Mask* had been a symbol of the cold and scorching storms of carnal passion, and which forms the background of *The Twelve*. This Russian wind of passion is again associated with the songs of the gipsy choruses of Petersburg and Moscow. Many great writers (including Derzhavin, Tolstoy, and Leskov) had understood before Blok the lure and glamour of the gipsy chorus. There was in the middle of the nineteenth century a man of great but abortive genius, Apollon Grigoriev, who was, more than anyone, full of this gipsy poetry. He wrote several extraordinary songs which have been appropriated by the gipsies, though they have forgotten his name. Blok prac-tically discovered Grigoriev as a poet (as a critic he had been well known always) and "took him up." He edited a collected edition of Grigoriev's poems (1915) and wrote a preface which is one of his few prose articles that are worthy of the great poet, and where he pays noble tribute to his forgotten predecessor.

Blok's love of Russia expressed itself in an acute sensibility for the destinies of his country, which sometimes verges on a genuine gift of prophecy. In this respect the lyrical fugue *The Field of Kulikovo* (1908) is especially remarkable: it is full of dark and ominous presentiments of the great catas-trophes of 1914 and 1917. Another remarkable poem (written in August, 1914) gives the full extent of Blok's strange and irrational love of his country. It begins:

> To sin shamelessly and uninterruptedly,
> To lose count of days and nights,
> And with a head heavy with drunkenness
> To insinuate oneself into God's temple.

Then, accumulating detail on detail, he draws a picture of the most repulsive and degraded Russian character possible, and suddenly winds up:

> Yes, and even in this form, my Russia,
> You are dearer to me than all the world.

It is impossible to give any detailed enumeration of Blok's shorter poems written between 1908 and 1916. Suffice it to mention such unforgettable masterpieces as *Humiliation* (1911) —the humiliation of venal love; *The Steps of the Commander* (1912), one of the greatest poems ever written on the eternal subject of retaliation; that terrible cry of despair, *A Voice from a Chorus* (1914), and *The Nightingale Garden* (1916), more "classical" and austere in style than most of his lyrics, a symbolical poem, unexpectedly reminiscent of that other great symbolical poem, Chekhov's *My Life*. Apart from the lyrics contained in the third volume stand two longer works of the same period: the narrative poem *Retaliation* and the lyrical tragedy *The Rose and the Cross*.

Retaliation was begun in 1910 under the impression of his father's death. It was planned to include three cantos, but only the first was completed. It is realistic in style and attempts to approach the methods of Pushkin and Lermontov. It is the story of his father and of himself, and Blok intended to make it a work of vast significance, illustrating the law of heredity and the consecutive stages of the disintegration of the Old Régime in Russia. Blok was unable to master his task, and the poem as a whole is not a success. But it contains many vigorous and beautiful passages. The beginning of the second canto reveals in Blok an unexpected gift of comprehensive historical vision: it is an excellent synthesis of Russia under Alexander III, which might almost be quoted in every text-book of Russian history.

The Rose and the Cross (1913) is more conventional and less immediately striking than anything Blok ever wrote. The scene is laid in Languedoc in the thirteenth century. The play is very well constructed and the lyrical quality of the poetry is on Blok's highest level. It is haunted, from beginning to end, as by a leitmotiv, by the burden of a mysterious song sung by the Breton Minstrel Gaëtan:

> Joy, oh, joy, that is suffering!
> Pain of unspeakable wounds!

The final scene is perhaps his greatest achievement in pathetic irony.

Blok's attitude to the Great War, like the attitude of a large part of the advanced *intelligentsia*, was one of passive pacifism. When his turn came to go to the front, he exhausted all the means in his power to escape mobilization and succeeded in avoiding military service by joining a civilian "building detachment" engaged in fortifying the rear. The moment he heard of the fall of the monarchy, he deserted his post and returned to Petersburg. He was soon appointed Secretary to the Extraordinary Examining Committee, which was to investigate the actions of the Ministers of the Old Régime that led to the Revolution.

During the Revolutionary year Blok came under the influence of the Left S.R.'s and of their spokesman, the "Scythian" Ivanov-Razumnik, who had evolved a sort of mystical revolutionary Messianism, which laid great stress on the revolutionary mission of Russia and on the fundamental difference of Socialist Russia from the bourgeois West. The Left S.R.'s joined hands with the Bolsheviks and took an active part in the overthrowing of the Provisional Government. So Blok found himself definitely on the Bolshevik side, together with his friend Bely, but against the great majority of his former friends, including the Merezhkovskys. Blok's Bolshevism was not an orthodox Marxian Communism, but it was not by chance that he became a Bolshevik. The Bolshevik Revolution with all its horrors and all its anarchy was welcome to him as the manifestation of what he identified with the soul of Russia—the soul of the Blizzard. This conception of the Bolshevik Revolution found expression in his last and greatest poem, *The Twelve*. The Twelve are twelve Red-Guardsmen patrolling the streets of Petrograd in the winter of 1917–1918, bullying the bourgeois and settling their quarrels among themselves for their girls, with the bullet. The figure twelve turns out to be symbolic of the Twelve Apostles, and in the end the Figure of Christ appears, showing the way, against their will, to the twelve Red soldiers. This is a homage to Ivanov-Razumnik's muddle-headed revolutionary mysticism, and a testimony to the essentially irreligious character of Blok's own mysticism. Those who are familiar with the whole of Blok's poetry will know that the name of Christ did not mean to him the same as it does to a Christian—it is a poetical symbol which has its own existence and its own associations, very different from those of the Gospels as well as from those of Church tradition. Every interpretation of "Christ" in *The Twelve* that would not take into account the whole of Blok's poetry would be merely meaningless. I have not place enough to discuss this problem here, but it is not its intellectual symbolism that makes *The Twelve* what it is—a great poem. The important thing is not what it signifies, but what it is. Blok's musical genius reaches in it its highest summit. From the point of view of rhythmical construction, it is a "miracle of rare device." The musical effect is based on dissonances. Blok introduces the rhythm and the diction of the vulgar and coarse *chastushka* (factory song) and draws from them effects of unutterable vastness and majesty. The poem is built with wonderful precision. It develops with a tremendous swing, passing from one rhythmical form to another, and fusing its dissonances into a superior harmony. In spite of its crude realism and of its diction bordering on slang, one is tempted to compare it with such another masterpiece of lyrical construction as *Kubla Khan* or the first part of *Faust*. There exist two English translations of *The Twelve*.

They may be read to have a general idea of the "argument," but they are inadequate and give no idea of the grandness and perfection of the original. The poem, on the face of it, is untranslatable, and to translate it well might seem an impossible miracle. This miracle, however, has been wrought by its German translator, Wolfgang Gröger, whose version of it is almost on the level of the original.

In the same month as *The Twelve* (January, 1918), Blok wrote *The Scythians,* a piece of intensely rhetorical invective against the Western nations for their not wanting to join in the peace proposed by the Bolsheviks. It is a powerful piece of eloquence but can hardly be called very intelligent, and is on an entirely inferior level as compared with *The Twelve.*

This was Blok's last poem. The new Government, who valued its few intellectual allies, gave Blok a lot to do, and for three years he was hard at work at various civilizing and translating schemes under the control of Gorky and Lunacharsky. His enthusiasm for the Revolution fell after *The Twelve,* and he subsided into a state of passive gloom, unbrightened even by the wind of inspiration. He tried to resume his work on *Retaliation,* but nothing came of it. He was dreadfully tired—and empty. Unlike most other writers, he did not suffer from hunger or cold, for the Bolsheviks looked after him, but he was a dead man long before he died. This impression is the leitmotiv of all accounts of Blok during this period. He died of heart disease on August 9, 1921. *The Twelve* had made him more widely famous than he had been before, but the Left literary schools in the last years of his life were united in depreciating him. His death became a signal for his recognition as a national poet of the first magnitude. That Blok is a great poet, there can be no doubt. But great though he is, he is also most certainly an unhealthy and morbid poet, the greatest and most typical of a generation whose best sons were stricken with despair and incapable of overcoming their pessimism except by losing themselves in a dangerous and ambiguous mysticism, or by intoxicating themselves in a passionate whirlwind.

10. ANDREY BELY

In the course of my account of Blok's life, I have more than
once mentioned the name of another remarkable writer—
Andrey Bely. If Blok was the greatest, Bely is certainly the
most original and the most influential of all the Symbolists.
Unlike Blok, whose nearest affinities are in the past with the
great Romanticists, Bely is all turned towards the future,
and of all the Symbolists he has most in common with the
Futurists. He is to-day by far the most living influence of
the Symbolist age, perhaps the only Symbolist who is still an
active force in the literary evolution. The example of his
prose especially has revolutionized the style of Russian prose-
writing. Bely is a more complex figure than Blok, or even
than any other Symbolist: in this respect he can easily vie with
the most complex and disconcerting figures in Russian litera-
tue, Gogol and Vladimir Soloviev, both of whom had their
say in the making of Bely. He is, on the one hand, the most
extreme and typical expression of the Symbolist mentality;
no one carried farther than he the will to reduce the world
to a system of "correspondences" and no one took these "correspondences" more concretely and more realistically; but
this very concreteness of his immaterial symbols brings him
back to a realism that is quite outside the common run of
symbolist expression. His hold on the finer shades of reality,
on the most expressive, significant, suggestive, and at once
elusive detail is so great and so original that it evokes the
unexpected comparison with that Realist of Realists, Tolstoy.
And yet Bely's world, for all its almost more than lifelike
detail, is an immaterial world of ideas into which this reality of
ours is only projected like a whirlwind of phantasms. This
immaterial world of symbols and abstractions appears as a
pageant of colour and fire, and in spite of the earnest intensity
of his spiritual life it strikes one rather as a metaphysical
"show," splendid and amusing, but not dead earnest. The
sense of tragedy is curiously absent from Bely, and in this
again he is in bold contrast to Blok. His world is rather an
elfland—beyond good and evil—like the Fairyland Thomas the

Rhymer knew; in it Bely moves like a Puck or an Ariel, but an undisciplined and erratic Ariel. All this makes some people regard Bely as a seer and a prophet, others as a sort of mystical mountebank. Whatever he is, he is strikingly different from all the Symbolists by his complete lack of hieratic solemnity. Sometimes he is comic against his will, but on the whole he has most audaciously fused his comic appearance with his mysticism, and utilized it with surprising originality in his works. He is a great humorist, perhaps the greatest Russian humorist since Gogol, and to the general reader this is his most important and attractive aspect. But it is a humour that disconcerts at first and which is very unlike anything else in the world. It took the Russian public some twenty years to learn to appreciate it, and it will hardly take by storm the unitiated foreigner. But those who have tasted of it will always recognize it as (in the strict sense of the word) unique—one of the choicest and rarest gifts of the great gods.

Like so many contemporary Russian writers, Andrey Bély became famous as a writer under a pseudonym which finally replaced his inherited name even in life. This name is Boris Nikolaevich Bugáev. He was born in Moscow in 1880, the same year as Blok. His father, Prof. Bugaev (who appears in his son's writings as Prof. Letaev), was a very eminent mathematician, a correspondent of Weierstrass and Poincaré, and Dean of the Faculty of Science of the University of Moscow. His son inherited from him a keen interest in the more abstruse mathematical problems. He studied at the private gymnasium of L. I. Polivanov, one of the best Russian educationists of his day, who infected him with a profound interest in the Russian poets. At the house of M. S. Soloviev, Bely used to meet Vladimir Soloviev and early became an adept in his mystical teachings. The years immediately preceding and following the beginning of the new century were for Bely and his precocious friend M. S. Soloviev's son, Sergey, an era of ecstatic apocalyptic expectations. They believed, with the most realistic concreteness, that the first years of the new century would bring a new revelation—the revelation of the Feminine Hypostasis, Sophia—and that her coming would

transform and transfigure the whole of life. These expectations were still more enhanced by the news of Blok's visions
and poetry. At the same time Bely studied at the University
of Moscow, where he remained for eight years taking degrees
in philosophy and mathematics. In spite of his brilliant capac-
ities, he was looked at askance by the professors for his
"decadent" writings—some of them even refused to shake hands
with him at his father's funeral! The first of these "decadent"
writings appeared in 1902 under the disconcerting title *Symphony (2nd dramatic)*. A small number of exceptionally
sensitive critics (M. S. Soloviev, Bryusov, and the Merezhkovskys) at once recognized in it something quite new and
of unusual promise. It is almost a mature work and presents
a full idea of Bely's humour and of his wonderful gift of
writing musically organized prose. But the critics treated it,
and the works that followed it, with indignation and scorn,
and for several years Bely replaced Bryusov (who was beginning to be recognized) as the stock target for all assaults
upon the "decadents." He was reviled as an insolent clown
whose antics desecrated the sacred precincts of literature.
The critics' attitude was certainly natural and pardonable:
in nearly all of Bely's writings, there is an unmistakable element of foolery. The "Second" Symphony was followed by
the First (*Northern, Heroic,* 1904), the Third (*The Return,*
1905), and the Fourth (*The Cup of Snow-storms,* 1908), and
by a volume of verse (*Gold in Azure,* 1904), all of which met
with the same reception.

In 1905 Bely (one has to repeat this detail in the life of
every one of the Symbolists) was carried away by the wave
of Revolution, which he tried to unite with his Solovievian
mysticism. But the reaction that followed produced in Bely,
as in Blok, a depression, and a loss of faith in his mystical
ideals. This depression found its expression in two books of
verse published in 1909: the realistic *Ashes,* where he took up
the traditions of Nekrasov, and *The Urn,* in which he related
his wanderings in the abstract wildernesses of Neo-Kantian
metaphysics. Bely's despair and depression have not the grim
and tragic bitterness of Blok's, and the reader cannot help

taking him somewhat less seriously, all the more as Bely's humorous gambols are always there to divert him. All this time Bely wrote voluminously, in prose, brilliant but fantastic and impressionist critiques, where he interpreted writers from the point of view of his mystical symbolism; and expositions of his metaphysical theories. He was highly valued by the Symbolists but hardly known to the general public. In 1909 he published the first of his novels, *The Silver Dove*. This remarkable work, which was soon to have such an enormous influence on the history of Russian prose, at first passed almost unnoticed. In 1910 he read a series of papers before the Poetry "Academy" of Petersburg on Russian prosody, from which one may date the very existence of Russian prosody as a branch of real knowledge.

In 1911 he married a girl who bore the poetical name of Asya Turgenev, and the next year the young couple made the acquaintance of the notorious German "anthroposophist" Rudolph Steiner. Steiner's "Anthroposophy" is a crudely elaborate, concrete, and detailed expression of the Symbolist mentality, which regards the human microcosm as a parallel in every detail to the greater universal macrocosm. The Belys fell under Steiner's spell and for four years they lived in his magical establishment at Dornach, near Bâle ("Goetheanum"). They took part in the construction of the Johanneum, which was all to be done by adepts without the intervention of profane workmen. During this period Bely published his second novel, *Petersburg* (1913), and wrote *Kotik Letaev*, which appeared in 1917. When the War broke out, he assumed a definitely pacifist attitude. In 1916 he was obliged to return to Russia to be mobilized. But the Revolution saved him from military service. Like Blok, he came under the influence of Ivanov-Razumnik and his "Scythian" revolutionary Messianism. He welcomed in the Bolsheviks an emancipating and destroying gale that would do away with the obsolete "humanist" civilization of Europe. In his (very weak) poem *Christ Is Risen* (1918), he identified Bolshevism with Christianity even more emphatically than Blok did.

Like Blok, Bely very soon lost his faith in this identity, but, unlike Blok, he did not fall into a gloomy prostration. On the contrary, precisely in the worst years of Bolshevism (1918–1921) he developed a feverish activity inspired with a faith in the great Mystic Renascence of Russia which was growing up in spite of the Bolsheviks. Russia, he thought, was before his eyes developing a new "culture of eternity" which was to displace the humanist civilization of Europe. Indeed, during these terrible years of starvation, destitution, and terror, there was in Russia a remarkable flowering of mystical and spiritualist creation. Bely became the centre of this fermentation. He founded the *Volfila* (*Free Philosophical Association*), where the most burning problems of mystical metaphysics in their practical aspect were discussed with freedom, sincerity, and originality. He edited *The Dreamers' Journal* (*Zapiski Mechtateley*, 1919–1922), a non-periodical miscellany which contains almost all the best works published during these worst two years. He gave lessons in poetry to the proletarian poets, and lectured with enormous energy almost every day. During this period he wrote, besides much minor work, a series of important works: *The Memoirs of a Crank*, *The Crime of Nicholas Letaev* (a continuation of *Kotik Letaev*), a long poem entitled *The First Meeting*, and *Recollections of Blok*. He was, together with Blok and Gorky (who were as good as dead, for they wrote nothing), the biggest figure in Russian literature, and far more influential than they. When, in 1922, came the revival of the book trade, one of the first things to be done by the publishers was to reprint most of Bely's work. In the same year he went to Berlin, where he became as central a figure among the *émigré littérateurs* as he had been in Russia. But his ecstatic and peaceless mind did not permit him to remain abroad. In 1923 he returned to Russia, for only there he feels himself in contact with what he believes to be the Messianic renascence of Russian culture.

One usually thinks of Andrey Bely as primarily a poet, and this is, on the whole, true; but his writings in verse are less in volume and in significance than his prose. In verse he is almost always making experiments, and no one did more than he to open up the hidden possibilities of Russian verse, especially of its more conventional forms. His poetry has not that accent of majesty and passionate intensity of Blok's. It is most easily and naturally assimilated if one takes it altogether as word-play. His first book is full of Teutonic reminiscences (in subject more than in form). Nietzsche with the symbols of Zarathustra, and Boecklin with his centaurs, are present on many pages, but already here we have the first fruit of his humorous naturalism. *Ashes*, his most realistic book, is also the most earnest in tone, though it also contains some of his best comical writing (*The Parson's Daughter and the Seminarist*). But the dominant note is one of grim and cynical despair. It contains what is perhaps Bely's most intensely earnest and concentrated lyric, *Russia* (dated 1907).

> Enough! Expect no more, nor hope.
> Fall to dust, my poor people,
> Into the spaces fall and break to pieces,
> Ye years on years of torment.
>
> . . . .

And it finishes:

> Disappear into the spaces, disappear!
> Russia, my Russia!

Ten years later, at the height of the Second Revolution, he rewrote the poem, finishing it up:

> Russia! Russia! Russia!
> Messiah of the days to come!

The Urn (written after *Ashes* and published simultaneously) is a most curious collection of pessimistic and whimsically ironical meditations on the non-existence of the world of realities revealed by the philosophy of Kant. Since then Bely has written few poems, and his last book of lyrics (*After the Parting*, 1922) is frankly a collection of verbal and rhythmical exercises. But his one longer poem, *The First Meeting* (1921), is a charming work. Like Soloviev's *Three Meetings*, it is a mixture of grave and gay, a mixture which is curiously inseparable in Bely. A large part of it will again seem to the uninitiated nothing better than verbal and phonetic play. It must be joyfully accepted as such, and as such it is most exhilarating. But the realistic part of the poem is better than that. It contains some of his very best humorous painting—the portraits of the Solovievs (Vladimir, Michael, and Sergey) and the description of a big symphony concert in Moscow about 1900 are masterpieces of verbal expressiveness, of delicate realism, and of delightful humour. This poem is most closely connected with his prose works, and, like them, it is all based on a very elaborate system of musical construction, with leitmotivs, "correspondences," and "cross-references."

In the preface to his first prose work (*The Dramatic Symphony*), Bely says: "This work has three senses: a musical sense, a satirical sense, and, besides, a philosophical-symbolical sense." The same may be said of all his prose, except that the second meaning is not always strictly satirical —realistic would be more comprehensive. The last meaning, the philosophical, is that which Bely probably thinks the most important. But for the reader the first way of enjoying his prose is not to take his philosophy too seriously and not to rack his brain in trying to discover his meaning. This would be useless, especially as regards his later "anthroposophic" work, the philosophy of which cannot be understood without a prolonged initiation at Dornach. But it is also unnecessary. Bely's prose loses nothing from his philosophical symbols' being taken as merely ornamental. His prose is "ornamental prose"—an expression that has by now become a technical term, and which covers almost all the better prose written in Russia since, say, 1916. In this ornamental prose the symbols (and sound-symbols) he uses to express his metaphysics are by no means the worst ornament. "Ornamental" is not the same as "ornate" prose. It is not necessarily marked by conventionally uplifted diction, as Sir Thomas Browne's or Vyacheslav Ivanóv's. On the contrary, it may be crudely realistic, or even aggressively coarse (some of the younger "ornamentalists" have gone in this respect much farther than any naturalist ever dared to.) * The essential is that it keeps the reader's attention to every small detail: to the words, to their sounds, and to the rhythm. It is the opposite of Tolstoy's or Stendhal's analytical prose. It is the declaration of independence of the smaller unit. Western masters of "ornamental" prose are Rabelais, Lamb, Carlyle. The greatest Russian ornamentalist was Gogol. Ornamental prose has a decided tendency to escape the control of the larger unit, to destroy the wholeness of a work. This tendency is fully developed in almost every one of Bely's followers. But in Bely's own work it is counterbalanced by the musical architecture of the whole. This musical architecture is expressed in the very name of the *Symphonies*, and it is attained by a most elaborate system of leitmotivs and "cross-references," crescendos and diminuendos, and parallel developments of independent but (by their symbolism) connected themes. However, the centrifugal tendencies of the ornamental style usually have the better of the centripetal forces of musical construction, and, with the possible exception of *The Silver Dove*, Bely's symphonies and novels are but imperfect wholes. They cannot compare in this respect with the supreme unity of *The Twelve*. The symphonies (especially the first, entitled the *Second, Dramatic*) contain much excellent stuff, chiefly of the satirical order. But they cannot be recommended to the inexperienced beginner. The best way to approach Bely is either through *Recollections of Alexander Blok* or through his first novel, *The Silver Dove*.

The Silver Dove is somewhat less wildly original than his other works. It is closely modelled on the great example of Gogol. It cannot be called an imitative work, for it requires a powerful originality to learn from Gogol without failing piteously. Bely is probably the only Russian writer who has succeeded in doing so. The novel is written in splendid, sustainedly beautiful prose, and this prose is the first thing that strikes the reader in it. It is not so much Bely, however, as Gogol reflected in Bely, but it is always on Gogol's highest level, which is seldom the case with Gogol himself. *The Silver*

* Mr. James Joyce's prose would be described in Russia as "ornamental."

Dove is somewhat alone also in being the one of Bely's novels which has most human interest in it, where the tragedy is infectious and not merely puckishly ornamental. The scene is laid in a rural district of Central Russia. The hero, Daryalsky, is an intellectual who has drunk deep of the choicest fruit of European and ancient culture, but remains unsatisfied and desires to find a new truth. From the West he wants to go eastwards. He is insulted by Baroness Todrabe-Graben, the grandmother of his promised bride, and this helps him to break away from Western civilization. He meets a set of peasants belonging to the mystical and orgiastic sect of the White Doves. He joins them and lives the life of a peasant. He feels himself sucked in by their sensual mysticism, and though he knows moments of ecstatic bliss in his new surroundings, he feels himself again attracted by the pure image of his forsaken "Western" love. He tries to escape from the White Doves, but he is lured into a trap and murdered by the mystics, who are afraid of the revelations he may make, once escaped from their spell. The novel contains much more narrative interest than most Russian novels do. It has a complicated and excellently disentangled plot. The characters are vivid— like Gogol's, characterized largely by their physical features— the dialogue, alive and expressive. But what is perhaps especially wonderful are the evocations of Nature, full of intense suggestiveness and pregnant poetry. The feeling of the monotonous and endless expanse of the Russian plain pervades the book. All this, together with the splendidly ornamental style, makes *The Silver Dove* one of the works of Russian literature that are most full of the most various riches.

Petersburg, like *The Silver Dove*, is also a novel on the philosophy of Russian history. In *The Silver Dove* the theme is the opposition between East and West; in *Petersburg*, their coincidence. Russian Nihilism in its two forms, the formalism of the Petersburg bureaucracy and the rationalism of the revolutionaries, is represented as the meeting-point of the devastating rationalism of the West with the destructive forces of the "Mongol" steppe. The two Ableukhovs, the bureaucrat father and the terrorist son, are of Tartar origin. *Petersburg* is connected with Dostoevsky as much as *The Silver Dove* with Gogol, but not with the whole of Dostoevsky: only *The Double*, the most "ornamental" and Gogolian of all Dostoevsky's writings, is reflected in Bely's novel. Its style is unlike that of its predecessor; it is not so rich and it is, like *The Double*, tuned to a dominating note of madness. The book reads like a nightmare, and it is not always easy to realize exactly what is going on. It has a great power of obsession, and, like *The Silver Dove*, the narrative is thrilling. The story turns round an infernal machine which must explode in twenty-four hours, and the reader is kept in suspense by the detailed and many-sided account of these twenty-four hours, and the hero's decisions and counter decisions.

Kotik Letaev is Bely's most unique and original work. It is the story of his own infancy and begins with his recollections of his life before his birth, in his mother's womb. It is built on a system of parallel lines, the one developed in the real life of the child, the other in the "spheres." It is certainly a work of genius, though the detail is disconcerting and the anthroposophical interpretation of the child's impressions as a repetition of the older experience of the race is not always convincing. The main thread of the story (if story it be) is the gradual formation of the child's idea of the external world. This process is expressed with the aid of two terms which may be rendered as "swarm" and "form" (in Russian, *roy i stroy*). It is the crystallization of chaotic and infinite "swarms" into strictly circumscribed and orderly "forms." The development is symbolically enhanced by the child's father being an eminent mathematician, a master of "forms." But to the anthroposophist Bely, the boundless "swarms" are the truer and more significant reality. The continuation of *Kotik Letaev*— *The Crime of Nicholas Letaev*—is much less abstrusely symbolical and may easily be read by the uninitiated. It is the most realistic and the most amusing of Bely's works. It is unfolded in a real world: it is the story of the rivalry of his parents—his mathematical father and his elegant and frivolous mother—over his education. Here Bely is in his best form as a subtle and penetrating realist, and his humour (though the

symbolism never ceases) reaches its most delightful expression.
The Memoirs of a Crank, though splendidly ornamental, are
better left unread by those who are not initiated in the mysteries
of anthroposophy. But his last long work, *Recollections of
Alexander Blok* (1922), is easy and simple reading. The
musical construction is absent, and Bely obviously concentrates on the exact notation of fact. The style is also less
ornamental, sometimes even rather untidy (which is never the
case in his other works). The two or three chapters devoted
to the anthroposophical interpretation of Blok's poetry must
be skipped. The remaining chapters are a mine of the most
interesting and unexpected information on the history of
Russian Symbolism, but, above all, they are delightful reading.
Though he always looked up to Blok as to a superior being,
Bely analyses him with wonderful insight and penetration.
The account of their mystical association in 1903–1904 is
extraordinarily vivid and convincing, so skilfully does he succeed in restoring the atmosphere of these connexions. But
perhaps the best thing in the whole *Recollections* are the portraits of the secondary personages, which are painted with all
the wealth of intuition, suggestiveness, and humour that Bely
is capable of. The figure of Merezhkovsky is especially a
masterpiece of the first order. It has already gone home to
the public imagination, and the tasselled slippers which Bely
introduces as his leitmotiv will probably go down to posterity
as the immortal badge of their wearer.

11. MINOR SYMBOLISTS

One of the principal effects of the Symbolist movement was
to multiply a hundredfold the number of poets, to raise in an
almost equal degree the average level of their workmanship,
and their social position in the estimation of the public and of
the publishers. Since about 1905 all new-comers in Russian
poetry have been more or less pupils of the Symbolists, and
since about the same date all except the illiterate succeed in
writing verse of a technical standard that was inaccessible
except to the greatest about the year 1890. The influence of

Symbolism went in several main directions: there was the meta-physical and mystical school; the school of rhythm and verbal pageantry; the academic school which imitated the mature style of Bryusov; the "orgiastic" school which aimed at the emancipation from the fetters of form towards a spontaneous expression of the "elemental" soul; the school of glorified vice; * and the school of sheer technical acrobatism.

The older metaphysical poetry of the early Symbolists may be exemplified by the austere and unsensational poems of Jurgis Baltrushàitis (b. 1873), a Lithuanian, who was a diligent translator of the Scandinavians and of D'Annunzio (we owe to him also an excellent version of Byron's *Vision of Judgment*), and who is now Lithuanian Minister to the Soviet. Sergey Soloviev (b. 1886), the precocious and brilliant mystic whom I have mentioned on several occasions in the paragraphs on Blok and Bely, turned out in his poetry to be nothing but a very accomplished disciple of the academic manner of Bryusov. In spite of his mysticism and genuine Orthodoxy (in 1915 he became a priest), his poetry is antique in the most heathen sense of the word. His life of his famous uncle, Vladimir,† is, on the other hand, one of the most charming biographies in the language.

What the public liked in the Symbolists was their verbal splendour and their caressing melodies. This pageantry of the Symbolists is best vulgarized in the poetry of Mme. Teffy, the well-known humorist; and the Balmontian intoxication with melodious rhythms, in the poetry of Victor Hoffman (1884–1911), who may be taken as the "typical minor" Symbolist—with his sentimental prettiness and wistfulness, and his para-phernalia, so vulgarized afterwards, of beautiful ladies and devoted pages.

More promise than in any one of these poets was thought to be discerned in the exhilarating early verse of Sergey Gor-odétsky (b. 1884). In his first book, *Yar'* (roughly, *vital sap*; 1907), he displayed a wonderful gift of rhythm and a curious

---

* I remember a dialogue between two young poets about 1907: "How I love the word razvrat [debauch]!"—"I prefer the thing."

† Prefixed to the 1915 edition of Vladimir Soloviev's poems.

power of creating a self-invented—quasi-Russian—mythology. For a moment he was regarded both by the élite and by the public as the greatest hope of Russian poetry, but his subsequent books proved how little breath there was in him; he degenerated rapidly into an easy and insignificant rhymester. *Yar'*, however, remains as the most interesting monument of its time when Mystical Anarchism was in the air, when Vyacheslav Ivanov believed in the possibility of a new mythological age, and when the belief was abroad that the vital forces of man's elemental nature were to burst the fetters of civilization and of the world order. This belief found its formula in three lines of Gorodetsky's:

> We will rouse ancient Chaos!
> We will shatter chained Cosmos!
> For we *can,* we *can,* we *can!*

A curious and isolated figure is that of Count Vasili Alexeevich Komaròvsky (1881–1914). He was almost all his life on the dangerous border of insanity, and crossed it more than once. This familiarity with madness gives a distinctive flavour to his very exiguous writings. His poetry, most of which is contained in his only book, *The First Stage* (1913), is exceedingly original, at once whimsical and ornate. There is in it a feeling of a terrible abyss over which he most light-heartedly weaves the sunlit spider-webs of his splendid diction and of his erratic humour. Probably no poet ever succeeded in giving his verse that absolutely indefinable touch of unique personality so well as Komarovsky did. Still more unique and indescribable is his prose (most of which is yet unpublished), where his whimsical wilfulness runs riot and the malicious and unaccountable twinkle in his eye is suggestive of the more than human freedom of a being that is supremely free from the laws of causation. There is nothing like Komarovsky's prose that I know of in any language, but one must be singularly free from pedantry and singularly open to unexpected enjoyments to appreciate it. Komarovsky had connexions with Symbolism, especially with Annensky and Henri de Régnier, but he was not a Symbolist, because he was not an "ist" of any kind.

12. "STYLIZATORS": KUZMIN

An important aspect of the Russian æsthetic revival—of which Symbolism was but the most important literary expression—was a revival of interest in the artistic production of the past, both national and foreign. It often took the form, both in painting and in poetry, of consciously imitating the manner of old artists and old writers. This kind of creative pastiche is known in Russian literary jargon by the name of "stylization." In literature it affected principally the domain of prose. The Symbolists had no fixed idea as to what sort of prose they wanted to write, and each of them went his own way; so that while there is a Symbolist school of poetry, there is no Symbolist school of prose. While some Symbolists solved the problem by subjecting prose to rules derived from poetry (Balmont, Sologub, Bely), and others indulged in a free impressionism (Hippius), others again, not relying on themselves, sought for the guidance of some external authority and came to imitate the prose of past ages. Such was the case of Bryusov, whose best prose is always a "stylization." The method was not confined to prose, and many minor poets of the period devoted themselves more or less entirely to pastiches, attaining sometimes a great delicacy in this art. Such, for instance, is Yuri Verkhovsky, a great authority on the age of Pushkin and a skilful *pasticheur* of its poets. But the greatest name in this connexion is Michael Alexeevich Kuzmin (b. 1875), who, though a member of the Symbolist set (and for several years an inmate of "The Tower"), as a writer stands apart from the Symbolist school. He is a pure æsthete. His favourite periods in the past are the Alexandrian age, the early Byzantine times, and the eighteenth century. On the other hand, he is firmly grounded in the Russian religious tradition and has a peculiar sense of sympathy for the Old Believers. There is a distinct religious strain in his work, but it is not like that of the Symbolists—it is not metaphysical, but devotional and ritual. This religious element is inseparable in him from a refined and perverse sensuality. The two make a piquant blend which is not to the taste of all. His poetry is

different from that of the Symbolists in that it is more concrete
and less solemn. The feeling he expresses in it is almost invariably love. His craftsmanship is very high and his verses
are often exquisite. His first poetical sequence, *Songs of
Alexandria* (1906), is also his best. It was inspired by the
example of Pierre Louÿs' *Chansons de Bilitis;* but there can
be no doubt that the Russian poet's reconstructions of Alexandrian love-songs are far more delicate, refined, and suggestive.
These songs were followed by the whimsically exquisite
"eighteenth-century" pastoral *The Seasons of Love* (1907),
where his wonderful, almost acrobatic skill in handling rhyme
is at its best.* His later poetry consists partly of rather
tedious allegorical love-poems in the style of Petrarch's
Trionfi, partly of exquisitely frivolous evocations of "the
charming trifles" of life, in which he has no equal. In prose he
vindicates the ideal of "beautiful clarity," inspiring himself by
the example of the late Greek romancers, the Lives of the
Saints, the Italian *novella,* and the French novel of the eighteenth century. His style is affected and advisedly Frenchified. Its charm lies in its piquant and perverse flavour, for
though he writes novels of pure adventure, he is curiously
lacking in the power to tell a story. His stories of modern
life (the longest is the novel *Gentle Joseph,* 1910) are indifferently constructed and seldom interesting. But what is
admirable in them is the dialogue, which goes even farther than
Tolstoy's in reproducing the actual accents and freedom of
spoken language. He has also written scenarios for ballets,
operettas, and plays. They are usually mischievous and frivolous, and their principal charm lies in the rhymed passages.
The most exquisite of all is *The Comedy of St. Alexis,* an early
work (1907), which is especially typical of his manner of treating sacred things and which contains some of his best songs.

13. KHODASEVICH

The poets born after 1880 contributed little or nothing to
the genuine achievement of Symbolism. An exception must be

* The music to the pastoral is also by Kuzmin, who is a composer.

made in the case of Vladislav Felixovich Khodasévich (in Polish, Chodasiewicz; b. 1886).   Though in his technique he is almost free from Symbolist influences, the general spirit of his poetry is much more akin to Symbolism than to that of the younger school; for, alone of the younger poets, he is a mystic.   His first book appeared in 1908, but he won general recognition only after the publication of his latest, post-Revolutionary books, *The Way of the Grain* (1920) and *The Heavy Lyre* (1923), which are full of mature and confident art.   Khodasevich is a mystical spiritualist, but in the expression of his intuitions he is an ironist.   His poetry is the expression of the ironic and tragic contradiction between the freedom of the immortal soul and its thraldom to matter and necessity.   This eternal theme is expressed in his verse with a neatness and elegance rather reminiscent of the wit of an older age.   Wit, in fact, is the principal characteristic of Khodasevich's poetry, and his mystical poems regularly end with a pointed epigram. This manner is very effective and goes home to the most unpoetical reader.   He sprang into popularity in 1919–1920, when, under the influence of their superhuman suffering, the Russian intellectuals were more than usually open to the lure of mystic moods.   But even such an unmystical (and unpoetical) man as Gorky considers Khodasevich the greatest living Russian poet.   And if we are to judge poetry by eighteenth-century standards, Gorky is right, for Khodasevich is the greatest living master of poetical wit.   In spite of his mystical faith, he is a classicist and his style is a skilful revival of the forms and fashions of the Golden Age of Pushkin.

1

THE Great War did not very deeply affect Russian literature. The Russian *intelligentsia* did not respond to it in the way the educated classes of Germany, England, France, or Italy did. Against the great number of German, French, English, and Italian men of letters who fought or fell, Russian literature can oppose only the solitary name of Gumilev. The spirit of National Liberalism propagated by Struve and his friends contributed to raise a warlike spirit in the rear, but, with a few exceptions, sent no one to the front. The fighting was done by the military class and those whose traditions were connected with it. The direct effect of the War on Russian literature began to be felt only when those young men of the "classes" 1895 and following who had begun life as soldiers, cadets, or volunteers had sufficient leisure to turn to writing. This happened only in 1921, after the end of the civil wars. As for the attitude of the *intelligentsia* towards the War, it was pretty equally divided between patriotism, indifference, and *défaitisme*. I have alluded to the effort of Blok to avoid mobilization, and Blok was no exception. This being so, it is scarcely astonishing to find that the War is much less interestingly reflected in Russian literature than in that of the Western nations. The little there is (with the exception of Gumilev's lyrics and with the exception of young writers who made their appearance after the War) is the work of war correspondents, not of soldiers.

The February Revolution of 1917 at first aroused general enthusiasm, but before long the turn things took put an end to all patriotic optimism. The optimistic stage of the Revolution has hardly at all been reflected in Russian literature. The growing pessimism, and the feeling of the end of all things, already find powerful expression in a work written as early as August, 1917—Remizov's *Lament for the Ruin of Russia*. Memoirs of 1917 are very abundant; few of them belong to literature, but among these few are such outstanding works as Remizov's *Chronicle* and Victor Shklovsky's *The Front and the Revolution* (first part of *A Sentimental Journey*).

The Revolution that inspired revolutionary poetry was the October Revolution, the Bolshevik Revolution. The greatest works inspired by it did not come from Communists, but from mystics who had little in common with the leaders and aims of the Revolution—from Blok and Bely. Both Blok and Bely were in 1917 and 1918 closely linked with the Left S.R.'s, one of whose leaders and theoreticians was Ivanov-Razumnik, a literary historian, who is responsible for the "Scythian" doctrine. The "Scythians" were mystical revolutionaries who believed in the religious essence of the Bolshevik Revolution and in the purifying power of destructive cataclysms. Many intellectuals who had nothing in common with the atheistic optimism of Lenin welcomed his Revolution in a spirit of ecstatic suicide. They hoped and believed that the old bourgeois world that had so ineffectively heaped up its mound of culture would be destroyed, and that a new mankind would be born to a new life on a new and naked earth. They believed that the destruction of material wealth, of political and economic greatness, gave more freedom to the spirit, and that the coming age would be a great age of spiritual culture—the culture of eternity, in a phrase of Bely's. This way of feeling is present in the works of Blok, Bely, Gershenzon, Voloshin, Remizov, Khodasevich, and other men of the Symbolist generation. It grew and spread during the worst years of hunger, destruction, and terror. Mysticism was extraordinarily vital in 1918–1920. In Petersburg it had its centre in the Free Philosophical Society (*Volfila*, founded by Andrey Bely), which united both men who "accepted Bolshevism" and those who, rejecting Bolshevism, accepted the new age as an age of material destruction and spiritual creation. Similar feelings were spread among Orthodox Churchmen, who, definitely condemning the evil force of atheistic Communism, prepared for a new era of "primitive Christianity" when the Church, persecuted and betrayed, would shine all the brighter with a purer mystical light.

2

Russian Bolshevism is a branch of Russian Marxism, and the characteristics of Bolshevik political literature are those of Russian Marxist literature in general. As a whole, it is difficult reading, written in a party jargon which is unintelligible to the reader unless he is himself well versed in Marxism. It is intensely dogmatic, and authority plays in it a far greater part than free inquiry—the Marxist is as devoted to authority as ever a mediæval Schoolman was. The works of Marx, of Engels, and (since his death) of Lenin are considered infallible. The writings of orthodox Marxists like Kautsky and Plekhanov are venerated in so far as they do not err into heresy. An argument from Marx is irrefutable, unless the opponent succeeds in giving it another interpretation. The texts of Marx are (and Lenin's are beginning to be) interpreted in as many fashions as the Bible has been, because outside Holy Writ there is no certainty.

Of all Bolshevik literature, the writings of Lenin himself are certainly from every point of view the most interesting. Lenin was certainly an admirable orator, both in his speeches and in his writings. His language is comparatively free from conventional jargon. His exposition is lucid. He had a keen gift of irony, and a genius for formulating his ideas, and the various twists and turns of his policy, in pithy and memorable form. His writings are those of a man of action. He had the temperament of an orator but no literary culture, and his writings and speeches are not literature in the sense, for instance, that Jaurès's speeches are. Trotsky in his writings is little more than a spirited and clever pamphleteer. His style is slovenly and journalistic, and disfigured by the usual Bolshevik jargon. It is Russian only in the broadest meaning of the word. He has indulged also in "literary criticism," and in this capacity he has given proof, for a Communist, of a comparatively liberal mind. But, like all official Bolshevik "criticism," it is not concerned with literary values, but only with the pedagogic usefulness for the education of the proletariate of the works discussed. The only difference between the several Bolshevik critics is that some, like Trotsky and Voronsky, understand education in a wider sense and include a certain degree of general culture, while others think it should be reduced to the driving in of Marxism and "Leninism."

The literary man *en titre* of the Bolshevik oligarchy is Lunachàrsky, the Commissioner of Education. But while Lenin and Trotsky, whatever we think of their literary and philosophical merits, have certainly left in their writings the impress of powerful personalities, Lunacharsky, for all his relatively superior culture and literary pretensions, is nothing better than a third-rate provincial schoolmaster with a dash of the journalist. His prose is below the level of decent journalese. His verse would have been considered hopelessly flat and ineffective even in the days of Nadson. His dramas— which have had such an inexplicably good reception in England (at least in the Press)—are piteously puerile attempts at allegories of the worst and most tiresome kind. Of course the piteous effect of his verse is somewhat lost in translation, but even in translation it is easy to discern his absolute inability to make his characters live, and the self-important and pompous hollowness of his would-be profound Symbolism. The distance between *The Tempest* and Leonid Andreev at his worst is less than the distance between this worst and Lunacharsky. Happily, perhaps, for Lunacharsky's reputation abroad, extreme bathos is as untranslatable as is absolute perfection.

From the very beginning, the Bolsheviks had the Futurists for their allies, but their attitude towards these dangerous friends has been rather suspicious and cautious, though the great success of Mayakovsky's *Mystery-Bouffe* and his remarkable achievements in political satire have taught the Communist leaders to value him. This, however, and the much desired and encouraged rise of a Proletarian school of poets will be discussed in the chapter devoted to contemporary poetry.

3

The civil wars, which lasted almost exactly three years (from the "October"—old style—Revolution on November 7, 1917, to the fall of Wrangel in the middle of November, 1920 *), reached farther and wider into Russian life than the Great War did. The greater part of the Russian territory saw actual fighting. From the parts that did not, all the young men were enrolled in the Red Army. The civil war was also a much more terrible business than the war with Germany. On all sides—White, Red, and Green—it was accompanied by nameless cruelty. Epidemic diseases (over ninety per cent of the armies that fought in South Russia went through typhus) and the breakdown of all material civilization increased the horror produced by war. The civil war has been abundantly reflected in literature and has become the favourite material of the new school of fiction. We shall hear more of it in the last chapter.

The result of the defeat of the White Armies was that large quantities of Russian citizens found themselves outside Russia. The number of these political refugees or *émigrés* must be estimated at certainly above a million,† and as the educated classes form a very high proportion among them, it was natural that a literature by *émigrés* and for *émigrés* should come into existence. Ever since 1920 Russian publishing-houses began springing up in all the temporary and permanent centres of "Russia abroad": Stockholm, Berlin, Paris, Prague, Belgrade, Sofia, Warsaw, Reval, Harbin, and New York have all had their part in the publishing of Russian books. In 1922, when Germany was the cheapest country in Europe, there was

* After that date, fighting was continued and resumed from time to time, but was only of local importance.

† 400,000 in France alone, other important centres being Germany, Czechoslovakia, Bulgaria, Jugoslavia, the "succession states," French Africa, China, the United States, Brazil and Argentina.

a tremendous boom in the Russian presses of Berlin, and they began working for both the *émigré* and the home market. But the stabilization of the mark, and the growing severity of Bolshevik censorship, which practically excludes from Russia Russian (and not only Russian) books printed abroad, have put an end to the prosperity of the Russian publishers of Berlin. Only a few have survived. At present the principal intellectual centres of the Russian *émigrés* are Paris—which combines relatively cheap living with all the attractions of the metropolis of western civilization—and Prague—where the Czechoslovak Government has opened a Russian university and Russian secondary schools.

The number of *émigrés*, especially of the higher intellectual classes, is constantly growing, and received a notable reinforcement in 1922–1923, when the Soviet Government expelled from Russia some of the most "suspicious" intellectuals. Today the principal names of the *émigré* literary world are: the novelists Kuprin, Bunin, Artsybashev, Shmelev, Zaytsev; the humorists Teffy and Averchenko; the poets Balmont, Zinaida Hippius, Marina Tsvetaeva; Shestov, Merezhkovsky, Berdyaev, Bulgakov, Muratov, Aldanov-Landau, Prince S. Wolkonsky. This list does not include many other writers who live, or have lived, abroad without abandoning their Soviet allegiance and without identifying themselves with the White *émigrés*.

On the whole, the eminent writers who have found themselves outside the Soviet pale have not preserved their creative vitality. Loss of touch with the native soil is a severe ordeal for a writer. And though Bunin and others have continued producing estimable work, Russian writers of imaginative literature have produced little outside Russia.* The worst thing to be said about the *émigré* literature is that it has no healthy undergrowth: not a single poet or novelist of any importance has emerged from the ranks of the young generation outside Russia.

The case is quite different with political literature (in the

---

* This does not apply to non-imaginative literature: Shestov, for instance, has written books since his exile which are by no means inferior to anything he wrote before.

broadest application of the term). This is natural, for only outside the U.S.S.R. can Russian political and national thought develop in those conditions of freedom of the press which are necessary for its existence. The number of interesting political writers of the older (pre-War) generation among the *émigrés* is considerable. It includes Berdyaev and Struve (of whom I have already spoken); Shulgin (whose political memoirs will be mentioned in a later chapter); the Churchman and Monarchist V. A. Ilyin (one of the intellectuals expelled in 1922); the moderate Socialist Aldanov-Landau, who will be further mentioned as an historical novelist; the S.R.'s Bunakov-Fundaminsky, the most interesting representative of Nationalist Democracy, and Fedor Steppun, who tries to reconcile Socialism and Democracy with the Orthodox Church. The most interesting of all is perhaps Gregory Landau, the author of *The Sunset of Europe* (which has grown round an essay originally published in December, 1914), where he discusses from the point of view of positive and scientific sociology the deterioration of European civilization consequent on the Great War and the Peace of Versailles. But, above all, Russian political thought outside Russia is not fruitless, as imaginative literature is, and its most interesting manifestations come from a group of young men, unknown before the Revolution, who have adopted the name of Eurasians. The Eurasians are extreme Nationalists and hold that Russia is a cultural world apart, different both from Europe and from Asia—hence their name. Their ideas partly go back to those of Danilevsky and Leontiev, but they are a distinctly post-Revolutionary formation. They accept the Great Revolution as an irreversible fact—not without a certain national pride in its destructive greatness—but they emphatically condemn its "conscious evil will directed against God and His Church." They are Churchmen but not "seekers after God"—they want to draw strength from religion, not to give away to it all of theirs. They are practical realists, and it is probable that they will leave a trace in history rather than in literature. What makes Eurasianism especially significant and interesting is the fact that it is undoubtedly in tune with certain important tendencies inside

Russia. In literature the Eurasians cut a comparatively poor figure: only one of their number, Prince N. S. Troubetzkoy (son of the philosopher Prince S. Troubetzkoy), in spite of his inclination to be an *enfant terrible*, is a genuinely gifted pamphleteer. His preface, especially, to a Russian translation of H. G. Wells's *Russia in the Darkness* is a masterpiece of scathing sarcasm.

In 1921, when the Bolsheviks began their shortlived policy of concessions, a few *émigrés* (chiefly extreme Imperialists) "discovered" that Bolshevism, though International in appearance, was in substance Imperialistic, and started a movement of repatriation. The movement, for a time subsidized by the Soviet Government, resulted in the return to Russia and to the Soviet allegiance of a few intellectuals (the most prominent was the novelist A. N. Tolstoy). But, on the whole, it met with little success. This was due to the illusory character of the Bolshevik concessions, but still more to the too obvious fact that the *Change-of-Landmarks-men* (*Smenovekhovtsy*—from the name of their first publication, named so in allusion to Struve's *Landmarks*) were all, with the exception of Professor Ustryalov, hired agents of Moscow and commanded no respect. As a whole, the *émigrés* have remained uncompromisingly hostile to the Communists, and if the convergence of Bolshevism and Nationalism is to take place, it will take other ways than those proposed by the *Smenovekhovtsy*.

4

Russian literature inside Russia has, like the rest of Russia, traversed two distinct periods separated by the NEP (New Economic Policy). The NEP was inaugurated in 1921 and consisted in the abandonment of strict economic Communism and in the permission of private trade, which had up to that date been a criminal offence punishable in many cases with death. During the first period the drastic enforcement of absolute State monopoly, coupled with wholesale political (and economic) terrorism, and the complete breakdown of the rail-

ways, made life in the towns of Soviet Russia, especially in
Petersburg, something so unspeakably terrible that any description of the actual facts arouses natural disbelief—so impossible does it seem that any human being may have lived
through three or four years of such unrelieved horror. It is
not my task to record the sufferings of the bourgeois of Petersburg (Moscow being the seat of Government and situated
nearer to the corn-producing provinces, the conditions there
were a shade better). The writers suffered comparatively
less, owing largely to the various "enlightening" contrivances
of Gorky, but even they had to live for months at a time on
$\frac{1}{8}$ pound of bread a day—and even this was not always forth-
coming. Most of them passed the winters of 1918–1919 and
1919–1920 without getting out of their fur coats, for the
shortage of fuel was even more serious than the shortage of
food. These conditions of literary life in Petersburg in 1918–
1920 are vividly evoked in Victor Shklovsky's *Sentimental
Journey.* Writing could bring no money, because in the
course of 1918 all the private publishing businesses died out
and the State Press practically monopolized all the printing
industry. To keep alive, writers had to work at translations
for Gorky's *World Literature* enterprise, or in the theatres,
or to lecture in various extension schemes. Even for this they
got only insignificant increases of their rations. Books bearing the dates 1919 and 1920, especially if not issued by the
State Press (*Gosizdat*), are exceedingly rare and in the future
will probably be of special interest to collectors. If literary
publication did not quite cease, it was due partly to a few en-
lightened profiteers, partly to the extraordinary inventiveness
of certain young authors who contrived to get hold of stocks
of paper and have their books printed for nothing (the Imaginists were particularly good at this), partly to the State
Press's publishing certain works of literary propaganda (Mayakovsky). As for the Terror, the literary world suffered
comparatively little from it: of course all the writers who were
not Communists passed a few months in prison, but Gumilev
was the only writer of note to be officially executed. A cer-

tain number of less prominent authors and university professors were killed in a less formal way in the provinces, or died in prison.

In spite of all these conditions, literary life did not cease. In Petersburg independent literary life centred round Bely's *Volfila* and similar groups, and assumed a pronouncedly mystical colouring. In Moscow it was much noisier and less dignified, and its principal centres were the poetical cafés where Futurists and Imaginists read their verse and fought out their literary battles. The characteristic features of these years all over Russia were the aggressive and noisy prominence of Left literary groups; an almost morbidly exaggerated interest in the theatre, coupled with an absolute disregard for the public (all the theatres lived on government grants and could thus dispense with the public's approval); an overwhelming predominance of verse over prose; and an extraordinary abundance of literary "studios," where young men were formally taught the rudiments of their art by eminent masters of the craft. The most notable of these studios were the one in Petersburg where Gumilev taught the art of poetry and Zamyatin the art of prose, and the officially supported studio of Proletarian poets in Moscow conducted by Bryusov.

The first effect of the NEP on literature was to put an end to numerous State-subsidized institutions, and was consequently harmful rather than otherwise. The second was to bring into existence a number of private publishing enterprises (most of which had their head-quarters at Berlin, but worked for the Russian market); most of these enterprises were shortlived, and to-day the State Press is again by far the most important publisher and issues more books than all the others put together.* The general atmosphere of literary life changed and became more normal, less nervous, and more like prerevolutionary conditions at their worst. A very serious censorship has been established and has grown more rigorous every year. What was possible in 1922 is no longer possible in

---

* This is brought about chiefly by the pressure exercised on the private presses by means of taxes, which make all business unprofitable. The State Press pays no taxes.

1925, and political journalism, except it be strictly Communist, is quite out of the question. Even the Communist journalists are submitted to the strict control of the *Lito* (Literary Department—the present name of the censorship). As in the days of Nicholas I, fiction and poetry comprise the only printed stuff which enjoys a certain extent of freedom. But even imaginative literature suffers severely from the censor's tyranny: we know of numerous works by the best authors which have not seen, and have no chance of seeing, the press as long as the present conditions last. In this state of things, especially after the expulsion of intellectuals in 1922, very few are the men of letters resident in the U.S.S.R. who have not in one way or another done active homage to its present rulers: Russian writers have since 1921 given proof of much greater servility than was their wont under the old régime. All the greater respect is due to those who have kept aloof from expressions of devotion. In spite of this, very few writers, apart from the Futurists, with whom Bolshevism is a pre-Revolutionary tradition, are Communists. There are Communists who have become writers, but hardly any writers who have become Communists.* This is due partly to the great severity of the tests imposed on prospective Communists by the party, but also to the fact that the spirit of contemporary Russian literature at home, and of the thinking part of the nation in general, though it may be Bolshevik, is not Communist: it is distinctly not International. Aggressive, self-confident, self-conscious nationalism and contempt for the nations of the West constitute the most obvious feeling in all their writings, and in the conversation of all those who come abroad. Russia was never so entirely nationalist in feeling as since she has become the seat of the International. The writers who do not openly oppose the Soviet Government, and who pay at least lip-service to the wisdom of Marx and the greatness of Lenin, go by the name of *poputchik*, which means "fellow travellers up to a certain point." The question of how to treat these *poputchiks* is one that divides the Communist party: its "liberal" wing (headed by Trotsky and the "critic"

* The principal exception is Bryusov.

Voronsky) is in favour of encouraging them as long as they are not openly harmful to the Communist education of the people. A left wing, consisting chiefly of ambitious but talentless young Communist writers,* maintains that only those writers should be admitted to the State periodicals who are directly useful for that education. At a discussion of the subject in May, 1924, a committee summoned by the Central Organ of the Communist Party adopted a resolution in favour of Voronsky's policy. Owing to this policy, the State Press can fill the columns of its literary magazines with the work of the *poputchiks*, who make a tolerable living by their writings.

* Chiefly members of the MAPP—Moscow Association of Proletarian Poets.

CHAPTER VI

1. GUMILEV AND THE POETS' GUILD

IN so far as the movement started by the Symbolists meant a widening of the poetical horizon, an emancipation of individual originality, and a raising of technical standards, it is in full swing and all the worth-while Russian poetry written from the beginning of the century to the present day belongs to the same school. But the *differentia specifica* of the Symbolist poets—their metaphysical ambitions, their conception of the universe as a system of significant cross-references, and their tendency to assimilate poetry to music—was not taken up by their successors. The poetical generation born after 1885 continued the revolutionary and cultural work of the Symbolists—but ceased to be Symbolists. About 1910 the Symbolist school began to disintegrate, and in the course of the next few years rival schools came into existence, of which the two most important are the Acmeists and the Futurists.

Acmeism (the rather ridiculous word was suggested with a satirical intention by a hostile Symbolist and defiantly accepted by the new school; the name, however, was never very popular and has scarcely survived) had its centre in Petersburg. It was started in 1912 by Gorodetsky and Gumilev as a reaction against the Symbolist attitude. They refused to regard things as mere signs of other things. "We want to admire a rose," they said, "because it is beautiful, not because it is a symbol of mystical purity." They wanted to see the world with fresh and unprejudiced eyes as "Adam saw it at the dawn of creation." Their doctrine was a new realism, but a realism particularly alive to the concrete individuality of things. They tried to avoid the pitfalls of æstheticism and proclaimed as their masters (a queer set) Villon, Rabelais,

Shakespeare, and Théophile Gautier. Visual vividness, emotional intensity, and verbal freshness were the qualities they demanded of a poet. But they also wanted to make poetry more of a craft, and the poet not a priest but a craftsman. The foundation of the Guild of Poets was an expression of this tendency. The Symbolists who had wanted to make poetry a religious activity ("theurgy") resented this development, and remained (especially Blok) distinctly hostile to Gumilev and his Guild.

Of the two founders of the new school, Gorodetsky has been mentioned elsewhere. By 1912 he had already outlived his talent. He requires no further mention in this connexion (except that after writing some exceedingly chauvinistic war verse in 1914, he became a Communist in 1918, and immediately after the execution of Gumilev by the Bolsheviks wrote of him in a tone of the most servile vilification).

Nikolay Stepanovich Gumilév, apart from his historical importance, is a true poet. Born in 1886 at Tsarskoe Selo, he studied at Paris and at Petersburg. His first book was published in Paris in 1905. It was kindly reviewed by Bryusov, whose influence is very apparent in it as well as in the books that followed it. In 1910 Gumilev married Anna Akhmatova. This marriage was shortlived and they were divorced during the war. In 1911 he travelled in Abyssinia and Gallaland, where he returned once more before 1914. He retained a peculiar affection for equatorial Africa. In 1912, as has been said, he founded the Guild of Poets. Its publications had at first little success. In 1914 he was the only Russian author to enlist as a soldier (in the cavalry). He took part in the campaign of August–September, 1914, in East Prussia, was twice awarded the St. George's cross, and in 1915 obtained a commission. In 1917 he was detailed to the Russian contingent in Macedonia, but the Bolshevik Revolution found him in Paris. In 1918 he returned to Russia, largely from a spirit of adventure and love of danger. "I have hunted lions," he said, "and I don't believe the Bolsheviks are much more dangerous." For three years he lived in or near Petersburg, taking part in the big translation enterprises initiated by Gorky, teaching the art of verse to younger poets, and writing his best poems. In 1921 he was arrested on the (apparently false) charge of conspiring against the Soviet Government, and, after several months of imprisonment, was shot by order of the Cheka on August 23, 1921. He was in the full maturity of his talent; his last book was his best and was full of further promise.

Gumilev's verse is contained in several books, the principal of which are *Pearls* (1910), *A Foreign Sky* (1912), *The Quiver* (1915), *The Pyre* (1918), *The Tent* (1921), and *The Pillar of Fire* (1921); *Gondla* (1917), a play of Icelandic history, in rhymed verse; and *Mik*, a tale of Abyssinia. His few stories in prose are not important; they belong to his early period and are under the very obvious influence of Bryusov.

Gumilev's verse is most unlike the common run of Russian poetry: it is gorgeous, exotic, and fantastic; it is consistently in the major key and it is dominated by a note that is rare in Russian literature—the love of adventure and manly romance. His early book *Pearls*, which is full of exotic splendours, sometimes in doubtful taste, contains *The Captains*, a poem in praise of the great sailors and adventurers of the high seas; with characteristic romanticism, it ends with an evocation of the Flying Dutchman. His war poetry is curiously free from all "political" feeling—the ends of the war is what interests him least. A new religious strain is present in these war poems which is rather different from the mysticism of the Symbolists—it is a boyish and unquestioning faith, full of a spirit of joyful sacrifice. *The Tent*, written in Bolshevik Petersburg, is a sort of poetical geography of Africa, his favourite continent. The most impressive poem contained in it—*The Equatorial Forest*—is the story of a French explorer among the gorillas and cannibals in the malaria-haunted forest of Central Africa. His best books are *The Pyre* and *The Pillar of Fire*. In them his verse acquires an emotional tenseness and earnestness that is absent from his early work. It contains such an interesting manifesto as *My Readers*, where he prides himself on giving them a poetical diet that is not debilitating or relaxing, and which helps them to play the man and be calm in the face of death. In another poem he expresses his wish to die a violent death, and "not in my bed, before my solicitor and my doctor." This wish was fulfilled. His poetry becomes at times intensely nervous, as in the strange and haunting *Stray Tramcar*, but more often it attains to a manly majesty and earnestness, as in the remarkable dialogue of himself with his Soul and with his Body—where the Body ends its soliloquy with the noble words:

> But for all which I have taken, or yet desire,
> For all my sorrows, and joys, and follies,
> As it befits a man, I will pay
> By irrevocable and final death.

The last poem in the book, *Star-Terror*, is a strangely weird and convincing account of how primeval man first dared to look in the face of the stars. When he died, he was working at another poem of primeval ages, *The Dragon*, a curiously original and fantastic cosmogony, of which only the first canto was completed.

The Poets of the Guild, on the whole, are imitators of Gumilev, or of that precursor of theirs, Kuzmin. Though they write agreeably and efficiently, they need not detain us—their work is "school work." They are memorable rather as the principal figures of that gay and frivolous *vie de Bohème* which was such a prominent figure of Tout Pétersbourg in 1913–1916, and which had its centre in the famous artistic cabaret of the Prowling Dog. But two poets connected with the Guild, Anna Akhmatova and Osip Mandelstam, are figures of greater importance.

2. ANNA AKHMATOVA

The greatest name connected with Acmeism and the Poets' Guild is that of Anna Akhmàtova. This is the pseudonym (but a pseudonym that has practically replaced the real name even in private life) of Anna Andreevna Gorenko (Akhmatova is her mother's maiden name). She was born in Kiev, in 1889.

In 1910 she was married to Gumilev, and in 1911 her verse was first published. In 1912 her first book, *Evening*, appeared, with a preface by Kuzmin, and attracted little attention outside the literary élite. But her second book, *Beads*, which appeared in 1914 a few months before the war, had an unprecedented success. It made her at once famous, and went into more editions than any other book of verse of the new school. A third book, *The White Flock*, appeared in 1917, and a fourth, *Anno Domini*, in 1922. After her divorce from Gumilev, she married Vladimir Kazimirovich Shileyko, a brilliant young Assyriologist (who is also a poet of great originality but exceedingly meagre output), but a few years later they were separated. She lives in Petersburg and, since the death of Blok, has been the *princeps* of the literary republic of that city. Her poetry is strictly personal and largely autobiographical, but all biographical comment is of course premature.

Akhmatova's success is due precisely to this personal and autobiographical character of her poetry: it is frankly "sentimental" in the sense that it is all about sentiment; and the sentiment is not interpreted in terms of symbolism or mysticism, but in simple and intelligible human language. Her main subject is love. It is always exceedingly actual, not only in sentiment but in treatment. Her poems are realistic and vividly concrete: they are easily visualized. They always have a definite background—Petersburg, Tsarskoe Selo, a village in the province of Tver. Many of them may be described as dramatic lyrics (a term not irrelevantly evocative of Browning): *Meeting at Night* and *Parting at Morning* might have been written by Akhmatova. The chief feature of these short pieces (they have seldom more than twelve and never more than twenty lines) is their great compactness. The technical perfection of her verse cannot be conveyed in a translation, but her manner of constructing her lyrics may be seen, for instance, from the following version by Mrs. Duddington: *

> True tenderness is not to be mistaken
> For any other thing—and it's quiet.

* *Adelphi*, November, 1923.

> It is no use carefully wrapping
> My breast and shoulders in furs.
> And it is no use your talking
> So humbly about first love.
> How well I know that staring,
> That greedy look in your eyes!

I will venture to give also my own version of another "dramatic lyric" in a somewhat different tone:

> Ever since St. Agrafena's day,
> He keeps a crimson shawl,
> He is silent, but rejoices like King David,
> In his frosty cell the walls are white
> And no one talks to him.
> I will come and stand on his threshold;
> I will say: give me back my shawl.

Both these quotations are specimens of her "first manner" which made her popularity and which dominates in *Beads* and in a large part of *The White Flock*. But in this last book a new style makes its appearance. It dates from the poignant and prophetic poems bearing the suggestive title *July, 1914*. It is an austerer and sterner style, and its matter is tragical— the ordeal her country entered on since the beginning of the War. The easy and graceful metres of her early verse are now replaced by the stern and solemn heroic stanza, and similar measures. At moments her voice reaches a rude and sombre majesty that makes one think of Dante. Without ceasing to be feminine in feeling, it becomes "manly" and "virile." This new style has gradually ousted her early manner, and in *Anno Domini* it has even invaded her love lyrics and becomes the dominant note of her work. Her "civic" poetry can scarcely be termed political. It is above the medley of parties, and is rather religious and prophetic. One feels in her voice the authority of one who has the power to judge, and at once a heart that feels with more than common intensity. Here is a characteristic poem dated 1919:

Is ours in any sense worse than any previous age,
Except that in the frenzy of grief and anxiety

It laid its finger on the blackest of our ulcers
And was powerless to heal it?

The earth's sun is still shining in the West
And the roofs of towns are aglow with its setting splendour.
But here white [Death] is already marking the houses with crosses,
And calling in the ravens, and the ravens are on the wing.

In her latest work, Akhmatova seems to be deliberately trying to rid herself of all that which attracted the public
towards her. From the delicate refinement of the concentrated, boiled-down love novels that are her "dramatic lyrics,"
she has turned towards an austere and ascetic "grand style"
which has little chance of meeting the taste of the many. The
advanced schools of poetry consider Akhmatova old-fashioned
and "reactionary," but there can be little doubt that her place
is safe in the pantheon of posterity, among the small number
of genuine poets.

3. MANDELSTAM

Osip (Joseph) Emilievich Mandelstam (a Jew by birth, who
afterwards became a Mennonite) made his first appearance at
the same time and in the same publication as Akhmatova
(1911). He is one of the least prolific of poets: all his work
is contained in two little books, *The Stone* (1916) and *Tristia*
(1922); together they contain rather less than a hundred
short poems. Mandelstam is a man saturated with culture.
He has an extensive knowledge of Russian, French, and Latin
poetry, and most of his poetry is on literary and artistic subjects. *Dickens, Ossian, Bach, Notre Dame, St. Sophia*, Homer's catalogue of ships, Racine's *Phèdre*, a Lutheran burial,
are among his characteristic subjects. All this is not introduced merely for decorative purposes, after the manner of
Bryusov, nor treated as symbols of some *Ens Realius* as they
would have been by Ivanov, but with genuine historical and
critical penetration as individual phenomena with a well-defined
place in the current of history. Mandelstam's diction attains
sometimes to a splendid "Latin" sonority which is unrivalled

by any Russian poet since Lomonosov. But what is essential
in his poetry (however interesting may be his historical views)
is his *form*, and his manner of laying stress on it and making
it felt. He achieves this by using words of various contradictory associations: magnificent and obsolete archaisms, and
words of everyday occurrence hardly naturalized in poetry.
His syntax especially is curiously mixed—rhetorical periods
tussle purely colloquial turns of phrase. And the construction of his poems is also such as to accentuate the difficulty,
the ruggedness of his form: it is a broken line that changes its
direction at every turn of the stanza. His flashes of majestic
eloquence sound especially grand in their bizarre and unexpected setting. His eloquence is magnificent and, based as it
is on diction and rhythm, it defies translation. But, apart
from all else, Mandelstam is a most interesting thinker; and
his prose essays (unfortunately uncollected) contain perhaps
the most remarkable, unprejudiced, and independent things
that have ever been said on modern Russian civilization and
on the art of poetry. When they are collected, they will form
a book that will be absorbingly interesting to the student of
poetry as well as to the historian of Russian civilization.

4. THE VULGARIZERS: SEVERYANIN

Symbolism was an aristocratic poetry, which appealed, all
said and done, only to the elect. Akhmatova's poetry is more
universally interesting, but if it does not require any intellectual preparation, at least it demands from its reader a finer
sensibility than that of the average newspaper-reader and
picture-goer. But the picture-goer and newspaper-reader aspired to have his own poetry, and the great widening of poetical
taste allowed by the Symbolists permitted to include within the
pale of poetry much that was not allowed by "Victorians."
The moment came when Vulgarity claimed a place on Parnassus
and issued its Declaration of Rights in the verse of Igor
Severyanin.

Severyánin (pseudonym of Igor Vasilievich Lótarev, b.
1887) called himself a Futurist (Ego-Futurist), but he has

little in common with the creative movement of Russian Futurism. His poetry is an idealization of the aspirations of the average townsman, who dreams of cars, champagne, elegant restaurants, smart women, and fine perfumes. The originality of Severyanin was that he had the boldness to present all this in its naked naïveté, and to give the philosophy of a hairdresser's assistant the gait of an almost Nietzschean individualism. He had a genuine gift of song and a considerable rhythmical inventiveness, and it was no wonder that his verse struck the jaded palates of the great men of Symbolism. Sologub, the most refined of them, wrote an enthusiastic preface to Severyanin's *Thunder-Seathing Cup* (1912), and Bryusov thought him the best promise in Russian poetry. All poetical Russia was for a moment dazzled and intoxicated by the richness of Severyanin's rhythms. The boom soon passed and Severyanin passed out of the limelight. But he had conquered in the meanwhile the masses, and for several years his books sold all over Russia better than those of any other poet. With genuine Futurism he has nothing in common. His claim to be a Futurist was based on his love of such modern things as cars and palace hotels, and on his profuse coining of new words— most of which were in complete disharmony with the genius of the language. His favourite method was to introduce into his verse ill-digested French expressions from the jargon of restaurants and hairdressing saloons. His later books do not possess even those merits which are to be found in *The Thunder-Seething Cup*, and to-day Severyanin (who lives in Estonia) seems to have been forsaken by his former public.

At first Severyanin's catchword of Ego-Futurism collected round him a group of young poets, but the better sort very soon abandoned his leadership and joined one of the two camps of Acmeism, or of genuine Futurism.

5. MARINA TSVETAEVA

Many poetesses flourished and met with more or less general recognition about the time Anna Akhmatova commanded the admiration of the reader. These poetesses had all very much in common: they were "sentimental," and between them they monopolized emotional poetry. The most notable of these ladies were Marietta Shaginyàn (b. 1889), an Armenian of Rostov, whose very successful *Orientalia* (1st ed., 1912) aimed at a "biblical" intensity of emotion and an oriental braveness of colour; and Marie Moràvsky, who united extreme sentimentality with interesting attempts to learn from the modern popular factory song (*chastushka*).

On a much higher level of creative poetic achievement, and entirely free from the doubtful amenities of ladyish poetry, is the remarkably original and fresh poetical talent of Marina Tsvetàeva (maiden name of Marina Ivanovna Efron, b. in Moscow, since 1922 resident in Prague). Her development was independent of all schools and guilds, but is representative of the general tendency of the most vital part of contemporary Russian poetry to escape from the fetters of "themes" and "ideas" into a free land of forms.

Her first book appeared in 1911. It was too obviously the work of a schoolgirl, but it seemed to promise something better. The promise has been richly fulfilled. During the revolutionary years Tsvetaeva published nothing, but the verse she wrote between 1916 and 1920 was circulated in manuscript in Moscow, and when after the revival of the book trade she almost simultaneously published several new books of verse it came as a revelation. She at once became one of the major lights of our poetical firmament. She writes much and evidently with great facility, and this sometimes reflects on the level of her work; much of it is second-rate and slovenly. But she is always original, and her voice can be mistaken for no one else's. For rhythmical swing she has few equals. She is especially a master of staccato rhythms which give the impression of hearing the sound of hoofs of a galloping horse. Her poetry is all fire, enthusiasm, and passion; but it is not sentimental, nor even in the true sense emotional. It "infects" not by what it expresses, but by the sheer force of its motion. This force is quite spontaneous, for she is not a great craftsman and the level of her work varies very greatly. At her worst she is painfully pretentious and obscure. But there is nothing more exhilarating than some of her short poems, simple, direct, full of breath. The very nature of her poetry makes it untranslatable. Besides, she is intensely Russian (though without a trace of mysticism or religion) and her poetry constantly re-echoes with the sounds of the people's songs. Her only long poem, *The King-Maiden* (1922), is in this respect a true marvel. Except Blok in *The Twelve*, no one has ever achieved anything of the sort with the aid of Russian songs: it is a wonderful fugue on a popular theme, and, unlike the greater poet's poem, it is free from every trace of mysticism.

As Marina Tsvetaeva is alive (and one is even tempted to add "and kicking"), the rule *aut bene aut nihil* does not apply to her, and it is only fair to say that the prose she has hitherto written is the most pretentious, unkempt, hysterical, and altogether worst prose ever written in Russian.

6. "PEASANT POETS" AND IMAGINISTS: ESENIN

In 1912, when Symbolism was disintegrating and the young schools seemed to offer little promise, and even such Leviathans as Sologub and Bryusov recommended Igor Severyanin as the great poet of to-morrow, the attention of the poetry-reading public was attracted by a little book of verse which bore the name of Nicholas Klyùev. It bore evident traces of Symbolist influence, but it was still more full of the genuine lore and imagery of the people. It was fresh and racy of the North Russian soil. Klyuev turned out to be a peasant from Lake Onego. The Onego country has preserved and developed better than any other district the ancient treasures of folk-poetry, of artistic handicraft, of wooden architecture, and of ancient ritual. His poetry was animated by a cult of the people. It united an ancient religious tradition with a mystical revolutionism. In 1917, when Ivanov-Razumnik preached his Scythian theories and Blok and Bely were of the number of his followers, it was natural that Klyuev, the poet of mystical "populism" and revolutionism, should be extolled to the skies by these Scythians. For a moment, together with the younger peasant poet Esenin, he seemed one of the largest lights of Russian poetry. But since then their fame as the poets of a mystical and revolutionary peasantry has faded, and their ways have parted. Esenin deserted the Scythian banner. Klyuev returned to his Northern home and, after publishing a satire against the renegade Esenin, has become silent. His poetry is the expression of a peculiar religion which accepts all the symbolism and ritual of the people's faith, but rejects its religious substance: Christianity is replaced by a cult of the people, and the images of Christian saints become holy not for what they represent but for whom they are worshipped by.

Klyuev's poetry is overloaded with ornament, with bold and gaudy metaphor and symbolism. In spite of his peasant origin, he is saturated with tradition and overloaded with ages of culture almost more than any other poet. He tries to give a mystical interpretation of the same style to the Bolshevik Revolution, and to identify it with the ancient religious movements of the Russian people. One of his most characteristic poems is *Lenin*, where he discovers in the Communist leader a kinship with the religious leaders of the Old Believers' schism!

The second peasant poet brought forward by the Scythians is Sergey Esénin (b. 1895). He is a product of South Great Russia (Ryazan), which has not the ancient and archaic civilization of the North, and where the peasant had always a tendency to be semi-nomadic with no firm roots in the soil. The Scythian revolutionism of Esenin was of a different kind from Klyuev's: he has no interest in religious symbolism and ritual; his mysticism is skin-deep, and the quasi-blasphemous poems he wrote in 1917 and 1918 were nothing more than his contribution to a fashion that raged among the belated Symbolists of the day. These poems, which seemed such profound revelations to the good Ivanov-Razumnik (and, later on, to a few good European critics also), are in point of fact the sheerest and most shamefaced nonsense. Fortunately for Esenin, his reputation does not stand and fall with these poems. He is a genuine poet and has a rare gift of song. He is genuinely akin to the spirit of the Russian folk-song, though he does not

adopt its metres.   This blend of wistful melancholy and insolent dare-devilry is characteristic of the Central Russian: it
is present in the Russian folk-song, and in Esenin it manifests
itself both in the pensive sweetness of his elegies and in the
aggressive coarseness of his *Confession of a Hooligan*.   There
is no genuine mystical or religious background in Esenin, but
a certain gay and careless Nihilism which every moment may
turn into a sentimental wistfulness, under the influence of love,
of drink, or of recollection.   There is no vigour in Esenin; if
Klyuev is a rural Byzantine or Alexandrian, Esenin is a sort
of peasant Turgenev, who sees the disappearance of all the
beauty that is dear to him, laments it, but submits to the inevitable.   His short lyrics are often very beautiful, though in
the long run monotonous.   All their charm lies in the sweetness of their melody.   His only longer work, the "tragedy"
Pugachov (1922), is not a tragedy at all but merely a succession of (often exquisite) lyrics put into the mouths of a famous
rebel and of his companions and enemies.

In life Esenin has ever since the Revolution of 1917 tried to
play up to his reputation of the "hooligan poet."   He was
the principal figure of the poetical cafés that flourished in
Moscow in 1918–1920, and in 1922 he acquired a world-wide
notoriety by his ephemeral marriage with Miss Isadora Dun-
can.   In his exploits he was backed by some other poets who
called themselves the Imaginists,* and were a very prominent
and noisy feature of literary life in Moscow.   During the
worst days of Bolshevik tyranny, when book-publishing had
become impossible, the Imaginists were a living reminder of undying freedom: they were the only independent group that
were not afraid to make themselves noticed by the authorities,
and they were wonderfully skilful in getting their slender little
collections and manifestoes printed by fair means or foul.   As
poets these Imaginists are not of any very great importance,
and the names of Shershenevich, Marienhof, and the "Cir-

---

* The Imaginists should not be thought of as the Russian counterpart of
the American Imagists.   These last have rather more in common with the
Acmeists than with the Imaginists.

cassian" Kusikov are not likely to survive. The theory of Imaginism was that the principal thing in poetry is "imagery," and their poetry (as well as much of Esenin's) is an agglomeration of "images" of the most far-fetched and exaggerated description. A principal point of their practice was not to distinguish between "pure" and "impure," and to introduce the coarsest and crudest images in the immediate neighbourhood of the pathetic and sublime. Some of the Imaginists were merely "hooligans," but in others a tragical "crack" (*nadryv*, to use Dostoevsky's word) is clearly present. They had a morbid craving for dirt, humiliation, and suffering, like the Man from Underground. The most "Dostoevskian" of these poets is Ryurik Ivnev, who, in spite of the hysterical substance of his inspiration, has sometimes succeeded in giving it a memorable and pointed expression, especially in certain poems on the tragical fate of Russia, which are unexpectedly reminiscent of Akhmatova's.

7. THE RISE OF FUTURISM

Russian Symbolism traced its tradition to a foreign source, but ultimately developed along national lines. Russian Futurism has nothing in common with the Italian movement of the name, except the name itself and its most general associations. It is one of the most purely domestic developments of modern Russian literature. If one were obliged to point out any Western movement most like the first stages of Russian Futurism, it would be the French Dada movement, which, however, belongs to a later date (1919–1920). In its further stages, Russian Futurism became very many-sided, and there is little in common between such poets as Khlebnikov, Mayakovsky, and Pasternak beyond a general will to escape from the poetical conventions of the past age and to air the poetical vocabulary.

As a whole, the work of the Russian Futurists may be summed up as follows: they *continued* the work, begun by the Symbolists, of revolutionizing and transforming metrical forms and of discovering new possibilities for Russian prosody; they fought against the Symbolist idea of the mystical essence of poetry, replacing the conception of the poet as priest and seer by that of the poet as workman and artisan; they worked to destroy all the poetical canons of the past by divorcing poetry from what is traditionally considered poetical, from every kind of conventional and ideal beauty; and they worked at constructing a new language that would be free from the emotional associations of current poetical diction.

Russian Futurism dates from 1910, when appeared Khlebnikov's, now famous, etymological poem, which was nothing but a series of fresh-coined derivatives from one word *smekh* (laughter). From 1911 to 1914 the Futurists did their best to *épater le bourgeois* in their aggressively unconventional publications, in their public conferences, and even in their personal appearance (for instance, they painted pictures on their faces). They were treated like lunatics or like insolent hooligans, but their principles and their work soon impressed themselves on their fellow poets and they soon became the most vigorous literary group in the country. There can be no doubt that their revolutionary work in rejuvenating the methods of the craft, and in exploding the mystical solemnities of Symbolism, was bracing and invigorating to Russian poetry, which was showing the most dangerous symptoms of anæmia caused by a too spiritual and fleshless diet.

All those who were rejected by "bourgeois" literature found hospitality with the Futurists. Many of these hangers-on of Futurism were merely insignificant and ambitious poetasters. But they also preserved the memory of at least one genuinely interesting writer—Elena Gurò (died young in 1910). Her delicate and sensitive writings in free verse and beautifully light prose had passed quite unnoticed by the Symbolists. Her two books, *The Hurdy-gurdy* (1909) and *The Little Camels of the Sky* (1912), are a wonderland of delicate and unexpected expression of the thinnest tissue of experience. They have never been reprinted and are practically inaccessible.* They will certainly be "discovered" some day and their author restored to the place she is entitled to.

The founder of Russian Futurism was Victor (or, as he renamed himself, Velemir) Khlébnikov (1885–1922), who died in extreme poverty when his friends were at the height of their popularity and official favour. Khlebnikov is an exceedingly curious and original figure. Unlike the other Futurists, he was a kind of mystic, or rather he had the mystically realistic mentality of primitive man. But his mysticism was a mysticism of *things* and words, not of ideas and symbols. In life he was strangely superstitious, and in his poetry he is rather a conjurer playing with the language than what we understand by the word "poet." Words and forms had for him an existence of their own, and his work in life was to create a new world of words. He had a deep, primary feeling for the nature of the Russian language. He is a Slavophil, but a pre-Christian, almost pre-pagan Slavophil. His Russia is a Russia free from all the scales of Christian and European civilization, a Russia which had been "scratched down to the Tartar." His vision of the primitive world was not the pageant of Gumilev's mythology, nor the virtuous simplicity of Rousseau: what he was after was not natural man, but magical man. All things were only a material for him to build up a new world of words. This world of words is without doubt a creation of genius, but it is obviously not for the general. He is not and probably never will be read except by poets and philologists, though an anthology *ad usum profanorum* might be selected from his works which would present him more attractively and accessibly than he chose to do it himself. As for the poets, they have found him an inexhaustible mine of good example and useful doctrine. They use his works as a granary whence they take the seeds for their own harvests. His work is also of great interest to the philologist, for he was a lord of language: He knew its hidden possibilities and forced

---

* I have not had the opportunity of re-reading them since 1914, and to my regret can give no more detailed account of them.

it to reveal them. His work is a microcosm reflecting on an enormously magnified scale the creative processes of the whole life-story of the language.

Khlebnikov in his creative linguistics was true to the genuine spirit of the Russian language; the method he uses is the same as that used by the language itself—analogy. Another Futurist (Kruchónykh) endeavoured to create an entirely new language or even to use a new language, created *ad hoc*, for every new poem. This movement led to little good, for Kruchonykh himself and most of his followers had no feeling for the phonetic soul of Russian, and their *written* inventions are, more often than not, simply unpronounceable. But when this "trans-sense" (*zaumny*) language is used in sympathy with the phonetic soul of the language, it produces rather amusing and interesting effects. The essential thing to make it alive is a good delivery which, adding to the "trans-sense" words the perfectly sensible intonation, gives the illusion of listening to "Russian as it might have been." The young Futurist Ilya Zdanévich (resident in Paris) is especially good at the game. A "trans-sense" play in his own delivery makes most amusing stuff to listen to. The "trans-sense" movement certainly contributed to the "de-Italianization" of Russian poetry, and favoured a return to the rougher and ruder phonetic harmonies of the language.

A more eclectic group of Futurists who also felt the necessity of invigorating and reforming poetical methods, instead of trying to create a new language or of going back to the primal roots of the old, tried to learn new methods from the old writers, especially those of the Golden Age (1820–1830)—especially Yazykov, who was a Futurist *avant la lettre*—and of the eighteenth century. They became diligent students of Russian poetry and continued the metrical researches of Andrey Bely, but their task, like that of the Futurists, was to find fresh forms and new strength. These scholarly Futurists have much in common with Mandelstam, and from their ranks came the remarkable poetry of Pasternak.

8. MAYAKOVSKY

All these manifestations of Futurism remained a sort of esoteric literature, important and necessary for the inner life of Russian poetry, but by their very essence incapable of attaining the public. To the general poetry-reader and to the man in the street, Futurism is synonymous with the poetry of Mayakovsky.

Vladimir Vladimirovich Mayakòvsky was born in 1893 in Transcaucasia. As a boy of thirteen or fourteen, he became a member of the Bolshevik party. In 1911 he came in contact with the beginning Futurists and began writing verse. He was hardly distinguished at first from the other Futurists, but gradually he began to emerge as something essentially different from the rest. His poetry was not intended for the studio, but for the street; it was free from "trans-sense"; it was full of human interest; and it was frankly rhetorical—only rhetorical in a very new and unexpected way. When, in 1916, his poems appeared in book form, under the characteristic title *As Simple as Mooing*, they met with a considerable success. In 1917 Mayakovsky shared the triumph of his party and became something like an official Bolshevik poet. Much of his poetry written in 1918–1921 is direct political propaganda (*A Mystery-Bouffe, 150,000,000*) or satires written more or less to order. Since 1923 Mayakovsky has been the "responsible editor" of the Communist-Futurist magazine *Lef*. He is also a designer, and in 1918–1920 his principal occupation was drawing propaganda posters.

Mayakovsky's poetry is extraordinarily unlike that of the Symbolists: he recognizes as the only poet who at all influenced him (except the Futurists) the satirist Sasha Cherny, whom I have already mentioned as the only man who wrote "unpoetical" verse during the reign of Symbolism. In prosody Mayakovsky is a continuer of the Symbolists; but the destruction of the classical syllabism of Russian verse which with them was only one of many tendencies becomes a fully developed system with Mayakovsky. His versification is based on the number of stress-accents (which in Russian is equivalent to the

number of words) in a line, and completely disregards all un-
stressed syllables. His rhyming system is also a development
of Symbolist tendencies, but here again Mayakovsky has made
a coherent system of what was only a tendency with the Symbolists: the principal stress is laid on the consonants preceding
and following the rhyming vowel; the quality and even the number of vowels that come after the stress is indifferent. He
revels in long rhymes composed of more than one word and in
punning rhymes—his whole method of rhyming would vividly
remind the English reader of Browning: *ranunculus* and
Tommy-make-room-for-your-uncle-us would be a good equivalent of the more conservative type of Mayakovskian rhyme.
Mayakovsky's new versification has had a very wide influence
on Russian poetry, but it has not succeeded in superseding the
old syllabic system, which is, after all, much more various and
full of resource than his.

Mayakovsky's poetry is very loud, very unrefined, and stands
absolutely outside the distinction between "good" and "bad"
taste. He uses the diction of every day in its cruder forms,
deforming it to suit his needs in a direction opposite to that
of the older poetical tradition. His language is free from
"trans-sense" elements; but, considered as a literary language,
it is a new dialect, a dialect which is entirely his own creation.
For the way he puts to use the elements of spoken language
makes them sound quite different from the usual. The harmony of his verse with its heavy emphatic beat and its rude
"unmusical" choice of sound is like the music of a drum or of
a saxophone. There is a certain affinity between Mayakovsky
and Mr. Vachel Lindsay. But, apart from the difference of
spirit animating the two poets, Mr. Lindsay's poetry is essentially musical, intended to be sung in chorus—Mayakovsky's
cannot be sung at all; it is declamatory, rhetorical—the verse
of an open-air orator. Judged but by "Victorian" standards,
his verse is simply not poetry at all; and judged by Symbolist
standards, it is no better. But it is largely owing to our Symbolist education, which has widened to such an extent our poetical sensibility, that we are capable of appreciating this rowdy
and noisy rhetoric. Mayakovsky is genuinely popular and

read by a very wide circle of readers. His appeal is direct and simple, his subjects can interest the most uncultured, while the high originality of his craftsmanship makes him a paramount figure in the eyes of the professional poet.

Mayakovsky's favourite method of expression comprises (besides purely verbal effects based on the utilization of "unpoetical" diction) metaphor and hyperbole. Both his metaphors and his hyperboles are developed in a realistic way, which recalls to a certain extent the *concetti* of the seventeenth century. He indulges in what his commentators call the "realization of metaphor," which is a powerful way of giving life to worn-out clichés: if he introduces the hackneyed metaphor of his heart burning with love, he heightens it by developing a whole realistic picture of a fire with firemen in casques and top-boots infesting the burning heart. If he symbolizes the Russian people in the colossal figure of the *moujik* Ivan, the champion of Communism, he describes in detail how he wades the Atlantic to fight in single combat the champion of capitalism, Woodrow Wilson. The inspiration of Mayakovsky's poetry is materialistic and realistic—this is his principal ground in common with atheistic Communism. His credo is expressed best of all in four lines of the prologue to the *Mystery-Bouffe:*

> We are fed up with heavenly candies,
> Give us real rye-bread to feed on!
> We are fed up with cardboard passions,
> Give us a live wife to live with!

But of the genuine spirit of Communism, there is very little in Mayakovsky, and the responsible Communists easily discern in him a dangerous individualism. Though "Mayakovsky," who is the hero of most of Mayakovsky's early poems, may be interpreted as a synthetic impersonation, he is more naturally taken as the actual man, and in his political poems the pathos is revolutionary, to be sure, and atheistic, but it is only superficially dyed in Socialist colours. Mayakovsky is not a humorist; in his satires he inveighs instead of ridiculing. He is an orator, and even his crudities and coarseness serve the ends of serious poetry. This is one of his most original features.

Mayakovsky's principal works are his longer poems. Those written before 1917 are mainly egotistic in inspiration. There is a distinct decadent and neurasthenic element at the bottom of their loud clamour. The most remarkable of these poems are *Man*, an atheistic apotheosis of self, and *The Cloud in Trousers*, a "sentimental" poem with definite revolutionary "premonitions." *War and Peace* is already a social poem. All these were written in 1915–1916. In 1917–1918 he writes the brilliant, exhilarating, and witty *A Mystery-Bouffe*, an Aristophanesque satire of the bourgeois world defeated by the proletarians. In 1920 he writes *150,000,000* (the figure represents the number of inhabitants in Russia), an invective against the "blockade" of Soviet Russia by the bourgeois West. After 1921 he writes satires of internal Soviet disorders but he also returns to egotistic poetry, most of which is on the subject of love. The lyrical poem *I Love* (1922) is perhaps the most immediately attractive of his poems for the general poetry-reader: it is free from excessive crudities, but constructed throughout on a system of elaborate *concetti*. His latest big poem is also on the subject of love. It is far less attractive, and, on the whole, is tedious. It appeared with the portrait of the woman to whom it is addressed, whose name is universally known and who is the wife of one of his literary and personal friends. It marks a certain decline of his powers, and the same is noticeable in all his recent work (written in 1923–1924), much of which is again satire or propaganda written to order.

9. OTHER LEF POETS

Mayakovsky is the head of the *Lef* (from Levy front—left front), the review of the Futurists who have whole-heartedly identified themselves with Communism.

The *Lefs* are aggressive and extreme in their denunciations of all "reactionary," "bourgeois," and mystical tendencies. But what interests them is revolution in art, much more than social revolution. So, in spite of their Bolshevik fervour, they are looked upon with suspicion by the official leaders of Communism. They are allowed a grant of money for their publication, but beyond this they have little influence with the powers that be.

The *Lef* opens its columns to all Futurists, including such essentially non-political poets as the late Khlebnikov, the "trans-sense" Kruchonykh, and Pasternak. But its principal poets are poets of Revolution. These include—besides Mayakovsky—Kamensky, Aseyev, and Tretiakov.

Vasili Kaménsky, one of the original Futurist squad, has much in common with Mayakovsky, but also not a little (especially in his pre-Revolutionary verse) with Igor Severyanin. He is an adept in "trans-sense." His best-known verses are the spirited *Songs of the Companions of Razin,* the famous rebel of the seventeenth century.

Nicholas Aseyev and Sergey Tretiakov began their career in the semi-Futurist publications of the pre-Revolutionary years. Like several other Futurists, they passed the years of the civil war in the Far East, where they actively served the Soviet cause. Both are better Communists than Mayakovsky. Tretiakov has written "trans-sense," but in the main he is a disciple of Mayakovsky. He has recently published a very clever poem of Asiatic propaganda, *Roar, China!* It is based on the phonetic utilization of the street cries of Peking.

Aseyev, like Mayakovsky, is an orator as much as a poet: he has been strongly influenced by that poet and by Pasternak, but he tends towards a more conventional and pathetic style of oratory: his poems often recall the invectives of Barbier, Hugo, or Lermontov. His verse is vigorous and nervous, and he has a great command of rapid, metallic rhythms. He has given forceful expression to the pet Communist idea of idealizing industrialism and machines: one of his books is called *The Steel Nightingale,* and the opening poem is an ode to this mechanical bird as preferable to the living one. Like Mayakovsky, Aseyev writes much purely propaganda work, a good instance of which is his poem *Budenny,* where he gives a rhymed biography of that famous leader of the Red Cavalry, in a style which is half-way between Mayakovsky and the folk-song.

10. PASTERNAK

If a vote were taken among Russian poets under forty for the name of the first of young poets, it is probable that the name of Boris Leonidovich Pasternàk would head the poll. He began publishing in 1913 in the *Centrifuga*, an association of "moderate," scholarly Futurists. For several years he was little more than one of a great number of more or less promising poets, and his only book published before 1917 attracted little attention. In 1917 he wrote that wonderful series of lyrics which forms the book *My Sister Life*. It was not published at the time, but was circulated in manuscript, and Pasternak gradually became the universal master and exemplar. Imitations of his style began to appear in print before his book was published, and very few poets have escaped his influence. Not only Futurists like Aseyev, but poets of very different schools, like Mandelstam and Tsvetaeva, were affected by it, and even Bryusov's last verse is a conscientiously studious imitation of Pasternak. The book appeared in print only in 1922. It was followed by a second volume, *Themes and Variations* (1923), which, though not always on the same level as the first, at times achieves even greater things. He has within the last year written some stories in prose in an equally original and interesting style. The public, unlike the poets, remained more or less cold to Pasternak, by reason of his excessive "difficultness."

It is very tempting to compare Pasternak with Donne: like Donne's, though not so long, Pasternak's poetry remained unpublished and unknown except to poets; like Donne, he is a "poet's poet" whose influence on fellow-craftsmen is far greater than his popularity with the reader. Passing to less external characteristics, Pasternak resembles Donne in his combination of great emotional intensity with highly developed poetical "wit"; like Donne's, one of his principal novelties is the introduction of technical and "vulgar" imagery in place of stock poetical diction; and, like Donne's, his verse consciously aims at avoiding the easy mellifluousness of the preceding period and

at destroying the "Italianate" sweetness of poetical language.*
In this respect, however, Pasternak is only one of the
Futurists.

Two things especially strike the reader in Pasternak: the
great intensity of his poetical passions, which has led to comparisons with Lermontov; and the extraordinary analytical
acuteness of his vision, combined with a deliberate freshness in
expressing it. Pasternak's landscapes and still-lifes are perhaps his most remarkable achievements. They give the impression of seeing the world for the first time; at first they seem
ludicrously far-fetched, but the oftener one re-reads them, the
more one realizes the almost mathematical precision and exactness of his imagery. This is, for instance, how he conveys the
idea of the very familiar Russian sight of a road so polished by
cart-wheels that it reflects the stars by night: "And you cannot cross the road without treading on the whole universe."
This is romantic in spirit. And here is a typical prosaic simile from a poem on *Spring:* "The air is blue like the bundle of
wash which a convalescent takes with him from the hospital."

Pasternak's rhythms are also remarkable; nowhere does he
attain such force as in the wonderful series of lyrics (*Themes
and Variations*) *The Quarrel,* on the subject of his final quarrel
with his mistress. For emotional and rhythmical force, these
nine lyrics have no rivals in modern Russian poetry. This
emotional element makes Pasternak very different from the
other Futurists, with whom he has in common only the will to
re-form poetical diction. The difference is emphasized by his
non-political attitude and by the absence of "trans-sense."
His obscurity, very real to a superficial reader, comes from the
novelty of his way of seeing and noting what he sees, but needs
no key to it, nothing more than attention. If Pasternak proceeds from any master, it is, above all, Annensky, who was obscure in somewhat the same way; but Annensky was decadent

---

* I must add, however, that any direct influence of Donne (whose poetry
is quite unknown in Russia) on Pasternak is exceedingly improbable. Besides, there is only a general similarity of tendencies, and no coincidence of
detail.

and morbid to the core—Pasternak is quite free from all morbidity; his poetry is bracing and all in the major key.

The few prose stories he has written are remarkable for the same courage of seeing for himself: the first strange impression produced by this disintegration of the world along new lines gradually changes into an acceptance of this new world, or rather of this new way of reducing its multiplicity to intelligible forms. There is ground to believe that he will develop into an interesting prose-writer, but he will primarily remain a great lyrical poet.

11. THE PROLETARIAN POETS

The Bolshevik poet laureate is Demian Bédny (Demian the Poor), who is not a poet at all, but a more or less skilful rhymester of comical and satirical verse, such as every provincial paper had on its staff before the Revolution. He is preferred by the leaders to Mayakovsky, because of his unquestioned orthodoxy, but he is as much outside literature as Lunacharsky.

Ever since the Revolution the Bolsheviks have tried to promote proletarian culture and have even created a special institution to look after it—the *Proletkult*. One of the *Proletkult's* duties was to organize proletarian poetry and to teach poetry-writing workmen to write verse properly and up to the standard of to-day. At first the principal proletarian studio was conducted by Bryusov, and the first contingent of proletarian poets was marked by his grandiloquent and empty rhetoric. This rhetorical school of proletarian poets has produced nothing of any interest, and has compromised to a certain degree the very idea of proletarian poetry. The only poet who could be put against them to the credit of proletarian poetry was A. Gastev, who wrote some prose poems in praise of machines and industrialism but, evidently realizing their emptiness, abandoned literature. Recent proletarian poets have risen to a higher technical level, learned from the most various masters, and for mere technical up-to-dateness are quite on a level with the bourgeois poets. But in spite of all this technical modernity, the poetry of Bezymensky and Obradovich, the two poets who are made most of by Communist critics, is little more than rhymed journalism, remarkable rather for the purity of its Marxist inspiration than for its poetical merits.

The only one of the proletarian poets who is more than a mere Marxist in verse is Vasili Kazìn, a young Moscow workman whose poetry has since 1921 attracted the sympathy of all lovers of Russian poetry. Though he has written hymns on the October Revolution, he is essentially non-political. The poetry of work and the beauty of the world are his principal subjects. The word "freshness" has inevitably occurred to everyone who writes of him. His verse is a magic wand which turns into the purest gold of poetry everything it touches: one of his most charming poems has for its subject the shavings left by his plane; another discusses whom of the two he prefers—the Sun or his uncle Semen Sergeevich, the tailor, who, "so carefully irons my trousers for me, that I may please my girl!" And no one has written with greater freshness and brightness and less banality on such subjects as spring and rain.

12. THE YOUNGER POETS OF PETERSBURG AND OF MOSCOW

The main line of development of Russian poetry has been carried on chiefly in Moscow, which is the seat of all the Left schools, and which has produced the principal poetical novelties since the Revolution. The northern capital of the Emperors is, on the contrary, the seat of poetical conservatism, and the work of its best poets, Gumilev, Akhmatova, Mandelstam, is more firmly rooted in the past than in the future. The younger poetical generations are also more conservative and traditional. Petersburg has, since 1917, produced less poetry of interest than Moscow. The typical young poets of Petersburg (its "proletarian" poets are insignificant) are the poets of Gumilev's Guild, united by a high technical level and by the absence of great boldness. One of the most interesting recent developments of this Guild poetry is the great vogue of the English ballad form: young poets, like Irina Odoevtseva and Vladimir Pozner, have written interesting ballads of revolution and

civil war in a style very similar to the genuine Border ballads.
The more independent Petersburg poets are united by a certain partiality for rhetorical intensity. This takes the form of exceedingly strained and unrelieved rhetoric in the poetry of Anna Radlova, the only one of the post-Revolutionary poets to whom mysticism and "big" Symbolist words are not taboo. The same tendency in a more condensed and pointed form appears in the verse of the most gifted of the young poetesses— Elizabeth Polònsky. The most original and promising poet of the northern capital is Nicholas Tikhonov, a Red Cavalry officer who made his appearance in the literary circles of Petersburg after the end of the civil wars. His poetry participates of the general Petersburg tendency to condensed and quintessential expression: it is very packed and terse, often to obscurity. His principal aim is to charge each stanza and each line with the utmost effectiveness. He has also a partiality for the ballad form, but he is more original in his treatment of it. Some of his best poems are highly condensed ballads of the civil war. They are strictly objective in tone, and are closely allied to the young school of civil-war fiction in the advisedly and studiously cool treatment of horror and cruelty.

In Moscow also there exist conservative and traditional poetical groups (the most important is headed by the Symbolist S. Soloviev), but the tone is given by the advanced poets. The most interesting of young poets of the Red capital is the "Constructivist" E. Selvinsky, who is, like Tikhonov, interested chiefly in concentrated expressiveness. But as he proceeds from the Futurists, he is more interested in the phonetic side of his verse, and often verges on the "trans-sense." He has written some admirably concentrated and expressive verse in which he aims at reproducing, for poetical ends, the intonations of spoken language. His gipsy songs are especially remarkable and succeed in giving the musical movement of the chorus by the mere arrangement of word and accent.

In spite of such interesting figures in the youngest poetical generation as Kazin, Tikhonov, and Selvinsky, it may be said in general that Russian poetry is on the ebb, and that after about fifteen years of hegemony (c. 1907–1922), poetry is to-day once again ceding its supremacy to prose. Since 1921-1922, by far the best forces of the young literary generation have given their attention to prose, and the last two or three years are characterized by a revival of prose.

CHAPTER VII

1. REMIZOV

THE Symbolists, victorious in poetry, did not at first succeed in finding a new style in prose. Their efforts in this direction remained disconnected and ineffective. Up to about 1910 imaginative prose was dominated by the writers of the Gorky-Andreev school. But in the long run the influence of Symbolism, and of writers connected with Symbolism, made itself felt. The recent development of Russian prose does not proceed from Gorky or Andreev or Bunin, but from two writers of the Symbolist party—Bely and Remizov. Bely's novels, his part in introducing ornamental prose, and the characteristics of his own prose have already been discussed in connexion with the rest of his work. Remizov's action has been in the same direction—towards more elaborate and conscious craftsmanship in the choice and arrangement of words, but with a difference. Bely's prose is rhythmical and "symphonic," Remizov's is primarily colloquial. The essence of his manner is expressed by the term *skaz*, which means the reproduction in written prose of the intonations of spoken language, with a particular eye for the individualization of the supposed narrator. This manner, which had been the manner of Leskov, has now become, under the influence of Remizov, the prevailing manner of Russian imaginative prose.

Alexey Mikhaylovich Rémizov is a pure Muscovite. He was born in 1877, in Taganka, in the "East End" of Moscow. His ancestors were wealthy merchants, but his parents had fallen out with the family and were reduced to rather straitened circumstances. So Remizov grew up in comparative poverty, and his early experiences were chiefly of the street life in the industrial quarters of the metropolis. This life is reflected in the sordid nightmares of his first novel, *The Pond*. He received,

however, the usual middle-class education at a secondary school
and became a student of Moscow University.   He began writing very early (his first works are dated 1896), but he did not
get into the press till 1902.   Meanwhile, in 1897, for a trivial
circumstance, he was expelled from the university and banished
into the provinces, at first to the comparatively civilized town
of Penza, afterwards to the remote Ust-Sysolsk, then again
to the larger centre of Vologda.   These ancient and out-of-
the-way little towns are the background of some of his most
characteristic stories—*The Clock, Stratilatov, The Fifth
Pestilence*.   In Vologda he married Serafima Pavlovna Dov-
giello, whose name appears in the dedication of all his books
and who is an eminent student of palæography (now Lecturer
in Russian Palæography at the Sorbonne).   In 1904 he was
released from the surveillance of the police and allowed to
choose his home.   He settled in Petersburg, where he remained
till 1921.   His works had since 1902 begun to appear in the
publications of the Modernists.   His first book was published
in 1907.   For a long time his works had very few readers,
and even the Modernists looked upon him with mild wonder,
and were not always willing to lend him their columns.   Thus,
in 1909, the editor of the *Apollon*, the principal Modernist
magazine of the time, refused to accept *The Story of Stratilatov*, which is now recognized as a masterpiece and the
fountain-head of almost all subsequent Russian prose fiction.
But in the inner circles of literature Remizov became an exceptionally popular figure.   His whimsical and mischievous
humour led him to imagine a whole organization of which he
was the Chancellor, the Great and Free House of Apes.   Most
eminent Russian writers and publishers are in possession of
charters granting them some dignity in the House of Apes,
written in a beautiful seventeenth-century cursive hand and
signed, *propria cauda*, by Asyka, King of Apes.   Among the
first officers of the order were the Chancellor's intimate friends,
the philosophers Rozanov and Shestov.   His rooms were a
menagerie of all manner of toy animals and goblins, and many
of his writings have them for their heroes.   Gradually, especially after *Stratilatov*, which became known before it was

published, Remizov became the head of a new school of fiction, and by the beginning of the War the literary press was full of imitations of this and similar stories. Prishvin, A. N. Tolstoy, and Zamyatin were the first in date to take up his lead. In 1916, when the selfish and short-sighted policy of the Entente insisted on Russia's mobilizing more men than she could arm, Remizov was also mobilized, but, after a hospital test, liberated on grounds of illness. After he left the university, Remizov never took any part in politics, but his writings during the War, in 1917 and in the years following, are remarkable for their extraordinary sensitiveness to the life of the nation. The atmosphere of Petersburg during those tragical years of 1914–1921 is nowhere so convincingly present as in such books of Remizov's as *Marà*, *The Chronicle of 1917*, and *The Noises of the Town*. Nor did he take sides in and after 1917. *The Lament for the Ruin of Russia*, written in August–September, 1917, though "political" in the best and broadest Greek sense of the word, is quite outside party politics. After living in Petersburg through the worst years of famine and cold, Remizov, whose health was seriously jeopardized by all these privations, was at length allowed by the Soviet Government to leave Russia. At the end of 1921 he came first to Berlin, then, in 1923, to Paris. In spite of his life abroad, Remizov continues to maintain a strictly nonpolitical attitude, even when he writes "politics." This has not prevented the Soviet Government from prohibiting the importation of most of his books to the U.S.S.R., for their mystical and religious character.

Remizov's work is one of the most varied in the whole of Russian literature—to such an extent that few of his admirers can embrace the whole of it in their admiration. Those who value the "underground" Dostoevskianism of *The Pond* will find little interest in the studied naïveté of *On a Field Azure;* those who like the lyrical eloquence of the mystery plays or of *The Lament for the Ruin of Russia* will be disgusted by such privately printed uncensored tales as *Czar Dadon*. To get hold of the essence of Remizov's personality, or to realize the unifying principle of his work, is the most difficult and baffling of tasks, so elusive and many-sided is he. He is the greatest of humorists, and at the same time he shows now and again a curious lack of humour which induces one to classify him with the most hieratic of Symbolists. With this literary school his relations are unmistakable. He belongs to the same stratum in the history of Russian civilization. But there is more in him than mere Symbolism, and what marks him off from all the rest of his contemporaries is that he is firmly rooted in the traditional Russian soil. All the Russian tradition, from the mythology of pagan times through all the Russianized forms of Byzantine Christianity to Gogol, Dostoevsky, and Leskov, has been absorbed and assimilated by Remizov. He is the most naturally Slavophil of modern Russian writers. His case, by the way, is one of those which refute the current and superficial idea of Russia as mainly a peasant country. All the most original and "Russian" of Russian writers—Gogol, Grigoriev, Dostoevsky, Leskov—neither belonged to nor knew the Russian peasantry. The same with Remizov: he has lived in the East End of Moscow, in Petersburg, in provincial towns big and little, but never more than a day or two in the country.

Remizov is very largely a man of books and papers; it is not for nothing that he married a palæographist. No one in Russia has spoken of books with such sincere affection; in no one's mouth does the word *knizhnik* (bookman, lover of books) sound so caressing and laudatory as in Remizov's. A large proportion of his writings are adaptations of folk-lore matter or of ancient legends. One of his books, *Russia in Writ*, is a running commentary on certain ancient manuscripts in his possession. He is a very laborious writer, and in more senses than one. Not only is his work at his style as elaborate and patient as was Charles Lamb's (with whom he has certain points of resemblance), but his actual handwriting is a most elaborate and skilful revival of the cursive writing of the seventeenth century.

Remizov's work may be divided into what we may conveniently call his prose and his poetry. In actual metre he has written practically nothing, but the difference of diction and artistic object between his stories and, say, *The Lament for the Ruin* justifies us in speaking of his poetry and in distinguishing it from his prose. Both intrinsically and historically, his prose is more important than his poetry. It is by his prose that he has exercised such a profound influence on the young generation of writers. In spite of its great variety, it is unified by one purpose—which is to delatinize and defrenchify the Russian literary language and to restore to it its natural Russian raciness. Russian literary prose, since the beginning of letters in the eleventh century down to the existent forms of journalese, has never been free from foreign grammatical influence. The Greek influence of the Slavonic translations of Church books, the Latin influence of the schools in the seventeenth and eighteenth centuries, the French influence paramount since Karamzin and Pushkin, all lie in thick layers on the Russian literary language of to-day and make it so very different from the spoken Russian of the people and from the pre-schoolmaster Russian of the upper classes. The difference lies principally in the syntax, and even writers who, like Tolstoy, were studiously colloquial in their diction could never go without a latinized and frenchified syntax. Only Rozanov in his "anti-Gutenberg" prose tried to create a more "spoken" form of written Russian. Remizov has gone farther in this direction. His prose, as I have already said, is *skaz*, that is to say, it reproduces the syntax and intonation of spoken language, and of the spoken language in its least literary and most native forms. He has a keen sense for words, for individual words and for grammatical composition. His prose, often very studious and elaborate, is always new and never falls into clichés. He has taught the Russian writer to value his words, to think of them as of independent beings and not to use them as mere signs, or as parts of ready-made verbal groups. He has gone often too far in this direction: he cannot resist the temptation of using a good old word he has chanced on in some old document, or of coining a new one to suit his needs. His action on the language has been largely parallel to that of the Futurists, who have also applied themselves to linguistic creation (Khlebnikov) and delatinizing the language.

Remizov's prose works consist of novels and stories of contemporary Russian life; of legends taken from the Prologue * or from the Apocrypha; of folk-tales and fairy-tales; of dreams; of memoirs and diaries; and of commentaries on old documents.

He is not a story-teller in the true sense of the word, and his influence over the younger generation has greately contributed to the disintegration of the narrative form. In his early stories the lyrical element is considerable. They are almost always concerned with the grotesque and the unusual, with a touch of Dostoevskian psychological weirdness. A typical example is *Princess Mymra* (1908), one of the latest and best in the series, which tells of the cruel disillusionment of a schoolboy who fell platonically in love with a harlot. A Dostoevskian atmosphere of intense shame and humiliation dominates the story. Other of his early stories deal with the fantastic—with the familiar devils and goblins of Russian popular fancy, whom Remizov usually speaks of with a semi-humorous twinkle in the eye, but who, for all that, are sometimes very seriously mischievous. The largest works of his early period are *The Clock* (written 1904; published 1908), a story of provincial life which is only an imperfect sketch in comparison with the ones that followed it; and *The Pond* (1902–1905), a novel of Moscow, in which he drew on the impressions of his childhood. There is still a lot of the untidy, poetical *moderne* in *The Pond* which recalls the disagreeable manner of certain Polish and German novelists; but it produces a very powerful impression. The Dostoevskian intensity of pain, of compassion with another one's pain, and of morbid attention to pain wherever it is to be found, reaches in *The Pond* its most quintessential expression. The book is almost one uninterrupted paroxysm of pain and racking compassion. The filth and cruelty of life are portrayed with a ruthless realism that struck with horror even those who

* See footnote to page 37.

were accustomed to Gorky and Andreev. The same theme is taken up in *The Sisters of the Cross* (1910), where the squalid misery of the inhabitants of a large block of buildings in Petersburg—"Burkov's house"—grows into a symbol of the world of misery. The principal theme of the book is the cruelty of fate to those "unanswering," defenceless, always unlucky and unsuccessful beings who come into the world to be the playthings of cruelty and treachery.

In 1909 Remizov wrote *The Story of Ivan Semenovich Stratilatov* (at first called *Neuyomny Buben—The Unhushable Tambourine*). In the way of formal fiction, it is his masterpiece. It is a story of provincial life centred round the character of the clerk Stratilatov, one of the most striking and extraordinary creations in the whole picture-gallery of Russian fiction. Like most of Remizov's characters, he is an underworld character, but with such peculiar touches as are quite out of the line of Dostoevsky. The story is a masterpiece of construction, though the plan of it is not strictly narrative. Remizov alone of all Russian writers is capable of these weird, uncanny effects, quite free from anything apparently terrible or uncanny, but which convey the unmistakable impression of the presence of minor devils. *The Fifth Pestilence* (1912) is also a provincial story. It is more piercingly human and less weird: it is the story of a scrupulously honest but cold and inhuman, and consequently intensely unpopular, examining magistrate against a background of provincial sloth, filth, and spite. The hated man is gradually forced to commit a glaring and unpardonable judicial blunder, and Remizov's poetic justice makes his ruin come as an expiation of his cold and inhuman integrity. To the same period belongs *Petushok* (1911), the piercingly tragical story of a little boy killed by a chance shot during the suppression of the Revolution. It has become one of the most influential of Remizov's stories owing to the great richness of its "ornamentally" colloquial style.

In his later stories Remizov's style becomes chaster and less exuberant, always remaining as racy and as careful. The years of the war are reflected in *Marà* (*Fata Morgana*, 1917), which includes *The Teapot*, an extraordinarily delicate story of. pity and. sensitiveness.   It is constructed with Chekhovian art, and belongs to a long series of stories of pity—characteristic of Russian realism—to which belong Gogol's *Greatcoat* and Turgenev's *Moomoo*. The Revolution and Bolshevik Petersburg are reflected in *The Noises of the Town* (1921), which also contains many lyrical pieces and legends.   His latest novel is *The Ditch*, planned on a vast scale, of which only part has up to the present appeared (in *Russkaya Mysl*, 1923–1924).   It contains a powerful piece of synthetic character-drawing in the person of the gloating pessimist, the "philosopher" Budylin, like Stratilatov, all in an aura of diabolical presences.

Somewhat apart from the rest of Remizov's fiction stands *On a Field Azure*, which he began in 1910 and which appeared in 1922; continuations of it have appeared since then.   It is the story of a girl, Olya, first at home in the country, then at school, and in the university, where she becomes an S.R. The story is one of his best: all the more so as he refrains in it from all the exuberance and originality of his style, but keeps its essential characteristic—the purity of colloquial diction.   It is remarkable for the subtly produced atmosphere—thin and delicate—of the old-world country home, and for the charming drawing of the heroine's character.   But it is not a novel—rather a series of glimpses of life, and of anecdotes.

In time Remizov grew always more willing to abandon the hard-and-fast limits of fiction, and to adopt freer forms. The most notable of these ventures are *The Chronicle of 1917*, a remarkably free and unjournalistic diary of his impressions during the Revolution; and *Rozanov's Letters* (1923), a worthy tribute to the memory of that remarkable man who was his intimate friend, but a book which is written by a Russian for Russians, and will appear wildly unintelligible to the foreigner.   The same tendency towards a freer and less formal expression appears in *Russia in Writ*, a book of commented documents, chiefly of the early eighteenth century.   In all these and in other fragmentary memoirs, Remizov remains the wonderful stylist he is; nowhere does his mischievous and whimsical humour appear more freely and strangely. This twinkle in the eye, which is at times merely playful, but at times becomes unexpectedly uncanny, is perhaps the ultimate and truest expression of Remizov's personality. It reappears in his *Dreams*, which are accounts of real, genuine, and quite ordinary dreams one sees every night, but which are revived with all their peculiar logic, so simply intelligible to the sleeping man and so wildly strange to him when he is awake. Introduced into *The Chronicle of 1917*, they give it that unique and peculiarly Remizovian touch which is so inimitable.

As dreams have a logic of their own, so also do folk-tales, and one which is very different from ours. This wonderful assimilation of the "fairy-tale" logic is the principal charm of Remizov's numerous and varied *skazki* (a word which it is customary but not quite exact to render by the English "fairy-tale." The German *Märchen* is a more exact equivalent). Some of these tales are his own and are connected with Olya, the heroine of *On a Field Azure*. They are perhaps the most delightful of all, so strangely and so convincingly alive are the hares, the bears, and the mice that inhabit them, so uncannily homely the goblins and devils, and so infectious their genuine dream-logic. These fairy-tales form a volume entitled *Tales of the Monkey King Asyka*. The same qualities, but without the same childlike atmosphere, reappear in *Tales of the Russian People*, which are founded on genuine folk-tales but become delightfully new in the hands of Remizov. The same style is reproduced in *St. Nicholas's Parables*, but these parables are more seriously meant and have a definitely religious object. The popular conception of the benevolent saint and miracle-worker Nicholas as a help in every work, who will even help to cheat and steal, and will always intercede before God for the poor man, is particularly near to the heart of Remizov. These *Parables* are a link between the fairy-tales and the legends. Some of the legends, especially those contained in *Travà-Muravà*, are merely humorous, complicated stories of adventures and wonders, in the style of the Greek romance—stories in which the absurdities of the narrative are brought out with affectionate emphasis. Such a story as *Apollo of Tyrus* is a delightful example in this manner, and a masterpiece of racy Russian.* Other legends are more rhetorical and ornate, and have a more definite religious message. This religious message is very much akin to Rozanov's cult of kindness. Remizov dwells on the well-known legend of the Virgin's visit to hell, where she was so moved by the sufferings of the damned that she wished to share them, and finally obtained from God a release of all the damned souls from hell for forty days every year. This legend, of Byzantine origin, became especially popular in Russia, and Remizov sees in it the fundamental religious conception of the Russian people—the religion of pure charity and compassion. Most of Remizov's legends are from old Slavonic books, canonical or apocryphal, and ultimately of Byzantine origin. But he does not shun other sources. Some of his legends are of Western origin. Recently he has undertaken a series of adaptations from the folk-lore of various primitive nations and has already published folk-tales, in his recension, of Caucasian, Siberian, Tibetan, and Kabylian origin.

Remizov's legends are the connecting-link between his prose and his poetry. If *Apollo of Tyrus* is in his purest colloquial manner, the legends of the early *Limonar* (1907) are written in an elevated Slavonic style with a lyrical colouring. His "poetry" (with few exceptions, it is not in metre, but in rhythmical prose) is almost as various as his "prose." It includes the charming prose lyrics which together with the Asyka tales originally formed the book *Posolon*, and its sequel *To the Ocean Sea*. It includes also some of the best pages of *The Noises of the Town*, inspired by the life of Petersburg in 1918–1921, such as the wonderful *Fences*, a lyric of spring after the "bestial" winter of 1919–1920: walking in a suburb of Petersburg as the last fences were being taken down for fuel, he suddenly sees a vista opened on the infinite sea. Many of his prose lyrics are full of pathos and rhetoric, but the rhetoric is redeemed by the exquisite workmanship of words, and by

---

* *Apollo of Tyrus* is a descendant of the same Greek romance of which Shakespeare's *Pericles* is the best-known English version.

the poignancy of the emotion. Such is the *Lament for the Ruin of Russia*, written in September, 1917. It is full of passionate love and passionate suffering for his country.

But, on the whole, Remizov's poetry is "secondary," derivative; it is a "bookman's" poetry, which would not have been written without the ancient poetry contained in old books, canonical and apocryphal. This derivativeness is also apparent in his mystery plays, which are also founded on apocryphal and popular plays. Those who love Remizov the humorist will find little to their liking in *The Devil's Comedy*, in *George the Brave*, and in *Judas, Prince of Iscariot*. The plays are ritual and hieratic, and saturated with ancient lore and symbolism. Even *King Maximilian* (1918), which is based on the amusing and absurd popular play of that name, is made into a mystery with profound symbols. Here more than anywhere is Remizov a contemporary of the Symbolists. The influence of his poetry and of his mystery plays has been as small as that of his prose style and of his provincial stories has been great. The principal difference between Remizov and his followers is that between the generation born before and after (roughly) 1885: the older generation in its greatest expression is mystical and symbolical—the younger one is not. Remizov the craftsman, linguist, and realist has a numerous following—the poet and mystic remains barren of influence.

2. A. N. TOLSTOY

A general characteristic of the writers of the post-Symbolist generation (as I have already shown in the previous chapter on the younger poets) is a certain deliberate flight from ideas in general. "Quests," problems, and mysticism of all kinds have become less fashionable and are by way of being quite tabooed. Life is accepted as it is, and a new Realism has arisen in the stead of the intricacies of Symbolism and of the fruitless searchings of Gorky and Andreev. This Realism and this absence of "ideologies" is very noticeable in the work of the first novelist of the new school who succeeded in winning the popular favour. A. N. Tolstoy must be counted with the new post-Symbolist school, first, because in point of fact his literary personality was formed under Symbolist influences in "the Tower" of Vyacheslav Ivanov and in the monkey-haunted flat of Remizov; secondly, because, though he is fundamentally the least mystical and metaphysical of writers, he is also quite free of those "ideological demands" which were necessary to the making of a pre-Symbolist writer of the orthodox Realistic school.

Count Alexey Nikolaevich Tolstoy was born in 1882, in the province of Samara. He belongs to a branch of the same family as his more famous namesake, and as his twofold namesake the poet Tolstoy. His mother was a Turgenev. He came of a class that had nothing in common with the *intelligentsia*. Even as a writer, he belonged from the very beginning to the new poetical and artistic Bohème of Petersburg, not to the old-fashioned, public-spirited literary world. In 1908 he appeared in print with a book of verse, which was followed in 1909 by a charming book of folk-tales, and in 1911 by a second book of poetry. He bade fair to become a very interesting poet, but before that date he had already begun writing stories, and in 1910 his first book of stories had a great success. After 1911 he wrote no more verse. In the years preceding and during the War, he was a prominent and popular figure in the literary world of Petersburg, and his stories and novels were read with pleasure by a numerous public. He began writing plays, which also had a certain success. But his War stories (he went to the front as a war correspondent) added nothing to his reputation and are by no means to his credit. During the civil war he found himself on the White side, and, after the evacuation of Odessa (1919), settled in France. But in 1921, when the *Change-of-Landmarks* campaign of reconciliation with the Bolsheviks was started, he was lured by the appearance of Bolshevik nationalism and went over to the Soviet. He was for some time the literary editor of a Bolshevik paper in Berlin, and afterwards returned to Russia. His "change of landmarks" had no effect on the *émigré* circles, for his moral and intellectual reputation had never stood high, and no one had ever taken his conduct seriously.

The most salient feature in the personality of A. N. Tolstoy is a very curious combination of very great natural gifts and a complete absence of brains. As long as he simply and confidently surrenders to the flow of his natural creative force, he is a charming and unique writer; the moment he tries to express ideas, he becomes piteous. As he very seldom completely refrains from ideas, very few of his writings are above censure. But for natural verve and for spontaneous force, he has few equals among contemporary writers, and is second perhaps to Andrey Bely alone. One of his best qualities is his admirable, racy, unbookish Russian, learned in his Samara home, and not so much influenced as let loose by the example of Remizov.

His poetry is for the most part on subjects of Russian folklore and has for its themes either mythological pictures of Nature, or popular legends. The mythological poems were keenly appreciated by the mytho-poetical mystics of "the Tower"; but Tolstoy's best qualities are much more apparent in the legendary poems that are free from all mythological afterthought: they are full of life, and even when they verge on the nonsensical, they infect one by their irrepressible vitality and spirit. The same may be said of *Magpie's Tales* (1909), which is so delightful and exhilarating precisely because it is so free from every intellectual and emotional ingredient: it is just the sheer delight of imagination set free from the laws of causation.

Of Tolstoy's stories, very few are quite satisfactory, and this is due, besides his constant efforts to transcend his intellectual limitations, also to a fundamental defect in his talent: he has an admirable narrative *manner*, but not an inkling of ability to *construct* a story. All his stories produce the impression of a strange, illogical giddiness: one never knows what will happen, nor why things happen. The law of causation is absent from his world, and his stories develop like dreams or like fairy-tales. This might not be a defect if Tolstoy had sincerely recognized this limitation and not tried to plaster up his defective logic by borrowed ideas and cardboard psychology. His merits are a wonderful verve, directness of narrative, and a supreme gift of making his personages live. Only here again his original intellectual defect comes in: he is capable only of making fools, cranks, simpletons, and idiots; in all his people, there is the inevitable mark of stupidity. When his first stories appeared, which were all about the decaying gentry of the Middle Volga, the stupidity of his characters was explained as the inevitable result of the degeneracy of the provincial gentry. Tolstoy himself cheerfully accepted this interpretation, but one has only to read the stories where he describes other *milieux* to see that the feature is inherent in the author rather than in his characters. His early stories are among the best: he avoids all sophistications, and some of them are even, as by chance, excellently constructed, as, for instance, the pathetic (and absurd) story of the silly romantic provincial squire *Aggey Korovin* in Petersburg. His longer novels written before the War are much less satisfactory: *The Treasures of the Earth* (1911) is the acme of absurdity; and *The Lame Squire* (1912) is disfigured by an entirely misplaced attempt to rival the psychological subtleties of Dostoevsky. His stories of War and Revolution (*Spook*, 1918) have his usual merits, but in so far as they are stories of War and Revolution, they are not worth much. His novel *The Way through Hell* (1920–1921), which attempts to be a synthesis of Russian life before and during the War, is also a failure in so far as it attempts that. *Aelita,* a story of men on Mars, in the style of H. G. Wells, seems to have been written for the sole purpose of showing up his limitations. All the scientific and fantastic part is ridiculously flat and absurd. But the book contains one of his most delightful character-sketches—the Red soldier Gusev with his matter-of-course and absolutely unastonished attitude to Mars and the Marsians. His last novel, *Ibycus* (of which only the beginning has appeared), is the story of the adventures of a new-made profiteer during the Revolution and civil war. Here Tolstoy's absurdity reaches its high-water mark, but this ab-

surdity is so unadulterated and light-hearted that it almost
ceases to be a defect and becomes a virtue.

Of all Tolstoy's stories, the best by far is *The Childhood of
Nikita* (written in France in 1919–1920). It is the story of
a boy of ten on his father's country estate near Samara. It is
without pretensions, without all the pitfalls that abound in his
other works. There is no plot, but several (for the most part,
trivial) episodes are told with admirable verve and sincerity.
Russian books on childhood are numerous, and some of them are
among the greatest books in the language, but A. N. Tolstoy's
Nikita must be assigned a very honourable place among them,
and a place that is unique for its unsophisticated vitality and
simple brightness.

What has been said of Tolstoy's lack of narrative construction applies still more to his plays, which do not give him a great
place among the playwrights. His merits are at their lowest
and his defects are exaggerated. But there is in them a healthy
and welcome strain of honest and unpretentious melodrama.

3. PRISHVIN

Mikhail Mikhailovich Prishvin is older than Remizov: he was
born in 1873. But his best work was written under the unmistakable influence of the younger writer. Prishvin began in literature as an ethnographer. His first two books, *Where Birds
Have Not Been Scared* (1907) and *After the Magic Ball*
(1908), are accounts of his travels in North Russia and contain
much valuable material for the study of the very peculiar peasant civilization of the country between Lake Onego and the
White Sea, and of the life and manners of the sailors of the
Arctic Ocean. These studies taught Prishvin to value the
originality of the uneducated Russian and the native force of
"unlatinized" Russian speech. Even after he came in contact
with Remizov, he did not give himself away to disinterested literature, and most of what he wrote was "civic" and "public-
spirited" descriptive journalism. Only the quality of his
Russian places these writings above the ordinary level of this

sort of thing. But in the years preceding the War, Prishvin wrote some short stories which give him an honourable place among imaginative writers. They are stories of provincial life, free from social preoccupations and permeated with the rough and acid scents of the forest soils of his province of Smolensk. They are, for the most part, stories of hunting and of animal life, of life that is at one with Nature. One of them, *The Beast of Krutoyarsk* (1913), is a masterpiece and stands quite alone as the best animal story in the Russian language. By virtue of this one story, Prishvin must be recognized as something like a classic. It is a story of the hunting squire Pavlik Verkhne-Brodsky and of his setter bitch Lady. The Remizovian provincial background is only a setting for the elemental force of Nature—the struggle for the female—which is the main subject of the story.

Since the Revolution, Prishvin has published one book, *Kurymushka* (1924), which has all the appearance of an autobiography. It is a very good book, full of delightful episodes and of a genuinely reproduced atmosphere of childhood. The subject of the first part is very much like that of *Kotik Letaev*—the gradual formation of a child's world as a process of explanation of words—but how different is Prishvin's manner from Bely's! What is especially remarkable in it is its extreme simplicity and absence of pretensions—so unlike the general spirit of modern Russian literature.

Another unpretentious writer who has been influenced by Remizov is Ivan Sokolov-Mikitov, whose "fairy-tales" and other stories, written in an admirable, pure, and racy Russian, breathe the genuine and unaffected spirit of folk-lore.

4. ZAMYATIN

Evgeni Ivanovich Zamyàtin, who ultimately developed into a very original writer, also began as a Remizovian. Born in 1884, at Lebedyan (province of Tambov, Central Russia), he studied shipbuilding at the Polytechnicum of St. Petersburg. In 1908 he received the degree of shipbuilding engineer and was invited to prepare for a chair. His first literary works were

technical articles on shipbuilding. His literary career began
in 1911, when he published *Uyezdnoe* (roughly, *Country
Town* *). During the War he lived in England, building ships
for the Russian navy. In 1917 he returned to Russia. He
became, together with Gumilev, the head of a literary studio,
and most of the young prose-writers of Petersburg have passed
through his classes. At the same time he lectures on shipbuilding at the Polytechnicum. This combination in one man
of the engineer and writer has not remained without its effect
on the writer: Zamyatin has been one of the strongest influences in shaping the "formal," technical attitude towards literature of the younger literary generation. The Soviet
authorities do not like Zamyatin and consider him one of the
most dangerous "*émigrés* left behind." He is a writer of very
small output, which is natural considering his engineering oc-
cupations and his elaborate manner of writing. All his work
consists of three volumes of short stories *Uyezdnoe* (and other
stories, 1916); *The Islanders* and *At the World's End* (*Na
kulichkakh*); of a small number of fairy-tales or rather satirical fables in prose (*Fables for Grown-up Children*); of one
play, *The Fires of St. Dominic* (all these books published in
1922); and of a novel (*We*) which will remain unpublished as
long as the Soviet censorship does not change its methods.

Zamyatin's early stories, contained in *Uyezdnoe*, are the
direct progeny of Remizov's *Stratilatov*. Provincial life is
given in its most vulgar, most grotesque, and most provincial
aspect. The stories are written in a studiously careful and
expressive Russian, with a marked predilection for rare and
provincial words. Uncannily inept vulgarity and lurid boredom form the atmosphere of these stories. In his later work,
Zamyatin tears himself away from the provincial Russian soil
and from the Remizovian vocabulary, and gradually evolves
a manner of his own which is founded on the heightening of
the expressive value of significant detail by an elaborate system of metaphor and simile. His style remains overloaded
with verbal expressiveness and imagery. This excessive richness of expressive means tends to disrupt the story and trans-

* *Winesburg, Ohio,* has been described as an American *Uyezdnoe.*

form it into a mere mosaic of details.   The method is akin
to the proceedings of Cubism in painting—his characters especially tend to become identified with the geometrical forms
he gives them.   Thus, squareness is the principal characteristic of the English hero of *Islanders.*   The two English stories
(*Islanders* and *The Man-hunter*) are distinctly satirical, as
is *At the World's End,* a grotesquely refined and exaggerated
caricature of the dreary and solitary life of an East Siberian
garrison.   It was published during the War and led to the trial
of its author.   Both in this and in the English stories, Zamyatin, in spite of the great conscientiousness and elaboration of
his artistic methods, shows a strange deficiency of information:
his knowledge of English and of Russian army life is insufficient.   This does not apply to his stories of Soviet life.   One
of the best of these, and perhaps his masterpiece, *The Cave,*
has been translated into English.   It is characteristic of his
methods: it is all one elaborate simile.   The life of a bourgeois
couple in an unheated room in Bolshevik Petersburg during
a Northern winter is likened to the life of palæolithic man in
his cave; the iron stove that heats their room for an hour
a day is the god of the cave, who is benevolent only when he is
satisfied with their sacrifices—of fuel.   This is Zamyatin's
method of giving unity to his stories: a large family of metaphors (or similes) dominated by one mother metaphor.   *We,*
of which one does not know when it will appear, is a scientific
romance of the future, written, according to accounts, in a
new and striking manner, which is a further development of
Zamyatin's Cubism.   *The Fires of St. Dominic* is feeble as a
play—too overloaded with that detail which Zamyatin cannot
forgo, and which is so out of place in a play.   It is a story of
the Inquisition and a very transparent allegory for the Cheka.
Fables for Grown-up Children is also pointedly satirical, and
both this satirical intention and the great elaboration of its
style make it recall the *Political Fables* Sologub wrote in 1905.

Zamyatin has had a very considerable influence as a master,
or rather as a teacher, of literature, and the great elaborate-
ness of contemporary fiction, especially in Petersburg, is largely

due to him. He is also an interesting critic, and his reviews
of current fiction are always worth reading.

5. MEMOIRS AND HISTORICAL NOVELS

The great events of 1914 and after have produced an abundant harvest of literature, which stands outside the main line
of professional literary development and which for the most
part is interesting only for the information it gives. But a few
works stand out for their literary merit.

The war produced little. The only book by a combatant
that may be quoted is *Memoirs of an Artillery Reserve Officer*
(1918), by Fedor Steppùn, who is an exceptionally thought-
ful and sincere thinker, as sincere a democrat as he is a patriot, and who has analysed with sympathy and insight the
tragical fate of the Russian army officer.

The war-books of Erenburg and Shklovsky will be discussed
elsewhere. There remains *The People at the Front* (1st ed.,
1918; numerous editions since), by Sofia Fedòrchenko. It
purports to be an exact record of soldiers' conversations and
soldiers' songs heard at the war. How far the author's imagination has had a part in it, cannot yet be discerned. It is
certainly a book of absorbing interest, and is indispensable
for every student of Russia's part in the War and of the
Russian soldier's mentality. Its principal literary merit consists in the admirable savour of the soldiers' language rendered
by Mme. Fedorchenko.

The most remarkable memoirs of the civil war produced by
the White side is *1920*, by Vasili Vitalievich Shulgìn, a Monarchist deputy of the Duma, who was member of the Parliamentary Executive Committee which legalized the February
Revolution, and one of the two delegates into whose hands
Nicholas II handed his abdication. *1920* is distinctly non-
literary: it is written in the belated journalistic style of
Doroshevich, with cheap and naïve effects that were good
twenty-five years ago. In spite of this, it is a book of extraor-

dinary value, for the great sincerity with which it is written. It is the history of the retreat of the Whites from Kiev to Odessa, and thence to the Rumanian frontier, of Shulgin's captivity in the hands of the Reds, of his conspiracies in Red Odessa, and of his escape to Wrangel's Crimea. The book is full of humour, often humour at his own expense, and the atmosphere of the times is evoked with remarkable vividness. Shulgin's other memoirs are less remarkable, but are also of considerable interest to the historian.

Shulgin's book has a deserved reputation among those who think, but the mass of the *émigré* reading public prefer the writings of General Peter Nikolaevich Krasnòv. In 1918– 1919 Krasnov was ataman of the Don Cossacks and showed in this capacity a great talent for organization. His memoirs of 1917–1919 are written in the lucid, direct, and unpretentious style of a man of action, and are important documents. The same cannot be said of his more "literary" work. His four-volume novel *From the Two-headed Eagle to the Red Banner* (1921–1922) has had a greater success than any other Russian book printed outside Russia since the Revolution. It is a very ambitious work, evidently planned to emulate and eclipse *War and Peace*. Among the older generation of *émigrés*, one often hears comparisons of the two novels which are not always in favour of Tolstoy's. In reality Krasnov's novel is simply not literature at all. It is written in the most shamefaced "boulevard" manner of Mme. Verbitsky. The love scenes and the "psychology" are quite painfully vulgar. Nor is the political side on a much higher level: Lenin and Trotsky are actually represented as receiving instructions from the Sages of Zion. The success of the novel among the *émigrés* is not to their credit. The only interesting pages in the novel (for, after all, General Krasnov is a good soldier) are the battle scenes, which are drawn with truth and simplicity.

An effect of the Revolution has also been an increased interest in the past, a sanctuary into which those who are out of tune with the present may escape and forget. This escape into the past is the mainspring of the memoirs of Prince Sergey Wolkònsky. Prince Wolkonsky (b. 1862) is known in America by his lecture tour of 1899. He was for a short time director of the imperial theatres. Later on he did much to popularize in Russia the ideas of Jacques Dalcrose. His books *Expressive Speech* and *Expressive Movement* are notable contributions to the theory of acting. Wolkonsky passed the worst years of Soviet chaos in Russia and escaped only in 1922. He has since published three volumes of memoirs, two of which are autobiographical, while the third (*On the Decembrists*) tells the story of his grandfather, the Decembrist Wolkonsky, and his wife. The subject is very familiar to the Russian reader (it is the subject of a famous poem by Nekrasov). Wolkonsky treats it in a tone of lyrical sentimentality and idealizes even more than is the custom his revolutionary grandparents. The "idea" of the book is a regret for the times when even revolutionaries were elegant and aristocratic. His autobiographical memoirs are also permeated with a lyrical idealization of the life of the old aristocracy, with a dash of exceedingly genteel and elegant Liberalism, when he speaks of the autocracy and of the bureaucracy. Post-Revolutionary Russia, which constantly appears in his memoirs, is nothing but a seething kettle of filth. His style is somewhat affectedly slipshod and desultory, and excessively fluent, but easy and agreeable.

Another refugee into the past is Peter Petrovich Muràtov, to whose importance as one of the Columbuses of old Russian art I have alluded in a preceding chapter: his *History of Old Russian Painting* (1914) is, up to the present, the most complete work on the subject. His *Sketches of Italy*, also written before the War, are in a style that is familiar to the English reader and might be described as Vernon-Lee-and-water. During the cold and hungry years of 1918–1921 he turned to imaginative literature and wrote *Egeria*, a novel of the Italian eighteenth century. It has a complicated love and political intrigue, and is saturated with a love for *barocco* Rome and the Roman Campagna. The style is closely imitated from Henri de Régnier's wonderful Roman novel, *La Double Maîtresse*. *Egeria* is not a work of great creative force, but it is the product of a very highly developed culture and of an intense love of beauty. It gets a peculiarly pathetic note

from the date that stands under it—Moscow, 1920.   Since then
Muratov has been able to see Italy once more and join in the
Italian enthusiasm for the rediscovered art of the *barocco*
painters.

Another retrospective writer is Mark Aldanov (pseudonym
of Mark Aleksandrovich Landau), but his historical novels
are not an escape from the present.   On the contrary, he
studies the past to understand the present, and his novels of
the French Revolution must be read in terms of the Russian
Revolution.   Aldanov is a "Latin" spirit, an ironist, and a
worshipper of common sense.   There is in him just a touch
of the Stracheyesque, though he is very far from the perfect
sense of measure of the author of *Queen Victoria*.   His first
novel, *Saint Helena* (1921), which has been translated into
English, is also the best: it is less overloaded with erudition
and with allusions to to-day than *9th Thermidor* (1923).   But
both are entertaining reading and are free from the sin of
over-sophistication which kills the historical novels of Merezhkovsky.   Aldanov is also a pungent and witty writer on modern politics.   His French book on *Lenin* (1921) is too
obviously biased, but an essay on *Clémenceau and Ludendorff*
published in the same year bears comparison with the most
brilliant personal pages of Mr. J. M. Keynes.

Another writer who may evoke comparisons with Mr. Lytton
Strachey is George Blok (a first cousin of the great poet),
whose excellent little essays on the life of Fet (especially *The
Making of a Poet*, 1924) are almost the first serious attempt
in Russian to write biography that would be both reliable as
information and readable as literature.

6. SHKLOVSKY AND ERENBURG

Post-Revolutionary Russian prose has developed an exaggerated attention to style, at the expense of "ideas" and "messages."   It has become openly and emphatically *formal*.   This
development is due to the example of Remizov, Bely, and
Zamyatin.   It was favoured by the rise of a new school of
literary criticism which is united by what is (somewhat er-

roneously) known as the *formal method*. The maxim of the "Formalists" was that "a work of art is equal to the sum of the *procédés* employed in producing it"—a formula that eliminates all "ideological" and "philosophical" interpretations and reduces the whole development of literature to the development of literary forms. I shall have more to say of these Formalists in the chapter on literary criticism, but it is here the place to deal with the most conspicuous of them, Victor Shklovsky.

Born in 1893 of a Jewish family which had already produced some notable men of letters, Shklovsky studied philology at Petersburg and was the principal initiator of the Formalist movement, and one of the founders of the *Opoyaz* (Society for the Study of Poetical Language), which was the battering-ram of the new doctrine. In 1916 he was mobilized, and served as an engineer in a motor-car section at Petersburg. He took a prominent part in the Revolution of February–March, 1917, as a member of the S.R. party, and was a member of the Petersburg Soviet; he was made *Commissar* of the Provisional Government at the front, first in Galicia (where he was wounded during the Kalusz-Halicz disaster), then in Persia. In 1918–1920 he spent part of his time developing his literary theories, and the other part in conspiring against the Bolsheviks, and fighting on their side against the Whites. In 1921 he was the most prominent literary figure of the younger generation in Petersburg, and taught them the theory of literature. In 1922 he escaped from Russia, and thus succeeded in evading trial for his conspiracies. But after a short stay at Berlin he returned to Russia and became reconciled with the Soviet authorities. As a theoretician he is certainly brilliant, though the style of his writings is affected and untidy, and though he is essentially superficial and lacks all historical perspective and all sense of proportion. But the ideas he has given general circulation are sound and have been very fruitful. As a critic he is skilful in applying his pet ideas to every literary work, ancient and modern, in explaining away its "ideas" and "philosophies," and in reducing it to its purely formal elements. His pet writer is Sterne, and, following the example of *Tristram Shandy*, he has demonstrated two of his favourite phenomena: "playing with the subject" and "laying bare the *procédé*." He has recently published an elaborate analysis of *Little Dorrit*, in which he demonstrates the technique of the "novel of mystery." He has not written any fiction himself, but his place in literature, and not merely in the theory of literature, is secure owing to a remarkable book of memoirs, the title of which is characteristically borrowed from his favourite, Sterne—*A Sentimental Journey* (1923); it is the story of his adventures from the February Revolution to 1921. The book seems to be so called as *lucus a non lucendo*, for its most remarkable feature is a studious absence of all sentimentality. The most horrid facts, as, for instance, the mutual massacres of Kurds and Assyrians in Urmiah, are described with studied calmness and with an abundance of matter-of-fact detail. In spite of its somewhat affectedly untidy and nonchalant style, the book is of absorbing interest. Unlike so many modern Russian books, it is full of intelligence and common sense. It is also very sincere and, though unsentimental, emotionally intense. In spite of its defects, it is the most remarkable book on its subject. After *A Sentimental Journey*, Shklovsky has published "a novel in letters," *Zoo* (1923; as it is the Berlin zoo, it must be pronounced *tsoe*). Here he exaggerates all the defects of his earlier book, without preserving its merits. It is affected, untidy, shrill, and dwells too complacently on the personal life of himself and of his friends. These features of Shklovsky's writings have, unfortunately, had as great an influence as his theories, and it has become the fashion for young men to begin their literary career by publishing an affectedly facetious and pre-tentious "autobiography." *

Shklovsky's influence has worked in the direction of shifting the centre of attention from the smaller to the larger unit, from style to construction. This is what is called to-day the "Western" tendency in prose, as opposed to the "Eastern" tendency of excessively ornamental writing. But Shklovsky himself is more interested in Sternian "play" with the plot

* The fashion was at its height in 1922, and seems to be dying out.

than in the plot itself. His influence was great on some of
the "Serapion Brothers," a literary fraternity of young men,
formed in 1921, which has produced some notable writers.
The most "Western" of the "Serapion Brothers" are V.
Kaverin (pseudonym of V. Zilberg) and Leo Lunts (1901–
1924), whose early death was a great loss to Russian letters,
and of whom I shall have more to say in the chapter on the
drama. Kaverin has applied himself to realizing in his stories
Shklovsky's idea of "playing with the plot," and has chosen as
his model the fantastic constructions of Hoffmann.

It is certain that the Russian public is fed up with ornamental prose and the hypertrophy of style and non-narrative
elements, and that it craves, even more than it ever did, solid
"Western" narrative. Many writers are trying to create a
novel of pure action, but they have not yet succeeded, and
so far as the literary public is concerned, the field still belongs
to the "ornamentalists" and non-narrative realists. As for
the less sophisticated and fastidious, they fall back on foreign
importations: since the revival of the book trade in 1922,
Tarzan has swept Russia like a conflagration, and is as popular to-day as Nat Pinkerton was in 1908.

The literary "Western" novel still remains to be created by
the Russian novelist. The man who has come nearest to it
is Erenburg.

Ilya Davidovich Erenburg is of Jewish descent and was born
in Moscow in 1891. He began by writing poetry in which he
showed an extraordinary adaptability to the taste of the times:
his poems from 1911 to 1922 may be used as a text-book of
the successive changes of poetical schools. He spent the years
before the War in Paris, and, of all Russian writers, is most
thoroughly imbued with the spirit of Montparnasse and of the
Rotonde. During the War he was a correspondent at the
French and Macedonian front, and wrote a book which is
among the best War books in Russian (*The Face of War*, 1st
ed., 1921). It is derivative and might have been better written
in French, but the little fragments, impressions, and pathetic
anecdotes that form it are not devoid of genuine significance.

The years 1917–1921 he spent in Russia, and after many wanderings and many fluctuations from party to party, he became a Bolshevik and a Futurist.

In 1921 Erenburg came to France, but was expelled as a Bolshevik. He took refuge in Belgium, and there wrote his most remarkable book, *The Extraordinary Adventures of Julio Jurenito*. Jurenito is a Mexican who has decided to do all he can to destroy and explode the rotten civilization of the West. His method is that of an *agent-provocateur:* he encourages all those sides of civilization which are surest to quicken its disintegration. His principal instrument is Mr. Coole, an American Puritan and millionaire, the embodiment of self-satisfied Anglo-Saxon hypocrisy. *Julio Jurenito* is written in a neutral "Latin" style, and the construction of the story is taken from the novels of Voltaire. It is full of a dry and concentrated irony, which is precisely what makes it a serious and significant book, genuinely subversive and nihilistic.

After *Jurenito*, Erenburg experimented with extraordinary rapidity in various styles of fiction, always succeeding in being superficially interesting and essentially cheap. He has gradually become the Russian novelist that sells best. This position has especially been confirmed by his latest book, *The Love of Jeanne Ney* (1924), which is a "Western" and a frankly sensational novel. It is in the style of the French "boulevard" novels of the forties, and of the later novels of Dickens. Like all that Erenburg writes, it is derivative, and leaves still unsolved the problem of creating a literary Russian novel after the Western pattern.

7. THE REVIVAL OF FICTION AFTER 1921

For a long time, ever since the triumph of the Symbolists, prose had been in the background of Russian literature. Its eclipse became complete in 1918–1921, when for three years practically no new novels or stories were printed. In 1921–1922 the first effect of the revival of the book trade was to bring out a profusion of verse written during the press-less years. But this was followed by a revival of prose fiction which is the most outstanding literary fact of these last three years (1922, 1923, 1924). The "Western" tendencies I have just been speaking about are but a side channel of comparative insignificance, and the new prose may be characterized first of all as profoundly, fundamentally, consciously, and even aggressively Russian. In spite of individual differences, it has several essential features that are characteristic of the whole movement: first of all, a much accentuated "formalism" and ornamentalism which lays the principal stress on style and manner, and tends to lose sight of the theme: the influence of Remizov in style, of Bely and Zamyatin in construction, is apparent everywhere. Only now, after 1921, can one fully realize the extent of their action on Russian literature. Remizov (and the older example of Leskov) is responsible for the almost exclusive prevalence of *skaz* (imitation of spoken language) and for the love of verbal curios; Bely, for a tendency to write in rhythm, and the method of "intersecting planes" and "disjointed surfaces," which excludes direct narrative and makes many Russian stories look like Cubist pictures.* But, for all that, the new fiction is realistic, and even aggressively realistic in the English sense of the word: extreme ornamentalism of style goes hand in hand with extreme naturalism in the description of everything disgusting, of everything that was taboo: Gorky and Andreev have been left far behind by Pilnyak and Babel.

Russian fiction lives under the very attentive and not always benevolent eye of the Communist party, of its censors and official critics. I have explained elsewhere the meaning of the word *poputchik* and the attitude of various sections of "the party" towards these "fellow travellers." The young novelists are all of them *poputchiks*, and answer more or less to the Communist demand that they should be "modern" and revolutionary. They are modern, for their subject is Russian actuality; they are revolutionary, for their actuality is Revolution; they are also Bolshevik, in a way, for their attitude

---

* Bely has been compared to Einstein, as the discoverer of the law of relativity in narrative.

towards the Revolution is not hostile; but there is not an ounce of the true Communist spirit in them, even if they chance to be members of "the party." * In this respect, even Maya-kovsky, not to speak of Aseyev, has no counterpart among the really significant prose-writers of to-day. The attitude of these young writers towards the Bolshevik reality they describe may be most easily described as one of "disinterested interest" and artistic admiration for the great cataclysms pro-duced by the will of the Russian nation, with an unmistakable touch of national pride in the exceptional, thoroughgoing, and original character of the Russian Revolution.

The writers I am going to speak of are not, of course, the whole of Russian post-NEP literature. There are besides them writers of the older generation whose recent work I have already discussed; there are also belated, old-fashioned realists who began to write late in life and consequently have the ap-pearance of youth (like, for instance, Panteleimon Romanov, b. 1884, who has published the first two parts of an enormous and very tedious novel, *Russia*, which purports to be a syn-thesis of recent Russian history); there are the proletarian writers, most of whom are mere clumsy fledgelings that must work and learn before they can produce anything of real value. The writers I am speaking of here are the literary pick of the generation born between (roughly) 1892 and 1900, and who are primarily writers, not journalists in fiction. These writers form the most interesting and worth-while fact about present-day Russian literature.

The first of the new writers to attract general attention was Boris Pilnyàk (pseudonym of Boris Andreevich Wogau, of mixed Russian and Volga German descent, b. 1894). He began writing before the Revolution (1915), but his early work is unoriginal and reflects various influences—most of all, Bunin's. In 1922 appeared his "novel" *The Bare Year*, which created something of a sensation by its subject-matter and by its new manner. This novel is not a novel at all: the non-narrative tendency of modern Russian prose reaches in it its high-water mark. It is rather a symphony unfolded along laws invented

* "The party" in Russia means the Communist party.

by the author and purporting to be a vast panorama of Russia in the throes of Revolution and civil war. The principal literary influence discernible in it is that of Bely's *Petersburg*. Like *Petersburg*, it is, first of all, a piece of historical philosophy: the only real character in the book is Russia, Russia as an elemental force and an historical entity. The Revolution to Pilnyak is the rising of the mass of peasants and lower classes against the un-Russian polity of the Petersburg Empire. *The Bare Year* was followed by *Ivan-da-Maria* (1923), *The Third Metropolis* (1923), and numerous shorter "stories" which may all be described in the same terms. The "novels" and "stories" of Pilnyak may be viewed as higher political journalism which has taken the form of a musical fugue. Unfortunately Pilnyak is too muddle-headed, fundamentally uncultured (in spite of a veneer of "Symbolist" culture), and devoid of ideas for his conceptions of Russian history to have any intrinsic interest. His manner, largely a further development of Bely's, is, however, in the details his own: it is based on vast sweeping panoramas and mass effects with a wealth of historical allusion and the deliberate utilization of "intersecting planes," so that the line of narrative (if it may be called narrative) is constantly broken abruptly and taken up at another point, geographically and constructively. He even goes so far as to quote, in the interest of "intersection" and "disjointure," passages from other people's books: *The Third Metropolis* contains long quotations from *The Gentleman from San Francisco* and from a story by Vsevolod Ivanov. As a whole, Pilnyak's manner is a complete impasse and is little more than a curio. His "novels" would be sorry stuff if he did not possess a genuine gift of vivid, realistic painting, which produces refreshing islands in the barren waste of his historical speculations. The chapter of *The Bare Year*—"Train No. 58"—describing travel in Soviet Russia in 1919, is an admirable example of his crude, unsweetened, and outspoken naturalism. The figure of Xenia Ordynina in *Ivan-da-Maria*, a girl of the gentry who has become an agent of the Cheka, and commits the worst cruelties on a basis of sexual perversion ("the Revolution," she says, "is all permeated with sex for me"), is a gruesome

and convincing, though by no means attractive, figure. Pilnyak has been in England (in 1923) and written a book of
English Tales (1924), but the least said of them, the better—
they are simply incredibly silly.

Pilnyak's manner has spread.   Many young writers imitate
him.   The most outstanding Pilnyakian is N. Ognév, whose
stories of the Revolution (*Eurasia* and *The Soup of the Republic*) reproduce Pilnyak's manner with somewhat more logic,
and introduce into it a more firmly built skeleton of narrative.
The influence of Bely in a milder form is apparent in the work
of Vladimir Lìdin (b. 1894), who began in 1915 as a Chekhovian, and whose recent books are devoted to the reproduction
of "Soviet week-days" in Moscow.   Like much in contemporary
Russian literature, it is description without narrative: an
elaborate and ambitious kind of higher journalism.

Leonid Maksimovich Leónov (b. 1899 in Moscow) belongs
to a younger generation.   His first stories appeared in 1922.
Most of his writings are in the orthodox Remizovian *skaz* manner, where the attention of the reader is primarily concentrated on the ornamental texture of the style.   He has not
yet shown his real face, but has given proof of extraordinary
literary gifts in works of very various styles.   He is largely
a *pasticheur*, but a superior *pasticheur*.   *The End of an Insignificant Person* is a masterly pastiche of Dostoevsky.   *The
Note-books of A. P. Kovyakin* reproduce to a nicety the semi-
educated jargon of a shop assistant of an out-of-the-way
country town.   The Communist critics discern in Leonov a
dangerous spirit of compassion and sympathy with the "insignificant man" whose welfare has been sacrificed to the Revolution, and tend to refuse him even the title of *poputchik*.
Apart from his other works stands *Tuatamur* (1924), a highly
original piece of work—a poem in prose written from the person of one of the lieutenants of Genghiz Khan, and describing
the defeat of the Russians at Kalka (1224) from the point
of view of the victorious Mongols.   The poem is written in
an admirably tense and dynamic style, and interspersed with
words and phrases in Turki.   It is full of the fierce and savage

poetry of the nomadic steppe. It is one of the most original productions of modern Russian prose.

In Petersburg the revival of fiction was centred round the "Serapion Brothers," * a fraternity of writers which was formed chiefly by students of Zamyatin's studio, was patronized by Gorky, and influenced by Shklovsky. It included the poets Tikhonov, Pozner, and Elizabeth Polonsky, the critic Gruzdev, the dramatist Lunts, and the novelists Kaverin, Slonimsky, Fedin, Zoshchenko, Nikitin, and Vsevolod Ivanov. There was a big boom round the Serapion Brothers in 1922, and their autobiographies (in the affected and nonchalant style introduced by Shklovsky) became known to the public before they had published any real work. There is little in common between the several Serapion Brothers, and even if one excludes the extreme Westerners Lunts and Kaverin, the others are united by no closer resemblance than are the majority of the young novelists. Nicholas Nikìtin (b. 1896) is a disciple of Zamyatin, an ornamentalist *à outrance* in whose elaborate stories it is almost impossible to discern the main line of the narrative. His most characteristic stories are episodes of the civil war, which are told with studied coolness and absence of sympathy. One of the best is *Stones*, an episode of the war in Karelia: the Whites come to a village, make the peasants deliver the head of their Soviet, execute him, and make them elect a *Starosta* (Old-Régime magistrate) ; then the Whites go and the Reds come, make the peasants deliver the Starosta, execute him, and again institute a Soviet. The moral of the story is that village life and the life of Mother Earth go on in the same way under the Reds as under the Whites, and the seasons continue uninfluenced by the strife of man.

Michael Zòshchenko (b. 1895) is a more narrative writer: he is also an ornamentalist, but his ornamentalism is a purely colloquial *skaz*, which proceeds from Leskov. His stories are simple anecdotes of war or Soviet life told in the amusing slang of a semi-educated corporal. Zoshchenko is, above all,

* The name is an allusion to E. T. A. Hoffmann's romance, *Die Serapionsbrüder*.

an excellent *pasticheur*. He has written admirable parodies, and the principal merit of his writings is the perfection of his imitative intonations. Michael Slonimsky and Konstantin Fedin have not yet found a manner of their own, but Fédin (b. 1892) is a writer of great promise. His first published story was a perfect and mature exercise in the style of Bunin (*The Orchard*, 1922), but he has not continued in this manner, and has recently published fragments of a large and ambitiously planned novel of great historical and social sweep in a direct, dynamic, and constructive manner that makes one expect the complete novel with impatience.

The most remarkable of the Serapion Brothers is Vsevolod Ivànov (b. 1895). But he stands apart from the rest—he is a Siberian and a self-made man. His life has been romantic and adventurous: he has been a conjurer and a compositor, and he went through the most various vicissitudes in 1918–1920, during the civil war in Siberia. More than once he escaped death by a hairbreadth. His first book was set by himself and published at Tayga Junction (Central Siberia) in 1919. In 1921 he came to Petersburg, was received by Gorky, and became one of the Serapion Brothers. He has chosen for the subject of his books the civil war in Siberia, a subject rich in the most sensational horrors and thrills. But Ivanov's manner of telling these horrors is to deal with them as a matter of course, almost in a parenthesis, or in a subordinate clause. He is very prolific and, though ornamental, his prose is not very careful. The lyrical element, of a pantheistic character, is very apparent in his early books, but he has been careful to prune it out of his later ones. He is a master of mass scenes, and the atmosphere of civil war, when all the country stands on end and everyone is everyone's enemy, and one does not know whom to avoid more carefully—a pack of wolves, or an armed fellow-creature—is conveyed with great power. His earlier novels lack a narrative skeleton, but he is gradually learning to tell a tale and in his latest novel, *The Return of Buddha* (1924), his manner acquires greater directness without losing the power of creating atmosphere. His masterpiece up to the present is *The Child*, a short story of great power and concentration and admirably constructed. It would be a pity to epitomize it, so unexpected and masterly is its development. It has been translated into French and would serve as an excellent introduction to modern Russian fiction for the English-speaking public.

Vsevolod Ivanov is not the only writer who has concentrated on Siberian civil war. It is also the subject of Vyacheslav Shishkòv's stories and of his novel *The Band* (*Vataga*, 1924). Shishkov is a good writer of Russian, and a more orthodoxly narrative novelist than most of his contemporaries. There is much stimulating melodrama in his novel, and he is even not quite free from a touch of sentimentality. Another Siberian is Lydia Seyfùllina (b. 1889, in the district of Orsk, not administratively part of Siberia, but on the Siberian side of the Urals). She is more old-fashioned and less audacious than Ivanov or Pilnyak, and writes ultimately in a good old nineteenth-century realistic manner with a touch of very stale (twenty-five-year-old) modernity in her style. The spirit of her writings is more compatible with orthodox Communism than that of any other writer of equal significance: the Revolution to her is not a whirlwind or a cataclysm, but a slow process of enlightenment. Her Communists are heroes of light, and the favourite subject of her stories (*Youthful Offenders, Manure, Virineya*) is the making of a Communist. Her merits are an honest and simple gift of narrative, and an excellent, scrupulously realistic dialogue. She is not a Communist, but with her qualifications it is easy to understand that she has become the spoiled child of Communist criticism.

A Communist by passport, but much less of an orthodox Communist in spirit, is Artem Vesély. He has written very little, but has shown himself a master of remarkable and refreshing originality. He is also an ornamentalist, put his ronamentalism is wonderfully free from anything bookish or "poetical." His prose is dynamic. It vibrates with such an intense life that it almost approaches verse in point of expressiveness. His method of construction is quite peculiar and is wonderfully suited for mass effects: his record of the Red Sailors revelling in Novorossiysk in the spring of 1918

(*Volnitsa*) is a masterpiece of remarkable originality—a po-
lyphony of voices uniting into one mass-picture of enormous
expressiveness. This sort of thing has never yet been attempted and gives Artem Vesély a place quite apart.

The latest great success in Russian prose is I. Bàbel, who
bids fair to eclipse all the other post-Revolutionary novelists.
Babel's first story appeared in 1916 in Gorky's *Letopis* and
was by no means strikingly promising. Then for seven years
he disappeared from literature. In 1920 he took part in the
Polish campaign with the cavalry army of Budeny. In 1923
his short stories began to appear in the literary press and
at once made him the reputation of a first-class writer. He
is to-day regarded by many as the first of all young writers,
and his fame has reached even the *émigré* press. His most
characteristic stories are those which will form the book *Konar-
mia* (*Cavalry Army*), impressions of his service with Budeny's
Cossacks. They are very short, seldom more than a few hundred words. They are in substance journalistic impressions—
choses vues—or tragical anecdotes. But they are told with a
concentrated power that makes them genuine art. They are
heroic in substance—fragments from a vast epic which is more
akin to the old ballads than to anything contemporary. *Taras
Bulba*, the heroic Cossack-romance of Gogol, has been mentioned in connexion with them; and, indeed, Babel does not
shun the most conventional beauty and the most conventional
pathos. Only he gives it a new setting. His stories are stories
of blood and death, of cold-blooded crime, of heroism and
cruelty. Single combats are among his favourite subjects.
There is always a grain of irony in him which does not destroy
but only enhances the heroic pathos. His favourite method
is to make his heroes speak for themselves; and the combination of the admirably reproduced slang of the Red Cossack full
of numerous dialectal solecisms and ill-digested revolutionary
clichés, with the epic character of his exploits, is peculiar to
Babel. The spicy mixture is further flavoured by a crudeness
that is exceptional even to-day when lack of reticence has become so common a virtue. Babel knows no taboos, and the
coarsest words stand next to almost Victorian poetry. His

world is a topsy-turvy world where people live according to
laws that are very different from those of a European drawing-
room, where it is as easy to kill as to die, and where cruelty and
filth are inseparable from courage and bravery.   Babel's great
talent makes the reader at once accept the laws of this world
and understand its logic.   He is a consummate master of *skaz*,
and this quality is present also in his *Odessa Tales*, which deal
with the remarkable exploits of a famous Jewish bandit, and
which are told in the characteristic Russian-Jewish jargon
of Odessa.

PARALIPOMENA

1. THE DRAMA

A HISTORY of the drama, in so far as it is not merely book-drama, cannot be written apart from the history of the stage it was intended for, and a history of the Russian stage within the last fifty years is a subject too vast to be tackled here. Of the dramatic work of those writers who were not exclusively dramatists, I have spoken in connexion with their other writings, and here I will do no more than give in briefest outline the main facts of the development of Russian dramatic literature in connexion with the evolution of the stage.

In the second half of the nineteenth century, the Russian stage was dominated by *byt*, which is an untranslatable Russian word meaning the life and manners of a particular part of humanity. The object both of the playwright and of the actor was first of all to reproduce types of contemporary life. In literature this school is dominated by the great figure of Ostrovsky, who from 1850 to his death in 1886 might have said: "The Russian drama—*c'est moi.*" The theatres which best embodied the ideals of *byt* realism were the Imperial Dramatic Theatres of the two capitals, especially the Little Theatre * of Moscow. Both actors and authors of the time concentrated exclusively on types and manners. Dramatic construction was neglected, and all its more obviously conventional aspects, everything smacking of *scribisme* and of "sardoudledom," carefully avoided. Ostrovsky, who was very prolific, did not leave a worthy successor. All the dramatists who followed in his footsteps were frankly second-rate, and by the end of the century Russian dramatic literature was in a state of stagnation, though the stage continued producing first-class *byt* comedians and though the output of *byt* plays never slackened. The most popular

* As opposed to the Big, or Opera, Theatre.

316

playwrights of this school were N. Ya. Soloviev (1845–1898), who had the honour of collaborating with Ostrovsky himself in several plays: Victor Krylov (1838–1915), for many years director of the repertoire of the Imperial Theatre of Petersburg; the novelist Potapenko; and Victor Ryshkov, whose work belongs already to the early years of the twentieth century.

The first revolution in the Russian drama were the plays of Chekhov and the foundation by K. S. Stanislavsky (Alekseyev) and Vladimir Nemirovich-Danchenko of the Moscow Art Theatre. The production of *The Seagull* by this cast in 1898 is the beginning of a new period. The principle of Stanislavsky was realism *à outrance*. It was the Russian counterpart of the Meiningen Troupe, and of the Théâtre Antoine. Everything "theatrical" and conventional was mercilessly hounded off the stage; the research of realism went so far as to make the actors sometimes speak with their backs to the public, and as to replace the traditional trapezoidal stage room by "realistic" rooms with corners at right angles. In this respect Stanislavsky was only continuing and exaggerating the old tradition. His really new departure was the absolute subordination of the actor to the producer, and a rigidly enforced equality of all actors between themselves. His was an all-star or rather no-star cast. This system was admirably suited to Chekhov's plays, which also eliminate the "hero" and carry "realism" to the point of suppressing all plot, and reducing the play to a series of "slices from life." Another essential feature of Chekhov's theatre was that it shifted the centre of interest from the social facts of manners and types to the emotional facts of psychology and atmosphere. I have dwelt at sufficient length on Chekhov's plays in the chapter devoted to him, and in the chapter on Gorky and Andreev I have pointed out the sad results to which the imitation of Chekhov led. The non-dramatic, psychological and ultra-realistic school of Chekhov was dominant only for a short time. It was too obviously an impasse, and the perfection attained by the absolute adequacy of player and playwright in the Stanislavsky productions of Chekhov was a sterile perfection: it had no to-morrow. The attempt to infuse a social meaning into the Chekhovian mould, in spite of the great success of *The Lower Depths* and of S. Naydenov's (1869–1923) problem play *The Children of Vanyushin* (1902), did not bring any lasting fruit. By 1910 Chekhovian realism (though of course not Chekhov's own plays) was even more dead than the old realism of Ostrovsky.

A new type of realism arose in the plays of Artsybashev, who (partly under the influence of Strindberg) attempted the psychological problem drama and succeeded in writing several rather crude but perfectly actable plays. Another direction was tried by Ilya Surguchév, who revived the ordinary nineteenth-century psychological drama. In 1914 he had a considerable success with *Autumnal Violins*, a well-constructed psychological drama on the old subject of a rivalry in love between a middle-aged woman and a very young girl. It is traditional in architecture, but is permeated with Chekhovian atmospheric details (and stage directions) and has a characteristically Chekhovian "blurred" ending. At the same time A. N. Tolstoy wrote his light-minded, frankly melodramatic plays with much action and little construction. But all this was not sufficient to breathe fresh life into the realistic drama and to revive a more dramatic manner of play-writing. Realism was doomed. Long before 1914 Stanislavsky had passed from ultra-realism to a new conventionalism *à la* Gordon Craig. Meyerhold had realized a strictly unrealistic theatre in 1906, and was advancing towards a still more subversive, purely spectacular, and anti-literary style of production.

The first anti-realistic growth in the drama was the symbolic and metaphysical drama in a conventional setting. The symbolic plays of Andreev (which held the stage in 1907–1910), besides being mediocre as literature, are tiresome as drama. They were merely dialoguized litanies in bad prose. Andreev's later manner, which is as bad from the literary, is much better from the dramatic point of view, and *He Who Gets Slapped* might have become a starting-point for the development of a crude popular melodrama with metaphysical pretensions. But it did not.

The genuine Symbolists were equally unsuccessful in creating a drama of their own, nor did they make any concerted efforts in this direction. Sologub's dramas, like Hugo von Hofmannsthal's, are merely lyrical recitals, to be judged by the poetical value of separate passages. Much more important and promising were Blok's essays in this direction. *The Puppet Show* (1906) and *The Stranger* (1907) are masterpieces of romantic irony in the tradition of Thieck and Gozzi, and, when produced, proved excellent shows. *The Rose and the Cross* (1913) is a first-class romantic tragedy, but, after all, Blok's plays are primarily poetry, and drama only by the way. Still they remain as the only really important achievements of Russian poetical drama within recent times.

The Symbolists made attempts to revive genuine tragedy. But Vyacheslav Ivanov's tragedies, obscure and heavily ornate, are only overgrown choric odes. The younger Symbolists and post-Symbolists turned to Corneille and Racine instead of to the too remote Athenians. Neo-classical tragedies were written by Gumilev and by Nikolay Vladimirovich Nedobrovò (1883–1919), a subtle critic and theoretician of Symbolism in its last stages. Both Gumilev's *Gondla* (1917, in rhymed anapæsts) and Nedobrovo's *Judith* (posthumous, in Alexandrines) are more remarkable for the intention than for the execution. Still, in both there are genuine merits—a true heroic spirit and a noble nudeness of design.

Closely connected with Symbolism are the work and the ideas of Nikolay Nikolaevich Evreinov (b. 1879), producer and playwright. His idea of the theatre as a great religious and solacing force which is the truest incarnation of the Deity led to the slogan of the "theatralization of life"—of making life a continuous joy and transfiguring its drabness by the exhilarating wine of dramatic art. This idea is most characteristically expressed in Evreinov's comedy, *The Principal Thing*, where the symbolical Paraclete (Consoler), assuming the most unexpected and varied masks, succeeds in bringing joy and enjoyment of life to the depressed and gloomy inhabitants of a vulgar and tiresome boarding-house by forcing them

to "act in life" and live on illusions. Evreinov's influence on
the stage is a thing of the past, and, on the whole, he stands
outside the main movement.

Of this main movement the most representative men are
Meyerhold in his later stages, and Tairov. The movement is
in the direction of "deliteratizing" the stage, of eliminating as
far as possible the author, and of absolutely eliminating ideas
and psychology. The play tends to become more spectacular—a matter of pure show, a *spectacle pure*. Tricks and buffoonery are gladly introduced by the new producers, and the
fool of Elizabethan drama has practically been revived in
Russia. This movement in its initial stages (before the War)
was closely allied with the great success of the humorous
"miniature" theatres, one of which (and not the best), the
Chauve Souris theatre of Balieff, has acquired such a world-
wide reputation. This type of theatre naturally enough
stands outside literature, though I have mentioned in another
connexion an author who contributed to it—the vaudevillist
Yuri Belyaev.

The Revolution, which was so destructive in every branch of
culture, was anything but destructive for the theatre. It had
the time of its life during the worst years of famine, wholesale Communism, and civil war. Never was Russia more
theatre-going than in the years 1918–1920. Every country
town, every junction, almost every unit of the Red Army had
one if not several theatres. Of course the level of these
democratic theatres was very low, but in the capitals the Left
producers were patronized by the State and could embody in-
tentions which were unthinkable when theatres were run com-
mercially. Left ideas in stage-producing naturally allied
themselves with Left ideas in painting and architecture, and
with literary Futurism. But the achievement of the Futurist
drama is not great, and is practically limited to the really
excellent *Mystery-Bouffe* of Mayakovsky, which was both a
clever piece of very crude propaganda and an admirably arranged show.

The official Bolshevik drama is represented first of all by
Anatoli Vasilievich Lunacharsky, whose numerous and inept

plays I have spoken of in Interchapter II.   All the authority
of the *Commissar* for Education cannot force even the official daily press to admire his plays.   The same style of play,
the revolutionary drama in a conventional setting, is cultivated
by numerous authors, some of whom, though on the same literary, stand on a higher dramatic level than Lunacharsky.
Such are, for instance, the plays of Wolkenstein.   But the
style in itself is capable of higher achievement, and in the
right hands may even become genuine tragedy.   The nearest
approach to this are the plays of Olga Forsch (b. 1875;
Rabbi).

Akin to this school, but free from revolutionary cant, and
much nearer to the true spirit of tragedy, are the plays of
the late Leo Lunts, who died in 1924 at the age of twenty-two.
He was the most uncompromising and extreme of the literary
"Westerners" and opposed the developed technique of the West
to the deep-rooted undramatic and un-narrative Russian tradition.   His tragedies *Outlawed* (1921) and *Bertrand de Born*
(1922) are tragedies of pure action, with a rapid and logical
development of the plot and with no irrelevant psychology.
Though they are full of thought, they are not problem plays
but tragedies of situation.   Still, they were only the first steps
towards real achievement.   Lunts's last play, *Justice City*
(1924), was a new departure towards a more philosophical
style of problem play.   Though none of his plays is in any
sense a masterpiece, he had a grip and a fixity of purpose
which promised real achievement, and his untimely death is a
serious loss to the Russian drama.

2. LITERARY CRITICISM

The prevalent form of Russian literary criticism in the second half of the nineteenth century was the "social" * criticism
introduced by Belinsky in the forties.   After his time, the
leaders of Radical opinion were also literary critics and exercised a sort of dictatorship over the literary opinion of the

* "Social" is the nearest possible rendering of the Russian word
obshchestvenny.

Liberal and Radical *intelligentsia*. Since 1870 the office of dictator was held by Mikhaylovsky, who exercised it to his death in 1904. The method of the "social" critics in dealing with works of imaginative literature was purely "social" and "civic"—that is to say, they viewed them only from the point of view of their social and political implications. The critics did not demand of the writer a definite political tendency, but reliable information on the present state of society that might be used by critics and publicists in their social speculations. But ultimately (especially after the classical period of the great novelists) writers came to be judged according to the public spirit that animated them, and all criticism went along party lines.

As a rule, these social critics had no qualifications to judge of literary facts, and are entirely negligible as critics. The exceptions are few. The most notable one is Mikhaylovsky himself, who had great critical gifts which he left more or less undeveloped, but which appear, for instance, in his penetrating essay on Dostoevsky.* Apart from Mikhaylovsky there is little to be said of the "social" critics, and only those need be mentioned here who wrote books of literary history that had a considerable influence on forming the average Russian's picture of the past of Russian letters, and which still, sometimes, have to be used for lack of anything better.

The oldest of these was A. N. Pypin (1833–1904), a Radical Democrat, the author of a four-volume *History of Russian Literature* from the origins to Gogol, where he views the whole subject as a conflict of Western, progressive, and national, reactionary ideas. The Populist A. M. Skabichevsky (1838–1910) wrote a *History of Modern Russian Literature* (1848–1893; 1st. ed., 1893), which is a caricature of the whole method, so naïvely tendentious and one-sided is it, but contains valuable biographical material. The Positivist D. N. Ovsyaniko-Kulikovsky (1853–1921), besides numerous monographs of social criticism (Gogol, Turgenev, Tolstoy), wrote a history of the Russian *intelligentsia* in three volumes, and edited a five-volume *History of Russian Literature in the*

* See Chapter I, 5.

Nineteenth Century (1910 and foll.). The youngest was Semen Afanasievich Vengerov (1855–1920), whose services to Russian bibliography and literary biography are inestimable. He also did noble work as Professor of Literature in the university of Petersburg, in encouraging young students towards literary studies. But his historical, critical, and editorial work (he edited a monumental edition of Pushkin, 1908–1915) does not give a favourable idea of his judgment.

The rise of Marxism brought with it a school of Marxist critics and literary historians, who, in addition to the general tendencies of social criticism, introduced a rigidly dogmatic system of interpretation of literary facts in terms of economic evolution. The earliest of the Marxist critics, Evgeni Andreevich Soloviev (1863–1905; pseud., "Andreevich"), had a genuine critical temperament, and his *Philosophy of the History of Russian Literature* (1905), for all its one-sided narrowness, is readable and worth reading. But the average Marxist critic and literary historian is the sorriest of sights. The critiques and literary histories of Fritsche, Kranichfeld, Kogan, or Lvov-Rogachevsky are merely more or less clever exercises in the entertaining game of fixing this or that literary work to this or that particular stage of economic development. Since the victory of the Bolsheviks, Marxist criticism has acquired an official position. Its method consists exclusively in the valuation of literary works from the point of view of their political, social, and educational effect, and in discerning the title of "proletarian writer," "*poputchik*," or "counter-revolutionary" to individual writers. The most conspicuous of these official critics is Voronsky, the editor of *Krasnaya Nov*, who cannot be refused a certain critical flair, for as editor he succeeds in making his magazine very good. The critical writings of Trotsky contain interesting remarks on the "educational" value of literary works.

But, apart from the present official position of Marxism, "social" criticism has, since the nineties, lost most of its influence, and its adepts have been infected by various heresies. In the works of Nestor Kotlyarevsky (b. 1863), for instance, the interest is shifted from social development to social psychology, after the manner of Brandes; which does not make them better criticism than Ovsyaniko-Kulikovsky's or Vengerov's. The work of Razumnik Vasielievich Ivanov-Razumnik is a curious cross between "social" and metaphysical preoccupations. His "Scythianism" * and his relations with Blok and Bely are more important to the literary historian than his own historical works. His *History of Russian Social Thought* (recently reprinted in a revised form as *Russian Literature*) is an elaborately scholastic account of the development of individualism (which he identifies with Socialism), substituted for the history of literature.

Social criticism was a creation but not a monopoly of the Radicals. Slavophil and Conservative criticism in the second half of the nineteenth century was also, for the most part, social. Only a few of the Conservative critics were capable of genuinely literary criticism. Strakhov, for instance, was as a rule purely "social" in his critiques, and only exceptionally (in *Notes on Pushkin*) faced literary facts as such. The great exception is Constantine Leontsev, whose wonderful book on Tolstoy is the *only* genuine book of literary criticism in the whole second half of the nineteenth century.

While social criticism was all-powerful in the magazines and even in the universities, two isolated scholars worked at giving the study of literature a solid scientific basis: Alexander N. Veselòvsky (1838–1906) laid the foundations of a natural history of literary forms, and A. A. Potebnyà (1835–1891) investigated the primary facts of poetry in connexion with the primary facts of language. But the influence of Veselovsky was limited to the study of mediæval literature, and had little influence outside the universities. The ideas of Potebnya were largely misrepresented by his disciples. They also remained restricted to academic circles, and were fruitful mainly in the study of folk-lore. In literary criticism his influence is apparent in the work of A. G. Gornfeld (b. 1867), who was for many years the only contributor to the Radical press to write about literary facts and realities, and not merely of sociological and journalistic abstractions.

* See Interchapter II.

The "æsthetic revival" of the eighties was favourable for the revival of a purely æsthetic criticism, and this did happen to a certain extent. But very few of the æsthetic critics were worth much. The amusing and truculent V. Burenin (1841–1919) degenerated into a professional Zoilus, who specialized on hounding down every young writer and ridiculing every new movement. The best critic produced by the eighties was S. A. Andreevsky,* whose *Literary Readings* (1st ed., 1890) was an important landmark in the emancipation of the Russian reader from purely social standards in literature.

But Russian literary criticism was not so easily to be emancipated from extra-literary tutelage. The decline of social criticism coincided with the rise of metaphysical criticism. The first to use the metaphysical method of interpretation was Vladimir Soloviev. This writer, in addition to all his other accomplishments, possessed a keen, if limited,† critical judgment, and his short notices on the Russian "Victorian" poets (in the Brockhaus encyclopædia) are always interesting. But his most notable critical work is his essay on *The Poetry of Tyutchev* (1896), which remains perhaps the masterpiece of the metaphysical method in criticism because its initial conception is firmly founded on fact, and is unfolded with convincing logic. Soloviev's interpretation of Tyutchev's poetry revolutionized the general idea one had of that poet, and deeply impressed itself on all thinking Russia.

Metaphysical criticism flourished in the hands of the "religious philosophers" and of some of the symbolists. Volynsky was the first to advance its theories. In his book on *Russian Critics* (1896), he condemned them for an absence of philosophical outlook, and put his theory into practice in his books on Leskov and on Dostoevsky's *Possessed* (*The Book of Great Wrath*). The great masters of metaphysical criticism were Rozanov, Merezhkovsky, Gershenzon, and Vyacheslav Ivanov. Rozanov was, without doubt, the greatest. His intuitive genius, even when it was on the most perverse tracks, saw with miraculous insight what was veiled from others, and certain

* See Chapter II, 6.

† He could see no good, for instance, in Tolstoy.

pages of his, especially on Gogol, belong to the highest summits of the higher criticism. But he is never primarily concerned with literary values, and his books are philosophy, not criticism. Valuable pages and chapters are to be found in Merezhkovsky (especially the first part of *Tolstoy and Dostoevsky*), in Gershenzon (*The Wisdom of Pushkin*), and in Ivanov (essays on Dostoevsky and on Pushkin's *Gipsies*), but as a whole the method is highly unsatisfactory, for it subordinates the criticized writer to the metaphysical convictions of the critic. The works of metaphysical critics may be (and often are) excellent literature and first-class philosophy; they are bastard criticism.

The metaphysical method was taken up by numerous younger writers, especially in the decade following the First Revolution, and is still practised, though its vogue has passed. A prolific critic of this school was the precocious and unfortunate Alexander Zakrzewski (1889–1918), whose numerous books published in the years preceding the Revolution, though valueless for the understanding of the writers discussed, are representative of a state of mind which is reminiscent of Dostoevsky's *Man from Underground* and was wide-spread at that time among the *intelligentsia*.

The Symbolists did not found a school of criticism of their own any more than they founded a school of prose fiction. Of the poets who were also critics, Ivanov was a pure metaphysician. Balmont and Annensky wrote lyrical rhapsodies in an impressionistic style, which is insipidly rhetorical in the case of Balmont, and aggressively capricious in Annensky's. Blok's criticism was intensely subjective: he used other people's work as a way of elucidating his own states of mind. When the writer he writes about is genuinely akin to himself, his criticisms are highly interesting, penetrating, and, in the best sense, imaginative. Such is his well-known essay on Apollon Grigoriev. Zinaida Hippius (who signed her critiques "Anton Krayni" *) and Bryusov were recorders of critical judgments: they were judges, not interpreters. Their appreciations are always of value, and Zinaida Hippius's are, besides, excel-

* See Chapter V, 4.

lently written. Bryusov, however, once at least wrote a critical work which is above the average. This is his essay on Gogol (*Ispepelenny—The Man Reduced to Ashes*, 1909), which, next to Rozanov's, contains the most worth-while things ever said of that great writer.

The most remarkable of Symbolist critics is Andrey Bely. Like most of his writings, his critical essays are full of flashes of genius and wonderful intuitive vistas. But he combines a strong metaphysical tendency with a style so troubled and hysterical, so lacking in restraint, and (sometimes) so wildly illogical that as literature his essays cannot be mentioned by the side of his poetry or of his novels. As criticism, apart from their frequent flashes of insight, they are too personal and subjective to be of more than relative value. His later criticisms (the critical chapters of *Recollections of Blok*) are unintelligible to anyone who is not an Anthroposophist. But apart from his metaphysical criticism, Bely is important as the reviver of Russian prosody. His study of the variations of the Russian octosyllabic ("four-footed iambus"), contained in the volume *Symbolism* (1910), was the starting-point for all those studies of poetical form which have become such a notable feature of Russian literary criticism.

The general tendency of criticism under the influence of the Symbolists was towards extreme subjectivism and impressionism. The most successful of these impressionist critics was Yuli Aichenwald (b. 1872), whose *Silhouettes of Russian Authors* (1st volume, 1907) has had many reprints and has even penetrated into the schools. Aichenwald is boundlessly eclectic and nauseously sweet. His style has been described as a dense layer of treacle beneath which it is impossible to distinguish between Turgenev and the vulgarest of lyrical journalists.

A much more enjoyable critic is Korney Ivanovich Chukovsky (b. 1883), whose first essays created a sensation in 1906–1907. His object was to make criticism readable and entertaining, and this object he certainly achieved. His style, rich in paradoxes, was formed under the influence of Oscar Wilde and Mr. Chesterton. His method of dealing with an author is to single out one or two violently contradictory characteristics, and then to group all the facts so as to corroborate the choice. The result, at its best, is a brilliantly convincing critical cartoon, which impresses itself on the mind of the reader. Naturally it is at its best when it is used as a weapon of ridicule, and Chukovsky's best essays are those in which he is most unkind. His essay on Artsybashev's *Sanin* is a masterpiece of killing criticism. But in most cases he either misses the point or simplifies to the point of vulgarity matters of extreme complexity, and, readable and entertaining though he is, Chukovsky is, above all, tremendously superficial. But he is a writer of great natural gifts. His memoirs (Andreev) and his essays in biography (Nekrasov), though quite as superficial and dashing as his critiques, are also excellent reading. His *Recollections of Leonid Andreev* have been translated into English, and described by reviewers as most amusing.

The latest development in Russian literary criticism is that connected with the so-called "formal method" and with the activities of the *Opoyaz* (O*bshchestvo izucheniya* Po*eticheskogo* Yazyka*—Society for the Study of the Language of Poetry). This movement is directed at once against all the existing methods of criticism—against the substitution of political or metaphysical for literary problems and standards, and against the irresponsible subjectivism of the impressionist critics. The formalists of the *Opoyaz* profess to abstain from all appreciation of values: they analyse and describe—they do not judge. The subject of their investigation are literary *forms* in the widest application of the term, which includes the *choice of themes* and the plot. (*The Plot as a Phenomenon of Style* is the characteristic title of an essay by Victor Shklovsky.) "A work of art is equal to the sum of *procédés* employed in it," is the principal tenet of the school. From the point of view of its origin, the school is a cross between the formal aspirations of Futurism and modern ideas in linguistics. The initiators of the movement were a group of young linguists connected more or less with the Futurist poets—Victor Shklovsky, Osip Brik, and Roman Yakobson. Their first works appeared before the Revolution, but their principal and most influential

manifesto was the collection of essays *Poetika* (*Poetics*), published in 1919 at the expense of Vladimir Mayakovsky. The new school is rich in talent, and its adherents are numerous and militant. They have succeeded in impressing themselves on the general literary opinion, and are now courageously fighting against official Marxist doctrines. They have a trusty ally in the Futurists, whose review, *Lef*, freely opens its columns to them. There are numerous shades of opinion within the school. The extremists tend to identify the study of literature and linguistics; they concentrate on the phonetic aspect of poetry, and are in favour of "trans-sense" diction. Of them, Osip Brik has published a notable analysis of the phonetic structure of Pushkin's verse, and Roman Yakobson a remarkable work on Czech prosody as compared with Russian. Of the brilliant, nonchalant, and dashing essays of Shklovsky I have spoken elsewhere.*
More moderate in their views are the Petersburg group—Boris Eichenbaum, Yuri Tynyanov, Boris Tomashevsky, and, especially, Victor Zhirmunsky. Their common characteristic is an intense interest in and acute insight into the historical process. Literary history to them is the history of the literary tradition, and their principal task is to explain the soil on which individual works grow up, and the organic continuity they form. The most brilliant is Eichenbaum, whose essay on Gogol's *Greatcoat* was the *clou* of the *Poetika* volume. His works on *The Young Tolstoy* (1922), on Nekrasov, and *Lermontov* (1924) are masterpieces of historical analysis which goes straight to the facts of literary expression, and works towards the construction of a really organic *évolution des genres*. Tomashevsky has concentrated on the study of Pushkin and his relations to French literature, and on prosody. Zhirmunsky, who is more of an eclectic, has written the first worth-while book on the much abused question of Byron's influence on Pushkin. All these works are not, in the strict sense, criticism, for they abstain on principle from all æsthetic appreciation.

But, connected with the formalists, a criticism is coming into existence which judges contemporary works without abandoning the solid historical outlook of the formalists. Of the formal-

* See Chapter VII, 6.

ists, Shklovsky and Tynyanov are judicious and acute critics of current literature; so is the novelist Zamyatin, whose always interesting reviews I have already alluded to.* A first-class critic is the poet Mandelstam.† But his eminently historical and fruitful mind does not always attain to articulate expression. His all-too-rare essays are so rich in thought and so brimful of ideas that the very abundance makes them difficult and confusing reading.

* See Chapter VII, 4.
† See Chapter VI, 3.

BIBLIOGRAPHY

This does not aim at being a complete, but only a working bibliography.

Under each heading the entries are grouped under three rubrics: (1) works in Russian; (2) in English; (3) in other languages, mainly French and German.

Under rubric 1, only the most complete, the most recent, or otherwise convenient editions are quoted; minor authors are omitted. Of biographical works, only the most important are mentioned. Critical works are referred to only in exceptional cases. Under rubric 2, I have tried to make a tolerably complete list of English translations. My sources were the Catalogue of the British Museum, and the *United States Catalog* only up to June, 1923; so the list of American editions will be found wanting in completeness. Obsolete translations have not been quoted, when better ones are available. Periodicals have not been searched, and references to them are exceptional. Of English books on Russian literature, and English anthologies, I have omitted to mention certain quite worthless books. Of the numerous books on Tolstoy, those which discuss him from religious, social, or pedagogical standpoints have not been included.

Rubric 3 includes French and German translations only of important works which have not been translated, or have been mutilated when translated, into English; a few have been included for their superior merits (e.g., Wolfgang Groeger's translation of *The Twelve*). French and German works have been mentioned only in exceptional cases.

GENERAL

In the following, P. stands for St. Petersburg, Petrograd, and Leningrad; M., for Moscow.

(1) (a) Indispensable works of reference are *Entsiklopedicheskiy*

331

Slovar' (Encyclopædia), 82 volumes, and 4 additional volumes, Brockhaus & Efron, P., 1890–1907; *Novyy Entsiklopedicheskiy Slovar'* (New Encyclopædia), incomplete, 29 volumes from A to O, Brockhaus & Efron, P., 1910–1917; and Vladislavlev, *Russkie Pisateli XIX–XXvv* (Bibliography of Russian Authors), 4th edition, State Press, P., 1924; the valuable handbooks by Prof. Peretts (*Metodologiya Russkoy Literatury,* Academia Press, P., 1922) and Prof. Piksanov (*Dva Veka Russkoy Literatury,* 2nd ed., State Press, M., 1924) cover only a small part of the present period.

(b) There is no satisfactory history of modern Russian literature. All the following are written from some political party point of view and have very little to do with literary facts (see also Appendix, 2. *Literary Criticism*).

Istoriya Novoy Russkoy Literatury 1848–1893, by A. Skabichevsky. 1 ed., 1893; numerous reprints; Populist.

Istoriya Russkoy Literatury XIX veka. 1800–1900, by N. Engelgart. 2 volumes, 1902; Conservative.

Istoriya Russkoy Literature XIX veka. 5 volumes, edited by Prof. Ovsyaniko-Kulikovsky; most of the contributors Marxists.

Russkaya Literature 1870–1922, by Ivanov-Razumnik. Skythen Verlag, Berlin, 1922; Left S.R.

Noveyshaya Russkaya Literatura, by V. Lvov-Rogachevsky. Tsentrosoyuz, M. 1923; Marxist.

Russkaya Literatura XX veka, 1890–1910, edited by Prof. S. A. Vengerov. 4 volumes, M., 1914–1915 (contains much valuable memoir and autobiographical matter).

(c) Anthologies: *Russkaya Muza,* 2nd ed., ed. by P. Ya. (the civic poet Yakubovich); *Russkiy Parnass,* ed. by A. & D. Eliasberg. Insel-Verlag, Leipzig, 1920; *Russkaya Lirika* (with notes), ed. by Prince D. Svyatopolk-Mirsky, Presse Française et Etrangère, Paris, 1924; *The Oxford Book of Russian Verse,* ed. by the Hon. Maurice Baring (Russian text; preface and notes in English), Clarendon Press, 1924.

(2)   (a)   *A History of Russian Literature,* by K. Waliiszewski,
Heinemann, London; Appleton, N.Y.; 1900 (super-
ficial and journalistic; the author is a Pole).

Russian Literature: Ideals and Realities, by P. Kropotkin. London, Duckworth & Co., 1905; 2nd ed., 1916;
Knopf, N.Y., 1915.

A Literary History of Russia, by A. Brückner, Professor of Slavonic Languages and Literature in the
University of Berlin; transl. from German by H.
Havelock, edited by Ellis H. Minns. London and
Leipsic. T. Fisher Unwin, 1908; Scribner, N.Y.,
1909. (The author is also a Pole; scholarly, but
treats literature exclusively from the political standpoint.)

Outline of Russian Literature, by the Hon. Maurice
Baring. Home University Library. London: Williams & Norgate; Holt, N.Y.; 1914.

Russia of the Russians, by Harold Whitmore Williams,
Ph.D.; Sir Isaac Pitman & Sons, London; Scribner,
N.Y.; 1914.   (Ch. III, *The Press;* Ch. VI, Litera-
ture; Ch. VIII, *The Theatre;* very valuable surveys
based   on   first-hand   knowledge.)   (Quoted   as
Williams.)

Contemporary Russian Novelists, by Serge Persky,
tr. from the French by F. Eisenmann; Palmer,
London, 1914; J. W. Luce, N.Y., 1913 (quoted as
Persky).

Essays on Russian Novelists, by William Lyon Phelps,
Lampson Professor of English Literature at Yale,
Macmillan, N.Y., 1916 (valuable bibliographies)
(quoted as Phelps).

Guide to Russian Literature (1820–1917), by Moissaye
J. Olgin, Ph.D.; New York: Harcourt, Brace &
Howe, 1920. (London: Cape.) (Contains valuable
bibliographical matter and curious extracts from
Russian critics.)   (Quoted as Olgin.)

The Spirit of Russia, Studies in History, Literature,
and Philosophy, by Thomas Garrigue Masaryk, tr.
from the German original by E. & C. Paul. 2 vol.
G. Allen & Unwin, London; Macmillan, N.Y.; 1918.
(A translation of *Russland und Europa.*)

(b) *Anthologies: Anthology of Russian Literature from the
Earliest Period to the Present Time* (Prose and
Poetry), by Leo Wiener, Assistant Professor of
Slavic Languages in Harvard University. (Part II,
The Nnieteenth Century.) Putnam, N.Y., 1902.
(Quoted as *Wiener.*)

Modern Russian Poetry. Texts and Translations
selected and translated with an introduction by P.
Selver. London: Kegan Paul; New York: E. P.
Dutton & Co.; 1917. (Ridiculous selection, but fairly
good translations.) (Quoted as *Selver.*)

Modern Russian Poetry: an anthology chosen and
translated by Babette Deutsch and Avrahm Yarmolinsky. New York: Harcourt, Brace & Co.,
1921; London: John Lane. (Quoted as *Yarmolinsky.*)

(3) (a) *Geschichte der Russischen Literatur,* by Arthur Luther,
Leipsic: Bibliographisches institut, 1924. (Mainly
a compilation from Russian text-books; numerous and
excellent illustrations.)

Russland und Europa, Erste Folge: Zur Russischen
Geschichts- und Religionsphilosophie, by T. G.
Masaryk. 2 vol. Eugen Diederichs, Jena, 1913. (A
thorough study of Russian political, historical, and
religious thought, from an anticlerical and democratic
standpoint.)

(b) *Anthologie de poètes Russes Contemporains,* by Jean
Chuzeville, Paris, 1914.

Russland in dichterischen Dokumenten, by Alex. Eliasberg and Joh. v. Guenther. 3 volumes, Munich,
1924.

PERIODICALS

The following periodicals contain much interesting matter:
The Slavonic Review (No. 1, June, 1922, three times a year),
published by the School of Slavonic Studies in the University of
London; *Russia* (in Italian), ed. by Prof. Ettore Lo Gatto, publ.
Riccardo Ricciardi, Naples.

CHAPTER I

Tolstoy: (1) *Works.* The editions published in Russia before
the Revolution are incomplete, many passages having been excluded, not by the Censorship, which
in 1906 ceased to have preventive functions, but
by the editors *in view of* the Censorship. Consequently post-Revolutionary or foreign editions are
preferable. But there is no complete edition of
this description. Separate works have been published by Ladyschnikow and by Slowo-Verlag, in
Berlin.

Letters: Pis'ma, 1848–1910, 2 vol. M., 1910.
Perepiska s gr. A. A. Tolstoy, 1857–1903. P.,
1911 and foll. *Novyy sbornik Pisem,* M., 1912;
Pis'ma k zhene, 1862–1910, M., 1913.

Diaries: Dnevnik (1895, etc.), M., 1916, etc.

Life, in four volumes by P. I. Biryukov, State Press,
1924 (other important biographical sources quoted
in their English form).

Of the critiques of the later work of Tolstoy, by far the most
important is:

Analiz, stil' i veyanie v romanakh gr. L. Tolstogo,
by Constantine Leontiev (Works, and separately.
M., 1911).

(2) The standard English version of Tolstoy's writings
is the "Maude" Tolstoy, not yet complete; it in-
cludes, up to the present, the following volumes:
Twenty-three Tales ("tales for the people");
The Kreutzer Sonata (and other stories);
Resurrection; Plays (complete); *Confession and
What I Believe in; Essays and Letters; What,
Then, Must We Do?* (ready shortly); all these
in the "World's Classics" series, Oxford Uni-
versity Press; *Tolstoy on Art,* by Aylmer
Maude (contains all Tolstoy's utterances on
the subject, including *What Is Art?*), Oxford
University Press, 1925.

The Complete Works of Count Tolstoy, 24 vol.,

tr. Leo Wiener. Dent, London; and Dana
Estes & Co., Boston (Mass.), 1904–1905.

The Death of Ivan Ilyich and other stories, tr.
Constance Garnett. Heinemann, London; Lane,
N.Y.; 1915.

The Dramatic Works of L. T., tr. N. H. Dole.
Harrap, London; Crowell, N.Y.; 1923.

Posthumous works: *Father Sergius and other stories and plays; The Forged Coupon and other
stories and dramas; Hadji Murad and other stories;* ed. by C. Hagberg Wright. Nelson, London; Dodd, N.Y.; 1911–1912. *The Forged Coupon and other stories,* tr. H. Bernstein; Ogilvie,
N.Y., 1912; *Posthumous Works,* tr. A. J. Wolfe,
3 volumes, International Book, N.Y., 1920.

Diaries: *The Diaries of L. T.,* tr. E. J. Hogarth
and A. Sirnis. Dent, London; Dutton, N.Y.;
1917.

The Journals of L. T., tr. Rose Strunsky. Knopf,
N.Y., 1917.

Letters: *Tolstoi's Love Letters,* tr. S. S. Koteliansky and Virginia Woolf. Hogarth Press, Rich-
mond, 1923.

The Life of Tolstoy, by P. I. Biryukov. Cassell,
London, 1911.

The Last Days of Tolstoy, by V. G. Chertkov
(Tchertkoff). Heinemann, London, 1922.

The Autobiography of Countess Sophie Tolstoi,
tr. S. S. Koteliansky and L. Woolf, Hogarth
Press, London; Huebsch, N.Y.; 1922.

Talks with Tolstoy, by A. B. Goldenveizer.
Hogarth Press, London, 1923.

Reminiscences of Tolstoy, by Maxim Gorky.
Hogarth Press, London; Huebsch, N.Y.; 1921.

The Life of Tolstoy, two volumes (*First Fifty
Years; Later Years*), by Aylmer Maude; Constable, London; Dodd, N.Y.; 1908, 1910.

The Truth about My Father, by Count L. L. Tolstoy. John Murray, London, 1924.

Reminiscences of Tolstoy by His Son, by Count

Ilya Tolstoy. Chapman & Hall, London; Century Co., N.Y.; 1914.

Cf. *Tolstoy*, by Janko Lavrin. Collins, London, 1924.

Tolstoy as Man and Artist, by D. S. Merezhkovsky. Constable, London; Putnam, N.Y.; 1902.

Tolstoy, by G. R. Noyes. Duffield, N.Y., 1918; John Murray, London, 1919.

Tolstoy, by Romain Rolland. T. Fisher Unwin, London; Dutton, N.Y.; 1911.

Count L. N. Tolstoy: His Life and Work, by Charles Sarolea. Nelson's Shilling Library, 1912.

Leskov: (1) Works, in 36 volumes, P., 1902–1903.

Zayachiy Remiz, M., 1923.

Life: biographical notice prefixed to *Works; Protiv Techeniy N. S. Leskov*, by A. I. Faresov. P., 1914.

Cf. *Leskov*, by A. Volynsky. P., 1898.

(2) *The Sentry and other stories*, tr. A. E. Chamot. John Lane, London, 1922; *Cathedral Folk*, tr. Isabel F. Hapgood. Knopf, N.Y.; John Lane, London; 1924 (printed U.S.A.).

(3) *Geschichten aus der Alten Zeit; Geschichten aus der Grossstadt; Legenden* (tr. by various hands), Becksche Verlagsbuchhandlung, Munich, 1924; *Ausgewählte Novellen*, tr. J. V. Guenther, 3 vol. Munich, 1923; and numerous editions of separate stories.

Gens de Russie, tr. Denis Roche. Paris, 1906.

Le voyageur enchanté, tr. V. Derély. Paris, 1892.

(A new version of this story is being prepared by *Les Editions de la Pléiade*.)

Mikhaylovsky: (1) Works, six volumes; and two additional volumes (1915).

(2) Cf. Kropotkin, Olgin, Masaryk.

(3) *Qu'est-ce que le Progrès? Examen des idées de Herbert Spencer*, Paris, 1897.

Sluchevsky: (1) Works, six volumes, P., 1898–1899.

(2) *Oxford Book*.

Pobedonostsev: Reflections of a Russian Statesman, tr. R. C.

Long, with a preface by Olga Novikoff. G. Richards, London, 1898.

Danilevsky: (3) *Russland und Europa,* tr. K. Nötzel. Stuttgart, 1920.

Strakhov: (1) Cf. Rozanov, *Literaturnye Izgnanniki,* P., 1913. (Contains a memoir and letters from Strakhov, annotated by Rozanov.)

(2) A correspondence between Strakhov and Tolstoy on the person of Dostoevsky. See *Criterion,* January, 1925.

Leontiev: (1) Works, nine volumes. M., 1912, etc.
Cf. *Pamyati K. N. Leontieva.* P., 1911 (contains a biography by Konoplyantsev and memoirs by various authors).
Stranitsy Vospominaniy (selected passages from memoirs), Parfenon, P., 1922.

(2) Cf. Masaryk.

(3) Selections from works: in *Ostliches Christentum,* herausgegeben von Hans Ehrenberg, Band 1, Munich, 1923.

CHAPTER II

Garshin: (1) Works in one volume, numerous editions; *What Never Happened* (and other stories): Russian text with accents. Clarendon Press, Oxford, 1920.
Cf. *Pamyati Garshina.* P., 1889.

(2) *The Signal* and other stories, tr. Rowland Smith. Duckworth, London; Knopf, N.Y.; 1915.
Wiener; cf. Williams, Olgin.

Boborykin: (2) Cf. Olgin.

Nemirovich-Danchenko: (2) *The Princes of the Stock Exchange,* tr. A. S. Rappoport. Holden & Hardingham, London, 1914.
Peasant Tales of Russia, tr. Claude Field. Robert Scott, London, 1917.
With a Diploma, and the Whirlwind, tr. W. J. Stanton Pyper, J. W. Luce, N.Y., 1915.

Potapenko: (2) *A Russian Priest,* tr. W. Gaussen. T. Fisher Unwin, London; Dodd, N.Y.; 1916; Wiener.

Mamin-Sibiryak: Cf. Olgin.

Mikulich: (2) *Mimi's Marriage, A Sketch* (Pseudonym Library, London: T. Fisher Unwin, 1893).

Ertel: (1) Works, seven volumes, M., 1904.

    Pis'ma (Letters). M., 1909.

    (2) Cf. Kropotkin.

Garin: (2) Cf. Olgin.

Yakubovich (Melshin): (2) Cf. Olgin.

    (3) *Im Reiche der Ausgestossenen.* Dresden, 1901.

Korolenko: (1) Works, nine volumes, Marx, P., 1914; selected stories, three volumes; and *Slepoy Muzykant (The Blind Musician),* State Press, 1923.

    Istoriya Moego Sovremennika (The History of My Contemporary), five volumes, Berlin, 1922; cf. Gorky *Vospominaniya.*

    (2) *The Blind Musician,* tr. S. Stepniak & W. Westall. Ward & Downey, London, 1890; J. W. Luce, N.Y., 1915; *The Saghalien Convict. Easter Eve.* The Pseudonym Library, T. Fisher Unwin, 1892; *The Murmuring Forest and other stories,* tr. Marion Fell. Duckworth, London; Duffield, N.Y.; 1916. Wiener: cf. Williams, Kropotkin, Olgin, Persky.

    (3) *Der Gerichtstag* (Yom Kippur), Leipsic, 1903; *Die Geschichte meines Zeitgenossen* (tr. by Rosa Luxemburg), Berlin, 1919.

Stepniak: (2) *The Career of a Nihilist.* A novel. W. Scott, London, 1890; Harper, N.Y., 1907. *Underground Russia,* translated from the Italian. Smith Elder & Co., London, 1883.

    (3) *La Russia Sotterranea.* Milan, 1882.

Kropotkin: (2) *Memoirs of a Revolutionist.* Smith, Elder & Co., London; Houghton, N.Y.; 1899; and Swan Sonnenschein & Co., London, 1906.

Bashkirtseva: (2) *The Journal of Marie Bashkirtsef,* tr. Mathilde Blind. Cassell & Co., London, 1890; do., tr. A. D. Hall, Rand, N.Y., 1908; *Journal of a Young Artist,* tr. Mary J. Serrano, Dut-

ton, N.Y., 1919; *The Further Memoirs of
M. B., together with a correspondence be-
tween M. B. and Guy de Maupassant.*
Grant Richards, London, 1901; *Letters,* tr.
Mary J. Serrano. Cassell & Co., London,
1891 (printed in U.S.A.).

New Journal, tr. Mary J. Safford, N.Y.,
1912.

Andreevsky: (1) *Literaturniya Chteniya,* 1891 (4th ed., *Literaturnye Ocherki,* P., 1913).

Kniga o Smerti. Reval: Bibliophil, 1921.

Nadson: (1) Poetical works, one volume, numerous editions.

(2) Wiener; Oxford Book; cf. *Poetry and Progress in
Russia,* by Rosa Newmarch. John Lane, London, N.Y., 1917 (p. 246 and foll.).

(3) *Gedichte,* tr. Fr. Fiedler. Leipsic: Reclam, 1898.

Apukhtin: (1) Works, one volume, numerous editions.

(2) *From Death to Life* (a spiritualist tale in prose),
tr. R. Frank and E. Huybers (Gems of Rus-
sian literature, 1), R. Frank, N.Y., 1917; *Oxford Book.*

Minsky: (2) Yarmolinsky; Selver; *Oxford Book.*

Lokhvitskaya: (2) Selver.

Soloviev: (1) Works, ten volumes, P., 1911–1914.

Poetical Works: *Stikhotvoreniya* (preceded by a
very valuable Life, by S. M. Soloviev).

Letters: *Pis'ma,* three volumes, P. 1908 and foll.;
additional volume, P., 1923. Nonsense plays:
Shutochnye Piesy, M., 1922. Soloviev's nonsense
verse has not yet been collected; some of it is included in *Pis'ma.*

(2) *The Justification of the Good,* tr. Natalie A.
Duddington. Constable's Russian Library, London, 1918; *War, Progress, and the End of History,
including a short history of Anti-Christ,* tr. A.
Bakshy. University Press, London, 1915; Yarmolinsky; Selver.

Cf. *Vladimir Soloviev: a Russian Newman,* by *M.*
D'Herbigny, tr. A. M. Buchanan. R. & T.
Washbourne, London, 1918.

The Philosophy of Vl. Soloviev, tr. A. Bakshy.
University Press, Aberdeen, 1916.
Cf. Masaryk; Williams; *Slavonic Review.*

(3) *La Russie et l'Eglise Universelle.* Paris, 1889.
(3rd ed., 1922); *Ausgewählte Werke,* Jena and
Stuttgart, 1914 and foll.

Chekhov: (1) Complete Works, 33 volumes, Commissariat for
Education, M., 1918–1919; 14 volumes, Slowo
Verlag, Berlin; separate works, Ladyschnikow,
Berlin.

Letters, six volumes (to each volume is prefaced
an outline of his life, within the period in hand,
by his brother, M. P. Chekhov), M., 1912–1914.
Letters of his wife (*Pis'ma k. O. L. Knipper*).
Slowo Verlag, Berlin, 1923.

(2) *The Tales of Tchehov,* 13 volumes, tr. Constance
Garnett. Chatto & Windus, London; Macmillan,
N.Y.; 1916–1922.

The Plays of Tchehov, two volumes, tr. Constance
Garnett. Chatto & Windus, London; Macmillan,
N.Y.; 1923–1924.

*The Note-books of A. Tchekhov. Together with
Reminiscences of Tch. by Gorky,* tr. S. S.
Koteliansky and Leonard Woolf. Hogarth
Press; Huebsch, N.Y.; 1921; *Letters of A.
Tchehov to His Family and Friends,* tr. Con-
stance Garnett. Chatto & Windus, London;
Macmillan, N.Y.; 1920.

The Life and Letters of A. Tchekhov, by S. S.
Koteliansky and Philip Tomlinson. Cassell, London, 1925.

Cf. *Anton Chehov: A Critical Study,* by William
Gerhardi. Richard Cobden-Sanderson, London,
1923.

INTERCHAPTER I

The relations between literature and revolution are one of the
principal subjects of most Russian histories of literature. On Russian Marxism, cf. especially Masaryk.

CHAPTER III

There is no special work on the subject of this chapter, but the writers discussed in it are, as a rule, the principal heroes of every general history of this period.

The principal publications to which they contributed were those of the publishing-houses: "Znanie" (Gorky, the writers mentioned in III, 3, Bunin till 1910, Andreev and Kuprin till 1907; especially the non-periodical miscellany *Sborniki "Znaniya,"* 1904, and foll.); "Shipovnik" ("Wild Rose"; Andreev, Kuprin, etc., also Sologub, Remizov, and others; non-periodical miscellany *Shipovnik,* 1907 and foll.); and "Knigoizdatel'stvo Pisateley" ("The Authors' Publishing-House," non-periodical miscellany *Zemlya* [The Earth], 1909 and foll.).

Gorky: (1) Works, sixteen volumes, State Press, 1924; separate editions of most of his works (up to 1922) for the foreign market were published by Ladyschnikow, in Berlin; *Moi Universitety (My Universities).* Kniga, Berlin, 1923; *Zametki iz Dnevnika (Notes from a Diary),* do., 1924; *Vospominaniya (Recollections,* including those of Tolstoy, Chekhov, Andreev, etc.), do., 1924.

(2) Early Works (1892–1899).

(a) *The Orloff Couple, and Malva,* tr. Emily Jakowleff and Dora B. Montefiore. Heinemann, London, 1901; *Twenty-six Men and a Girl (Tchelkash. My Fellow Traveller. On a Raft).* Duckworth, London; Stokes, N.Y.; 1902; tr. R. Nisbet Bain: *Tales from Gorky,* Funk, 1902; *Chelkash and other stories,* Knopf, 1917; tr. J. K. M. Shirazi: *Creatures That Once Were Men* (with a brilliant but very uninformed introduction by G. K. Chesterton), Alston Rivers, London; Boni & Liveright, N.Y.; 1905; tr. A. S. Rappoport: *The Individualists, and A Strange Companion* (i.e., *My Fellow Traveller*), Maclaren, London, 1906; *Heartache, and The Old Woman Izergil,* do.; *A Naughty Girl (Varenka Olesova),* do.; tr. H. T. Schnittkind and Isaac Goldberg:

Stories of the Steppe (*Makar Chudra, Because of Monotony*), Stratford Co., 1918; tr. anon: *Orloff and His Wife, Tales of the Barefoot Brigade,* Scribner, 1901; *The Outcasts* (*Byvshie Lyudi*), and other stories, T. Fisher Unwin, London, 1902; *Chelkash and other stories,* Hodder & Stoughton, London, 1916; *Tales* (*Twenty-six and One, Tchelkach, Malva*), Brentano's, 1923; *Twenty-six Men and a Girl* (Ten-cent pocket ed.), Haldeman-Julius Co., Girard, Kansas, 1922.

(b) Novels, etc., 1899–1912: *Foma Gordyeef,* tr. Isabel F. Hapgood; T. Fisher Unwin, London; Scribner, N.Y.; 1901; *Foma Gordeyev,* tr. H. Bernstein; Ogilvie, 1912; *Three of Them,* T. Fisher Unwin, London, 1902; Knopf, N.Y., 1922; *The Spy,* Duckworth, London, 1908; do., tr. T. Seltzer; Huebsch, 1908; *Mother,* Appleton, N.Y., 1921; *A Confession,* tr. from the German by W. F. Harvey; Everett, London, 1910; do., tr. Rose Strunsky; Stokes, 1916; *Tales of Two Countries* (America and Italy), Werner Laurie, London; Huebsch, N.Y.; 1914; *Through Russia: A Book of Stories,* tr. C. J. Hogarth; Dent, London; Dutton, N.Y.; 1922.

(c) Later Works, 1913–1924: *My Childhood;* and *In the World* (*V Lyudyakh*) tr. Mrs. Gertrude M. Foakes, Werner Laurie, London; Century, N.Y.; 1915 and 1917; *Reminiscences of Tolstoy,* tr. S. S. Koteliansky and L. Woolf, Hogarth Press, London; Huebsch, N.Y.; 1920; *Fragments from My Diary,* P. Allen & Co., London, N.Y., 1924; *Reminiscences of My Youth* (*My Universities*), tr. Veronica Dewey, Heinemann, London, 1924; *My University Days* (the same), Boni & Liveright, N.Y., 1924; *Fragments from My Diary,* tr. Marie Budberg, McBride, N.Y., 1924; *Reminiscences of L. Andreyev,* in the *Dial,* July and August, 1924.

(d) Plays: Poet Lore Plays (R. G. Badger, Boston) include: *Night's Lodging,* 1910; *Children of the Sun,* 1910; *Smug Citizen,* 1912; *Summer Folk,* 1912—*The Lower Depths,* tr. Lawrence Ivvry, T. Fisher Unwin, London; Duffield, N.Y., 1910; *Submerged* (same play), tr. Edwin Hopkins, Four Seas Co., Boston, 1915; *The Lower Depths,* tr. Jennie Coran (Moscow Art Theatre Series), Brentano's, 1922.

(e) Poems, in *Hours Spent in Prison,* by Gorky, etc. tr. M. Galinska; Simpkin, Marshall & Co., London, 1909. Cf. *Maxim Gorky: His Life and Writings,* by E. J. von Dillon; Isbister & Co., London, 1902; Williams; Kropotkin; Olgin; Wiener; Phelps; Persky.

(3) Numerous German translations of separate works; *Gesammte Werke,* I Serie, eight vols., Berlin, 1923; *Ein Jahr Russischer Revolution* (political articles), Munich, 1918.

L'Annonciateur de la Tempête (with a critical and biographical Introduction by E. Séménoff), Paris. *Hôtes d'Eté,* Paris, 1905; *Ecrits de Révolution,* Paris, 1922.

Cf. *Maxime Gorky. L'Œuvre et l'homme,* by Vicomte Melchior de Vogüé, Paris, 1905.

Chirikov: (2) Cf. Olgin; Persky.

(3) German translations of several of his works.

Veresaev: (2) *The Confessions of a Physician,* tr. S. Linden. Grant Richards, London, 1904; cf. Olgin; Persky.

(3) German translations.

Skitalets: (2) *Publican and Serf,* tr. J. K. M. Shirazi. Alston Rivers, London, 1905; *The Czar's Charter,* tr. P. L.; Hendersons, London, 1907.

Gusev-Orenburgski: (2) *The Land of the Fathers,* tr. Nina N. Selivanova. Cape, London, 1925; cf. Olgin.

Yushkevich:

(2) Cf. Olgin; Persky.

(3) *Ghetto (The Jews),* Vienna, 1905; and other German translations.

Muyzhel: (2) Cf. Olgin.

Kuprin: (1) Works, Moskovskoe Knigoizd, M., 1916 and foll.; Berlin, 1921 and foll.

(2) *Olessia, a Novel* (an early work), tr. Major A. E. Harrison, Sisley's, London, 1909; *The Duel,* Allen & Unwin, London; Macmillan, N.Y., 1916; *Shulamite,* J. W. Luce, N.Y., 1915; *The River of Life, and other stories,* tr. S. S. Koteliansky and J. M. Murray, The Modern Russian Library, London, J. W. Luce; N.Y., 1916; *A Slav Soul, and other stories* (including *Captain Rybnikov*), Constable, London; Putnam, N.Y.; 1916; *The Bracelet of Garnets, and other stories,* tr. Leo Pasvolsky, Duckworth, London; Scribner, N.Y.; 1919; *Sasha* (and other stories), tr. Douglas Ashby, Stanley Paul, London, 1920.

Cf. Olgin; Phelps; Persky.

(3) *La Fosse aux Filles* (Yama), Bossard: Paris, 1923.

Bunin: (1) Pre-Revolutionary editions: Poems, three volumes; *Pereval* (stories, 1892–1902); *Zolotoe Dno* (stories 1903–1907); *Razskazy* (stories and poems, 1907–1910); *Derevnya (The Village)*; *Sukhodol* (stories, 1911–1912); *Ioann Rydalets* (stories and poems, 1912–1913); *Chasha Zhizni (The Cup of Life,* and stories and poems, 1913–1914); *Gospodin iz San Frantsisko* (stories and poems, 1915–1916).

Post-Revolutionary editions: *Derevnya* (including *Sukhodol*). Povolozky, Paris, 1920; *Gospodin iz San Frantsisko* (a reprint), do., 1920; *Krik* (stories from the *Sukhodol* and *Ioann Rydalets* volumes, Berlin, 1921; *Roza Ierikhona* (stories and poems), Slowo Verlag, Berlin, 1924.

(2) *The Village,* tr. Isabel Hapgood. Secker, London; Knopf, N.Y.; 1923; *The Dreams of Chang, and other stories* (including *The Gentleman from San Francisco*), tr. B. G. Guerny, Secker, London; Knopf, N.Y.; 1923; *The Gentleman from San Francisco, and other stories,* tr. D. H. Lawrence, S. S. Koteliansky, and L. Woolf, Hogarth Press, London; Seltzer, N.Y.; 1922; poems in Selver and in Yarmolinsky.

Cf. Olgin.

(3) *Le Calice de la Vie* (including *Au Pays des Morts* i. e. *Sukhodol*), Paris, 1923; *Erzählungen* (early stories), Munich, 1903.

Andreev: (1) Works, Prosveshchenie, P., 1911 and foll.; separate editions of most of works by Ladyschnikow, Berlin.

Life: *Kniga o Leonide Andreeve* (reminiscences by Gorky, Blok, Chukovsky, and others), Grschebin, Berlin, 1922; *Molodye Gody Leonida Andreeva* (Early Years of L. A.), by N. N. Fatov, M., 1924; recollections, by his brother, P. N. Andreev, in *Literaturnaya Mysl*, III, Mysl, P., 1925; letters to his mother, in *Russky Sovremennik*, No. 4, 1924.

(2) (a) *The Little Angel, and other Stories,* Hodder & Stoughton, London; Knopf, N.Y.; 1915; *The Crushed Flower, and other Stories,* Duckworth, London, 1917; do., tr. H. Bernstein, Knopf, 1916; *Silence, and other Stories,* tr. W. H. Lowe, Francis Griffiths, London, 1910; *Silence,* tr. John Cournos, Brown Brothers, N.Y., 1908; *An Abyss,* in *Hours Spent in Prison,* tr. M. Galinska, Simpkin Marshall & Co., London, 1909; *The Red Laugh,* tr. Alexandra Linden, T. Fisher Unwin, London, 1905; Duffield, N.Y., 1915; *Red Laugh* (ten-cent pocket series), Haldeman-Julius Co., Girard, Kansas, 1922; *And It Came to Pass that the King Was Dead,* tr. M. Magnus, C. W. Daniel, London, 1921; *When the King Loses His Head, and other stories,* tr. A. J. Wolfe, International Book, N.Y., 1919; *His Excellency the Governor,* tr. M. Magnus, C. W. Daniel, London, 1921; *Judas Iscariot, forming with "Eleazar"* (*Lazarus*) *and "Ben Tobit" a biblical trilogy,* tr. W. H. Lowe, F. Griffiths, London, 1910; *Lazarus,* etc., tr. A. Yarmolinsky, Stratford Co., 1917; *The Dark,* tr. L. Magnus and K. Walter, Hogarth Press, 1922; *The Seven That Were Hanged,* tr. H. Bernstein, Ogilvie, N.Y., 1909;

do., tr. Th. Seltzer, Boni & Liveright, 1918; do.
(ten-cent pocket series), Haldeman-Julius Co.,
N.Y., 1922.

(b) Plays: *To the Stars,* tr. M. Magnus, Plays
for a People's Theatre: London, C. H. Daniels:
N. Y., 1921; do., Poet Lore Plays, R. G. Badger,
1912; *Savva, and The Life of Man,* tr. Th. Selt-
zer, Boni, 1914; *The Life of Man, tr. C. J.*
Hogarth, Allen & Unwin, London; Macmillan,
N.Y.; 1915; *Plays (The Black Maskers, The
Life of Man, The Sabine Women),* tr. Clarence
L. Meader and F. N. Scott, Duckworth, London;
Scribner, N.Y.; 1915; *King Hunger,* Poet Lore
Plays, R. G. Badger, 1912; *Anathema,* tr. H.
Bernstein, Macmillan, N.Y., 1910; *Katerina,* tr.
H. Bernstein, Brentano's, N.Y., 1924; *The Waltz
of the Dogs,* tr. H. Bernstein, Macmillan, N.Y.,
1922; *Love One's Neighbour,* tr. Th. Seltzer,
Shay, 1917; *The Dear Departing* (same play),
tr. J. West, Heinemann, London, 1916; *He Who
Gets Slapped,* tr. G. Zilboorg, Brentano's, N.Y.,
1924.

(c) Late Works (War and Revolution): *The
Sorrows of Belgium, a play in six scenes,* tr. H.
Bernstein, Macmillan, N.Y., 1915; *The Confes-
sions of a Little Man during Great Days,* tr. R.
S. Townsend, Duckworth, London; Knopf, N.Y.;
1907; *Satan's Diary,* tr. H. Bernstein, Boni &
Liveright, 1920; *Russia's Call to Humanity:
Save Our Souls. An Appeal to the Allies,* Rus-
sian Liberation Committee, London, 1920.

Cf. *Leonid Andreyev: A Critical Study,* by
Alexander Kaun. Huebsch, N.Y., 1924; Williams; Olgin; Phelps; Persky.

(3) Numerous German translations of all his works.

Artsybashev: (1) Works, Moskovskoe Knigoizd, M., and foll.

(2) *The Millionaire (Ivan Lande. Nina),* tr. Percy
Pinkerton, with an introduction by the author;
Secker, London; Huebsch, N.Y.; 1915; *Tales
of the Revolution,* tr. Percy Pinkerton, Secker,

London; Huebsch, N.Y.; 1917; *Sanine,* tr. Percy Pinkerton, Secker, London; Huebsch, N.Y.; 1915; *Breaking-Point,* Secker, London; Huebsch, N.Y.; 1915; *War, a play in four acts,* tr. Thomas Seltzer, Knopf, N.Y., 1916 (Borzoi Plays); do., tr. Percy Pinkerton and Ivan Ohzol, Grant Richards, London, 1918. Cf. Olgin; Phelps; Persky.

(3) *Eifersucht. Drama.* Munich, 1914.

Sergeyev-Tsensky: (1) Works, Knigoizdatelstvo Pisateley, M.

Preobrazhenie (Transfiguration), part I, Crimean State Press, Simferopol, 1923.

(2) Cf. Olgin; Persky.

(3) *Babajew,* Berlin, 1910.

Dymov: (2) *The Flight from the Cross,* tr. G. M. Foakes. T. Werner Laurie, London, 1916.

Nju, an everyday tragedy, tr. Rosalind Ivan (Borzoi Plays), Knopf, 1917.

Cf. Persky.

Grebenshchikov: (3) *Les Tchouraïev,* Roman. Paris, 1922.

Shmelev: (2) *That Which Happened,* tr. C. J. Hogarth, Dent, London, 1924.

(3) *Garçon!* Bossard, Paris, 1925.

Savinkov (Ropshin): (2) *The Pale Horse,* tr. Z. Vengerova. Modern Russian Library, 1917.

What Never Happened, tr. Th. Selzer. G. Allen & Unwin, London, 1919; Knopf, N.Y., 1917; *The Black Horse,* Williams and Norgate, London, 1924.

Cf. Olgin.

Zaytsev: (2) Cf. Olgin; Persky.

(3) *Novellen,* Berlin, 1923.

Doroshevich: (2) *The Way of the Cross,* with an introduction by Stephen Graham. Constable, London, 1916.

Averchenko: (3) *Grotesken,* Munich, 1914; *Das Verbrechen der Schauspielerin Maryskin, und andere Grotesken,* Munich, 1919.

CHAPTER IV

The principal publications connected with the "religious philosophers" were *Mir Iskusstva* (see ch. IV), 1899–1904; *Novyy Put'* (*The New Way*), P., 1903–1904;*Voprosy Zhizni* (*Problems of Life*), P., 1905; after 1909, *Russkaya Mysl.*

Benois: (1) His principal work is *Istoriya Zhivopisi* (*History of Painting*), incomplete, 1911–1917; his art criticisms have not been collected in book form.

(2) *The Russian School of Painting,* tr. A. Yarmolinsky, Knopf, N.Y., 1916; T. Werner Laurie, London, 1919.

Merezhkovsky: (1) Works, Wolff, P., 1912–1913 (seventeen volumes); *Chetyrnadtsatoe Dekabrya* (December 14th), Pavolozky, Paris, 1921.

(2) (a) Novels: *The Death of the Gods* (*Julian*), tr. Herbert Trench, Constable, London; Putnam, N.Y.; 1901; *The Forerunner* (*Leonardo da Vinci*), tr. Herbert Trench, Constable, London, 1924; Putnam, N.Y., 1917; *Peter and Alexis,* Constable, London; Putnam, N.Y.; 1905; *December the Fourteenth,* tr. Natalie Duddington, Cape, London, 1923.

(b) Miscellaneous prose: *The Life Work of Calderon* (*Ibsen, Montaigne, Pliny the Younger, Flaubert, Marcus Aurelius, The Acropolis, Dostoevsky*), tr. G. A. Mounsey, 8 parts; Alexander Moring, 1908–1912; *Tolstoi as Man and Artist. With an Essay on Dostoevsky* (abridged translation of *Tolstoy and Dostoevsky*), Constable, London; Putnam, N.Y.; 1902; *The Menace of the Mob,* tr. B. J. Gurney, N. L. Brown, N.Y., 1921.

(c) Poems: Selver; Yarmolinsky.

Cf. Williams; Wiener; Olgin; Persky.

(3) *La Naissance des Dieux,* Bossard, Paris, 1924. *Le Mufle Roi.—L'Avènement de*

Cham, Paris, 1916; *Le règne de l'Antéchrist* (together with *Mon Journal sous la
terreur,* by Z. Hippius), Paris, 1921; *Ewige
Gefährten, Munich,* 1922; *Michel Angelo,
und andere Novellen,* Leipzig, 1907; *Kaiser
Pauls Tod, Tragödie,* Berlin, 1910; *Alexander I, Roman,* Munich, 1913.

Rozanov: (1) Principal Works: *Legenda o velikon inkvizitore,*
with important appendixes, mainly on Gogol,
4th ed., P., 1906; the same, but without the appendixes, Berlin, 1922; *V mire neyasnago i
nereshennago (Among Riddles and Mysteries),* 2
vol., P., 1901; *Semeynyy Vopros v Rossii (The
Family Problem in Russia),* 2 vol., P., 1903;
*Okolo tserkovnykh sten (In the Shade of the
Church's Walls),* P., 1906; *Russkaya Tserkov'
(The Russian Church),* P., 1906; *Kogda Nachal-
'stvo Ushlo (When the Authorities Were Away),*
P., 1909; *Temnyy Lik (The Dark Face),* 1911;
Lyudi Lunnago Sveta (Moonlight Men), P.,
1913; *Literaturnye Izgnanniki* (Letters of Strakhov, annotating Rozanov), P., 1913; *Uedinnenoe,*
2nd ed., P., 1916; *Opavshie List'ya (Fallen
Leaves),* P., 1913; the same, *Korob vtoroy (Second Basketful),* P., 1915; *Iz Vostochnykh Moti-
vov (Oriental Motives),* 5 *issues,* 1915–1917;
Apokalipsis Russkoy Revolyutsii, Sergiev-Posad,
1918–1919.

Cf. *V. V. Rozanov,* by E. Gollerbakh, P., 1922;
Pis'ma Rozanova (Letters to Gollerbakh), Berlin, 1922; *Kukkha* (Rozanov's letters, and recollections of him), by A. Remizov, Berlin,
1924; for Rozanov's first wife and her relations with Dostoevsky, see article by L. Gros-
man in *Russky Sovremennik,* No. 3, 1924.

(2) *Ontology, or the Metaphysics of Pure Being,* by
Fedor Shperk, tr. G. L. Calderon, with a preface by W. Rosanow. Hudson & Co., London,
1897.

Shestov: (1) *Shekspir i ego Kritik Brandes,* P., 1898; *Dobro v
uchenii Tolstogo i Nitsshe,* new ed., Berlin, 1922;

Dostoevskiy i Nittsshe, new ed., Berlin, 1922;
*Apofeoz Bezpochvennosti (Apotheosis of Ground-
lessness),* P., 1905; *Velikie Kanuny (Great Eves),*
P., 1910; *Nachala i Kontsy (Beginnings and
Ends),* P., 1908; *Potestas Clavium,* Berlin, 1923.

(2) *All Things Are Possible* (an arbitrary title for the
book entitled *Aɩpotheosis of Groundlessness*), tr.
S. S. Koteliansky. Secker, London; McBride,
N.Y.; 1921; *Anton Tchekhov and other essays,*
tr. S. S. Koteliansky and J. M. Murray, Modern
Russian Library, London, 1916; the same, as
Penultimate Words, J. W. Luce, N.Y., 1917.   (All
these translations are highly unsatisfactory.)

(3) *Les Révelations de la Mort.   Dostoïevsky—Tolstoï*
(with a preface by Boris de Schloezer), Plon-
Nouvrit, Paris, 1923; *La Nuit de Gethsémani*
(Pascal), "Les Cahiers Verts," Grasset, Paris,
1924; *Tolstoj und Nietzsche,* Marcon Verlag,
Cologne, 1924; *Dostojewsky und Nietzsche,* do.,
1924.

Cf. preface by Boris de Schloezer to *Les Révéla-
tions de la Mort,* an admirable introduction to the
personality and philosophy of Shestov.

E. Troubetzkoy: (2) *Saint Sophia, Russia's Hope and Calling:
A lecture,* tr. Lucy Alexeiev, Faith Press,
London, 1916.

Cf. *The Successors of Soloviev* (Troubetzkoy, Bulgakov & Florensky), by N.
O. Lossky, in *Slavonic Review,* No. 7,
1924.

Bulgakov: (2) *At the Feast of the Gods, a dialogue,* in *Slavonic
Review,* Nos. 1, 2, 3, 1922–1923; articles in
Russian and *Slavonic Review;* cf. *The Succes-
sors of Soloviev* (see under Troubetzkoy).

Berdyaev: (1) *Smysl Tvorchestva (The Meaning of Creativeness),* P., 1915.

Florensky: (1) *Stolp i Utverzhdenie Istiny (The Pillar and
Foundation of Truth),* M., 1914.

(2) Cf. *The Successors of Soloviev* (see under Troubetzkoy).

Gershenzon: (1) See Vyacheslav Ivanov.

352 CONTEMPORARY RUSSIAN LITERATURE

Landmarks: (1) *Vekhi,* 1st ed., M., 1909.
Boldyrev: (1) Articles in *Russkaya Svoboda,* 1917.

CHAPTER V

There is no work on the Symbolist movement as a whole. *Noveyshaya Russkaya Poezia* (*Modern Russian Poetry*), by E. Anichkov, is of little value. *Recollections of Blok,* by Bely, is important (see Bely). The memoirs of Zinaida Hippius on Bryusov, Sologub, etc., have not yet appeared in book form. The anthologies (quoted under General Works) of Selver, Yarmolinsky, and Chuzeville are largely devoted to the Symbolists. Valuable remarks on the Symbolist style will be found in the books of Prof. Zhirmunsky and of B. Eichenbaum, quoted under Bryusov, Blok, and Akhmatova (Ch. VI).

The principal publications connected with the Symbolists were: *Mir Iskusstva,* P., 1899–1904 (see ch. IV, 2); *Severnye Tsvety* (*Northern Flowers;* once a year), M., 1901, 1902, 1903, 1905, and 1911; *Vesy* (*The Scales*), M., 1904–1909; *Zolotoe Runo* (*The Golden Fleece*), M., 1906–1909; *Apollon,* P., 1909–1917. After 1910 most of the Symbolists contributed to Struve's *Russkaya Mysl,* where Bryusov was the literary editor. Of Post-Revolutionary publications, *Zapiski Mechtateley* (*The Dreamers' Journal;* non-periodical; six parts, 1919–1922), conducted by Bely, had a definitely Symbolist character.

Balmont: (1) All his best poetry is contained in the first four volumes of his Collected poems (*Sobranie Stikhov*), M., 1908 and foll.

(2) Selver; Yarmolinsky; cf. Williams; Olgin.

(3) *Visions Solaires* (selections), tr. Ludmila Savitsky, P., 1923; *Balmont und Briusow. Gedichte,* tr. Wolfgang Groeger, Berlin, 1921.

Bryusov: (1) The poetry of his best period is contained in *Puti i Pereput'ya* (*Ways and Crossways*), 3 volumes, M., 1908–1909; *Ognennyy Angel* (*The Fire Angel*), 1st ed., 2 vol., M., 1908; cf. *Valeriy Bryusov i Nasledie Pushkina* (V. B. and the tradition of Pushkin), by V. Zhirmunsky, P., 1921.

(2) *The Republic of the Southern Cross, and other stories,* Constable, London, 1918; McBride, N.Y., 1920; Selver; Yarmolinsky; cf. Williams; Olgin.

(3) See Balmont; *Erduntergang, Tragödie,* tr. J. V. Guenther, Munich, 1909; *Der Feurige Engel,* Munich, 1910; *Der Siegesaltar,* Munich, 1913.

Hippius: (1) Poems: *Sobranie Stikhov,* M., 1904; 2nd book, M., 1910; *Stikhi 1911–1921* Slowo Verlag, Berlin, 1922.

Criticisms: *Literaturnyy Dnevnik (Literary Diary),* by Anton Krayni, P., 1908.

(2) *The Green Ring, a Play,* tr. S. S. Koteliansky, C. W. Daniel, London; C. H. Daniels, N.Y.; 1920; Poems: Selver, Yarmolinsky.

(3) *Le Pantin du diable,* Paris, 1924; *Des Teufels Puppe,* Munich, 1912; *Mon journal sous la Terreur;* see Merezhkovsky, *Le Règne de l'Antéchrist.*

Sologub: (1) Works, P., 1913 and foll.

(2) *The Little Demon,* tr. J. Cournos and R. Aldington, Secker, London; Knopf, N.Y.; 1916; *The Created Legend* (first part only), tr. J. Cournos, Secker, London; Stokes, N.Y.; 1916; *The Old House, and other tales,* tr. J. Cournos, Secker, London; Knopf, N.Y.; 1915; *The Sweet-scented Name, and other fairy-tales, fables, and stories,* Constable, London; Putnam, N.Y.; 1915; *Little Tales (Skazki),* tr. J. Cournos, Russian translations, London, 1917 (limited edition); poems: Selver; Yarmolinsky; cf. Williams; Persky; Olgin.

(3) *Das Buch der Märchen,* Munich, 1908; *Kleine Politische Fabeln und Märchen,* Munich, 1921; *Schatten* (early stories), Berlin, 1912; *Süsser als Gift, Roman,* Munich, 1922.

Annensky: (1) *Tikhiya Pesni (Quiet Songs),* 2nd ed., Academia, P., 1923; *Kiparisovyy Lavets (The Cypress Chest),* 2nd ed., P., 1923; *Posmertnye Stikhi,* P., 1923.

Vyacheslav Ivanov: (1) *Kormchiya Zvezdy (Pilot Stars),* P., 1903; *Prozrachnost' (Transparency),* M., 1904; *Cor Ardens,* two volumes, M., 1911; *Perepiska iz dvukh uglov (Correspondence between Two Corners,* with Gershenzon), Berlin, 1922;

Zimnie Sonety (*Winter Sonnets*) in
Erenburg: *Poezia Revolyutsionnoy
Moskvy,* Mysl, Berlin, 1922.

(2) Yarmolinsky: cf. Williams; Olgin.

(3) *Die Wintersonette,* in *Vivos Voco,* März–
April, 1923.

Chulkov: (2) Yarmolinsky.

Voloshin: (1) *Demony Glukhonemye* (*Demons Deaf and Dumb*),
Berlin, 1923.

(2) Yarmolinsky.

Blok: (1) Works, 10 volumes, Epocha Verlag, Berlin, 1922–1924.
Life: *A. A. Blok,* by (his aunt) M. A. Beketova, P.,
1922; recollections, by A. Bely (see Bely); cf.
Poeziya A. Bloka, by V. Zhirmunsky, P., 1922 (important for a general view of Russian Symbolism).

(2) *The Twelve,* tr. C. E. Bechhofer (with illustrations by
M. Larionov), Chatto & Windus, London, 1920;
Twelve, tr. Babette Deutsch and A. Yarmolinsky,
Huebsch, N.Y.; 1920; Selver; Yarmolinsky; cf.
Williams (portrait).

(3) *Die Zwölf,* tr. Wolfgang Groeger (a masterpiece), Ber-
lin, 1921; and three other German translations;
Gedichte, tr. W. Groeger, Berlin, 1920; *Rose und
Kreuz,* tr. W. Groeger, Berlin, 1923; *Les Douze,* tr.
A. Sidersky, Paris, 1923.

Bely: (1) (a) Poems: *Stikhotvoreniya* (a "selected-collected"
ed.), Grschebin, Berlin, 1922; *Pervoe Svidanie*
(*First Meeting*), Berlin, 1922.

(b) Prose: *Serebryanyy Golub'* (*Silver Dove*) 2 vol.,
Epocha, Berlin, 1922.

Peterburg, 2 vol., do., *Kotik Letaev,* P., 1922.

Prestuplenie Nikolaya Letaeva (*The Crime of N. L.*),
in *Sovremennyya Zapiski* (see Interch. II bibliography), Nos. 11 and 12 (1923).

Recollections of Blok, in *Epopeya,* Nos. 1–4, Berlin,
1922–1923.

(2) Yarmolinsky: cf. Olgin.

(3) *Die Silberne Taube,* Frankfurt a. M., 1912; *Petersburg,* Munich, 1919; *Auf der Wasserscheide* (critical
and philosophical essays), Stuttgart, 1922.

Baltrushaitis: (2) Yarmolinsky.

Gorodetsky: (2) Yarmolinsky.

V. Hoffmann: (2) Yarmolinsky.

Kuzmin: (1) *Seti* (including *Songs of Alexandria*), 3rd ed.,
  "Petropolis," Berlin, 1923; *Kuranty Lyubvi* (*Seasons of Love*), words and music, M., 1910.

    (2) Yarmolinsky.

    (3) *Alexandrinische Gesänge,* tr. J. v. Guenther, Munich,
  1919; do., tr. A. Eliasberg, Munich, 1921; several
  German translations of novels and stories.

Khodasevich: (1) *Putem Zerna* (*The Grain's Way*), 2nd ed., P.,
  1921; *Tyazhelaya Lira* (*The Heavy Lyre*),
  Grschebin, Berlin, 1923.

INTERCHAPTER

Sofia Fedorchenko: *Narod na Voyne* (*The People at the Front*),
  2nd ed., M., 1923.

For Shulgin, Shklovsky, and Erenburg, see Ch. VII, 5 and 6.

Lenin: Lef No. 1 (1924) contains interesting articles by
  Shklovsky, Eichenbaum, Tynyanov, Tomashevsky, etc.,
  on "the style of Lenin."

Trotsky: Literatura i Revolyutsia, 2nd ed., State Press, 1924.

    The principal literary periodicals of the *émigrés* are: *Sovremennyya Zapiski* (*Les Annales Contemporaines*), Paris, about six times a year, Right S.R., from the literary point of view the best; *Russkaya Mysl* (*Russian Thought*), Prague, nominally monthly, but in reality non-periodical. Ed. by Peter Struve; nationalist; literary part poor; *Volya Rossii* (*Russia's Will*), Prague, fortnightly, S.R.; *Zveno* (*le Chaînon*), Paris, weekly; Left Liberal (Milyukov's group).

Gregory Landau: (1) *Zakat Evropy* (*The Sunset of Europe*),
  Berlin, 1923.

Eurasians: (1) *Evropa i Chelovechestvo* (*Europe and Mankind*),
  by Prince N. Troubetzkoy, Sofia, 1920; *Iskhod
  k Vostoku* (*The Exodus towards the East*), by
  Troubetzkoy, Suvchinsky & Savitsky, Sofia,
  1921; *Na Putyakh,* by the same, Berlin, 1923;
  etc.

    (2) *Iskhod k Vostoku,* reviewed in the *Times Literary
  Supplement,* May, 1922.

    Russian Post-Revolutionary Nationalism, by the

present author, in the *Contemporary Review,*
August, 1923.

Literary conditions in Soviet Russia:

K voprosu o Politike RKP v khudozhestivennoy literature
(Stenogram of conference on the "literary policy" of the
Communist Party, May, 1924), *Krasnaya* Nov', M., 1924.

*Pisateli ob Iskusstve i o sebe (Authors on Art and on Them-
selves),* articles by Pilniak, Seyfullina, Ognev, A. N. Tolstoy,
Zamyatin, etc., M., 1924.

Letopis' Doma Literatorov (a periodical published by the independent men of letters of Petersburg), eight numbers,
1920–1921; suppressed in 1921, continued as *Literaturnye
Zapiski* (three numbers), finally suppressed early in 1922.

At present the best periodicals are: *Krasnaya Nov' (Red Fal-
low),* ed. Voronsky, since 1922; State Press, Moscow; much of
the best fiction appears in it; critical section strictly Marxist, of
the "Liberal" wing; *Pechat' i Revolyutsiya (Press and Revolution),* State Press, Moscow; only critical; good bibliography;
Lef, Moscow Futurists (see Chapter VI, 9); *Russkiy Sovremennik
(Russian Contemporary),* P., 1924; independent, non-political, excellent literary material, and critical reviews.

CHAPTER VI

Two good (though by no means complete) anthologies by Ilya
Erenburg: *Poeziya Revolyutsionnoy Moskvy,* Mysl, Berlin, 1922;
and *Portrety Russkikh Poetov,* Berlin, 1922.

The Futurists publish a magazine, *Lef* (M., since 1923), which
is one of the best literary magazines in Russia.

Gumilev: (1) His best poetry is contained in *Kolchan (The
Quiver),* 2nd ed., "Petropolis," Berlin, 1923;
Koster (The Pyre), Grschebin, Berlin, 1922;
Ognennyy Stolp (The Pillar of Fire), Petrop-
olis, P., 1921.

Akhmatova: (1) A uniform edition has been published jointly by
"Petropolis" and "Alkonost," Berlin, 1923, in
three little volumes: *Chetki* (9th ed.), *Belaya
Staya* (4th ed.), and *Anno Domini* (2nd ed.);
cf. *Anna Akhmatova,* by B. Eichenbaum, P.,
1922.

(2) See in *Adelphi* (Nov., 1923), tr. by Natalie A.

Duddington; also *Slavonic Review;* Yarmolinsky.

Cf. *Times Literary Supplement,* Nov. 20, 1924.

Mandelstam: (1) *Kamen' (The Stone),* 2nd ed., State Press, M., 1924; *Tristia,* "Petropolis," Berlin, 1922.

Igor Severyonin: (2) Yarmolinsky.

Tsvetaeva: (1) *Versty (Versts),* M., 1921.

    Remeslo (My Craft), Berlin, 1923.

    Psikheya (Psyche), Grschebin, Berlin, 1923.

    Tsar'-Devitsa (The King Maiden), Epocha, Berlin, 1922.

Klyuev: (2) Yarmolinsky.

Esenin: (1) *Sobranie Stikhov (Collected Poems),* Grschebin, 1923; *Pugachov,* Berlin, 1922.

    (2) Yarmolinsky.

Marienhof (2) Yarmolinsky.

Khlebnikov: (1) Cf. article by G. Vinokur, *Russky Sovremennik,* 1924, No. 4; recollections by D. Petrovsky, *Lef,* No. 1, 1923.

Mayakovsky: (1) *13 Let Raboty (13 Years' Work),* 2 volumes, M., 1923; *Izbrannyy Mayakovskiy (Selections),* Berlin, 1923.

    (2) *A Bolshevik Satire,* by the present author, in the *Literary Review (New York Evening Post),* May 27, 1922.

Pasternak: (1) *Sestra Moya Zhizn (My Sister Life),* Grschebin, Berlin, 1922.

    Temy i Variatsii (Themes and Variations), Helikon, Berlin, 1923.

CHAPTER VII

An anthology of contemporary Russian prose with portraits and autobiographies; edited by Vladimir Lidin: *Literaturnaya Rossiya,* Part I, M., 1924; Part II has not yet appeared; quoted as Lidin.

Remizov: (1) Works, eight volumes, P., 1910–1912. Principal post-Revolutionary editions: *Krestovyya Sestry (Sisters of the Cross),* Grschebin, Berlin, 1923; *Povest' o I. S. Stratilatove,* Berlin, 1922; *Pyataya Yazva (Fifth Pestilence),* Grschebin, Berlin, 1923; *V pole blakitnom (On a Field Azure),* Ber-

lin, 1922; *Petushok*, Mysl, Berlin, 1922; *Mara*
(stories, 1914–1916), Epocha, Berlin, 1922; *Zga*
(stories of spooks), Prague, 1925; *Shumy Goroda*
(*The Noises of the Town*, stories, legends, prose
lyrics, 1917–1920), Bibliophil, Reval, 1921;
Trava-Murava (legends), Efron, Berlin, 1922;
Skazki Obez'yan'yago Tsarya Asyki (*Tales of
the Monkey King Asyka*), Berlin, 1922; *Skazki
Russkago Naroda* (*Tales of the Russian People*),
Grschebin, Berlin, 1923; *Zvenigorod Oklikannyy*
(*St. Nicholas's Parables*), Alatas, Paris, 1924;
Rossiya v Pis'menakh (*Russia in Letters*), Berlin,
1922; *Kukkha* (Recollections of Rozanov), Ber-
lin, 1924; *Ognennaya Rossiya* (contains *The
Lament for the Ruin of Russia*), Bibliophil,
Reval, 1921.

(2) *The Clock* (and three prose lyrics from Shumy
Goroda), tr. J. Cournos; Chatto & Windus, London, 1924; an edition of *Stratilatov* and *The
Fifth Pestilence* is being prepared by the same
publishers; see also *Slavonic Review*, No. 7, 1924.
Cf. Williams; *Times Literary Supplement*, February 21, 1924.

(3) *Die Schwestern im Kreuz*, Munich, 1913; *Prinzessin
Mymra. Novellen und Träume*, Weimar, 1917;
Legenden und Geschichten, Leipsic, 1919; *Die
Goldene Kette. Weltpassionen. Altrussische
Legenden*. Munich, 1923; *Russische Frauen*,
Munich, 1923; *In Blauem Felde*. S. Fischer
Verlag, Berlin, 1924; *Die Fünfte Plage*. Pro-
pyläen-Verlag, Munich, 1925. *Sur le Champs d'Azur*, Plon-
Nourrit, Paris, 1925; *Pierrot* (Petushok), Ed. de
la Pleïade, Paris, 1925.

A. N. Tolstoy: (1) Works, 10 volumes, M. *Detstvo Nikity*
(*Nikita's Childhood*), State Press, 1923,
and Berlin, 1922; *Aelita*, State Press, 1923,
and Berlin, 1923; *Khozhdenie po Mukam*
(*The Way through Hell*), Berlin, 1922; etc.

(3) *Im Nebel*, Munich, 1919; *Höllenfahrt*,
Munich, 1922; *Zar Peters Werktag*,
Reichenberg, 1922; *Die Liebe, ein goldenes*

Buch. Komödie, Munich, 1923. *Le Lieutenant Demianof. Récits de Guerre 1914–
1915*, Paris, 1916; *L'Enfer sous l'eau* . . .
Récits de guerre 1916–1917, Paris, 1924;
L'Amour, livre d'or. Comédie, Répertoire
du Vieux Colombier, Paris, 1922.

Prishvin: (1) Stories and Sketches, three volumes. Znanie, P.,
1914. *Kurymushka*, M., 1924.

    (3) *Der Schwarze Araber*, Munich, 1917.

Zamyatin: (1) *Uyezdnoe*, P., 1916.

    Ostrovityane (Islanders). Grschebin, Berlin,
1922.

    Na Kulichkakh (At the World's End), do., 1923.

    *Vzroslym Detyam Skazki (Fables for Grown-up
Children)*, do., 1922.

    (2) *The Cave*, tr. by the present author, in the
Slavonic Review, No. 4, 1923.

Wolkonsky: (2) *Lowell Lectures. Pictures of Russian History
and Russian Literature*. Lamson Wolffe &
Co., Boston (Mass.), 1897; *My Reminiscences*,
tr. A. E. Chamot, two volumes. Hutchinson,
London, 1925.

Krasnov: (2) *From the Double-headed Eagle to the Red Banner*,
Brentano's, London, 1923 (printed in Germany).

Aldanov: (2) *Saint Helena: Little Island*, Jarrold, London;
Knopf, N.Y.; 1924.

Shulgin: (2) See *Slavonic Review*, No. 2, 1922.

    Cf. article by the present writer in the *Literary
Review*, Sept. 2, 1922.

Shklovsky: (1) *Sentimental'noe Puteschestvie*. Helikon, Berlin,
1923.

    (3) A fragment (describing literary life in Petersburg
in the winters 1918–1920) in the Italian review *Russia*, 1923, No. 3.

Erenburg: (1) *Neobychaynye Pokhozhdeniya Khulio Khuvenito*.
Helikon, Berlin, 1922; *Lik Voyny (The Face
of War)*, 1st ed., Sofia 1920; 2nd ed., M., 1923.

    (3) *Die ungewöhnlichen Abenteuer des Julio Jurenito*,
Munich, 1923; *Les aventures Extraordinaires
de Julio Jurenito, La Renaissance du Livre*,
Paris, 1925.

Pilnyak: (1) *Golyy God (The Bare Year)* and two volumes of
stories.   M., 1924.
>   Cf. Lidin.
>   (2) *Tales of the Wilderness,* with a preface by the
>   present author.   Routledge, London, 1924; Knopf,
>   N.Y., 1925.

Leonov: (1) *Tuatamur.*   M., 1924.   Cf. Lidin.

Zoshchenko: (1) *Razskazy   Sinebryukhova.   Epocha,   Berlin,*
1922.

Vsevolod Ivanov: (1) *Partizany,* 3rd ed., M., 1924; *Bronepoyezd,*
>   Nos. 14, 69, 2nd ed., M., 1923; *Tsvetnye
>   Vetra,*   Berlin,   1922;   *Vozvrashchenie
>   Buddy,* Berlin, 1923.

>   Cf. Lidin.
>   (3) *Panzerzug   nr.   1469.*   Hamburg,   1923;
>   *L'Enfant,* in *La Revue Européenne,*
>   Nov., 1924.

Seyfullina: (1) *Peregnoy (Manure),* 3rd ed., M., 1924.
>   Cf. Lidin.

Babel: (1) His stories have not yet been published in book form;
see *Lef, Krasnaya Nov', Russky Sovremennik,* 1923
and 1924.

Artem Vesely: (1) Nothing yet in book form; see *Lef* and
Krasnaya Nov', 1924.

PARALIPOMENA

1. THE DRAMA

See also under Tolstoy, Chekhov, Gorky, Andreev, Artsybashev, Blok, etc.

For a good general view of the modern Russian Stage see: *Russky Teatr Nachala XX veka* (*Russian Theatre in the early twentieth century*), by E. Znosko-Borovsky. Prague, "Plamja," 1925.

There are several works in English on the modern Russian stage, viz.: *The Russian Stage, a Sketch of Recent Russian Drama,* by G. Calderon, from the *Quarterly Review,* July, 1912; *The Russian Theatre,* by O. M. Sayler. Brentano's, London and N.Y., 1922; *The Path of the Modern Russian Stage,* by A. Bakshy. Palmer & Hayward, London, 1916; J. W. Luce, N.Y., 1918; *The New Theatre and Cinema of Soviet Russia,* by Huntly Carter. Chapman & Dadd, London, 1924; Williams, ch. VIII.

Moscow Art Theatre: (2) *My Life in Art,* by Constantin Stanislavsky, tr. J. J. Robbins. Little, Brown & Co., Boston, 1924; *The Moscow Art Theatre Series of Russian Plays,* ed. by O. M. Sayler. Brentano's, N.Y., 1923.

Evreinov: (2) *A Merry Death, a harlequinade, and The Beautiful Despot, the last act of a Drama,* in *Five Russian Plays,* tr. C. E. Bechhofer. Kegan Paul, London, 1915.

The Theatre of the Soul, tr. Marie Potapenko and Christopher St. John. Hendersons, London, 1915.

Lunacharsky: (2) *Three Plays: Faust and the City, Vasilisa the Wise, The Magi,* tr. L. A. Magnus and K. Walter. Routledge, London, 1923 (Broadway translations).

Lunts: (1) see *Beseda,* 1923–1924 (Berlin), No. 2 (*Vne Zakona*), No. 3 (*Na Zapad—Westward Ho*), No. 5 (*Gorod Pravdy—Justice City,* and obituary notice by Gorky).

2. LITERARY. CRITICISM

See General Works, and under Mikhaylovsky, Leontiev, Andreevsky, Soloviev, Merezhkovsky, Rozanov, Hippius. Marxist Criticism: *Khudozhestvennaya Literatura v otsenke Marksistkoy Kritiki* (an anthology), by R. S. Mandel'shtam. State Press, 1924.

Volynsky: (2) See *A Russian Anthology in English,* by Bechhoffer. Cf. Olgin.

Chukovsky: (1) Among other books, Chukovsky wrote in 1915 a book of pro-British propaganda, *Zagovorili Molchavshie* (*The Silent Ones Have Begun to Speak*).

(2) *Reminiscences of Andreyev,* in the *Dial,* 1924.

The Formalists: (1) *Poetika.* P., 1919.

Eichenbaum: (1) *Molodoy Tolstoy* (*The Young T.*). P., 1922; *Skvoz' Literaturu* (*Through Literature*). P. 1923; *Lermontov.* State Press, 1924.

(3) An article on Pushkin in the Italian *Russia,* 1924, No. 1.

ADDENDA

Chapter I. 2. In my account of Tolstoy's work after 1880 I make no mention of the autobiographical notes written by him in the early years of the century at the request of P. I. Biryukov, and included by that author in his *Life of Tolstoy.* They are not strictly literature, of course, and Tolstoy authorised their publication only on the condition of it being expressly stated that the notes in question had been just jotted down and not revised by him. But they are among the most interesting of his later writings. They breathe the idyllic atmosphere of *War and Peace* and the intense physiological sensibility characteristic of that great novel is carried in them to an even further degree of penetration and refinement.

Chapter III. 2. Gorky's short stories written within the last years have appeared in book form (Berlin, 1925).

Chapter III. 5. Bunin has published (in *Sovremennya Zapiski,* 1925, books 23 and 24) a new nouvelle *Mitya's Love,* which is superior to all he has written since 1918, and shows that the writer has by no means uttered his last word.

Chapter III. 9. Savinkov committed suicide in a Bolshevik prison (May, 1925).

Chapter IV. 6. Gershenzon died in March, 1925.

Chapter VI. 3. Mandelstam has published a book of memoirs (*The Noise of Time, Shum Vremeni,* Petersburg, 1925) which definitely gives him one of the first places among contemporary Russian prose-writers. It is an invaluable historical evocation of the atmosphere of pre-revolutionary Russia, especially of the years 1900–1907.

Chapter X. 10. Pasternak's prose has appeared in book-form (*Razskazy,* Moscow, "Krug," 1925). The book includes *The Childhood of Lüvers,* a story that stands quite apart from the rest of contemporary Russian fiction. It is a masterpiece of intelligent and acute observation. It has drawn from critics comparisons with Marcel Proust, but it is as concise and concentrated as the work of the French novelist is vast and ample.

Chapter VII. 7. Babel's *Stories* have appeared in book-form (State Press, 1925).

——Fedin's novel, *Cities and Years,* has appeared in full, (State Press, 1924). It has justified the expectations it aroused, and is no doubt the most significant work of fiction of its size by any writer of the younger generation. Its central subject is the moral bankruptcy of the Russian "intelligent" placed face to face with the Revolution.

——An English translation of *The Child* (*Dityò*), by Vsevolod Ivanov appeared in *The Nation and Athenæum,* June 27 and July 4, 1925.

INDEX

A NOTE ON THE TYPE IN
WHICH THIS BOOK IS SET

This book is composed (on the Linotype), in Scotch. There is a divergence of opinion regarding the exact origin of this face, some authorities holding that it was first cut by Alexander Wilson & Son, of Glasgow, in 1837; others trace it back to a modernized Caslon old style brought out by Mrs. Henry Caslon in 1796 to meet the demand for modern faces brought about by the popularity of the Bodoni types. Whatever its origin, it is certain that the face was widely used in Scotland, where it was called Modern Roman, and since its introduction into America it has been known as Scotch. The essential characteristics of the Scotch face are its sturdy capitals, its full rounded lower case, the graceful fillet of its serifs and the general effect of crispness.

SET UP, ELECTROTYPED AND PRINTED
BY THE VAIL-BALLOU PRESS, INC.,
BINGHAMTON, N. Y. · PAPER MAN-
UFACTURED BY W. C. HAMIL-
TON & SONS, MIQUON, PA.,
AND FURNISHED BY W. F.
ETHERINGTON & CO., NEW
YORK · BOOKS BOUND
BY H. WOLFF ESTATE,
NEW YORK.